DICKENS STUDIES ANNUAL
Essays on Victorian Fiction

DICKENS STUDIES ANNUAL
Essays on Victorian Fiction

EDITORS

Michael Timko
Fred Kaplan
Edward Guiliano

DICKENS
STUDIES
ANNUAL

Essays on Victorian Fiction

VOLUME
21

Edited by
Michael Timko, Fred Kaplan,
and Edward Guiliano

AMS PRESS
NEW YORK

DICKENS STUDIES ANNUAL
ISSN 0084-9812

Dickens Studies Annual: Essays on Victorian Fiction is published in cooperation with Queens College and the Graduate Center, CUNY.

International Standard Book Number
Series: 0-404-18520-7
Vol. 21: 0-404-18541-X

Dickens Studies Annual: Essays on Victorian Fiction welcomes essay and monograph-length contributions on Dickens as well as on other Victorian novelists and on the history of aesthetics of Victorian fiction. All manuscripts should be double-spaced, including footnotes, which should be grouped at the end of the submission, and should be prepared according to the format used in this journal. An editorial decision can usually be reached more quickly if two copies are submitted. The preferred editions for citations from Dickens' works are the Clarendon and the Norton Critical when available, otherwise the Oxford Illustrated or the Penguin.

Please send submissions to the Editors, *Dickens Studies Annual,* Room 1522, Graduate School and University Center, City University of New York, 33 West 42nd Street, New York, N.Y. 10036: please send subscription inquiries to AMS Press, Inc., 56 East 13th Street, New York, N.Y. 10003.

Manufactured in the United States of America

All AMS books are printed on acid-free paper that meets the guidelines for performance and durability of the Committee on Production Guidelines for Book Longevity of the Council on Library Resources.

Contents

List of Illustrations

Preface

The editors continue to be grateful for the services of the members of the editorial and advisory boards. Special thanks go to those who wrote the comprehensive review essays. We also thank the participants in the annual Santa Cruz Dickens Conference, especially John Jordan. Alicia Carroll, the editorial assistant from CUNY, and Jack Hopper, AMS Press, deserve special commendation.

We note and express our gratitude to those in administrative posts in different institutions who continue to provide supports of various kinds: Chancellor Anne Reynolds, CUNY; President Florence Horowitz; former Provost Stephen Cahn; Executive Officer, Ph.D. Program in English, Joseph Wittrich, The Graduate School and University Center, CUNY; Dean of Humanities Michael Spitzer, The New York Institute of Technology; President Shirley Strum Kenny, Dean John Reilly, and Chair, English Department, Charles Molesworth, Queens College, CUNY; and Gabriel Hornstein, President, AMS Press, whose encouragement has always been a constant source of strength.

—THE EDITORS

Notes on Contributors

CHRIS R. VANDEN BOSSCHE has recently published *Carlyle and the Search for Authority* (1991). He is also the author of articles on Dickens, Scott, Tennyson, Ruskin, and Pre-Raphaelite art. He is currently researching representations of the literary debates on copyright, censorship, canon, and curriculum.

JEROME H. BUCKLEY, Gurney Professor Emeritus of English Literature, Harvard University, is author of *The Victorian Temper, Tennyson: the Growth of a Poet, Season of Youth: The Bildungsroman from Dickens to Golding*, and other studies in nineteenth-century literary and intellectual history. He has edited texts of Victorian poetry, *The Worlds of Victorian Fiction*, and recently the Norton Critical *David Copperfield*.

JULIE F. CODELL, Director, School of Art, Arizona State University, is professor of art history and Women's Studies. She has published 55 articles and book reviews in *Victorian Studies, Victorian Review, Art History, The Journal of Pre-Raphaelite Studies, Nineteenth-Century Contexts*, and in several books and encyclopedias. She recently won an NEH Fellowship to prepare a book-length study on artists' careers and the image of the artist in England, 1870-1914.

RICHARD A. CURRIE is Associate Professor of English at the College of Staten Island. He has published articles on Esther Summerson in *The Dickens Quarterly* and Amy Dorrit in *English Studies* and co-edits the *Victorian Studies Bulletin* for the CUNY Victorian Committee.

H. M. DALESKI is a Professor of English at the Hebrew University, Jerusalem. He is the author of *The Forked Flame: A Study of D. H. Lawrence, Dickens and the Art of Analogy, Joseph Conrad: The Way of Dispossession, The Divided Heroine: A Recurrent Pattern in Six English Novels*, and *Unities: Studies in the English Novel*.

EDWIN M. EIGNER is a Professor of English at the University of California, Riverside. He has published three books on nineteenth-century fiction, two of them on Dickens, and has co-edited an anthology of Victorian criticism of the novel. The current essay was first delivered as a paper at the University of California's Dickens Universe, which Professor Eigner helped to found.

RICHARD T. GAUGHAN is an Associate Professor of English at the University of Central Arkansas.

ROBERT E. LOUGY is on the English faculty of the Pennsylvania State University, where he teaches graduate and undergraduate courses in the nine-teenth-and twentieth-century novel and in critical theory. This article is part of a larger on-going study of textual repression and representations of the body in a number of nineteenth-century texts.

MALCOLM MARSDEN has served on the English staff at Syracuse University and South Dakota State University and is currently Dana Professor of English at Elmira College, Elmira, N.Y. He has published articles in such journals as *The New England Quarterly, Twentieth-Century Literature,* and *The Journal of General Education.* In recent years he has contributed frequently to *The Mark Twain Society Bulletin* and has served on the Advisory Board to The Center of Mark Twain Studies at Quarry Farm, Elmira, N.Y.

JEROME MECKIER is Professor of English at the University of Kentucky and the author of *Hidden Rivalries in Victorian Fiction: Dickens, Realism and Revaluation* (1987) and *Innocent Abroad: Charles Dickens's American Engagements.* A sub-editor of *Dickens Studies Annual* volumes 1–7, Professor Meckier is currently Vice-President of The Dickens Society and is co-editing the Norton Critical edition of *Great Expectations.*

NANCY AYCOCK METZ is an Associate Professor of English at Virginia Polytechnic Institute and State University. She has published articles on Dickens and Trollope and is currently working on the *Martin Chuzzlewit* volume for the Dickens Companions Series edited by Susan Shatto and Michael Cotsell.

LILLIAN NAYDER, Assistant Professor of English at Bates College, teaches courses on the English novel and the literature of imperialism. Her articles on Dickens have appeared in *Victorian Literature and Culture* and *Studies in*

English Literature. Dickensian Displacements, the book she is currently writing, examines the relation of imperial and social histories is selected works by Dickens and Collins,

ROBERT A. STEIN teaches at the University of Massachusetts/Lowell. His recent publications are on *Little Dorrit* and *Great Expectations.*

MARGARET L. SHAW is currently an Assistant Professor at Virginia Polytechnic Institute and State University where she is completing a book on Charlotte Brontë and cultural politics. She is also working on women's literacy issues of the 1840s and '50s which are being repeated and revised in the 1990s.

KAY HEATHERLY WRIGHT teaches in the Department of English and American Literature at Showa Women's University in Tokyo, Japan, She is currently finishing a Ph.D. in Literature from the University of Wisconsin, Madison.

Shakespeare, Milton, Dickens and The Morality of the Pious Fraud

Edwin M. Eigner

Early in 1848 Dickens and his group of amateur actors were engaged in the business of selecting a play to perform (Forster 468–69). The occasion was a series of benefits for the playwright James Sheridan Knowles, whose declaration of bankruptcy Dickens had just been made aware of. The acting group wanted two plays so that they could show something different on successive evenings, but one of them, it was already settled, would be a revival of Ben Jonson's *Every Man in His Humour,* which the group had successfully staged three years previously. For the other, they considered a number of works— Jonson's *The Alchemist,* Fletcher and Massinger's *The Beggars' Bush,* Goldsmith's *The Good Natured Man,* Douglas Jerrold's *The Rent Day,* and Bulwer Lytton's *Money*—before deciding on *The Merry Wives of Windsor.* They also chose a pair of farces to fill out the programs: Mrs. Inchbald's *Animal Magnetism* and James Kenney's *Love, Law, and Physic.*

What is distinctive about this group of plays is that they are all of them based on deceptions. The tricking of Falstaff is, of course, the sport of the merry wives. *The Alchemist* and *Animal Magnetism* exploit stylish frauds of their respective times, alchemy and Mesmerism, and show how clever servants can make dupes of their greedy and foolish "betters." *The Beggar's Bush* deals with an exiled ruler who lives disguised as the King of the Beggars. Jerrold's *The Rent Day,* which owes a debt to Shakespeare's *Measure for Measure,* includes a disguised absentee landlord who spies on his corrupt agent. In *Love, Law, and Physic* Dickens had an opportunity to play, of all things, a benevolent lawyer, who engineers a series of hoaxes so that his friend can rescue his sweetheart from a forced engagement to a rich and objectionable rival. Bulwer Lytton's *Money,* which was one of Dickens'

1

sources for *Our Mutual Friend,* is about a young man who pretends to have become a pauper because he is afraid of being married for his fortune. And in Goldsmith's play, *The Good Natured Man,* there are several deceptions, the most interesting of which, at least for our purposes, is Sir William Honeywood's scheme to involve his soft-touch of a nephew "in fictitious [monetary] distress" so that he will see his false friends in their true colors (8).

No doubt that some of these works were rejected for fear of offending Sheridan Knowles with all their talk of debt and bankruptcy, but I think the plays may have suggested themselves to Dickens in the first place because Knowles's most successful play, *The Hunchback* (1832) was structured around a deception, one which is, moreover, quite similar to those in both *Money* and *The Good Natured Man.*

Dickens was much more than simply aware of Knowles's *The Hunchback.* He owned a well-thumbed, 1832 edition of the work (*The Flint and the Flame* 325) and as late as 1854 he referred to it as "the play of modern times best known to an audience,"[1] as indeed it probably was, having achieved an initial sensation not only at a number of London theaters but also in New York, Edinburgh, Glasgow, and Cork, and having enjoyed numerous revivals and reprintings over the years. Dickens also had a personal reason to remember it, for *The Hunchback* was indirectly responsible, as he recalled years afterwards, for his becoming a novelist rather than an actor. In 1832, when Dickens asked for a try-out, the managers of Covent Garden were unable to see him immediately because, as he wrote to Forster, "they were busy getting up the Hunchback."[2] A fortnight later, when the audition was scheduled at last, Dickens was ill and thus lost his chance to go on the stage. Finally, as Earle Davis has shown, *The Hunchback* provided Dickens with the most controversial plot in all his fiction, Noddy Boffin's pious fraud in *Our Mutual Friend.*[3]

Just how closely Dickens followed Sheridan Knowles will be apparent from a summary of *The Hunchback.* Because of his deformity, the title character has been living under an assumed name, Master Walter, and pretending to be his daughter Julia's guardian rather than her father. After educating her in the uncorrupting countryside, and finding in Sir Thomas Clifford an attractive and noble-minded lover for her, Master Walter decides to finish Julia's upbringing with a brief exposure to the city, where, unfortunately, she quickly loses all the values of her country education. And when Clifford overhears her telling a friend that she plans to go through with the marriage, not for love, but only to obtain money and a title, he angrily renounces her. Now begins the pious fraud. Master Walter arranges for Clifford to hear that he has lost both his fortune and his title, and then he encourages Julia to engage herself to an empty-headed Lord, for whom the now impoverished Clifford, like John Harmon in Dickens' novel, has gone to work as a secretary. Julia slowly begins to understand that she really does love Clifford, after all, but Master Walter will not let her off the hook until she has completely proved herself. When Clifford sends her a letter, the Hunchback pretends, like Mr. Boffin, to vituperate:

He's a bankrupt! stripped of title,
House, chattels, land and all! A naked bankrupt,
With neither purse nor trust. Would'st read his letter?
A beggar! Yea, a beggar! fasts, unless
He dines on alms! How durst he send thee a letter? (65)

Even after he has by indirection brought his daughter to tell *him* that in marriage love must outweigh all other considerations, and then arranged a meeting between Clifford and Julia so that the lovers can renew their broken promises to one another, Master Walter continues to denounce Clifford as a traitor and to insist on her marriage to the Lord. Only at the wedding, does he reveal the fraud and give the grateful lovers to one another.

Thus, an elaborate deceit informs the structure, creates the suspense, provides the surprises, and redeems the characters of this work which had so large an influence on Dickens' life and career, and his recollection of *The Hunchback* may, as I began by suggesting, have directed Dickens' attention in 1848 to plays involving deceptions.

On the other hand, it might have been difficult for Dickens to have happened on a comedy or melodrama which did not involve a deceit. The stage is a place of deceptions, and part of the fun of comedy has always consisted of characters, who are, of course, impersonated by actors to begin with, impersonating still other characters. In Greek Old Comedy, as in Shakespeare, a boy plays a girl pretending to be a boy. In *Charley's Aunt,* a middle-aged actor appears as an undergraduate dressed up as a wealthy widow. And, of course, this sort of thing was the meat and bread of the Pantomime, perhaps the most popular form of entertainment in Dickens' England.

But while one finds a fraud virtually everywhere one turns in dramatic literature, *pious* frauds, where the purpose of the deception is to benefit the character being deceived, are surprisingly hard to come by. They occur frequently in Shakespeare, not only in comedies and romances like *Much Ado, Cymbeline, The Tempest,* and *The Winter's Tale,* but even in a tragedy like *King Lear,* where Edgar pretends to lead Gloucester to the Dover cliff, trifling with his father's despair, as he says, in order to cure it. Nevertheless, of all the plays Dickens considered in 1848 for the Sheridan Knowles benefit, only Goldsmith's play can be said to contain a pious fraud. The others use deception in ways that are relatively common in the theater: to test a lover *(Money)*, to unmask a villain *(The Rent Day)*, to save one's own life *(The Beggar's Bush)*, to make money *(The Alchemist)*, to discountenance an unsuitable lover *(Animal Magnetism* and *Love, Law, and Physic)* and for plain, good fun *(The Merry Wives of Windsor)*. And even in Goldsmith the deception is not really central to the resolution of the plot.[4] Nevertheless, *The Good Natured Man* and *The Hunchback* contain, I believe, the only pious frauds, not only on Dickens' mind in 1848, but in all of English dramatic literature outside of Shakespeare.

There is at least one important precedent in the British novel. The mother of Darsie Latimer, the hero of Scott's *Redgauntlet,* deceives her son by withholding from him the truth that he is the heir of the heroic and rebellious Redgauntlets and having him brought up under a false name in the house of a loyal, Whig attorney.

> "she adopted," said Lilias, "every precaution her ingenuity could suggest, to keep your very existence concealed from the person whom she feared [Darsie's uncle, who would raise the boy to lead a revolution to restore the Stewarts and get vengeance for his father's execution]—nay from yourself; for she dreaded ... that the wildfire blood of the Redgauntlet would urge you to unite your fortunes with those of your uncle." (435)

This plot, moreover, is probably the source for the similar deception in an important novel written after Dickens' death, George Eliot's *Daniel Deronda.* A difference is that Scott believes that Darcie's mother acted for the best, while George Eliot clearly thinks it was wrong to attempt to deprive Daniel of his Jewish heritage. But both mothers are sure their fraud is pious.

Dickens' pious frauds are unambiguous and they occur throughout his novels. He uses the term not only in *Our Mutual Friend,* but in several of his novels, as, for instance, when he wants to describe Aunt Betsey's benevolently intended lie to David Copperfield about the loss of her fortune. But he did not coin it. Victorians employed the expression simply to indicate a deception practiced for any virtuous purpose,[5] and Addison had used it in a *Spectator Paper* of 1712 in a way which seems especially relevant to Dickens' own practice. Writing about the fantastic in literature, Addison noted that "The Ancients have not much of this Poetry among them; for, indeed, almost the whole Substance of it owes its Original to the Darkness of Superstition of later Ages, when pious Frauds were made use of to amuse mankind and frighten them into a Sense of their Duty" (VI, 95). So understood, pious frauds, involving fear, the supernatural, and a moral lesson, had been the *modus operandi* of a good deal of Dickens' shorter fictions beginning with "The Story of the Goblins Who Stole a Sexton" from *Pickwick Papers,* and continuing through the first two of the Christmas Books, *A Christmas Carol,* and *The Chimes,* which is subtitled, *A Goblin Story.* The fraud becomes more domestic, but no less pious in *The Cricket on the Hearth: A Fairy Tale of the Home,* where the benevolent agent reassures rather than frightens, and, beginning with *The Battle of Life* (1846), the deceptions operate in Dickens without the help of the overtly supernatural, although Aunt Betsey, John Jarndyce, and Mr. Boffin are realistic characters only when we take care not to look away from them for a single moment.

In one highly significant respect, Dickens' pious frauds resemble at least one of Shakespeare's and differ even from Goldsmith's, Scott's, George Eliot's, and Sheridan Knowles's: like Shakespeare in *The Winter's Tale,*[6] Dickens deceives not only his characters but his readers. Sir William Honeywood's pretended disinheritance of his nephew is explained in the first scene. In neither Scott nor George Eliot are we encouraged to conclude a false paternity, and in both cases the narrative is so handled that the reader discovers the truth as soon as it is revealed to the hero, who, in the case of Scott, is also the principal narrator. And the alert theater-goer, at least, should have been on to the Hunchback's benevolent deception, for he tells the disillusioned and angry Clifford at the end of Act II:

> Go to! Thou art a boy
> Fit to be trusted with a plaything, not
> A woman's heart. Thou know'st not what it is!
> Which I will prove to thee, soon as we find
> Convenient place. Come on, Sir! you shall get
> A lesson that shall serve you for the rest
> Of your life. "I'll make you own her, Sir, a piece
> Of Nature's handiwork, as costly, free
> From bias, flaw as ever yet
> Her cunning hand turn'd out.

In the next acts, Master Walter puts on such a good show that I would guess most Victorian audiences quickly forgot this speech, but they could not complain, as they could in both Dickens and Shakespeare, that fair warning had not been given. For there is not the slightest clue in *The Winter's Tale* which might lead the audience to suspect that Hermione, who was reported in Act III to have died of grief for her dead son and her imputed honor, will surprisingly return to the action as a living statue in the very last scene of the play; and Dickens, of course, customarily goes some distance out of his way to tempt us into false conclusions.[7]

The remainder of this paper may be regarded as a meditation, the subjects of which are (1) a plot device, the pious fraud, employed frequently by the two greatest and most influential writers in the language, but imitated by virtually no one else, and (2) a technique, which, among English writers, they alone, with the possible exception of Milton, appear to have practiced, the technique of including the readers or audience among those to be benevolently deceived. I can speak with less confidence regarding Continental literature, but except for the pious frauds in the fairy tale tradition, the only examples which spring to my mind are the deception practiced on the hero and the readers of *Don Quixote* and *Wilhelm Meister's Apprenticeship,* and on the lovers and the audience of Mozart's *The Magic Flute.* Shakespeare, Cervantes, Milton, Dickens, Mozart, Goethe, and virtually no one else: this business of the pious fraud seems to be in the province only of the greatest moguls of art.

It is not a question of lesser talents not daring to aspire; they seem not even to be tempted. Few writers, and very few indeed among the realists who were Dickens' contemporaries, are interested in confusing their characters—they are usually too busy disillusioning them—and both writers and critics, at least critics of Dickens, are frequently contemptuous of the practice of deceiving the reader.

Strangely, the fraud on the audience of *The Winter's Tale* has not raised hackles. Critics of earlier generations worried a great deal about the bed trick in *All's Well that Ends Well,* and they have begun to argue about the morality of the Duke's disguise in *Measure for Measure,* but not about the deception on the jealously murderous Leontes, who clearly deserves all the suffering he gets, or about the fraud on our innocent selves. Perhaps this is because we want so much for the wronged Hermione to be alive, or perhaps it is because *The Winter's Tale* is a play, not a novel, and, since there is no narrator, we are less conscious of having been deceived by a manipulating author. In any event, the deception has usually been admired, and it was especially esteemed in the nineteenth century. In Cervantes the deceptions on the reader (I am referring, of course, to the two instances in Part II when the bachelor Samson Carassco appears in disguise to challenge Don Quixiote) are abandoned as quickly as possible, in the next chapters after they occur. *The Magic Flute* is an opera in which anything goes, and, no one worries about the deception in *Wilhelm Meister,* either, probably because not many readers are sufficiently interested in the action to *get* upset.

But with Dickens we are helplessly caught up in the characters and in the story, and we are fully conscious of an authorial presence which appears clearly to have hoodwinked us. Even before *Our Mutual Friend,* an angry critic, J.C. Jeaffreson, found Dickens "as deceitful, deceiving, and wittingly dishonest a describer as can be found in the entire range of living authors" (II, 272), and in our own generation Robert Garis has objected to Dickens' "theatrical mystification," which exploits our moral stupidity.[8] More recently still, Charlotte Rotkin in *Deception in Dickens* argues "that *Little Dorrit* is a deceptive presentation of deception. It deludes the reader with false images of its most significant characters. It overwhelms the reader with stimuli in order to hide the ambiguities which undermine the false images of characterization. It misleads the reader by presenting, but not quite approving, Victorian standards of morality" (1)[9] A critic with whose position I find it much easier to sympathize, Grahame Smith, speaks, I must suppose, for countless readers who have felt cheated by the pious fraud of *Our Mutual Friend.*

> Boffin belongs to the tradition of Dickens' genially eccentric old benefactors, and yet we feel convinced that Dickens is prepared to sacrifice him in the interests of artistic truth. His failure to do so is damaging ... to the entire novel, but it makes nonsense of the earlier stages in which we watched Boffin's breakdown.... Such manipulation of people, in life or in art, is at once arrogant and frivolous. It cannot be denied that the weakness of the Boffin strand seriously undermines the novel's artistic unity. We sense in it a failure of nerve. (182–83)

This is not only anger; it is criticism taking itself and literature seriously, as Dickens would have it do, and we must consider his charge at some greater length.

In the fifteenth chapter of the *Adventures of Huckleberry Finn,* Huck, returning to the raft after having been lost in the fog, and finding Jim asleep from worry and exhaustion, decides to have some fun. He makes Jim believe the events of the night were only a dream, and he encourages him to interpret them. After Jim, who prides himself on his oracular powers, has ingeniously explained the meaning behind all the sounds and sights which he now supposes were warnings and predictions, Huck springs the trap on him. He points out some real leaves and rubbish on the raft, evidence that it was no dream after all, and he asks Jim what "*these* things stand for." After some reflection, Jim tells him:

> "What do dey stan' for? I's gywne to tell you. When I got all wore out wid work, en wid de callin' for you, en went to sleep, my heart wuz mos' broke bekase you wuz los', en I didn' k'yer no mo' what become er me en de raf'. En

when I wake up en fine you back agin, all safe en soun', de tears come en I
could a got down on my knees en kiss yo' foot I's so thankful. En all you wuz
thinkin 'bout wuz how you could make a fool uv ole Jim wid a lie. Dat truck
dah is trash; en trash is what people is dat puts dirt on de head er dey fren's en
makes 'em ashamed." (105)

Admittedly, there was nothing pious about Huck's fraud, but it is questionable whether Jim would have felt differently about it if there had been. As we
have just heard Grahame Smith say, "Such manipulation of people, in life or
in art, is at once arrogant and frivolous." Jim, who does not moralize past the
particular instance, puts his emphasis on the violated friendship, and in this
respect his objection to Huck's deceit is similar to Anthony Trollope's criticism of deceptive narrators like Dickens. Thus, in *Barchester Towers*
Trollope wrote that "the author and the reader should move along together in
full confidence with each another. Let the personages of the drama undergo
ever so complete a comedy of errors among themselves, but let the spectator
never mistake the Syracusan for the Euphesan. Otherwise he is one of the
dupes, and the part of a dupe is never dignified" (Chap. 15). Like Jim,
Trollope gives companionship, quietly and respectfully travelling along
together, his highest priority. If we can believe *An Autobiography,* it is why
he wrote fiction in the first place.

Dickens also valued his readership, and, as Fred Kaplan emphasizes in his
recent biography, friendships were at the center of his life. It is questionable,
however, that he defined his relationship with his readers and with the audiences at his public readings as a companionship. He wanted, rather, to be a
teacher to his public. More than this, he wanted, following Carlyle's injunc-
tion, to be his century's priest. And for teachers and priests, ironically, there
had long existed a tradition justifying deceit. Indeed, the *OED* definition for a
pious fraud is "a deception practiced for the furtherance of what is considered
a good object; *esp.* for the advancement of religion," and Dostoevsky's Grand
Inquisitor was certainly not the first or the only cleric to conclude that deception was allowable when it led sinners to God or even to the church, or when
it worked to redeem their souls.

Educators, we know, are another set of frauds. Alice Miller's brilliant new
book on education, translated under the title *For Your Own Good,* explains
how generations of teachers and parents in Germany and elsewhere have tried
to instill moral values, such as the virtues of honesty, by resorting to lies and
deceptions (63–64). Miller provides a number of examples, but perhaps none
more apt or more frighteningly Dickensian as one my wife witnessed while
she was living in Germany. During the Christmas season, she has told me, the

children of a Franconian family may be visited by a pair of amateur actors, dressed up, the one as Saint Nicholas and the other as Pelzmaertl, a furry, gnomic figure of terror. Nikolo carries a sack full of presents for all the good children, but Pelzmaertl scolds the naughty ones and threatens to carry them off in his sack, which is always empty. My wife tells me she has seen a terrified little boy being stuffed into one of these sacks and carried screaming, and then beyond screaming, for five hundred yards or so before being tumbled out onto the cold, hard ground.

Such sadistic and repressive education Alice Miller would term "poisonous pedagogy," aimed at mastering the child and destroying his spontaneity, almost certainly calculated, she would say, to produce a Hitler. But even Rousseau, the father of up-front, liberal, progressive education, who can write eloquently against lying to children, is ingenious at constructing elaborate little life-dramas, which can only be called pious frauds, aimed at teaching the child such things as respect for the property of others or not exercising a stubborn will by going out of the house alone. Before Rousseau reads the fable of the fox and the crow to Emile, he arranges for the boy to be made a fool of through flattery so that there will be no chance of his identifying with the wrong character. Emile is even taught not to lie by means of such fictions, for, as Rousseau says

> Punishment as punishment ought never to be inflicted on children, but it should always happen to them as a natural consequence of the bad action. Thus you will not declaim against lying; you will not precisely punish them for having lied; but you will *arrange* it so that all the bad effects of lying—such as not being believed when one tells the truth, or being accused of the evil that one did not do although one denies it—come in league against them when they have lied. (101)

It remains a live issue in Rousseau studies as to whether the author of *Emile* was really a liberal or a totalitarian, but no educational theorist seems to have objected to these deceptions.

What is more, educators continue to "arrange" such object lessons for the benefit of students. Just a few years ago, for instance, several of the high schools in my city cooperated with the police in staging scenes just outside the school grounds, so that when the unsuspecting students walked out of the building at recess, they were confronted with the apparently dead body of a popular classmate, lying in the street, the victim, it was made to seem, of a drunk driver, who was just then being arrested by the police. Some of the students who had been taken in were angry when they learned of the deception, but most of them conceded they had been taught a valuable lesson. Is it justified?

Let us try, as Captain Ahab says, the little lower layer. In recent years the
topic of animal rights has become a legitimate philosophical endeavor, and it
might be asked, therefore, whether it is immoral to practice pious frauds on
the members of other species. Yet one of the most outspoken animal advocates, Vicki Hearne, has written the following in a 1983 article, published in
Raritan. Hearne is a poet, a philosopher, and even a Dickens buff, but she is
also a dog trainer, faced with the problem of a pointer bitch named Salty, who
has become addicted to hole-digging in the garden:

> Here corrections won't work. I may yell, scream, lay for her and deliver out
> corrections all I like, but these will have little or no effect. She learns to make
> sure I am distracted, perhaps by listening for the sounds of the typewriter, and
> has her holedigging fix as often as she can. Any corrections and punishments
> are just part of the fun, accepted as a dedicated athlete accepts aches and
> injuries. I don't mean she *likes* being walloped, but she is not deterred by wal-
> loping as she was so deterred when the issue of puddling on the rug came up.
> Puddling on the rug wasn't sacred.
>
> So, I submit myself to the holy discipline of hole digging. Dressed in gardening
> clothes, I go into the backyard and Discover the Hole. I rejoice. I dance a jig
> around the hole in celebration of the Mystery. I congratulate Salty on the hole
> and, still dancing, get out spade and shovel, with a view of making this perfect
> thing even more perfect. Salty is delighted, and helps me dig the hole. We per-
> fect its form, making it diamond or heart-shaped. I dance another jig when
> we're done, and, still dancing, I go get the garden hose and fill the hole with
> water. Then, still rejoicing, I put Salty's head in the Hole. She emerges quite
> quickly (she's a very strong, agile dog) gasping in astonishment and outrage. I
> am surprised, and say, "But, I thought you loved hole digging!"
>
> I do this every day for three weeks. If there is no new hole, I redig the old one.
> It is not long before Salty starts hanging back as far as she can when I start
> humming my hole digging hymn as I get out my overalls. Her face begins to
> express something like, "Christ! She's crazy! Hole digging is not fun!" And she
> stops digging holes and devotes herself to preventing the very thought of
> holes…. I … have become [to the dog] the sort of animal who has this crazy
> response to the sight of a hole and this is an incurable fanaticism; the only way
> to handle it is to keep me away from holes. (24–25)

The author of this pious fraud, who, as I said, is deeply concerned with the
ethics of dog training, insists that *"this has nothing to do with punishment or
authority"* (25), but it certainly seems to involve manipulation, and we
appear indeed, to be back to the place from which we started when we quoted
from *Huckleberry Finn,* for, like the dog, Jim was Huck's best friend, and the
issue of Black rights stood in Huck's day about where the issue of animal
rights stands today. Is it all right then to lie to your pointer bitch when it is for
her own good?

Are these instances (glaring instances, Dickens might have called them) of arrogant manipulation, or does it make a difference when the relationship is between teacher and student rather than author and reader? Perhaps it is a question of an implied contract, which the author violates when he takes the liberties of one whom we have employed to educate our children or to redeem our souls, whom we have, so to speak, licensed to deceive us, in the case of the clergyman, or to lie to our children or our pets? If so, how is an author to know for what purpose his readers have purchased his book? And if he could know, is he morally bound to honor such a contract?

A certain class of readers who like to be deceived, but who insist on a strictly honest contractual relationship with the author, are the devotees of detective stories. Such readers insist on what they call the principle of fair play. As Earl F. Bargainnier writes, "The author is expected to be fair; that is, whatever is needed for the reader to solve the mystery should be available to him" (17). Howard Haycraft, the pioneer critic of detective fiction, explains this requirement in greater detail:

> To say that the detective story must play fair means much more today than the obvious necessity of laying all the clues before the reader. It means, as well, that no evidence shall be known to the reader which remains unknown to the detective ... that false clues are automatically forbidden; that fortuity and coincidence are outlawed as beneath the dignity of the self-respecting craftsman ... and that no extraneous factors (such as stupidity and "forgetting") shall be allowed to divert or prolong the plot in any essential manner. (225–26)

But, although Dickens is regarded as one of the fathers of detective fiction, the very title of the chapter from which the preceding passage is taken expresses an essential difference between his aims and the requirements of such readers. The chapter is called "The Rules of the Game." Well, Dickens wasn't *playing* games. He saw himself not as a self-respecting craftsman, but as an artist, and he held fellow novelists in contempt when they did not take their art seriously enough, or even when they modestly affected not to. He never really forgave Thackeray because, as Dickens wrote in his obituary tribute to his great rival, "he feigned a want of earnestness, and ... made a pretense of undervaluing his art, which was not good for that art that he held in trust."[10] Nor would Dickens have been amused by W. H. Auden's cynical put-down of Shelley's "Defence of Poetry": "The unacknowledged legislators of the world," Auden quipped, "describes the secret police, not the poets" ("Writing" 27). So much for pious frauds.

Auden, by the way, who confesses himself an addict of detective fiction, insists nevertheless that such stories "have nothing to do with works of art"

("Vicarage" 147). He does not say that their purpose is simply to pass the time of day harmlessly, but he sees the form, nevertheless, as an essentially conservative one, indulging in the reader "the fantasy of being restored to the Garden of Eden, to a state of [unearned] innocence" ("Vicarage" 158). The best whodunnits take place in the country and begin with "an innocent society in a state of grace":

> a society where there is no need of the law, no contradiction between the aesthetic individual and the ethical universal, and where murder, therefore, is the unheard-of act which precipitates a crisis (for it reveals that some member has fallen and is no longer in a state of grace). The law becomes a reality and for a time all must live in its shadow, till the fallen one is identified. With his arrest, innocence is restored, and the law retires forever. ("Vicarage" 150)

The reader is driven to read such novels, according to Auden, because he suffers from "a feeling of guilt, the cause of which is unknown to him" ("Vicarage," 158), and the purpose of the story is simply to offer Kafka's Joseph K an analgesic for temporary relief. Neither the characters nor the readers are supposed, in any way, to be changed by the experience ("Vicarage" 148).

There is in Dickens, also, a certain amount of hankering after Eden, but, notwithstanding the disappointments of social critics, his message is not conservative. As Northrop Frye writes, "For all its domestic and sentimental Victorian setting, there is a revolutionary and subversive, almost a nihilistic quality in Dickens's melodrama that is post-Romantic, has inherited the experience of the French Revolution, and looks forward to the worlds of Freud, Marx, and the existential thriller" (80). He did not write with the expectation or even the hope of overturning governments, at least not directly or in his own generation, but he certainly intended to redeem the minds and hearts of his readers.

This is not to say that he believed his readers wanted to be redeemed. As they kept reminding him, what they wanted from him were more *Pickwick Papers*. No one knew better than the inventor of the Circumlocution Office that "the genius of the country ... tends to being left alone," and so Dickens understood that he had no license from his readers to deceive them into virtue. But, of course, he didn't look for their permission. A writer who begins with the belief that his readers need to be saved and that he is the man to do it, provides his own license.

Is this arrogance? No doubt, it sounds like it to the reader being duped, but I suppose the answer to this question has more to do with the attitudes of the authorial dupester, especially in regard to his victim. I am pretty clear, for instance, on the arrogance of Huck's fooling Jim, and not because the fraud lacks a virtuous motive. Huck's action would be just as arrogant if he believed that Jim needed, for his own good, to be cured of his penchant for interpreting dreams. Huck is wrong because he shows a disrespect for Jim's personhood, for his essential being, a being which includes a close, oracular relationship with nature and the world of dreams. The novel expresses the deepest respect for such a relationship, and so usually does Huck, except when he loses his moral bearings temporarily in the fog or when he submits himself to the values of Tom Sawyer and civilization, which, of course, has no respect for any relationship with nature. By making Jim ashamed, which is, according to Mark Twain, civilization's chief educational ploy, Huck threatens what is both natural and valuable in his friend.

I am worried about the philosophical hole-digger. It is not that she does not understand the problems. "The trainer," she writes "has occasion to be aware as few people are that human authority is corrupt to the core, and that any trope of human ascendancy creates the stink of the immodest, the self-righteous, and the sadistic" (3). Moreover, in most instances she shows a deeper respect for the animal than most educators display for people, and a deeper respect still for what is natural in the dog. "Dog training," she writes, "is one of the arts concerned with the imitation of nature" (13), and the train-er's task is to help the dog realize his vision of himself, as a fighter or a hunter or a companion, etc., a vision implanted by nature itself. Yet in the case of the hole-digging fraud, she dupes the pointer into abandoning an activity which she recognizes as sacred to its nature, and not because this will transform the dog into a more transcendental hunter, but because it interferes with an object which has a strong hold in the trainer's own imagination, "such as tidy lawns and flower beds" (25). In spite of the earlier rhetoric, civ-ilization seems to be winning out again.[11]

The dog trainer's rhetoric goes back to Rousseau, as does the conviction that the teacher must never punish, only make corrections which have the force of natural consequences,[12] and, most significantly, the faith in the uncor-rupting power of nature. As the dog trainer tries to help the dog realize his natural vision of himself, so Rousseau seeks to give the child what Allan Bloom calls "a healing education which returns him to himself." *Emile,* writes the critic, "is an experiment in restoring harmony to [the] ... world by reordering the emergence of man's acquisitions in such a way as to avoid the imbalances created by them while allowing the full actualization of man's potentials" (3). In other words, Rousseau has invented a highly artificial sys-tem of education, which includes deceptions, in order to counteract the false vision of the world that has been painted by the artifices of a corrupt society. He thus justifies his educational revolution, which is, in large measure, a reaction to John Locke's thoughts on the same subject, by using Locke's own method of justifying the English political revolution of 1688, not as change, but as the restitution of the natural state of things. The pious frauds of Rousseau, therefore, like the Glorious Revolution, seem less arrogant, because they respect the essential nature of the child. There would be more arrogance, perhaps, if Rousseau presumed to understand nature's intentions and to effect them in his pupil, but usually he simply seeks to undo or prevent the contamination of the rival system, society's system, and he counts on unhindered nature itself to supply the positive instruction.

Shakespeare had not heard of the noble savage, but his frauds in *The Winter's Tale,* both the fraud on Leontes and the fraud on the audience, can be justified by a similar argument. Leontes' problem, as critics have pointed out, is similar to the problem of Othello, drawn this time to a romance conclusion. Both men lose faith in the chastity of their perfectly innocent wives, and in both cases this loss of faith is emblematic, as the philosopher Stanley Cavell has pointed out, of a general profession of lost faith, called skepticism, insisted on by the entire Western world. While Shakespeare himself was unwilling to admit impediments to the marriage of true minds, his lesser but more representative and intellectually respectable contemporary, John Donne, was ready enough to "Swear, / No where, / Lives a woman true and fair," and most of us regard Donne, not Shakespeare, as the realist. Cavell writes that philosophy, at least as constituted at present, has no answer to Othello's problems, because his skepticism, his failure of faith, is not based on an ignorance which philosophy might remedy. Rather, like the rest of us living in the post-Renaissance world, he knows far too much. Tragedy can't answer it either, for Renaissance tragedy, according to Cavell, is itself "the outcome of the problem of knowledge... the dominance of modern philosophical thought by it" (482). Romance, however, offers possibilities which lie beyond what he calls the claim of reason, and, in *A Winter's Tale,* art, as represented by the living statue of Hermione and by Paulina's pious fraud, is able to defeat Leontes' skepticism. Nothing else could have done it, for the problem of other minds is impenetrable except by the imagination. The audience of *The Winter's Tale* had also to be deceived because, infected by the Renaissance, it shared Leontes's lack of faith, not his lack of faith in Hermione, who was after all only a character in a play to them and easy enough to believe in, but a lack of faith in the real women and the real world around them. Thus, as in Rousseau, Shakespeare's pious fraud does not teach a new supposedly good lesson; it unteaches an old and obviously bad one. His deception does not arrogantly make us over according to his own vision; rather it returns us to ourselves, just as it restores Leontes as the lover he had been before the advent of a skepticism which no dose of reason, however honest, could ever have cured.

As you must have noted from the quotations I used earlier, Sheridan Knowles was the most self-consciously Shakespearean of all Victorian playwrights, and a similar justification might absolve his Hunchback. Master Walter has brought Julia up according to principles derived from Rousseau, and he seeks, by the deception, simply to undo the false education of society and to reestablish her natural values, to prove her, as he says, "a piece of Nature's handiwork." He does so not only through his pious fraud, but in a scene reminiscent of the masque scene in *The Tempest,* by showing his daughter an allegorical tapestry. The statue of Hermione, like all the various contrivances and deceptions of Shakespeare and The *Hunchback,* are the white magical tricks by which benevolent art strives to unwind the black spells of social conditioning, and by supernatural means to set captive nature free.

And as with the Hunchback, so it is with the benevolent goblins and godparents of Dickens' romances. We have already seen that pious frauds were an important aspect of his art in the Christmas Books of the 1840s. Interestingly, the device gets incorporated into his longer fiction in a serious way with *David Copperfield,* the novel which he wrote immediately after the Sheridan Knowles benefits. It is Aunt Betsey who perpetrates most of the pious frauds on the characters and readers of this novel, but so that we can see how Dickens confronts a problem similar to those in *Othello* and *A Winter's Tale,* and before we get on to Noddy Boffin, Dickens' most benevolent fraud, I want to deal with a deception which has no agent within the plot, but is aimed entirely at the reader. I mean the Annie Strong plot.

With the help of Mr. Wickfield's infectious skepticism regarding human motivations, Dickens has encouraged us to believe that Annie, a young girl, married to an old but virtuous man, is in love with her worthless cousin, Jack Maldon, and that she is his lover, or in danger of being seduced by him. As it turns out, Annie has never wavered in her love for her husband; indeed, she had outgrown her cousin long before she entered the action of the novel, and during most of the time we were worried about her, she has refused even to talk to him when they are not in public. But although she is easily as innocent as Hermione or Desdemona, everyone reading the novel and most of those taking part in it lose faith in her. Uriah Heep capitalizes on her supposed fall, and David grieves over it. Even her husband, who refuses to believe that she has done or could do anything evil, and who nobly blames himself rather than her, allows himself to conclude that she does not love him.

If the deception has not disturbed very many readers, it must be because the sub-plot involving the Strongs fails to get our sympathetic attention, but when a critic does become interested in it, he responds with some confusion. Thus, Earle Davis:

> Perhaps it is Dickens's point that Annie should not have encouraged Jack Maldon at all. His intent in the story is not clear, I think. As the earlier scenes are presented, and Mr. Wickfield gets Maldon away to India on an appointment, I felt that it was a fine interpretation of a girl in a difficult situation, admiring and loving her elderly husband, and fighting a passion which she really knows to be wrong. But this interpretation is ruined by the denouement which comes later in the story. From the conclusion, the reader is asked to believe that she never even thought of loving Maldon—a conclusion which is hard to accept when one sees her on her knees looking up at the doctor on the night after Maldon has departed for India.[13]

Davis, like some readers of the Boffin plot in *Our Mutual Friend,* suspects a changed intention.

Even if the same fraud on the reader, with the same resolution, had not been used in *The Cricket on the Hearth,* the placement of the Annie Strong plot within the structure of *David Copperfield* should suggests otherwise. As Dickens ultimately made clear by the four-book pattern of *Our Mutual Friend,* his twenty-part novels are usually divided into quarters. At the midpoint of the mature novels a catastrophe occurs which has been preparing since the beginning of the sixth number—the Dombeys have married; the Dorrits have been released into the larger prison of the real world; Esther Summerson has been stricken cold and blind; Little Emily has run off with Steerforth. The title of the first chapter of *Dombey and Son*'s eleventh number—"The Wooden Midshipman Goes All to Pieces"—expresses what is to happen throughout the rest of the third quarter. During the next five numbers the values of the novel come under the most serious of attacks. Carker appears to be making progress in the seduction of Edith, and Dombey's rejection of Florence builds to a climax. In other novels during these same chapters Richard Carstone sinks helplessly into Chancery while Jo the Crossingsweeper dies; the Dorrits are degenerating in Italy, and Mr. Merdle's complaint is becoming the Condition of England. In *David Copperfield,* David has fallen out of love with Dora, Emily is still lost, Uriah Heep has become Mr. Wickfield's partner, and Annie Strong's marriage, which showed signs of weakness in the first two numbers of the *second* quarter, seems to be breaking up in the last two numbers of the third.

This doubt regarding the novel's Strong marriage (pun fully intended) has thus framed the darkness of *David Copperfield,* a darkness which has had as much to do as *Othello* with fears regarding the faithfulness of women. "My life upon her faith!" the Moor says of Desdemona, and David might say the same of his redeemer, Agnes Wickfield, whose chastity is threatened during these chapters by the almost phallic rise of Uriah Heep. Annie Strong is to Agnes what the prostitute Martha Endell was to Little Em'ly, another fallen woman. And just as Daniel Peggotty feared that Martha's society might pollute Emily, so Mr. Wickfield dislikes the intimacy between Annie and his daughter. David, moreover, confesses regarding Annie that "The innocent beauty of her face was not so innocent to me as it had been; I mistrusted the natural grace and charm of her manner, and when I looked at Agnes at her side, and thought how good and true Agnes was, suspicion arose within me that it was an ill-assorted friendship" (Chap. 19). With this doubt of Annie Strong, which includes a want of perfect faith in Agnes, her friend, the novel's universe rocks on its foundations. "If she be false," as Othello says, "O, then heaven mocks itself!"

But, of course, Agnes is not false, and neither is Annie Strong, as Dickens lets us know in the fifteenth number, at precisely the spot in all the late novels where, after giving us our darkest moment, Dickens lets in the ray of light which is to expand and illuminate the comedy of the last five numbers. With the help of Mr. Dick, Annie not only vindicates herself but sounds the keynote of the concept of the disciplined heart, which is ultimately to win Agnes for David. And in the chapter after the conclusion of this fraud, David even learns that the supposedly lost Emily has run away from Steerforth.

The significance of the fraud seems clear, but what was its purpose? Why did David need to be misled by appearances? Why did the reader need to be misled by Dickens? My theory is that Dickens did not see it this way at all, that he regarded the reader as already misled, as David was, by the appearances of life as interpreted by nineteenth-century skepticism. Mr. Wickfield's lack of faith in human nature, which infects everybody in regard to Annie Strong, was the germ of *David Copperfield.* "What would you think of this for the notion of a character?" Dickens asked Forster in a letter of 19 January 1849. "Yes, that is very true; but now, *What's his motive?*" This, of course, becomes Wickfield's tag-line. Distrust of human nature was the disease Dickens sought to cure in *David Copperfield,* and his method, here as elsewhere, was to encourage the delusion until it reached the proportion of a glaring instance, until its significance became obvious, until its danger became apparent. And since, like Shakespeare, Dickens believed that faith was the *natural* condition, and doubt merely the result of a bad education administered by civilization, he did not hesitate to use his imagination as a counterforce.

As usual, Dickens understood his readers correctly. The proof of this is in the ease with which he deceives us. For it is not, as Robert Garis would have it, our moral stupidity which Dickens exploits; it is our sophistication, our presumed knowledge of the world. We despise Annie Strong's worldly mother, the Old Soldier, but we go along with her assumption that a blooming girl like Annie could not possibly have married old Doctor Strong out of love. We know too much of the world to swallow that one. We are so sophisticated that we do not even blame Annie much if she is having an affair, although we regret it for the Doctor's sake. The more sophisticated of our fraternity tote up the number of June and December marriages in the novel and conclude that the thirty-seven year old author must have been a dirty old man.[14] Dickens could not have had it better. Any con man will tell you it's easier to dupe a sophisticate than a fool; indeed, the con game, strictly defined, depends on the victim's distrust of human nature. Dickens encourages this sophistication with an array of artistic devices.

But the main reason we are so easily taken in by Boffin's fraud in *Our Mutual Friend* is that we were skeptical about Boffin's honesty to begin with. We read through the first half of the book, sadly nodding our heads over the mounting evidence which seemed to prove what we already knew, that money can indeed corrupt anybody. Boffin seemed to be an exception, but then he was only a fairy-tale character of the sort we were loftily ready to excuse the unrealistic Dickens for indulging in. Dickens encouraged us to patronize him in this fashion by pretending to be trying to fool us about the identity of John Harmon. He didn't get away with that one, did he? After all, we know his tricks, and, like Ralph Nickleby, we know the world. At least we think we do. But then, suddenly, the novel started getting really interesting in a truly *adult* way. Even Boffin began feeling the influence of money. Perhaps there was hope for Dickens, after all, and maybe, at the end of his career, he was finally growing up and becoming a realist, becoming, at last, as wise as his readers. When my students read these pages they are unhappy about the fall of Noddy Boffin, but they have to admit that at least the picture was a realistic description of the way things are. About this time, Dickens pulled the rug out from under us with the revelation that Boffin was only pretending.

It was a dirty trick. There we were like Mark Twain's Jim, ready to welcome Dickens back from the fog of wish-fulfillment to the raft of reality, so glad to see him "safe en soun" we could a got down on our knees "en kiss his foot." And all he could think about was how he could make a fool of us with a lie. Is he really that arrogant? Does he actually think so little of readers, his friends who have been so faithfully forgiving of him since *Pickwick*? If not, why did he deceive us?

The answer lies, I think, in the reason for Boffin's fraud on Bella. Boffin does not feel arrogantly superior to the victim of his deception even before her redemption. Bella herself knows that it is Old Harmon's fiction, not Boffin's, which aimed to make a fool of her. Since he doesn't believe Bella is mercenary at bottom, Boffin isn't trying to change her. He's only trying to change her bad story about herself, to prove to her that she is already better than she thinks she is. A piece of Nature's handiwork. In the process he wants also to prove to John Harmon that his story of his own worthlessness, taught by his father's cynical will and the world's *im*pious frauds—the everyday theatricals of the Weggses and the Veneerings and the Podsnaps—are wicked falsehoods.[15]

And in the same process Dickens wants to prove to us that we also are better than we think we are. Not wiser or more dignified,[16] but better. From his point of view, we have all read a lot of bad stories, stories which call themselves realistic and have as their moral a curiously comforting despair about the hopelessness of the human condition. All is Vanity Fair, saith the preacher. He wants to give us a new story. It's based on a lie, but, then, so was the old one. As Plato well knew, all poets lie. And he didn't kick them out of the Republic on moral grounds, but because he needed to get the competition out of the way so that he could pull off some pious frauds of his own, "contrived falsehoods," he called them, like the myth of the metals, according to which all those students who flunked their Scholastic Aptitude Tests were to be reconciled to an inferior class status with the story that Mother Earth had mixed base metals in their bodies because she intended them to be members of the lower classes.

The Boffin fraud takes place in the part of *Our Mutual Friend* which was occupied in *David Copperfield* by the Annie Strong fraud, that is to say, in the third quarter of the novel.

In the fifteenth number, as we might expect, we find the golden dustman at his worst. Bella Wilfer, faced with this glaring instance, this grotesque exaggeration of her own vision of reality, wakes up to a nobler conception of herself, and, as in *David Copperfield* and the other novels, the third quarter ends on a positive note.

But the *reader* has also been faced with a nightmare. Like Trotty Veck in *The Chimes*, he has been treated to a horrifying vision of the consequences of his complacently held world-view, but in this case it has been presented according to the structural pattern of the mature, long novels. Once again, there is great confusion at the keystone. Denounced by her brother, Lizzie Hexam has disappeared in the tenth number, perhaps to become Eugene Wrayburn's mistress. John Harmon, despairing of Bella, has buried himself deeper under a mountain of dust. The old power of the pure heroines to redeem the heroes appears to have been lost from Dickens. In the next five numbers, during which Boffin's apparent degeneration is gradually chronicled, all the tokens of a secure universe seemed to have disappeared. Bradley and Eugene have gone out of control, and even Lizzie, when we find her safe again, tells us that she doesn't know whether, if Eugene persists, she, our one sure token, will be strong enough to remain chaste. The thirteenth number is organized around the motif of insane pursuits: Eugene pursuing Lizzie, Bradley pursuing Eugene—or is it Eugene pursuing Bradley? The fourteenth number is a melodrama, fueled by hatred, revenge, and Nietzschean *ressentiment*. Bradley and Rogue want revenge on Eugene because of his contempt for them; Fledgeby wants revenge on Twemlow because of his class attitudes and revenge on Lammle because of his beard; Wegg wants revenge on Boffin for God knows what. It is a world of hatred, weakness, and distrust in which the originally benevolent and fearless Boffin is apparently afraid of everyone and ready even to quack like a duck at poor, dead John Rokesmith.

Faced with this glaring instance of how bad a vision of reality he has permitted himself to adopt, is not the reader ready at last to change for a better story? Here, perhaps, Dickens may have overestimated his readers. As any therapist will tell you, it's not so easy to get rid of a story we have become committed to, one which, no matter how destructive, seems to make sense of the universe. But if anyone can give us a compellingly new story, it ought to be the poet, especially those master story tellers like Shakespeare and Dickens who truly believe in their art and in the power of the illusions it permits them to create.

What I am arguing for Dickens and Shakespeare is a position somewhat similar to that which Stanley Fish posits for Milton in *Surprised by Sin: The Reader in Paradise Lost*. "Milton's method," according to Fish, "is to re-create in the mind of the reader (which is, finally, the poem's scene) the drama of the Fall, to make him fall again exactly as Adam did.... Milton consciously wants to worry his reader, to force him to doubt the correctness of his responses.... The ambivalence of the response," Fish goes on to say, "is meaningful because the reader is able to identify its components with different parts of his being: one part, faithful to what he has been taught to believe (his 'erected wit') and responsive to the unmistakable sentiments of the poem's official voice, recoils in the presence of what he knows to be wrong; but another part, subversive and unbidden (his 'infected will') surprises and overcomes him and Adam [in his rebellion] is secretly applauded. It would be a mistake to deny either of these impulses; they must be accepted and noted because the self must be accepted before it can be transformed.... [Thus] a description of the total response would be, Adam is wrong, no, he's right, but, then, of course he is wrong, and so am I.... In the pattern I discern in the poem, the reader is continually surprised by sin and in shame, 'sore displeased with himself.' his heart 'riseth against it'" (1–2, 42–43).

If for Adam we substitute Pecksniff and Mrs. Gamp and all the other vital though negative Dickensian characters of whose party, according to such critics as James Kincaid and Robert Polhemus, the novelist, without knowing it, was, then we can understand the device of the pious fraud in the context of the didactic tradition from which it comes. Fish suggests an analogue for Milton's technique in the form of a Platonic dialogue, with the epic voice taking the role of Socrates, and the reader in the position of a Phaedrus or a Cratylus, continually forced to acknowledge his errors, and in this way moving toward a confirmation in the truth (49), and, in a passage which is even more relevant to Dickens, Fish argues a precedent in the scene in the *Aeneid* when, immediately after forcing us to sympathize with Dido and to conclude that Aeneas is a cad for leaving her, Virgil refers to his hero as "Pious Aeneas."

> The experience of the scene redefines heroism completely, as does our experience of Satan in the first six books of *Paradise Lost*. Satan's initial attractiveness owes as much to a traditional idea of what is heroic as it does to our weakness before the rhetorical lure. He exemplifies a form of heroism most of us find it easy to admire because it is visible and flamboyant.... Because his courage is never denied (instead Milton insists on it) while his virtue and goodness are (in the "allegations" of the epic voice), the reader is led to revise his idea of what a true hero is.... Perhaps the most important aspect of the process I have been describing—the creation of a reader who is fit because he knows and understands his limitations—begins here at I. 125 when Milton's authorial corrective casts the first stone at the ideal of martial valour and points us towards the meaningful acceptance of something better. (48–49)

A similar re-education and restitution of the reader's values, especially as regards what is truly heroic behavior, is what I am arguing as the purpose behind the pious fraud and the deception of the reader in Dickens.

But it is not only a didactic intent which makes Dickens, Milton, and Shakespeare the only writers of pious frauds in English. Additionally, they may be the only ones who possess a supreme confidence in the imagination. Realists are characteristically respectful of their readers and make only the most modest claims for their art, which they usually prefer to call their craft. It is a modesty based perhaps on a lack of faith in the power of the imagination. Most of them would agree not only with Auden's quip about the secret police and the unacknowledged legislators, but with his much better known pronouncement in the Yeats elegy that "Poetry makes nothing happen." I suppose most of us readers believe this, too. But then, alas, we're not Dickens or Shakespeare or Milton, are we? We are only the poor, "bedayed" intellectuals, the tragical skeptics whom they tried so hard to save. Speaking for her creator, Amy Dorrit, at once the most modest, the most natural, and the most imaginatively deceitful of Dickens' heroines, justifies the pious fraud most succinctly: "I hope there's no harm in it. I could never have been of any use, if I had not pretended a little." (211)

NOTES

1. Letter to Mr. John Saunders, 26 October 1854. Quoted in T. Edgar Pemberton, *Dickens and the Stage* (London: George Redway, 1888), p. 240.
2. Letter to Forster. Quoted in Forster's *Life*, p. 60.
3. *The Flint and the Flame*, pp. 264–66. Davis also points out that the Gaffer Hexam plot is taken from Knowles's melodrama, *The Daughter* (1836), and, as with *The Hunchback*, the borrowing is obvious to anyone who takes the trouble to read the play. The only wonder is that earlier critics did not identify these sources. *The Hunchback* remained popular throughout the century, and, in fact, was enjoying a London revival as *Our Mutual Friend* was appearing. Even T. Edgar Pemberton, who writes on *Our Mutual Friend* in *Dickens and the Stage* and on *The Hunchback* in his book on *The Birmingham Theatres: A Local Retrospect* (Birmingham: Cornish Brothers, 1889) fails or does not bother to point out the connection. Moreover, Dickens must have been confident that no one would notice, for if anyone had, there would have been no surprise when the fraud is revealed.
4. Honeywood is cured when Leontine, who believes Honeywood has betrayed his plan to elope with Olivia, angrily tells him that everyone holds him in contempt for his good nature. This revelation, and not his uncle's fraud, gets to him because his benevolence was at least partly motivated by a desire to be well thought of. He is thus cured of a symptomatic behavior but not of the disease and certainly not according to his uncle's plan.
5. The *OED* (IV, 516) quotes Milman in *Latin Christianity* (1864), II, vii, 143, where the term is used to describe the action of a nurse who substitutes her own child to be murdered in the place of the Emperor's youngest. Dickens uses the term in a letter of 18 November 1842 when he plots to use Thomas Beard, the recipient of the letter, as the dummy buyer of a painting by Daniel Maclise, who would not have accepted money from Dickens because of their friendship. He uses it in at least three of his novels: *Martin Chuzzlewit, David Copperfield*, and *Our Mutual Friend*.

6. It is possible that the audience of *King Lear* was similarly deceived about Edgar's deception on the Dover cliffs. A bare Elizabethan stage would have no way to indicate that the characters are not in fact at the precipice which Edgar describes, and, although Gloucester does not hear the sea and thinks the ground is even, the audience might have gone along with him in accepting Edgar's explanation that the blind man's "other senses grow imperfect." The two most recent British television productions of *King Lear* pictured the characters in this scene only from the waist up, thus confusing, I would suppose, although I would not venture to say intentionally, some first-time viewers of the play.

7. Indeed, when John Leech mistakenly did a misleading illustration for *The Battle of Life* which confirmed the deception of that work, Dickens actually allowed it to be published, although, as he wrote to Forster, it was only out of regard for the pain Leech would feel at having his error pointed out (Forster, pp. 439–40). The illustration showed Marion Jedler eloping with Michael Warden. Everyone in and out of the story assumes until near the end that this elopement took place, but it is not presented except in Leech's illustration because, of course, it did not in fact happen.

8. *The Dickens Theatre* (Oxford: Oxford UP, 1965), pp. 55–56. Critical objection to the poetic meters in which some of Dickens' death scenes are written may also be motivated by outrage at the discovery that we have been manipulated. Of course, an author accustomed to being moved by the mood music of the melodrama might have a hard time understanding the point, and critics who have been similarly moved by the background music of films ought perhaps to be more sophisticated, although I understand such music is now included in the condemnation.

9. A more perceptive treatment of the deceptions in *Little Dorrit* can be found in Janice M. Carlisle's *"Little Dorrit:* Necessary Fictions," *Studies in the Novel,* VII (1975), 195–214.

10. "In Memoriam: W. M. Thackeray," *Cornhill Magazine,* Feb. 1864. Reprinted in *Collected Papers* (London, 1938), I, 98. The classic example of the unserious artist in Dickens is, of course, Henry Gowan in *Little Dorrit.*

11. I have shown this part of the essay to Vicki Hearne, who justifies the training technique by pointing out that she had insisted, both in the article and later on in her book, *Adam's Task* (New York: Knopf, 1988), that no deception is involved. The dog trainer must actually become the maniacal hole-digger for the correction to work. As I understand her, the trainer's action is justified because she is putting her sanity at risk by hallucinating in the same way that G. H. Lewes claimed Dickens did when he imagined his characters ("Dickens in Relation to Criticism," *Fortnightly Review,* 17 (February 1872), 141–54). She could end up a life-long digger. Hearne believes further that Mr. Boffin's "deception" in *Our Mutual Friend* is similarly justified because anyone who permits his imagination such free rein (Hearne is also a horse trainer) is in danger of being carried away. Boffin is in serious danger of becoming the miser whose role he has so assiduously researched and assumed. According to this explanation and justification, it would seem, the trainer, teacher, or fictionist is not manipulating the pupil so much as he or she is manipulating him- or herself.

12. This principle is also strong in Dickens' contemporary, Herbert Spencer, who appears never to have read Rousseau, but differs from him in that he will allow no pious frauds. Any improved consequences, like pretending not to believe true statements of the child you have caught lying, will give him as false a picture of reality, according to Spencer, as it would to believe his obvious lies to save his feelings. See *Education: Intellectual, Moral, and Physical* (New York and

London: D. Appleton, 1860), p. 182.

13. "The Creation of Dickens's *David Copperfield:* A Study in Narrative Craft," *Bulletin: Municipal University of Wichita,* XVI (1941), p. 21.

14. See, for instance, Brian Crick's "'Mr. Peggotty's Dream Comes True': Fathers and Husbands; Wives and Daughters," *University of Toronto Quarterly,* 54 (1984), 38–55.

15. Michael Cotsell argues that a main purpose of Boffin's fraud is to redeem John Harmon, who has suffered a failure of confidence ("Secretary or Sad Clerk? The Problems of John Harmon," *Dickens Quarterly,* 1 (1984), 134–35. An anecdote reported in T. Edgar Pemberton's book on *The Birmingham Theatres* makes me hesitate to make the same claim regarding the education of Sir Thomas Clifford in *The Hunchback.* According to Pemberton, the actor who played Clifford "for the very life of him could not make out whether Sir Thomas Clifford was a party to, or innocent of, the harmless plot to bring out Julia in her true colours. In his anxiety he went to the fountain head, and consulted Knowles himself. 'Good gracious, my dear fellow, *I don't know,'* said the author of the plot within the play. 'What do you think about it yourself?'" (p. 81).

16. For an earlier and less complete statement of this position, see my *The Metaphysical Novel in England and America: Dickens, Bulwer, Hawthorne, Melville* (Berkeley: U. of California P, 1978), p. 203. Rosemary Mundhenk makes a similar point in "The Education of the Reader in *Our Mutual Friend, Nineteenth-Century Fiction,* 34 (1979), 41–58. "Dickens," she says, "does for the reader what Boffin does for Bella."

WORKS CITED

Addison, Joseph, Number 419, July 1, 1712. *The Spectator,* London: J. and R. Tonson and S. Draper, 1753.

Auden, W. H., "The Guilty Vicarage," *The Dyer's Hand and Other Essays,* New York: Random, 1962.

———"Writing," *The Dyer's Hand and Other Essays.* Bargainner, Earl F., *The Gentle Art of Murder: The Detective Fiction of Agatha Christie,* Bowling Green, Ohio: Bowling Green, 1980.

Bloom, Allan, "Introduction," *Emile,*

Carlisle, Janice, *"Little Dorrit:* Necessary Fictions," *Studies in the Novel,* VI (1975), 195–214.

Cavell, Stanley, *The Claim of Reason: Wittgenstein, Skepticism, Morality, and Tragedy,* London: Oxford UP 1979.

Cotsell Michael, "Secretary or Sad Clerk? The Problems of John Harmon," *Dickens Quarterly,* 1 (1984), 134–35.

Crick, Brian, "'Mr. Peggotty's Dream Comes True': Fathers and Husbands; Wives and Daughters," *University of Toronto Quarterly,* 54 (1984), 38–55.

Davis, Earle, "The Creation of Dickens's *David Copperfield:* A Study in Narrative Craft," *Bulletin: Municipal University of Wichita,* XVI (1941).

———, *The Flint and the Flame: The Artistry of Charles Dickens,* Columbia: U of Missouri P, 1963.

Dickens, Charles, "In Memoriam: W. M. Thackeray," *Cornhill Magazine,* Feb, 1864. Reprinted in *Collected Papers,* London, 1938.

———, *Little Dorrit,* Harmondsworth: Penguin Books, 1978.

Eigner, Edwin M., *The Metaphysical Novel in England and America: Dickens, Bulwer, Hawthorne, Melville* (Berkeley: U of California P 1978.

Fish, Stanley Eugene, *Surprised by Sin: The Reader in Paradise Lost,* London: Macmillan, 1967.

Forster, John, *The Life of Charles Dickens,* (ed.) J. W. T. Ley, London: Cecil Palmer, 1928.

Frye, Northrop, "Dickens and the Comedy of Humours," in *Experience in the Novel: Selected Papers from the English Institute* (ed.) Roy Harvey Pearce, New York: Columbia UP, 1968.

Garis, Robert, *The Dickens Theatre,* Oxford: Oxford P, 1965.

Goldsmith, Oliver, *The Plays of Oliver Goldsmith* (ed.) C. E. Doble, London: Henry Frodse, 1909.

Haycroft, Howard, *Murder for Pleasure: The Life and Times of the Detective Story,* New York and London: D. Appleton-Century, 1941.

Hearne, Vicki, "How to Say Fetch," *Raritan,* III (1983).

Jaeffreson, J. Cordy, *Novels and Novelists, from Elizabeth to Victoria,* London: Hurst and Blackett, 1858.

Kaplan, Fred, *Dickens: A Biography,* New York: Morrow, 1988.

Kincaid, James, *Dickens: The Rhetoric of Laughter,* Oxford: Oxford U P, 1971.

Knowles, James Sheridan, *The Hunchback,* London: E. Moxon, 1832.

Lewes, G. H., "Dickens in Relation to Criticism," *Fortnightly Review,* (February 1872), 141–54.

Miller, *Alice, For Your Own Good,* (trans.) Hildegard and Hunter Hannum, New York: Farrar, Straus, Giroux, 1983.

Mundhenk, Rosemary, "The Education of the Reader in *Our Mutual Friend,*" *Nineteenth-Century Fiction,* 34 (1979), 41–58.

Pemberton, T. Edgar, *The Birmingham Theatres: A Local Retrospect,* Birmingham: Cornish Brothers, 1889.

———, *Dickens and the Stage,* London: George Redway, 1888.

Polhemus, Robert, *Comic Faith: The Great Tradition from Austen to Joyce,* Chicago: U of Chicago P, 1980.

Rotkin, Charlotte, *Deception in Dickens' Little Dorrit,* New York: Peter Lang, 1989.

Rousseau, Jean-Jacques, *Emile: or On Education* (trans.) Allan Bloom, New York: Basic Books, 1979.

Scott, Sir Walter, *Redgauntlet: A Tale of the Eighteenth Century,* London: Nelson, 1905.

Smith, Graham, *Dickens, Money, and Society,* Berkeley: U of California P, 1968.

Spencer, Herbert, *Education: Intellectual, Moral, and Physical,* New York: D. Appleton, 1860.

Trollope, Anthony, *Barchester Towers.*

Twain, Mark, *Adventures of Huckleberry Finn,* Berkeley: U of California P, 1985.

"Quoth the Raven":
The Role of Grip in *Barnaby Rudge*

Jerome H. Buckley

"Halloa!" cried a hoarse voice in his ear. "Halloa, halloa, halloa! Bow wow wow. What's the matter here! Hal-loa!"

The speaker—who made the locksmith start as if he had seen some supernatural agent—was a large raven, who had perched upon the top of the easy-chair....

"Look at him!" said Varden, divided between admiration of the bird and a kind of fear of him. "Was there ever such a knowing imp as that! Oh he's a dreadful fellow!"

The raven, with his head very much on one side, and his bright eye shining like a diamond, preserved a thoughtful silence for a few seconds, and then replied in a voice so hoarse and distant, that it seemed to come through his thick feathers rather than out of his mouth.

"Halloa, halloa, halloa! What's the matter here!

Keep up your spirits. Never say die. Bow wow wow. I'm a devil, I'm a devil, I'm a devil. Hurrah!"—And then, as if exulting in his infernal character, he began to whistle. (*Barnaby Rudge* 50–51)

Thus quoth the raven Grip, introducing himself in the sixth chapter of *Barnaby Rudge*. Grip's exuberance at the outset seems far removed from the dark foreboding of traditional ravens and quite unlike the dismal croak of Poe's "ghastly grim and ancient Raven," the Nevermore bird, of which he was nonetheless the almost certain source (Grubb 209–21). For Grip voices a life-affirming hope rather than a doleful gloom, and his "devilry," which he will continue to allege, seems more ironic than nefarious. Gabriel Vardon's divided response recognizes at once the creature's uncanny awareness and perplexing ambiguity. Whether a force for good or, like most of his kind in literature, an ill omen, Grip readily detects something the "matter" in the scene he has just witnessed and perhaps, by extension of his prescience, in the events that are to follow and even, we might fancy, in the troubled fortunes of Dickens' strange fifth novel over the past one hundred and fifty years.

In 1971, when reviewing the critical heritage of *Barnaby Rudge,* Philip Collins noted that the tale had "attracted little serious attention, and not much enthusiasm" (Collins 92). Most of its early readers thought it inferior to its enormously popular predecessor, *The Old Curiosity Shop,* and many later Dickensians, judging it melodramatic in characterization, disproportionate in plotting, too heavily sardonic in its intermittent humor, assigned it a very low place in the master's canon. Poe, considering it a failed murder mystery, claimed to have guessed the identity of the murderer long before the "exceedingly feeble and ineffective" denouement. (Collins 110) John Forster complained of the abrupt break in structure structure (I:245). Wilkie Collins declared *Barnaby* "the weakest book that Dickens ever wrote" (Collins 588). And G. K. Chesterton believed that the sum of its vivid pictures "hardly [made] a novel" (125–26).

On the other hand, among its relatively few admirers, Bulwer-Lytton lauded it as Dickens' finest work "in point of art," and Thomas Hood, in one of the first reviews, found it "better built" than any of the earlier novels.[2] Swinburne contrasted it with *A Tale of Two Cities,* convinced that the latter had "nothing of the rich and various exuberance which makes of *Barnaby Rudge* so marvellous an example of youthful genius in all the glowing growth of its bright and fiery April" (Swineburne 50). And George Gissing, less hyperbolically, concluded that *Barnaby,* fashioned in a "language full of subdued energy" was "perhaps the best written" of all Dickens' works.[3] In more recent scholarship and criticism, especially since 1970, the novel has received a good deal of close analysis, much of it prompting a newly positive assessment.[4] But even its staunchest defenders have confessed to its anomalous place among the fifteen novels as an "awkward stepchild, impossible to ignore and difficult to love" (Folland 406). And none has paid much heed to the presence or function of Grip the raven.

Barnaby Rudge in fact was a long deliberated and seriously planned fiction, and Dickens, as the letters of 1841 bear witness, was strenuously engaged in its composition and generally pleased with his achievement. Though he complained that the demands of weekly serialization frequently left him feeling cramped for space, he declared a total absorption in his narrative; when "I sit down to my book, some beneficent power shows it all to me, and tempts me to be interested, and I don't invent it—really do not—*but see it,* and write it down" (Letters [Pilgrim] II:411). He repeatedly sought "strong" effects. As he approached the climax of the story, he believed it was "progressing ... to good strong interest" (II:325). A month later he told

Forster he was steadily "warming up very much about *Barnaby"* and hoping "the interest will be pretty strong—and in every number, stronger" (II:351). And again he affirmed his confidence: "I was always sure I could make a good thing of *Barnaby,* and I think you'll find it comes out strong to the last word" (II:356). An earlier letter promises the raven a measure of that strength; as he is to appear in Chapter X, "Grip will be strong." (II:219). And the last words of the novel affirm Grip's strength, his capacity to endure indefinitely, to survive history itself.

On commissioning his illustrator, Dickens described his odd intention in choosing his titular hero: "Barnaby being an idiot, my notion is to have him always in company with a pet raven who is immeasurably more knowing than himself. To this end, I have been studying my bird and think I could make a very queer character of him" (II:197–98) Grip, then, had a living orig-inal— or rather more than one, for Dickens writes often and at length, in his 1841 correspondence, of his three successive ravens, one devoted to devious mischief, one highly vocal, but none achieving the longevity or semi-mythi-cal status of Barnaby's companion.[5] Describing the last and most intelligent of the three, however, Dickens seems to have reversed the influence and to have granted him attributes already assigned to Grip in the fiction, since this bird, schooled in a Yorkshire alehouse, "loves to see human Nature in a state of degradation, and to have the superiority of Ravens asserted. At such times he is *fearful* in his Mephistophelean humour,"[6] repeating no doubt Grip's cry, "I'm a devil, I'm a devil."

Though few of us nowadays, I suppose, keep talking ravens, or crows (the names are virtually interchangeable), such birds presumably were not uncom-mon as household pets in the nineteenth century. Byron included an unruly crow, "tame (but not *tamed)"* (*Letters and Journals* VIII:13), in his menagerie at Ravenna. Scott reportedly was much amused by his raucous Corbie's attack on a surly dog.[7] And Dickens seems to have had no difficulty in acquiring replacements for the original Grip.

But, whatever the availability of pet ravens, the fictional Grip has at least as certain a lineage in literature, folklore, and popular myth as in actual fact. Ravens had long been regarded as creatures of mystery and ill omen, pre-sagers of doom and death—no doubt from their observed appetite for carrion. Their alleged longevity was legendary—as in Tennyson's passing reference in "Locksley Hall" to "the many-wintered crow." In the medieval bestiary the crow appeared as "a long-lived bird, ... much used by diviners to foretell the future, ... fond of spying upon the doings of men, particularly in their treach-ery," issuing warnings of retribution, yet knowing nothing of "the secrets of

God."[8] The Bible presents the raven as an ambiguous symbol: the unreturning messenger released from the ark, an unclean creature proscribed by the dietary laws, yet also, as Dickens remembered (Letters II:232) an agent of pity bringing food to Elijah in the wilderness. Shakespeare writes variously of the "hateful," the "boding," and the "fatal" raven, and, in *Hamlet*, of "the croaking raven [that] doth bellow for revenge," but conversely, in *Titus Andronicus*, concedes that "Some say that ravens foster forlorn children"—a notion clearly pertinent to the ministry of Grip.

A more specific raven, answering to the name "Ralpho," enters Smollett's *Roderick Random*. Here Roderick and Strap, stopping at a country inn, are frightened out of their wits by the large ominous bird suddenly perched at the foot of their bed. "As this creature," Roderick explains, "is reckoned in our country as a common vehicle for the devil and witches to play their pranks in, I verily believed we were haunted, and, in a violent fright, shrunk under the bed-clothes." The next morning he learns that Ralpho's keeper is "the land-lord's father, who had been an idiot some years, and diverted himself with a tame raven, which, it seems, had hopped away from his apartment in the night."[9] Dickens, as we know, had been familiar with *Roderick Random* ever since boyhood, but he may also have seen an 1831 edition of the novel with five illustrations by his friend George Cruikshank, one of which depicted Ralpho's intrusion. In any case, the mad old man's raven, though, after all, merely a bird, seems to anticipate the queer character of Barnaby's more pervasive and more-than-avian Grip.

Ravens, then, have had a certain prevalence in English literature, at least from the time of the medieval ballad "The Twa Corbies" through Ted Hughes's ironic sequence, "Crow" (1970).[10] But Dickens alone assigns his bird a recurrent place in a realistic narrative, and we may still wonder at his choice and the intention and effect of Grip in the completed novel. One modern critical reader suggests resolving the problem by taking Grip quite literally and simply at his own "Mephistophelean" word. Grip so interpreted becomes "a clear symbol of evil, a kind of externalized demon" in possession to the very end of the demented Barnaby's soul.[11] But the text as a whole, I believe, hardly warrants so direct a reading. For Grip is neither truly diabolic nor effectively benevolent. He remains throughout most of the narrative enigmatic and ambiguous, observant but detached, existing by choice in an animate non-human dimension of his own.

Grip, of course, frequently does present an apparently sinister aspect. As we have seen, Gabriel Varden, whose very name suggests more angelic propensities, mingles fear with admiration in his appraisal of the bird as the "sharpest and cunningest of all the sharp and cunning ones" (v, 42), and he is half-persuaded that "If there's any wickedness going on, that raven's in it, I'll be sworn" (vi, 53). At Haredale's gloomy Warren, when Barnaby and his mother are in flight from London, Grip, "strictly in unison with the rest" and "with the air of some old necromancer," looks "like the embodied spirit of evil biding his time of mischief" or, again, like "a very sly human rascal" overhearing private conversation (xxv, 192, 195). Even Barnaby at one point confesses to being in thrall to Grip (though he does not think of the mastery as a devil's command): "He calls me, and makes me go where he will. He goes on before, and I follow. He's the master, and I'm the man" (vi, 51). But later Barnaby describes Grip as his "friend" and his "brother" rather than his master, to which the raven answers "by an affectionate croak" (lvii, 435). In fact Grip leads Barnaby into no serious mischief of any kind. He is a vocal presence, a sort of chorus character commenting with ironic effect on the current mood, but always the passive observer and never an efficient cause of unrest or mounting violence. He is apparently happiest when he and Barnaby are rollicking through the open fields and hills or playing innocent games with Hugh and his dog. He does hoarsely echo, perhaps in mockery, the Gordonites' cry, "No Popery" (lviii, 445). But he is immediately downcast, with drooping head and rumpled feathers, by Barnaby's arrest since he appears "to comprehend and to partake, his master's fallen fortunes" (lviii, 448). Again, on the other hand, in the prison yard when he sees Barnaby embracing the evil Rudge as his lost father, he hops excitedly around the pair, "as if enclosing them in a magic circle, and invoking all the powers of mischief" (lxii, 478). Yet when Barnaby's death by hanging seems imminent, the bird eager to reassure him with "Never say die," lacks "the heart to get through the shortest sentence" (lxxiii, 561). And when Barnaby's mother is bidding her son what seems to be a last farewell, Grip "utter[s] a feeble croak" as if "half in encouragement.... and half in remonstrance," but wants "heart to sustain it, and lapse[s] abruptly into silence" (lxxvi, 584). Thereafter the horrors of the prison and the riots apparently weigh so heavily upon Grip that he remains speechless for a whole year after the troubles have passed until at the end he can be contentedly assured of an edenic peace regained, such as could please no veritable devil.

Whereas Grip can approach or simulate human responses, Barnaby seeks to realize the attributes of a bird. He garbs himself in fluttery old ruffles and ribbon-ends like bedraggled plumage and bedecks his hat with peacock feathers, long since limp and broken, which hang loosely down his back. The most vivid (and grotesque) of Phiz's illustrations (xvii, 136) depicts a distrait recumbent Barnaby with the raven perched upon his raised knee, the eyes of each fastened hypnotically on the other. Barnaby's birdlike fear emerges in his account of a bad dream in which "something ... was always hiding and crouching, like a cat in dark corners," ready to pounce upon him (vi, 48). And he fancies—presumably as Grip would view a scarecrow—that clothes hanging out to dry are animate beings, moving ominously in the breeze, hatching evil plots against nature. For Barnaby, who is essentially a child of nature, below but also beyond human intelligence—"a sort of natural" (or half-wit), as Mr. Willet calls him—is convinced that it is "much better to be silly" in a world of innocent imaginings than to be bound by the cold calculation of a "wise" man like John Chester.[12]

Barnaby excitedly tells Chester that he can see "eyes in the knotted panes" and "swift ghosts" in the hard-blowing wind," and hear "voices in the air." And Mr. Willet obtusely explains the delusion, "He wants imagination, ... that's what he wants" (x, 82). But it is in Barnaby's vivid imagination that we may find a clue to the vibrancy of the novel, a kind of primitive animism which ascribes human qualities not only to Grip but to a whole world of sometimes benign but more often threatening material objects. For an anthropomorphic vision—more controlled, of course, than Barnaby's—pervades Dickens' descriptive method, lending a strange intensity to the documented history. The very houses and their furnishings come alive. The Maypole Inn nods in its sleep, its bricks "grown yellow and discoloured like an old man's skin, [its] sturdy timbers ... decayed like teeth" (1, 2). The fireside of its guest chamber, selling its momentary warmth to strangers, is as mercenary as "a very courtezan" (x, 78). The beer kegs broken by the rioters become "the mere husks of good fellows whose jollity had departed, and who could kindle with a friendly glow no more" (lv, 417). Haredale's Warren lingers for a while as "the very ghost of a house, haunting the old spot in its old outward form" (xiii, 102), and a London tenement vegetates "like an ancient citizen, ... dozing on in its infirmity until ... it tumbles down, and is replaced by some extravagant young heir" (iv, 30). The narrative is likewise animated by dynamic active verbs, as, for example, in Chapter LXIV, where one tremendous sentence, with nearly forty verbs or verbal forms, describes the flames of riot behaving with the diabolic savagery of the pyromaniacs who are feeding them. Again and again the fiction moves into an eerie surrealism, the world of Grip and Barnaby, which involves omen and symbol and defies measurement by the rational standards of the historical novel that the tale of the Gordon riots on one level appears to be.[13]

The shift in title from the original *Gabriel Vardon, the Locksmith of*

Straps. fright at the Raven.

London, Printed for Cochrane & Pickersgill 1831

George Cruikshank illustration for 1831 edition of Smollett's *Roderick Random*. (Courtesy of Print Collection, The New York Public Library, Astor, Lenox, and Tilden Foundations.)

Barnaby and Grip
(*p. 135*)

H. K. Browne ("Phiz") illustration for *Barnaby Rudge*. (Courtesy of Special Collections Office, The Research Libraries, New York Public Library.)

Barnaby in Newgate

H. K. Browne illustration for *Barnaby Rudge*. (Courtesy of Special Collections Office, The Research Libraries, New York Public Library.)

In the Condemned Cell

H. K. Browne illustration for *Barnaby Rudge*. (Courtesy of Special
Collections Office, The Research Libraries, New York Public Library.)

London to *Barnaby Rudge,* before the serialization began, signals an altered conception and tone. The admirable Gabriel remains the efficient hero he was apparently meant to be, insofar as his benevolent sanity helps achieve the positive resolution. But Gabriel's kindly commonsense, which at the outset makes him suspect the raven, blunts his understanding of mystery and impending violence, which Grip readily intuits and in which Dickens himself as narrator seems at times a vicarious participant.[14] Gabriel has no personal affinity to the pervasive force of the irrational that envelops the novel, either as harmless fantasy or tumultuous passion. Barnaby, on the other hand, though his active role is secondary to Gabriel's, serves in his "silliness" as counterpart or analogue to a madness far deeper than his own, the militant unreason that enlists his innocent and witless support.

Whether or not Dickens' view of the mass demonstration culminating in the exultant overthrow of Newgate seems confused and ambiguous, the text clearly presents the riots as an urban affront to nature. Barnaby the helpless "natural" in his country retreat is seduced by the blind rogue Stagg into thinking city crowds preferable to the tranquillity of the rural scene. London then, fiercely animated, proves the cruel antagonist.[15] Hugh, who is Barnaby's instinctive friend, has already been co-opted by the rioters, until he is no longer, as he was in his proper setting, an independent natural man, "like a handsome satyr," half animal and half woodland deity (xxi, 159). In the implicit conflict between town and country, society and nature, that betrays both Barnaby and Hugh (and even silences Grip), the Maypole, which has long stood as symbol of rural stability and continuity, is sadly desecrated. But by the end of the novel, when the antagonist has been subdued, nature has recovered, and Barnaby, though inarticulate about his urban fears, has found peace in the restored Maypole farm and in his firm resolve never again to venture into the city. And by that time Grip has once more found his voice and his cheerful impish identity, "I'm a devil, I'm a devil, I'm a devil!" over and over, almost as if the irrepressible Dickens, speaking through him, were slyly punning on his own name.

NOTES

1. Forster on *BR*. Despite misgivingings about the structure, Forster finds the description of the riots vivid and "masterly" (I, 246). Edgar Johnson considers *BR* "the least satisfactory of all Dickens' full-length books," the hero Barnaby having "no organic connection" with its "clumsy and broken-backed plot": *Charles Dickens: his Tragedy and Triumph*, 2 vols. (New York: Simon and Schuster, 1952), I, 330.

2. Hood on *BR*, see *Critical Heritage*, pp. 103–4, from Hood's enthusiastic *Athenaeum* review of Jan. 22, 1842. Bulwer, quoted by Andrew Lang, ed. *Works*, Gadshill Edition, 34 vols. (London: Chapman and Hall, 1897), XII, xii.

3. George Gissing, *Charles Dickens* (1903, reprinted, New York: Haskell House, 1974), p. 187; also, p. 190, "The impression aimed at is obtained with absolute success."

4. Among the more positive estimates of *BR*, see Tillotson, "Introduction"; Jack Lindsay, *Charles Dickens: a Biographical and Critical Study* (London: Dakers, 1950), pp. 212–17; Steven Marcus, *Dickens: from Pickwick to Dombey* (New York: Basic Books, 1965), pp. 169–212; James K. Gottshall, "Devils Abroad: the Unity and Significance of *Barnaby Rudge*," *Nineteenth-Century Fiction*, 16 (1961), 133–46; Harold F. Folland, "The Doer and the Deed: Theme and Pattern in *Barnaby Rudge*." Rudge," *PMLA*, 74 (1959), 406–17; T. J. Rice, "Variable Focus in *Barnaby Rudge*," *Nineteenth-Century Fiction*, 30 (1975), 172–84; Thelma Grove, "Barnaby Rudge: A Case Study in Autism," *Dickensian*, 83 (1987), 139–48; and Juliet McMaster, "Better to be Silly: From Vision to Reality in *Barnaby Rudge*," *Dickens Studies Annual*, 13 (1984) 1–19. T. J. Rice offers a comprehensive survey of secondary sources in his *"Barnaby Rudge": An Annotated Bibliography* (New York: Garland, 1987).

5. See *Letters*, II, 202, 230–32, 303–4, 412.

6. Letter of Dec. 2, 1841, after the completion of *BR*.

7. See Captain Basil Hall's account of the incident in John Gibson Lockhart, *The Life of Sir Walter Scott*, 7 vols. (Edinburgh: Cadell, 1837–38), V, 410–11.

8. *A Cloisters Bestiary*, ed. Richard H. Randall, Jr. (New York: Metropolitan Museum of Art, 1960), p. 44. See also T. H. White, *The Book of Beasts* (London: Cape, 1954), p. 142.

9. *Roderick Random* (London: Cochrane, 1831), ch. xiii, pp. 70–71. F. D. Wierstra calls attention to this passage in his *Smollett and Dickens* (Amsterdam: De Boer, 1928), p. 74.

10. Hughes's Crow has been compared to the Trickster hero of American Indian myth as the wanderer, apart from normal notions of good and evil, a realist in a "world of harsh natural necessities and instincts," an ironic contemplator of the scene, enigmatic, resilient in longevity; see David Perkins, *A History of Modern Poetry*, 2 vols. (Cambridge, Mass.: Harvard University Press, 1976, 1987), II, 455–58. A note on Hughes by David Daiches ascribes to him "an ambivalent attitude to nature—seen as both startlingly apart from human sensibilities and simultaneously parallel to and symbolic of the human situation" (*Norton Anthology of English Literature*, 4th edition, 2 vols. [New York: Norton, 1979], II, 2487).

11. Dickens' view of Grip's world seems very similar. On Grip as a devil or diabolic agent, see Gottshall, p. 141. Lindsay, p. 216, also associates Grip with "the dark forces."

12. On Barnaby, see Grove's piece on autism and especially the McMaster essay, which finds Barnaby's unreason essential to "a novel about the eruption of the

unconscious" (p.15). An earlier defence of Barnaby against many detractors is
E. E. Polack's "Was Barnaby Rudge Mad?" *Dickensian*, 7 (1911), 298–99.

13. *BR* has been both defended and attacked as an example of the historical novel.
Lindsay finds the "mass movement" [the Gordon riots] "treated in its own right,
an integral part of the story, not as a mere background" (p. 212). Georg Lukács
claims that history *is* primarily background in *BR*, where it "provides purely accidental circumstances for 'purely human' tragedies": quoted by Stephen Wall,
Charles Dickens: A Critical Anthology (Harmondsworth: Penguin Books, 1970),
p. 433.

14. *Cf.* Johnson, 311: "Dickens obviously shared with the rioters an orgiastic joy in
the flaming demolition of Newgate." Marcus (p. 172) argues that Dickens "unconsciously... identified himself with the rioters who burned into Newgate" but at the
same time was deeply distrustful of violence and mob action.

15. *Master Humphrey's Clock*, which introduced and serialized *BR*, suggests that the
city is to be its central theme; *cf.* the long digression on the "heart of London," its
poverty, homelessness, and crime, and the failure of its citizens to know or care
much about the lives of their unfortunate neighbors. See (Cambridge, Mass.:
Riverside Press, 1869), pp. 156–58.

WORKS CITED

Chesterton, G. K., *Charles Dickens*. New York: Dodd Mead, 1906.

Collins, Philip. ed., *Dickens: The Critical Heritage*. New York: Barnes & Nobles, 1971.

Dickens, Charles, *Barnaby Rudge*, London: Oxford UP, 1954.

Folland, Harold F. "The Doer and the Deed: Theme and Pattern in Barnaby Rudge" *PMLA*, 74, (1959) 406–17.

Forster, John, *The Life of Charles Dickens*. Philadelphia: Lippincott, 1873.

Gissing, George. *Charles Dickens*. 1903, rptd. New York: Haskell House, 1974.

Gottshall, James K. "Devils Abroad: the Unity and Significance of Barnaby Rudge" *Nineteenth-Century Fiction*, 16, (1961).

Grove, Thelma. "Barnaby Rudge: A Case Study in Autism," *Dickensian*, 83, (1987), 139–48.

Grubb, Gerald G. "The Personal and Literary Relations of Dickens and Poe," *Nineteenth Century Fiction*, 6 (1950), 209–21.

Johnson, Edgar. *Charles Dickens: His Tragedy and Triumph*, 2 volumes, New York: Simon and Schuster, 1952.

Lindsay, Jack. *Charles Dickens: A Biographical and Critical Study*. London: Dakers, 1950.

Marcus, Steven. *Dickens: from Pickwick to Dombey*. New York: Basic Books, 1965.

McMaster, Juliet. "Better to be Silly: From Vision to Reality in Barnaby Rudge," *Dickens Studies Annual*, 13, (1984).

Rice, T. J. *Barnaby Rudge: An Annotated Bibliography*, New York: Garland, 1987.

———. "Variable Forms in Barnaby Rudge" *PMLA*, 74, (1959) 406–17.

Swinburne, Algernon. *Charles Dickens*. London: Chatto and Windus, 1913.

Wall, Stephen. *Charles Dickens: A Critical Anthology*. Harmondsworth: Penguin Books, 1970.

Repressive and Expressive Forms: The Bodies of Comedy and Desire in *Martin Chuzzlewit*

Robert E. Lougy

He who has eyes to see and ears to hear may convince himself that no mortal can keep a secret. If his lips are silent, he chatters with his fingertips; betrayal oozes out of him at every pore.[1]

PIMPLES, NOSES, AND GAPING MOUTHS:
THE BODY AS TEXT

Dickens is intrigued by those depressions and protuberances inscribed upon the surface of the human body, by noses, pimples, Adam's-apples, beards and bare cheeks, bare legs and wooden legs, by snowy breasts and waving hands, mouths with teeth and mouths without them, by various bodily odors and emanations, and by the ways in which bumps, abrasions, or errant thoughts can cause the surfaces and appendages of our body to change shape or color, become moist or dry, larger or smaller, hotter or colder. We witness, in fact, the changing contours of the body early in *Martin Chuzzlewit,* as we hear of the collision between Pecksniff and a wind-blown door and of the subsequent goose-egg, "an entirely new organ, unknown to phrenologists, on the back of his head" (10). Throughout the novel, Dickens is fascinated by those bodily concavities and convexities that shatter, disrupt, or violate the images of wholeness and intactness we attempt to present to the world. He is drawn not to the individual body per se, but rather to its capacity for sudden growths, eruptions, and transformations. The bodies we find in *Martin Chuzzlewit* are not seamless texts, but are instead characterized by various shapes and often bizarre combinations of parts and pieces, invested with their own configurations and power to intrigue and attract.

In speaking of Rabelais's fascination with the grotesque body, Mikhail Bakhtin observes that "all these convexities and orifices have a common characteristic; it is within them that confines between bodies and between the body and the world are overcome: there is an interchange and interorientation" (*R,* p. 317). Dickens too is interested in such interchanges and interorientations, as in the scene where young Martin becomes, as Meckier describes him, "a violated man" (7), his body carefully scrutinized by several Americans:

> Two gentleman … agreed to divide the labour. One of them took him below the waistcoat; one above. Each stood directly in front of his subject with his head a little on one side, intent on his department. If Martin put one boot before the other, the lower gentleman was down upon him; he rubbed a pimple on his nose, and the upper gentleman booked it. He opened his mouth to speak, and the same gentleman was on one knee before him, looking at his teeth, with the nice scrutiny of a dentist.... They had him in all points of view: in front, in profile, three-quarter face, and behind.... New lights shone in upon him, in respect of his nose. Contradictory rumours were abroad on the subject of his hair. (316)

Priggish and rather stuffy throughout much of the novel, Martin is in this scene the grotesque body of orifices and protoberances (the gaping mouth and pimpled nose) examined from all angles, from the rear as well as from the front and sides.[2] If young Martin's body, like his contradictory hair, is open to various interpretations, Dickens's attitude towards the bodies that populate his fictional landscape in *Martin Chuzzlewit* is similarly ambiguous. "Spitting to Dickens," S. J. Newman has observed, "is as shitting to Swift" (109), and Dickens seems to find the body and its functions to be disturbing and unsettling. But Dickens' imagination is fueled rather than constrained by such misgivings, drawn, whether in fascination, horror, or both, to images of the body that break down boundaries, collapsing the categories of inside and outside, self and other, body and earth. He is also fascinated with those dynamics of the body that participate in the processes of inundation or assimilation, and if eating and drinking swallow the things of this earth, absorbing the outside into the inside, spit, like dung, urine, and death, participates in the other end of this cycle, as the body returns to the earth that which has come from it.

If we interpret such images in Dickens' novels as simply serving the cause of satire, we not only diminish his fiction, but cheat ourselves as well. These textualized images of the human body are, of course, hardly limited to *Martin Chuzzlewit* alone. We have only to think, for example, of his earliest novel,

The Pickwick Papers, with its extensive ceremonies of eating and drinking as well as its multitude of variously configured bodies—from the rotundity of Pickwick himself or the insatiable and narcoleptic plumpness of Joe the fat boy to the gangly and bony sharpness of its numerous spinsters. Or, for that matter, we might also turn to his last novel, *Our Mutual Friend*, with those corpses that Gaffer and Lizzie Hexam retrieve from the river, Sials Wegg's wooden leg, erotically elevated by the thought of money, the pink-faced Fledgeby, with his jealousy of the bearded Lammle and other men, the intense sexual desire and frustration evident in the body and physical gestures of Bradley Headstone, or the deformed figure of Jenny Wren, surrounded by the "golden bower" of her incredibly beautiful hair. But Dickens wrote a good number of novels, most of them populated with such bodies, and, given the constraints of time and space, I would like to focus my attention on *Martin Chuzzlewit.* In reading *Martin Chuzzlewit,* for example, we must follow the methodology of the curious Americans, for its fictional landscape is filled with bodies, often dismembered or fragmented, its world resembling at times the fecundity and corporeality of a Fellini film, at other times the *corps morcele* of Salvador Dali's canvasses. Challenging or rewriting what Bakhtin identifies as "the new bodily canon," with its representation of "an entirely finished, completed, strictly limited body" (*R,* 320), Dickens' art is a subversive enterprise, undermining or parodying those ideologies and structures that privilege such wholeness or completeness.

Bakhtin's analysis of the "the bodily canon," (*R,* pp. 320–23), however, identifies not only the ideological biases and assumptions involved in the production of canonical images, but also the ways in which the body itself becomes an ambiguous text, inviting readings and misreadings. This particular ambiguity of textuality has been spoken of by Edward Said and others, and their remarks can, I think, help illuminate better the body in *Martin Chuzzlewit* and the problems of interpretation posed by it. Said observes, for example, how Freud's theory of language makes it necessary for us to revise our understanding of the act of reading or interpretation. Because words carry with them "a considerable freight of the unknown," Said points out, "any interpretive act necessarily involves us in a regressive movement away from the text to what the words carry along with them, whether that is the memory of the writing or of some other, hidden, and perhaps subversive power" (75). Writing of the body of the text as well as of the text of the body, Roland Barthes has observed how such sites of hidden and subversive power can be discerned by means of abrasions or fissures, by rough edges or seams that destroy smoothness or intactness (7).[3]

In reading the body in *Martin Chuzzlewit,* we need to be aware of its fissures, abrasions, and distortions, of extraordinary or unusual gestures and movements through which the repressed can find articulation. We need to pay attention, in other words, to those Freudian pores through which secrets ooze. Like Dickens' rude Americans, I too want to examine the body in *Martin Chuzzlewit* and the various ways in which Dickens textualizes it as he explores the dynamics of expression and repression.

I will look first at one of Mrs. Gamp's later monologues, examining the ways in which the comic impulses in *Martin Chuzzlewit* are often located in Dickens' carnivalesque imagery and iconography of the human form. Like the dream or the joke, such impulses within the novel enable the repressed to find expression and, as such, they destabilize those moral or social values which, if we take Dickens at his word, the novel advances and defends.[4] Secondly, I want to turn my attention to a particularly memorable scene involving Jonas Chuzzlewit, Charity Pecksniff, and Tom Pinch, and at the ways in which secrets are betrayed by the body's various disfigurements, transformations, and gestures. Permeated with blood and violence, this scene not only contains one of the most developed sexual puns in Dickens' canon, but also testifies to the power with which the repressed can return. In the new bodily canon, "all orifices of the body are closed," suggests Bakhtin (R, p. 320), but in *Martin Chuzzlewit,* the text, like young Martin's mouth, gapes open, its libidinized sites, identified by bloody wounds, flushed faces, and tumescent organs, testifying to unspoken narratives.

NOSES, BEARDED WOMEN, AND
SHAKESPEARE'S LEGS

"What jokes whisper may be said aloud: that the wishes and desires of men have the right to make themselves acceptable alongside of exacting and ruthless morality."[5]

The first scene tales place late in the novel, just before Pecksniff is unmasked, and in it, Sairey appropriates center stage as she senses that this valued space is in danger of becoming inhabited by Poll Sweedlepipe and young Bailey. However, her linguistic occupation of this position is tenuous, since she, like Pecksniff, is soon upbraided by old Martin, the novel's embodiment of Freud's "exacting and ruthless morality." Before this happens, however, she shares a final anecdote about Mrs. Harris and then disappears into silence, led out of the room in a "walking swoon." As always, her words deserve to be heard in their entirety:

"Which, Mr. Chuzzlewit," she said, "it is well beknown to Mrs. Harris as has one sweet infant (though she do not wish it known) in her family by the mother's side, kep in spirits in a bottle; and that sweet babe she see at Greenwich Fair, a travellin in company with the pink-eyed lady, Prooshan dwarf, and livin skelinton, which judge her feelins wen the barrel organ played, and she was showed her own dear sister's child, the same not bein expected from the outside picter, and performing beautiful upon the Arp, which never did that dear child know or do; since breathe it never did, to speak on, in this wale! (696)

The ostensible motive behind this monologue—Mrs. Gamp's wish to become a companion for the recently widowed Mercy Pecksniff—recedes into the background as her words generate their own energy, testifying to the immense differences between the nineteenth-century's response to death and that of our own age. For if our age tends to isolate or conceal death, the nineteenth-century adult and child knew death as an immediate and accessible presence. Edgar Johnson, for example, recounts Dickens's description of how he was taken as a child by his nurse to visit a woman who had just recently gone through the ordeal of childbirth:

"At one little green grocer's shop," he wrote, there had been a lady "who had had four children (I am afraid to write five, though I fully believe it was five) at a birth"; and he saw "how the four (five) deceased young people lay, side by side, on a clean cloth on a chest of drawers," reminding the little boy by their complexion "of pigs' feet as they are usually displayed at a neat tripe-shop" (12)

Freed early in its life from this "wale of tears," the tiny corpse of Gamp's anecdote is kept in a bottle of spirits, accompanied by other grotesque variations of human form, including a "pink-eyed lady, Prooshan dwarf, and living skelinton," co-members of a carnival freak-show advertised by misleading billboards, as Mrs. Harris discovers when "she was showed her own dear sister's child, the same not bein expected from the outside picter, and performing beautiful upon the Arp, which never did that dear child know or do" (696).

Drawn from scenes familiar to almost all Victorians, this passage subverts those sentimental and morally edifying images that become more dominant as the novel moves rapidly toward closure. J. Hillis Miller suggests that Sairey's "way is very firmly rejected by Dickens when he includes her among the villains exposed in the denoument" (120), but it is possible that this final anecdote, postponing as it does that moment of exposure, testifies to Dickens' recognition of the sadly diminished world which will exist when there is no longer any room for Mrs. Gamp. Dickens' vision, articulated by a woman he loves but soon must destroy through the patriarchal admonitions of old Martin, is abusive and cruel, violent, vindictive, and profoundly comic; as

Fellini and Flannery O'Connor would later do for our own age, he submerges us in the folk-culture of his world—its fairs, circuses, puppet shows, street vendors, organ grinders, and, as J.W.T. Ley has shown, its popular songs and folk ballads—and, in doing so, he invokes images of the carnivalesque, an icon for Dickens (for example, *Hard Times)* of subversive and anarchic energies. As such, Dickens drew upon those same sources Bakhtin and Freud turned to when they explored the origins of the novel and humor. Bakhtin, for example, locates the "authentic folkloric roots of the novel" (21) in what he describes as "popular laughter," observing that its "folklore and popular comic-sources" helped the novel to restructure the image of the individual by providing us with the "comic familiarization of the image of man" (35). Lacan reminds us of how Freud, an encyclopedic and eclectic reader, turned to similar sources while writing some of his radical early texts, such as *The Interpretation of Dreams* and *Jokes and their Relation to the Unconscious:* "to interpret the unconscious as Freud did," writes Lacan, "one would have to be as he was, an encyclopedia of the arts and muses, as well as an assiduous reader of the *Fligenda Blätter,"* a German comic newspaper of the late nineteenth and early twentieth centuries (169).

In Dickens' case, he turned to a London that he knew as few have ever known the city. George Lear once commented, for example, that "I thought I knew something of the town, but after a little talk with Dickens I found that I knew nothing. He knew it all from Bow to Brentford," adding that "he could imitate, in a manner that I never heard equalled ... the low population of the streets of London in all their varieties, whether mere loafers or sellers of fruit, vegetables, or anything else" (*Johnson,* I, 55). At the center of this city in *Martin Chuzzlewit* is Sairey Gamp, Kincaid's "high priestess" (156), who, like the folk culture within which she is rooted, challenges the "exacting and ruthless" morality of her age. Like the joke or the carnivalesque, she is inherently subversive, cutting through the repressed or the concealed to tell us of what goes on behind closed shutters: "we never know what's hidden in each other's breasts," she observes, "and if we had glass winders there, we'd need to keep the shutters up, some on us, I do assure you" (400). "The body," writes Bakhtin, "that figures in the expression of the unofficial speech of the people is the body that fecundates and is fecundated, that gives birth, devours and is devoured, drinks, defecates, is sick and dying" (*R,* 319), and Mrs. Gamp, as wife, mother, widow, mid-wife, and layer-out, belongs to such speech. "Gamp is my name, and Gamp my nater," she tells us (367), and her "nater" is familiar with secret desires and human mysteries, giving expression to them through her body when they cannot be said aloud, as when she reminds Mercy Chuzzlewit of how she will eventually need a midwife:

> And with innumerable leers, winks, coughs, nods, smiles, and curtseys, all
> tending to the establishment of a mysterious and confidential understanding
> between herself and the bride, Mrs. Gamp, invoking a blessing upon the house,
> leered, winked, coughed, nodded, smiled, and curtseyed herself out of the
> room." (367)

Patterns of repetition and return pervade *Martin Chuzzlewit*—young
Martin's and Mark Tapley's return from Eden and from America and young
Bailey's coming back from "death" are just two examples among many—
and, indeed, the novel seems haunted by the dynamics of repression and
exposure, by the ways in which the repressed returns, translating itself into
our gestures, language, and actions—into the wink, the leer, the cough, the
blush that will not remain concealed. In this respect, *Martin Chuzzlewit* is the
joke writ large, and like Freud's tendentious joke or Sairey herself, it is variously obscene, hostile, and aggressive.[6] It is the half-opened door, the shutters
with a crack in them, the slip of the tongue, the blush, the dream, the drunken
rambling—whatever enables us to penetrate behind facades and screens and
to see what is really going on behind them.

Too strong to be completely excised or silenced, these comic impulses
challenge or threaten the moral concerns of the novel, such as Dickens's
desire as expressed in his "Preface to the Cheap Edition" (1850) of *Martin
Chuzzlewit*, to "show how Selfishness propagates itself" (717). Various readers have pointed out, for example, how figures such as Pecksniff and Mrs.
Gamp inhabit a realm comparable to Nabokov's "aesthetic bliss," transcend-
ing through their language and elasticity of spirit the moral strictures within
which the novel attempts to contain them.[7] Often disturbing and unsettling,
the novel participates in Bakhtin's "comical operation of dismemberment,"
which allows one to "disrespectfully walk around whole objects; therefore,
the back and rear portion of an object [and also its innards, not normally
accessible for viewing] assume a special importance" (23). During such a
moment, that which should be hidden, not seen, is suddenly exposed. The
text, Barthes suggests, "is (should be) that uninhibited person who shows his
behind to the Political Father" (53); and although nineteenth-century England
did not allow Dickens openly to represent backsides or insides, he nevertheless found ways, especially in his earlier novels, of looking "below the waist-
coat," and of mooning those same canonical images the novel would seem to
embrace.

This "comical operation of dismemberment" is evident as Mrs. Gamp speaks of her preference for soft foods: "in consequence of tender teeth, and not too many of 'em, which Gamp [her husband] himself ... at one blow, being in liquor, struck out four, two single, and two double." Her teeth are not only knocked out, but acquire a peripatetic fate afterwards: "[Gamp's teeth] was took by Mrs. Harris for a keepsake, and is carried in her pocket at this present hour, along with two cramp-bones, a bit o' ginger, and a grater like a blessed infant's shoe, in tin, with a little heel to put the nutmeg in" (602). Dislodged teeth in Dickens's novel seem to wander widely, but wooden legs, such as that which once belonged to Mr. Gamp, move towards a stasis brought about, as Sairey observes, through excessive intimacy with winevaults: "and as to husbands, there's a wooden leg gone likeways home to its account, which in its constancy of walkin' into winevaults, and never comin out again till fetched by force, was quite as weak as flesh, if not weaker" (535).

There are, however, numerous other examples of such dismemberment or fragmentation. Foremost among these is Mercy Pecksniff's nose, much adored by Moddle:

"Oh, Mrs. Todgers, if you knew what a comfort her nose is to me."
"Her nose, sir!" Mrs. Todgers cried.
"Her profile in general," said the youngest gentleman, "but particularly her nose." (439)

And those female legs ignored by Shakespeare:

"Shakespeare's an infernal humbug, Pip! What's the good of Shakespeare, Pip? I never read him. What the devil is it all about, Pip? There's a lot of feet in Shakespeare, but there an't any legs worth mentioning in Shakespeare's plays, are there, Pip? Juliet, Desdemona, Lady Macbeth, and all the rest of 'em, whatever their names are, might as well have no legs at all, for anything the audience knows about it, Pip.... What's the legitimate object of the drama, Pip? Human nature. What are legs? Human nature. Then let us have plenty of leg pieces...." (p. 391).

Martin Chuzzlewit gives us "plenty of leg pieces," or at least plenty of what leg pieces synecdochically represent. We find, however, not only noses and legs existing independent of the body, but various scenes of either real or potential fragmentation, death, or disaster. Mrs. Gamp bestows a ghoulish benediction upon Mrs. Prig, who, like Mrs. Gamp, not only midwives, but also tends to the sick, the dying, and the dead—"wishin you lots of sickness, my darlin creetur," as she entertains a private fantasy of meeting Prig "at a large family's, where they all takes it regular, one from another, turn and turn about, and has it business like" (403). Entertaining peculiar erotic fantasies about the apparently dying Lewsome, Sairey pins "his wandering arms against his side, to see how he would look if laid out as a dead man. Hideous as it may appear, her fingers itched to compose his limbs in that last marble attitude. 'Ah,' said Mrs. Gamp, walking away from the bed, 'he'd make a lovely corpse'" (353). The epicene Poll Sweedlepipe, a barber attracted to the facial hair of Mrs. Prig, whom he declares, "in admiration of her beard, to be a woman of transcendent charms" (404), applies his razor to the beardless adolescent cheeks of young Bailey, but not without Bailey's nervous admonition, "gently over the stones, Poll. Go a-tiptoe over the pimples" (396-397).

Jokes are like dreams, Freud reminds us, in that both "bring forward something that is concealed or hidden" (SE, VIII, 13–14), and Dickens, a writer haunted by dreams and possessed by the comic impulse, exposes the concealed and the shameful. "The legs of the human subject, my friends, are a beautiful production," observes Pecksniff, "compare them with wooden legs, and observe the difference between the anatomy of nature and the anatomy of art" (134). Standing forth on the upstairs landing of Todgers's, drunk and half-naked in his nightshirt and still sexually aroused by his earlier flirtations with Mrs. Todgers, Pecksniff rhapsodizes about the comfort of bare legs, of having that which is normally hidden or concealed exposed or released from confinement: "'this is very soothing', said Mr. Pecksniff after a pause. 'Extremely so. Cool and refreshing; particularly to the legs'" (134). The sexual subtext of Pecksniff's remarks becomes evident as he wonders aloud what Mrs. Todgers's notion of a perfectly designed wooden leg might be: "'Do you know … that I should very much like to see Mrs. Todgers's notion of a wooden leg, if perfectly agreeable to herself'" (134). Jokes make possible the satisfaction of an instinct, either hostile or lustful or both, that cannot be satisfied otherwise (SE, VIII, 101), and in the case of Pecksniff, the leg, endowed with phallic significance, enables Pecksniff to speak of what is normally concealed, turning his attentions, both lustful and hostile, towards Mrs. Todgers.

Mrs. Todgers too exposes that that which should be concealed when Pecksniff unexpectedly enters her room:

> And then Mr. Pecksniff peeped smilingly into the room, and said, "May I come in, Mrs. Todgers?"
> Mrs. Todgers almost screamed, for the little door of communication between that room and the inner one being wide open, there was full disclosure of the sofa bedstead in all its monstrous impropriety." (p. 117)

"Language is not immaterial," writes Lacan, "it is a subtle body, but body it is" (87); its subtlety is evident in the above passage, which begins with Pecksniff's unsolicited intrusion into forbidden enclosures and testifies to an eroticized space that assumes the contoured shapes of Mrs. Todger's concealed female body, whose wide-open "little door" of communication reveals the inner room behind it. Unlike Mrs. Todgers's repressed scream, that which should be hidden is suddenly exposed, and within the center of this space is the sofa-bedstead "in all its monstrous impropriety," testifying to the human sexuality it metonymically represents.

Along with Nadgett, the novel's detective and quintessential voyeur, Dickens might very well say that "nothing has an interest in it to me that's not a secret." Like the partially opened door or the cracked shutter, the body in *Martin Chuzzlewit* both conceals and reveals, hides and makes the hidden known. Fascinated with that which is usually concealed, but needs to expose itself (in this respect, the scene involving the half-naked and drunken Pecksniff is emblematic of the comic or artistic impulses behind the novel, the artist in performance both as voyeur and exhibitionist), Dickens is similarly intrigued with the mechanisms of repression and with how these mechanisms are subverted, gotten around, betrayed by a body within whose gestures and configurations the unconscious is inscribed.

THE WOUND, THE FLUSHED FACE, AND THE ERECTION

"There is no other way of conceiving the indestructibility of unconscious desire—in the absence of a need which, when forbidden satisfaction, does not sicken and die.... It is the truth of what this desire has been in his history that the patient cries out through his symptom, as Christ said that the stones themselves would have cried out if the children of Israel had not lent them their voice. (*Écrits,* 167)

Secrets in *Martin Chuzzlewit* are betrayed by the body. Gamp enters the Mould residence announced by harbingers that are, like Shelley's words, carried upon the wind, as Dickens likens her bodily emanations to the gastric disturbances of an ethereal creature: "at the same time, a peculiar fragrance was borne upon the breeze, as if a passing fairy had hiccuped, and had previously been to a wine vault" (347). Among other things, this particular vignette suggests that it is difficult to keep our secrets hidden, for we are not only betrayed by words whose often hidden and subversive meanings slip through our conscious nets, but by our bodies as well. Such is the case with an especially rich and problematic scene in chapter twenty-four which, like Gamp's carnival anecdote, calls our attention to the enigmatic textuality of human forms and gestures.

Given the length of *Martin Chuzzlewit,* a brief synopsis of this particular scene might be helpful. It begins with a fight between Jonas Chuzzlewit and Tom Pinch that results in Jonas being struck on the head with his own walking stick. Along with Tom Pinch, Jonas soon returns to the Pecksniff residence, where his wounds are tended to by Pecksniff and his daughter, Mercy, while Pecksniff's other daughter, Charity, recently jilted by Jonas, sits quietly by with a strange smile on her face. The second section takes place later that same evening when Charity, having already guessed the origin of Jonas's injury, comes to Tom Pinch's room, and, with unusually intimate gestures, expresses her gratitude to him and tells him that she wants to be his friend. During the third section, Tom contemplates the significance of Charity's visit as well as the implications of his earlier fight with Jonas. Reflecting upon his position within the ambiguous and shifting entanglements of the Pecksniff and Chuzzlewit families, Tom's thoughts or dreams—the whole passage is ambiguously suspended between sleep and wakefulness—turn to Mary Graham and conclude with what one critic has characterized as "one of the most remarkable passages in Dickens" (184):

> It must be acknowledged that, asleep or awake, Tom's position in reference to this young lady was full of uneasiness. The more he saw of her, the more he admired her beauty, her intelligence, the amiable qualities that even won on the divided house of Pecksniff…. When she spoke, Tom held his breath, so eagerly he listened; when she sang, he sat like one entranced. She touched his organ; and from that bright epoch even it, the old companion of his happiest hours, incapable as he had thought of elevation, began a new and deified existence (340).

Michael Steig suggests that "Dickens would no doubt have expunged this last sentence had he been consciously aware of its extended sexual pun" (184). Perhaps Dickens would have, perhaps not. In any case, this sexual pun was not deleted and, as Steig argues in "The Intentional Phallus," it is difficult to conceive of such a passage as the result of a mere accident (53–55). Steig raises the question of authorial intentionality, but such questions, while interesting, remain extremely problematic since, at best, we can only hazard a guess about what Dickens intended and whether such intent is inscribed in the design and/or execution of the particular text under examination.[8] More importantly, however, if Freud, Lacan, Derrida, and countless artists have taught us anything, it is that because we are not unified subjects and not in full control of the meaning of the words we use or the language we create, we are not the authors of our own texts. Moreover, this passage involving Tom

Pinch does not exist in isolation, but rather, like the fight between Jonas and Tom and Charity's visit to Tom's room, it provides exemplary evidence of how the body is a theater within which our psychic symptoms are acted out, a text upon which is transcribed narrative histories repressed by language.[9] As such, these three sections or textual moments exemplify Peter Brook's concept of "textual binding," in which textual energies are organized into a "servicable form," such as repetition, recurrence, or symmetry, that "allows us to bind one textual moment to another in terms of similarity or substitution rather than mere contiguity" (101).

THE WOUND

Dickens knew of the ways in which the body speaks, and in each of the three moments that constitute this scene, secrets are betrayed by means of libidinized sites marked by the sudden appearance of blood—namely, Jonas wound, Charity's flushed face, and Tom's erection. Thus, it is only appropriate that the scene itself begins with a violent fight between Tom Pinch and Jonas Chuzzlewit:

> He [Jonas] flourished his stick over Tom's head; but in a moment, it was spinning harmlessly in the air, and Jonas himself lay sprawling in the ditch. In the momentary struggle for the stick, Tom had brought it into violent contact with his opponent's forehead; and the blood welled out profusely from a deep cut on the temple. (338)

A shaken Tom Pinch later confesses to Charity that "I didn't mean to hurt him so much" (339), but even more significant than Tom's ambiguously phrased admission (how much is "so much"?) is the disclosure of a capacity for violence on Tom's part that is both registered and erased by a text that informs us that his "apparently" violent designs are in fact "really" directed towards healing:

> Tom Pinch, in his guilty agitation, shook a bottle of Dutch Drops until they were nothing but English Froth, and in his other hand sustained a formidable carving-knife, really intended to reduce the swelling, but apparently designed for the ruthless infliction of another wound as soon as that was dressed (338–39).

What is most peculiar about this scene, however, is not so much the fight itself, since Jonas' beligerence virtually forces Tom's hand, but rather Jonas's response to his wound. Throughout the novel, he has been a man moved quickly to anger, easily offended, and, as Montague Tigg later discovers, dangerous to cross, and yet his subdued response to his injury is so out of character that even Tom is bewildered, interpreting it as evidence of a new magnanimity on Jonas's part. With a passivity insufficiently accounted for by his mild concussion, Jonas stares at his blood-stained handkerchief ("several times he took his handkerchief from the cut to look vacantly at the blood upon it" [338]), as if he were attempting to interpret the stain itself. Gayatri Spivak has spoken of how certain textual signs, such as the overstated or understated expression, the awkward or engimatic word or scene, alert us to those places within the text where the subject is least in control, where the repressed is most likely to return (xliv), and this particular scene would seem to exemplify such a moment. If we are to understand Jonas's wound, we need to regard it as the site of psychic as well as physical trauma, a symptomatic mark or hieroglyph, like the blood stain, through which the repressed escapes and makes itself known.

This wound, however, is not only experienced by Jonas, for Dickens is also concerned in *Martin Chuzzlewit* with the wound as the metonymic cultural scar inflicted upon us by virtue of the fact that we are inserted into human culture and history. The first chapter of *Martin Chuzzlewit* suggests that it will examine not only the Chuzzlewit family, but the nature of "human nature" itself and those conflicts, jealousies, and desires found within the family structure. Just as the original title of the novel identified the centrality of kinship and filiation to the novel, offering its reader a key that would enable them to enter "the House of Chuzzlewit," so too did its original motto—"Your homes the scene. *Yourselves* the Actors, here"—make it clear that the novel was concerned with those conflicts and desires found in all "houses," not just Chuzzlewit's.[10] In this respect, the Chuzzlewits not only embody those tensions, conflicts, and desires inscribed within the family romance, but also what Dickens refers to as those "innumerable repetitions of the same phase of character" passed on from one generation to the next.

Such repetitions are also the stuff of metaphor and myth. In her study of Jacques Lacan, for example, Anika Lemaire observes how "the Oedipus is the unconscious articulation of a human world of culture and language; it is the very structure of the unconscious forms of society" (92). It is within the context of this structure and its determinative presence within the individual and collective patterns of human history (Dickens informs us, again in the first chapter, that these patterns can be traced as far back as the earliest families) that Guy Fawkes's otherwise inexplicable presence in the Chuzzlewit family tree (2) makes sense. His story of regicide testifies to the continuing presence of Oedipal patterns (of which regicide is but a variation) within human history, and, as such, Guy Fawkes is both the heir and ancestor of Oedipal conflicts and desires woven throughout this novel, and most power-fully realized in the figure of Jonas.

Dreams, Nietzsche observes, enable us to reach "some primeval relic of humanity ... we can scarcely reach any longer through a direct path" (cited by Freud, *SE,* V, 549), and the story of Jonas and Anthony, like a dream, moves in "a direct path" towards the exploration of forbidden desires. Woven into the novel as an Oedipal Ur-plot that amplifies or brings other tensions (for example, those between Tom Pinch and Pecksniff and between young and old Martin) into sharper focus, Jonas's story is unusual not because it tells of parricidal desires, but rather because such desires have escaped inter-diction.[11] It is through Jonas's wound as mark or fissure that his blood, at once hidden and familiar (Freud's definition of the uncanny) pours forth, inscribing an enigmatic text upon his handkerchief.[12] This blood-stained handkerchief also shows up later in the novel, reappearing as Montague Tigg's clothes, "stained with clay, and spotted with blood" (675), retrieved by Nadgett from the river into which Jonas threw them.

The repressed returns in other ways as well. The strength of the symbolic father as dead father derives from the fact that his prohibitions are internal-ized after his death by the sons, who yield to his patriarchal interdictions through what Freud characterizes as "deferred obedience" (*SE* XIII: 143). Anthony's judgment returns from beyond the grave through the choric voices of Chuffey and Lewsome to tell of the violation of such prohibitions, thus set-ting into motion the punishment that follows. Jonas's passive response to his wound and his "reading" of his blood acknowledge the strength of the dead father's presence, and, as fissure or mark, Jonas' wound also prefigures his later attempts to atone for his crime through self-inflicted punishment. Before such atonement can take place, however, Jonas's body is once again marked or scarred, this time with the taboo, and exposed to public scrutiny and repul-sion. The intensity of the horror Jonas's presence invokes suggests that the community is responding not so much to the murder of Montague Tigg as to his attempted murder of his father: "they turned away," Dickens writes,

> from him as if he were some obscene and filthy animal, repugnant to the sight.... As he crouched on the floor, they drew away from him as if a pesti-lence were in his breath. They fell off, one by one, from that part of the room, keeping him alone on the ground (671, 675).

Situated within an ambivalent field of desire, the taboo arises in response to our most powerful longings and unconscious desires, and the strength of our repulsion depends upon the power of these desires (*SE,* XIII: 35). Regarded as contagious because of the community's "fear of an infectious example" (SE, XIII: 71–72), Jonas, isolated and feared as if he were the carrier of a deadly pestilence, evokes such a response precisely because the community is in fact already "infected" with Jonas's disease, finding in him the embodiment of their own unconscious desires. Having actually done (or tried to do) that of which they have only dreamt, Jonas, when he observes at one point in the novel that "I dare say I'm no worse than other men. We're all alike, or nearly so" (545), is more correct than he realizes.

Ritualistically summoned to public exposure and punishment by the patriarchal voice of old Martin, who still presides over the house of Chuzzlewit—"'Let no one leave the house,' said Martin. 'This man is my brother's son. Ill-met, ill-trained, ill-begotten'" (666)—Jonas is condemned; and in a brilliant intuitive stroke on Dickens' part, Jonas is unable to hang himself, but instead must die his own death through a gesture involving yet still more repetition, as Jonas drinks poison, thus killing himself by the same instrument of destruction he had attempted to use against his father. Like the hero of Kafka's "The Judgment," Jonas is condemned to death by an internalized patriarchal voice and carries out the sentence himself.

THE FLUSHED FACE

As Mercy Pecksniff and her father tend to Jonas's wounds, Charity does not help, instead sitting "upright in one corner, with a smile upon her face" (338). But as in Jonas's case, the textual body articulates that which language attempts to repress, literally speaking in this case through its pores. Similar to the scene in *Great Expectations* when Estella first allows Pip to kiss her after she secretly witnesses a fight between himself and Herbert Pocket, this moment is similarly situated within the erotic dynamics of violence. "Underlying eroticism," writes Bataille, "is the feeling of something bursting, of the violence accompanying an explosion" (93), and Charity's flushed or blood-suffused face reveals the *jouissance* she experiences through her vicarious participation in the scene between Jonas and Tom Pinch. In *Martin Chuzzlewit,* the opening of that which should be closed alerts us to the escape of the repressed or the forbidden, and like Gamp's shutters or Jonas's wound, the scene involving Charity and Tom Pinch begins with such an opening. For as Charity quietly sneaks to Tom's room and knocks on his door, Tom "heard a gentle tap at his door, and opening it, saw her, to his great astonishment,

standing before him with her finger on her lip" (339). The gesture of the "finger on her lip" calls attention to the precarious containment of secrets which
theaten to escape through the fissures or seams of the body and Charity's
body, her gesture of conspiratorial silence notwithstanding, testifies to the
presence of such secrets, as she elaborates upon her remark to Tom that "I am
your friend from tonight. I am always your friend from this time" (339):

> She turned her flushed face upon Tom to confirm her words by its kindling
> expression; and seizing his right hand, pressed it to her breast, and kissed it.
> And there was nothing personal in this to render it at all embarrassing, for even
> Tom, whose power of observation was by no means remarkable, knew that she
> would have fondled any hand, no matter how bedaubed or dyed, that had bro-
> ken the head of Jonas Chuzzlewit (339).

Dickens' feeble narrative disclaimer ("there was nothing personal in this
to render it at all embarrassing") cannot be taken seriously except in so far as
it calls our attention to the transgressive nature of erotic gestures directed
towards someone who occupies the position of her brother within the
Pecksniff household. The blush, David-Ménard observes, "points up the
insistence of a long experience of pleasure that has always been situated at
the point of articulation between body and language" (60), and like the
Victorian novelist's "virginal blush" that belies its adjectival demure, the
flushed face also testifies to sublimation or displacement, when that which
originates below is transported above. As such, Charity's face, as well as
those movements on her part that translate into gesture what her face has
already articulated, anticipates the final paragraph of this scene and Tom
Pinch's sexual apotheosis.

For although the "kindling expression" of Charity's flushed face "confirms
her words," her words themselves, with their allusions to a wished-for friendship, attempt to evade or avoid the desire that empowers them. The erotics of
the scene, however, are identified not only by the configurations of Charity's
body or by blood that will not remain repressed, but also by a series of acts
that complete or provide closure for the desire articulated by her blood: as she
"fondles" Tom's fetichized hand, which has been marked ("bedaubed or
dyed") by association with the blood or violence of Jonas's wound, first
pressing it to her breast and then kissing it (gestures that both recall and preempt those "snowy breasts" that threw kisses at Tom because they saw "no
harm" in him), she enacts, through a series of gestures, a pantomime of sexual activity and pleasure, caught up within the dynamics of violence that permeate this scene. In the specific choreography of Charity's gestures—from
the knock on the door and her finger pressed against her lips to her flushed

face and the blood "bedaubed" hand she presses against her breast and kisses—we find an eroticized movement as the form of her particular gestures articulates a previously repressed history of desire.

THE ERECTION

If the narrator wilfully attempts to misread Charity's gestures, Tom does not. And if we in turn are to understand Tom Pinch, we cannot, like Barbara Hardy, dismiss him as a "grossly sentimental figure" (112). Mould, the undertaker, alerts us to the significance of surnames in *Martin Chuzzlewit,* and Tom Pinch's surname suggests not only his distorted and prematurely wizened nature, but also the pain associated with his body. Anticipating *David Copperfield's* Mr. Dick, Tom is an early Dickensian version of the man-child as sage and artist who hides behind his simplicity or even simple-mindedness values and perceptions against which the rest of the characters are judged. He is, however, problematic in ways that Mr. Dick is not, for while Mr. Dick remains essentially asexual, we find in Tom an ambiguous but nevertheless discernible growth of sexual awareness and erotic desire.

Tom's body is the arena within which this growth is registered, and both as Dickens describes it and Hablot K. Browne draws it, it is an ambiguous text that resembles his clothes, "twisted and tortured into all kinds of odd shapes." The unconscious expresses itself through the body and someone familiar with its articulations or "symptomatic acts," Freud suggests, might "feel like King Solomon who, according to oriental legend, understood the language of animals" (*SE,* VI: 199). However, such articulations can be puzzling, and Tom's body is an enigmatic text. He is, we read,

> an ungainly, awkward-looking man, extremely shortsighted, and prematurely bald.... He was far from handsome certainly; and was dressed in a snuff-coloured suit, of an uncouth make at the best, which, being shrunken with long wear, was twisted and tortured into all kinds of odd shapes; but notwithstanding his attire, and his clumsy figure, which had a great stoop in his shoulders, and a ludicrous habit he had of thrusting his head forward, by no means redeemed, one would not have been disposed ... to consider him a bad fellow by any means. He was perhaps thirty, but he might have been any age between sixteen and sixty: being one of those strange creatures who never decline into an ancient appearance, but look their oldest when they are very young, and get over it at once. (17)

The distorted bodies of Gamp's carnival anecdote, the "pinkeyed lady, Prooshan dwarf, and livin skelinton," exemplify divergences from the anticipated lines or configurations of the human form and, as such, they have been narrativized, made the stuff of theatre. Unlike these bodies, however, Tom's has not been mythicized or turned into material for theater and magic; but it too bewilders and intrigues us—even concealing its true age—as we attempt to decipher it and to uncover its history. It is similarly misread by other erotic bodies.

> Sparkling eyes and snowy breasts came hurriedly to many an upper casement as he clattered by, and gave him back his greeting; not stinted either, but seven-fold, good measure. They were all merry. They all laughed. And some of the wickedest among them even kissed their hands as Tom looked back. For who minded poor Mr. Pinch! There was no harm in *him*. (59, emphasis Dickens').

If the "sparkling eyes and snowy breasts" look upon Tom as a eunuch, a man who has "no harm" in him, he is likewise regarded by John Westlock as lacking that which a man should possess: "you haven't half enough of the devil in you," he tells Tom (20).[13] Although it invites misinterpretation by others, however, Tom's body also reveals the truth. "A perturbed stomach or mind ... they mean the same thing," Betteredge tells Franklin Blake in Wilkie Collin's *The Moonstone,* and Tom's knowledge, registered as both somatic and psychic pain, is experienced as moments of "uneasiness" or discomfort that arise when that which has been previously repressed or concealed makes itself known.[14] Thus, although the narrator denies any "personal" significance to Charity's gestures, Tom Pinch knows better:

> That there should be any such tremendous division in the family as he knew must have taken place to convert Charity Pecksniff into his friend, for any rea-son, but, above all, for the real one; that Jonas, who had assailed him with such exceeding coarseness, should have been sufficiently magnanimous to keep the secret of their quarrel; and that any train of circumstances should have led to the commission of an assault and battery by Thomas Pinch upon any man call-ing himself the friend of Seth Pecksniff, were matters of such deep and painful cogitation, that he could not close his eyes. His own violence, in particular, so preyed upon the generous mind of Tom, that coupling it with the many former occasions on which he had given Mr. Pecksniff pain and anxiety (occasions of which the gentleman often reminded him), he really began to regard himself as destined by a mysterious fate to be the evil genius and bad angel of his patron. But he fell asleep at last, and dreamed—new source of waking uneasiness— that he had betrayed his trust, and run away with Mary Graham (339–40).

Like Jonas' wound and Charity's flushed face, Tom's discomfort brings to light that which has been concealed or repressed. Reflecting upon familial patterns of secrets, betrayals, and violence that he did not notice earlier, Tom becomes aware not only of a "tremendous division" within the Chuzzlewit family, but also of his own ambiguous position within these divisions. As Tom realizes, his "assault and battery" of Jonas, the "friend of Seth Pecksniff," was also a reenactment of earlier assaults upon Pecksniff, and thus he correctly associates or "couples" his violence toward Jonas with those occasions on which he had also caused Pecksniff "pain and anxiety." Regarding himself as "destined by a mysterious fate to be the evil genius and bad angel of his patron," Tom sees himself as taking part in hidden scenarios, the actor in a script not of his own making, but rather one situated in Lacan's "censored chapter."

"The text itself," Barthes suggests, "can reveal itself in the form of a body, split into fetish objects, into erotic sites" (56), and the wound that flows from Jonas's temple, the blood suffusing Charity's face, and the tumescence of this scene's final paragraph all tell of the word made flesh. Like the two earlier sections (with their corresponding gestures, the violent "touch" that wounds Jonas and Charity's touching of Tom's hand to her breast and lips), the libidinized area is identified by the touch and thus calls our attention to the particular site of Tom's *jouissance*. If the sliding of signified under signifier becomes unusually transparent in this scene, the musical metaphor barely containing the elevated organ it only half-heartedly attempts to conceal, it is because of symptoms that demand to be heard, of desires, such as those that empower Tom's dreams, that will not remain silent.

INTERDICTED DESIRE AND PATRIARCHAL RAGE

However, the presence of the Oedipus within the family romance disturbs patterns of kinship and filiation, creating what Edward Said refers to as "a tangling up of the family sequence" (170). Such entanglements pervade *Martin Chuzzlewit,* a novel especially haunted by Oedipal dynamics, and the above passage concerning Tom's fantasies is situated within such an ambiguous or shifting web. Some time ago, Orwell spoke of the "incestuous atmosphere" (448) in Dickens' novels, and Tom's uneasiness or discomfort has its origin not only in his feelings of violence or aggression towards Pecksniff, but also because Mary's presence within his fantasies only partially screens even more forbidden desires.

Later in the novel, this screen momentarily collapses and the text, like Gamp's opened shutters, discloses to Tom and Ruth Pinch that which should be hidden. Within the entanglements created by the Oedipus, identities and kinship structures remain unstable and in this particular scene, the identities of Mary and Ruth merge into one another as the unspoken name discloses those desires which were both hidden and revealed by Tom's earlier fantasies. Once again initiated by the opened door and the violent gesture, the scene begins with young Martin bursting into Tom's apartment and accusing him of an unnamed treachery or betrayal. This textual moment seems particularly overdetermined, riddled with fissures or abrasions through which the hidden can only partially escape, for although Tom repeatedly asks young Martin to be more explicit, we never do find out what Tom is specifically accused of or why Martin will not be more direct.

The large gaps of silence in the midst of Martin's speech gives this scene a peculiar or enigmatic quality, as if that which should have been said has been left unspoken. Young Martin leaves the room, but his refusal to name his accusation lingers, and Tom and Ruth Pinch, moving to fill in such silences, begin to speak of secrets, but create silences of their own as they refuse to name the subject of their discourse. Responding to a sudden burst of tears on Tom's part, Ruth tells him that "I know your secret heart. I have found it out; you couldn't hide the truth from me. Why didn't you tell me" (654). Answering her by saying that "I am glad ... that this has passed between us ... because it relieves my mind of a great weight" (655), Tom continues:

> "My dear girl," said Tom: "with whatever feelings I regard her," they seemed to avoid the name by mutual consent; "I have long ago—I am sure I may say from the first—looked upon it as a dream. As something that might possibly have happened under very different circumstances, but which can never be." (655)

As with Martin's outburst, what is most striking about this passage is its evasiveness, not what is said, but unsaid. Circling around the subject, tentatively coming close to it, but never approaching it directly, Tom and Ruth participate in such a circuitous dialogue that the narrator actually interrupts it, observing how they "seemed to avoid the name by mutual consent." But just as his earlier narrative disclaimer confirmed what it intended to deny, here his narrative aside calls attention to the missing name, that which has been censored.

Like Jonas's body, the name is avoided, empowered with the taboo, because it is invested with those forbidden desires attached to it. Testifying to the chasm between desire and need as well as to the indestructibility of unconscious desires, Tom and Ruth both cry out in their symptoms, afraid of coming any closer, but also afraid of moving apart. Tom dreams of a world in which desire might find fulfillment, but his vision of closure, rooted in fictional scenarios no longer available to him, is haunted by death as well by

Warm reception of Mr Pecksniff by his venerable friend.

H. K. Browne ("Phiz"), "Warm reception of Mr. Pecksniff by his venerable friends," *Martin Chuzzlewit*.

desire—"someone who is precious to you might die," he tells Ruth, "and you may dream that you are in Heaven with the departed spirit, and you may find it a sorrow to wake to the life on earth" (656). Incest, Peter Brooks observes, "is only the exemplary version of a temptation of short-circuit from which protagonist and text must be led away, into detour, into the cure that prolongs narrative" (109), and Tom realizes that such a short-circuit cannot be. The murder of the father, according to Lacan, "is the fruitful moment of debt through which the subject binds himself for life to the Law [and] the symbolic Father is, in so far as he signifies this Law, the dead Father" (199), and although Tom Pinch "kills" Pecksniff when he denies his existence, Pecksniff remains very much alive within the Oedipal armature as the Dead Father or Symbolic Father, binding the subject to law and culture, what Tom refers to as "life on earth." The laws of culture, Tom's "higher justice," stand between Tom and the fulfillment of that "poetical justice" that haunts his dreams.

   Dominating the center of the novel's final illustration, "Warm Reception of Mr. Pecksniff by his Venerable Friend," is old Martin, Freud's "obscene, ferocious figure" of the primordial father (*Écrits,* 176), his face distorted by rage and his walking stick raised high ready to strike, revenging himself upon Pecksniff, who cowers by the desk while other members of the clan look on with expressions of relief, bemusement, and curiosity. A patriarchal bust presides over this scene from atop the bookcase, and a copy of *Paradise Lost,* also concerned with patriarchal figures, lies on the floor, one more victim of the violence of this scene.[15] Standing in front of the bookcase are Tom and Ruth Pinch, their arms and hands entangled and their bodies touching, as if they have been interrupted in the midst of an embrace, enacting, even in the presence of patriarchal rage, interdicted desires. Hablot K. Browne's brilliant final illustration is visual testimony to the novel's refusal to separate brother and sister, as they are bound together in a *ménage à trois* legitimized by Ruth's marriage to John Westlock, itself a screen for deeper motives that we find articulated in Ruth's insistence to her future husband that she will not tolerate separation from her brother. Both are destined to reenact, in a Sadean comedy of erotic terror and joy, narrative scripts wherein *jouissance* is always anticipated, the fulfillment of desire forever deferred.

NOTES

1. "Fragment of an Analysis of a Case of Hysteria" (1905), perhaps better known as the case-history of Dora. In *The Standard Edition of the Complete Psychological Works of Sigmund Freud,* ed. James Strachey. 7 (London: Hogarth Press, 1960), VII, 77–78. All future references to Freud's writings will be to this edition, here-

after cited as SE. Both volume and page number will be given.

2. Bakhtin observes that the "most important of all human features for the grotesque is the mouth. It dominates all else. The grotesque face is actually reduced to the gaping mouth" (R, 317)

3. Following a similar line of inquiry, Jacques Lacan writes of how the body is a text in whose symptoms we can find repressed narratives, what Lacan calls "the censored chapter":

> The unconscious is that chapter of my history that is marked by a blank or occupied by a falsehood: it is the censored chapter. But the truth can be rediscoved; usually it has already been written down elsewhere. Namely: in monuments: this is my body.

In *Écrits: A Selection*, trans. Alan Sheridan (New York: W.W. Norton, 1977), p. 50. All future references to Lacan, unless otherwise noted, will be to this edition.

4. The most important study of the subversive power of comedy is still Freud's *Jokes and their Relation to the Unconscious*. For other studies of the comic vision in Dickens, see Roger B. Henkle's *Comedy and Culture: England 1820–1900* (Princeton: Princeton UP, 1980), pp. 135–45, James Kincaid's *"Martin Chuzzlewit:* the Comedy of Accommodation," in *Dickens and the Rhetoric of Laughter* (Oxford: Clarendon, 1971), pp. 132–61, S.J. Newman's *"Martin Chuzzlewit:* the Novel as Play," in *Dickens at Play* (London: Macmillan, 1981), pp. 101–123, and especially Robert M. Polhemus's "Dickens's *Martin Chuzzlewit:* the Comedy of Expression," in *Comic Faith: The Great Tradition from Austen to Joyce* (Chicago: U of Chicago P, 1980), pp. 88–123.

5. Sigmund Freud, "Jokes and their Relation to the Unconscious," *SE,* VIII, 110.

6. Polhemus, for example, observes how Dickens "imagines and plays with fantasies of aggression—particularly against children and parental figures—and of madness, omnipotence, liberty, sex, anarchy, and—most important of all—death" (121).

7. See Henkle, Kincaid, and Polhemus on this point.

8. Steig observes that we cannot determine the answers to such questions, for "we simply do not know on the basis of any verifiable hypothesis" (54).

9. Steig observes that "in fact *in* the context of the novel it [the passage describing Tom Pinch and his elevated organ] makes absolute sense" (53, emphasis Steig's).

10. The rather cumbrous original title of *Martin Chuzzlewit,* used only during its serial publication, explicitly identified the concern of the novel with questions of kinship structures, filiation, and inheritance: "The Life and Adventures) of Martin Chuzzlewit) His Relatives, Friends, and Enemies/Concerning/All His Wills and Ways;/With a Historical Record of What He Did,/And What He Didn't:/Showing, Moreover,/Who Inherited The Family Plate, Who Came in for the Silver Spoons, (And Who for the Wooden Ladles./The Whole Forming a Complete Key to the

House of Chuzzlewit." Dickens never did use his motto, dropping it upon the advice of John Forster, who feared that Dickens might offend his readers.

11. Steig regards the Pinch-Pecksniff story line as a "detailed parody of the Oedipal conflict" (184). In referring to Tom Pinch, Steig speaks of how one can "successfully resolve his oedipus complex" (185). Freud and Lacan have taught us, on the other hand, that one can repress this complex, sublimate it, or reenact it, but not "successfully resolve" it.

12. Freud defines the uncanny as that "which is secretly familiar *[heimlich-heimisch]*, which has undergone repression and then returned from it" (XVII: 245). Manifesting itself in patterns of repetition and recurrence, the uncanny can be found, Freud tells us, in the presence of similar crimes (for example, Dickens's "innumerable repetitions" of family conflict and aggression) and the appearance of the same name (such as the two eponymous heroes of *Martin Chuzzlewit*) through several generations (XVII: 234).

13. Steig similarly suggests that "the point is clearly that 'no harm' means no danger of sexual feelings" (182).

14. David-Ménard observes that the question of "how a thought can be diverted into bodily innervation [e.g., in cases of hysteria] while at the same time it remains a thought" constitutes one of the central problems of psychoanalysis from Freud to Lacan (13). In his case history of Dora, for example, Freud observes that "we must recall the question that has so often been raised, whether the symptoms of hysteria are of psychical or somatic origin, or whether, if the former is granted, they are necessarily all of them psychically determined" (*SE*, VII, 40). Ned Lukacher suggests that David-Ménard, trying to find a way out of this epistemological paradox, locates the "body of jouissance" neither in the psychical or physiological, but rather in "the realm of signifying discourse" (x). David-Ménard observes that

> Reality exists for us only inasmuch as language structures our desire, inasmuch as grammar contributes its resources to the construction of that desire. If this is true of our relation to objects of the world, it is hard to see how our relation to our own bodies could be any different (66).

"Our bodies," she suggests, "exist for us inasmuch as we symbolize them" (66).

15. See chapter five, "Paradise Lost," (pp. 59–73) of Alexander Welsh's *From Copyright to Copperfield* for an extensive examination of the importance of Milton's text to Dickens' novel.

WORKS CITED

Bakhtin, M.M. *The Dialogic Imagination*. Ed. Michael Holquist. Trans. Caryl Emerson and Michael Holquist. Austin: U of Texas P, 1981.

———. *Rabelais and His World*. Trans. Hélène Iswolsky. Bloomington: Indiana UP, 1984.

Barthes, Roland. *The Pleasure of the Text*. Trans. Richard Miller. New York: Hill and Wang, 1975.

Bataille, Georges. *Erotism: Death and Sensuality*. Trans. Mary Dalwood. San Francisco: City Lights, 1986.

Brooks, Peter. *Reading for the Plot: Design and Intention in Narrative*. New York: Vintage, 1985.

David-Ménard, Monique. *Hysteria from Freud to Lacan: Body and Language in Psychoanalysis*. Trans. Catherine Porter. Ithaca: Cornell UP, 1989. First published in French in 1983.

Dickens, Charles. *Martin Chuzzlewit*. Ed. Margaret Caldwell. Oxford: Oxford University Press, 1984.

Freud, Sigmund. "Jokes and their Relation to the Unconscious." In *The Standard Edition of the Complete Psychological Works of Sigmund Freud*. Trans. James Strachey. London: The Hogarth Press, 1955. Vol. VIII.

———. "The Interpretation of Dreams." *Standard Edition*. Vols. IV and V.

———. "Totem and Taboo." *Standard Edition*. Vol. XIII.

———. "The Uncanny." *Standard Edition*. Vol. XVII.

Hardy, Barbara. *"Martin Chuzzlewit."* In Dickens and the *Twentieth Century*. Ed. John Gross and Gabriel Pearson. London: Routledge and Kegan Paul, 1962, 107–120.

Henkle, Roger B. *Comedy and Culture: England 1820–1900*. Princeton: Princeton UP, 1980.

Johnson, Edgar. *Charles Dickens: His Tragedy and Triumph*. Boston: Little, Brown, 1952. Vol. I.

Kincaid, James. *Dickens and the Rhetoric of Laughter*. Oxford: Clarendon Press, 1971.

Lacan, Jacques. *Écrits: A Selection*. Trans. Alan Sheridan. New York: W.W. Norton, 1977.

Lemaire, Anika. *Jacques Lacan.* Trans. David Macey. London: Routledge and Kegan Paul, 1977.

Ley, J.W.T. "More Songs of Dickens's Day." *Dickensian,* 28 (1932), 20–22.

———. "Sentimental Songs in Dickens." *Dickensian,* 29 (1933), 49.

———. "Some Comic Songs that Dickens Knew." *Dickensian,* 27 (1931), 33–38.

Meckier, Jerome. *Innocent Abroad: Charles Dickens's American Engagements.* Lexington: UP of Kentucky, 1990.

Miller, J. Hillis. *"Martin Chuzzlewit."* In *Charles Dickens: the World of His Novels.* Cambridge, Mass.: Harvard UP, 1958: 98–142.

Newman, S.J. *Dickens at Play.* London: Macmillan, 1981.

Orwell, George. "Charles Dickens." In *The Collected Essays, Journalism and Letters of George Orwell.* Ed. Sonia Orwell and Ian Angus. New York: Harcourt, Brace, and World, 1968. Vol. I, pp. 413–60.

Polhemus, Robert M. *Comic Faith: The Great Tradition from Austen to Joyce.* Chicago: U of Chicago P, 1980.

Said, Edward. *Beginnings, Intention and Method.* New York: Basic Books, 1975.

Spivak, Gayatri Chakravorty, ed. Jacques Derrida, *Of Grammatology.* Baltimore: The Johns Hopkins UP, 1974.

Steig, Michael. "The Intentional Phallacy: Determining Verbal Meaning in Literature." *JAAC* 36 (1977), 51–61.

———. *"Martin Chuzzlewit:* Pinch and Pecksniff." *Studies in the Novel* 1 (1969), 181–88.

Welsh, Alexander. *From Copyright to Copperfield: The Identity of Dickens.* Cambridge, Mass.: Harvard UP, 1987.

Dickens' Mr. Micawber and Mark Twain's Colonel Sellers: The Genesis of an American Comic

Malcolm M. Marsden

The year before his death, a forgetful Mark Twain told his official biographer Albert Bigelow Paine that, except for *A Tale of Two Cities,* he had never been able to read the novels of Charles Dickens. The Mark Twain scholar Howard Baetzhold has recently explained this denial and demonstrated that Mark Twain had indeed read Dickens off and on all his life and, "consciously or unconsciously, had borrowed important elements for a number of his own works" ("Twain and Dickens" 189). Both the plot and the narrator's moral development in Mark Twain's *Adventures of Huckleberry Finn* (1885), for example, have been shown to run parallel to the plot and the narrator's moral development in Dickens' *Great Expectations,* which had appeared in 1861 (Mills & Ridland). Likewise, Dickens' exposure of the vulgarity and corruption of the village of Cairo, Illinois (or Eden, as Dickens called it in *Martin Chuzzlewit),* presumably inspired, some thirty years later, Mark Twain's depiction of Stone's Landing in *The Gilded Age* (1873). Dickens' *A Tale of Two Cities* (1859), which Mark Twain admitted having read, suggested several episodes in *Huckleberry Finn* and both episodes and major themes in *A Connecticut Yankee in King Arthur's Court* (1889). In *The Adventures of Tom Sawyer* (1876), Mark Twain very likely based the juvenile courtship between Tom Sawyer and Becky Thatcher on the model which Dickens had provided for him twenty-six years previously in *David Copperfield* (1850), in which a callow David carries out with exaggerated care the Victorian rites of courtship with Dora, his child-wife-to-be. But a major Dickensian influence on Mark Twain that has long been noted but never fully explored is evident in the parallelism between Mr. Micawber (and to a lesser extent Mrs. Micawber) in *David Copperfield* and Colonel Beriah Sellers in Mark Twain's *The Gilded Age*. Baetzhold can sympathize with the older Mark Twain's convincing himself that he owed nothing to Dickens and might thus perceive of himself as a "self-made original from Missouri and the West." Yet Baetzhold believes that Mr. Micawber was in fact "among the several models for Colonel Sellers" ("Twain and Dickens" 198–207).

Mark Twain's habitual contention that he based his writing on his personal experience has some substance, for, in creating the character of Colonel Sellers, he clearly had in mind his mother's cousin, James Lampton: "I merely put him on paper as he was.... He was not a person who could be exaggerated" (*Autobiography* 1: 89). This sounds plausible since both James Lampton and Colonel Sellers were once so poor that they each served a guest a meal of water and cold turnips and then tried to save face by praising turnips as so good for the health that all wise men were clamoring to eat them. Both Lampton and Sellers were apt to order expensive items only to discover that they had forgotten to carry their wallets, thus forcing their guests to pay the bills. Both Lampton and Sellers shared the little they did have with others so generously that their families "spent their days in poverty and at times were pinched with famine" (French 165–69; *Gilded Age* 60, ch. 7; 192, ch. 25).

Cousin James Lampton, moreover, was not the only real life model: Mark Twain also derived much of Colonel Sellers's character from his own. Both Sellers and Samuel Clemens were compulsive speculators. While Sellers continuously speculated in railroads, Clemens poured money into "a steam generator that would not generate, ... a steam pulley that would not pull, a marine telegraph that never carried a message, and ... a chalk-plate engraving process that was vanquished by its successful rival, photoengraving." Clemens refused—or so he said—Alexander Graham Bell's offer to sell him potentially priceless shares in telephone stock; but he invested a fortune in the Paige typesetting machine only to be bankrupted when the Mergenthaler linotype proved to be superior (French 172–74). Clearly, Mark Twain derived almost as much of Colonel Sellers from himself as he did from his cousin James Lampton.

And yet, the personal experience of all writers includes their exposure to the writing of the past. Writers have always taken full advantage of the literary tradition which they have inherited and great writers have developed this tradition in ways that future writers might, in turn, build on. Although the example of James Lampton undeniably helped to inspire the author's conception of the character of Sellers, Mark Twain also built on a pre-existing foundation—his literary inheritance, one which included great comic characters provided by earlier master writers of the comic.

It is very likely, for example, that Mark Twain was unconsciously influenced by his memory of Oliver Goldsmith's *The Citizen of the World,* Letters LIII and LIV. Goldsmith's character Beau Tibbs, after ostentatiously asking his wife to cook costly food for his guest, then decides that the guest would prefer the inexpensive peasant food ox-cheek instead. Could this have alerted Mark Twain to the literary possibilities of his recollection of Cousin James Lampton's serving of turnip? (Baetzhold *Twain and Bull* 271–72). It has also been argued that Colonel Sellers recalls both Shakespeare's Falstaff and Cervantes's Don Quixote (Canby 236–37). But the chief literary source which critics have suspected ever since *The Gilded Age* was first reviewed is Mr. Micawber in Charles Dickens' *David Copperfield* (Baetzhold "Twain and Dickens" 189, 200, 215). This paper will explore the parallelism between Mr. Micawber and Colonel Sellers and, to a lesser extent, between Mrs. Micawber and Sellers.

To anyone who has studied both Dickens and Mark Twain, it is not surprising that such a parallelism should exist, for the authors' personal lives and their attitudes toward life had much in common, and both drew heavily on their intimate knowledge of close relatives.

As children not yet in their teens, both authors lost the support of a father—Dickens through his father's financial ineptitude which finally led to his incarceration in debtor's prison, and Clemens through his father's death. As a result, both authors as boys had to drop out of formal schooling and to earn their living performing menial labor. Largely self-educated, both authors began their writing careers by submitting comic vignettes to newspapers and gradually developed into full-time writers of short satirical newspaper features and then into writers of full-length books.

Having known through painful experience a socio-economic system which had capriciously disrupted their education and youthful aspirations, both authors attacked the callous willingness of the upper classes to exploit and degrade the vulnerable masses. Dickens attacks the heartlessness of the contemporary upper classes in *Dombey and Son, Little Dorrit,* and *Hard Times* and Mark Twain attacks it in *A Connecticut Yankee in King Arthur's Court.*

This common hostility of Dickens and Mark Twain toward the wealthy often led them to attack that greed which knows no satisfaction. Always a theme in Dickens' writing, greed became a major motif in *Our Mutual Friend* (1864–65), the last novel which Dickens completed. In it, the dust heaps at

Harmon's Bower in London symbolize the desire for material possessions that pits such innate virtues as "love, generosity, and communal responsibility" against socially engendered vices such as the hunger for wealth (Kaplan 473). Only six years after Dickens published this attack, Mark Twain likewise castigated the greed he had encountered in New York and Washington. In September, 1871, the New York *Tribune* printed Mark Twain's "The Revised Catechism," a parody of the Westminster Shorter Catechism, in which the author declares the passion for money to be the actual religion of his countrymen:

> What is the chief end of man?—to get rich. In what way?—dishonestly if we can: honestly if we must. Who is God, the one only and true: Money is god. Gold and greenbacks and stock—father, son and the ghost of same—three persons in one; these are the true and only God, mighty and supreme; and William [i.e., Boss] Tweed is his prophet. (Vogelback 72–73)

Despite these attacks on those who pursue and control wealth, one side of both authors reacted to the memory of childhood poverty by avidly pursuing the very high economic and social status which the other side was attacking. This is symbolized in Dickens' case in his purchase of Gad's Hill, a Kentish country manor which he associated with Shakespeare, and in Mark Twain's case in his constructing an extravagantly lavish mansion at Nook Farm, a fashionable area in Hartford. In short, when Mark Twain printed "The Revised Catechism" in the New York *Tribune* denouncing the pursuit of money, Mr. Samuel Clemens was living on a scale in keeping with his wife's wealthy heritage.

Although the fathers of both Dickens and Clemens failed to provide adequate support for their growing families, both fathers were able to ignore current troubles because they temperamentally expected that the future would bring them prosperity. One is not surprised, then, to find that the sons of such fathers stress the pernicious results of spending one's life in the expectation of acquiring great wealth. In Dickens' *Bleak House,* lawyers' fees for litigating the suit of Jardyce vs. Jardyce leave not a penny for the penniless heirs; this theme reappears in Dickens' *Great Expectations,* in which Pip is encouraged to fritter away his youthful time and energy in the naive assurance that he is soon to be left a fortune. As for Clemens, his father had invested in 70,000 Tennessee acres which he believed until his death were destined to make his family wealthy Virginia aristocrats:

> It kept us hoping and hoping during forty years, and forsook us at last. It put our energies to sleep and made visionaries of us—no occasion to work. It is good to begin life poor; it is good to begin life rich—these are wholesome; but

to begin it poor and *prospectively* rich! The man who has not experienced it cannot imagine the curse of it.

Just as Dickens' family experiences provided him with literary material, Clemens's family's faith in a poor investment ironically furnished him, he said, with "a field for [the character Colonel] Sellers and a book" (*Autobiography* 1: 94). This ambivalent attitude toward the pursuit of wealth enabled Dickens and Mark Twain to conceive of such comic characters as Mr. Micawber and Colonel Sellers. For one side of the authors can identify with and support Micawber's and Sellers' refusal to succumb to greed, to meanness, to de-humanization, while another side can identify with the characters' confidence that the future will bring them social and financial security.

Both Dickens and Mark Twain, moreover, use their aptitude for the comic in two ways: to affirm the goodness of human existence and to attack those who endanger this goodness. In *David Copperfield*, Dickens elicits our laughter as he reveals the weaknesses of Mr. and Mrs. Micawber; but he does so in such a manner that we love the Micawbers and applaud their tendency to rely on words as a means of making the world seem to be a more humane place than it actually is. But Dickens also uses a second kind of comic expression to attack the enemies of joy, such as Uriah Heep in *David Copperfield*, by revealing that Heep merely pretends to be humble while secretly seeking to attain power over others (Kincaid 177–81, 186). Likewise, Mark Twain also uses his aptitude for the comic to expose Colonel Sellers's weaknesses, but once again the effect is to make the Colonel lovable. In his later criticism of an actor's interpretation of the Colonel in the dramatized version of *The Gilded Age*, Mark Twain insisted: "The real Colonel Sellers, as I knew him in James Lampton, was a pathetic and beautiful spirit, a manly man, a straight and honorable man, a man with a big, foolish, unselfish heart in his bosom, a man born to be loved …" (*Autobiography* 1: 90). But Mark Twain, like Dickens, could also use a second, lower, form of the comic in making an attack. In *The Gilded Age* he makes the reader despise, rather than love, the corrupt and piously hypocritical Senator Dilworthy. Although this second kind of comic attack is effective, it elicits none of the joy that the depiction of Colonel Sellers brings to us.

Since the physical circumstances, as well as the attitudes and values, of Charles Dickens and Mark Twain run so parallel, one is not surprised to learn that their famous comic characters have as much in common as do the authors themselves. Besides the fact that the Micawbers have two children and one set of twins, and that the Sellers have four and two sets, there are, perhaps, more important similarities.

Although the Micawbers and Sellers explicitly profess their respect for the laws of capitalism, they implicitly attack the entire institution of capitalism. Mr. Micawber, while prudently advising David Copperfield to live within his income, blithely increases his own indebtedness on the flimsy hope that some lucrative position will soon "turn up." Temperamentally, Micawber cannot take money seriously. In a business-like manner, he keeps careful records of the IOU's which he dispenses, but it never occurs to him that a single IOU will ever be paid off (*DC* 615, ch. 57). Micawber further undermines the basis of capitalism by inducing the reader to feel that he does genuinely repay his debts not in money but in language, in exhilarating whiskey punch, in happiness. If he fails to take money seriously he at least takes joy seriously (Kincaid 185). Like genuine capitalists, Micawber is also capable of sustained hard work, but the projects on which he works are somehow always devoted to the welfare of somebody else, not his own family. Both Mr. and Mrs. Micawber almost welcome the disasters inflicted by a commercial society in order that they may rely on words to transform these disasters into triumphs. When financial pressure forces the Micawbers to leave London, Mrs. Micawber, who has lost everything, creates a kind of wealth through professing her loyalty:

> I never will desert Mr. Micawber. No! ... I never will do it! It's of no use asking me! ... Mr. Micawber has his faults. I do not deny that he is improvident. I do not deny that he has kept me in the dark as to his resources and his liabilities, both ... but I never will desert Mr. Micawber ... He is the parent of my children! He is the father of my twins! He is the husband of my affections ... and I ne—ver—will—desert Mr. Micawber!" (*DC* 137–38, ch. 12).

Mark Twain makes his indirect attack on capitalism by having Colonel Sellers invest all of his (and his friends') money in enterprises which are destined to fail. Throughout the book, the Colonel expresses his faith in capitalism so fervently that he invests without restraint, believing only in profit and ignoring the possibility of loss. When he begs his friends to invest their every cent in the construction of a railroad pushing through the wilderness, he gets so carried away with his own rhetoric that his words become more real to him than the actualities which they describe:

> Just see what a country... [the railroad] goes through. There's your onions at Slouchburg—noblest onion country that graces God's footstool; and there's your turnip country all around Doodleville—bless my life, what fortunes are going to be made there when they get that contrivance perfected for extracting olive oil out of turnips—if there's any in them.... Then you've got a little stretch along through Belshazzar that don't produce anything now—at least nothing but rocks—but irrigation will fetch it. Then from Catfish to Babylon

it's a little swampy, but there's dead loads of peat down under there somewhere.... Next is the sassparilla region. I reckon there's enough of that... to fat
up all the consumptives in all the hospitals from Halifax to the Holy Land
(*Gilded Age* 202–203, ch. 27).

Part of the reason why the Micawbers and Sellers are able to survive in a
world of laissez-faire capitalism is that all are unusually resilient. The more
they are crushed down, the higher they "rebound automatically, like a rubber
ball" (Kincaid 178). After David Copperfield receives a letter from Micawber
confessing his imminent economic doom and signed "the Beggared Outcast,"
David decides to seek him out and offer "a word of comfort. But, half-way
there, I met the London coach with Mr. Micawber up behind …, the very picture of tranquil enjoyment, smiling at Mrs. Micawber's conversation, eating
walnuts out of a paper bag, with a bottle sticking out of his breast pocket"
(*DC* 207, ch. 17). Likewise, at the end of Mark Twain's *The Gilded Age*,
Colonel Sellers's protégé Washington Hawkins is totally disillusioned with
his dream of acquiring wealth; but Sellers, who has failed at every practical
project he has ever touched, is now dreaming of a new career in law, his
"native element": "There's worlds of money in it," he states and he now
expects to "climb, and climb, and climb—and wind up on the Supreme
Court" (*Gilded Age* 456, ch. 61).

This extreme resiliency reflects a tendency in the Micawbers and Sellers to
view an unlikely possibility in the distant future as more real, more interesting,
more important, than are actual circumstances. As the Micawber family prepares to sail from England to seek employment in Australia, Mr. and Mrs.
Micawber, oblivious to the uncertainty that awaits them, involve themselves in
an extended argument as to whether Mr. Micawber should allow his native
England to share the honor which his future success in Australia is certain to
bring: "I cannot forget the parent-tree," Mrs. Micawber declares, "and when
our race attains to eminence and fortune, I own I should wish that fortune to
flow into the coffers of Britannia.... I wish Mr. Micawber to take his stand
upon that vessel's prow, and firmly say, 'This country I am come to conquer!
Have you honours? Have you riches? Have you posts of profitable pecuniary
emolument? Let them be brought forward. They are mine!'" (*DC* 616–17, ch.
57).

Colonel Sellers is also so resilient that he brushes aside the collapse of his
Columbus River Slack-water Navigation Company, which has once more
thrust him and his large family into poverty. "Cheer up and don't you fear,"
he tells his wife: he will build a railroad and the entire community will thereby become rich. In a *tour de force* of extravagent comedy, he then proceeds

so to arrange the eating utensils and toilet articles on the dining room table as to suggest the course which this future railroad will take through the wilderness (*Gilded Age* 202–203, ch. 27). This resiliency has the effect of making all these comic characters virtually unteachable. As the books end, they react to life's challenges precisely as when the books begin.

Like Dickens and Mark Twain themselves, Mr. Micawber and Colonel Sellers are lifelong theatrical performers. To them, life is a stage on which the individual puts on a dramatic show. Micawber's manner of dress, his gestures and his language are all calculated to help him act his part. While delivering his eloquent denunciation of Uriah Heep, Mr. Micawber is so satisfied with the artistry of one sentence that he pretends to lose his place in order that he have an excuse to go back and re-state the choice lines (*DC* 573–74, ch. 52). Likewise, the Colonel's strong flair for the dramatic enabled Mark Twain to rework his novel into a play entitled *Colonel Sellers,* which was produced again and again between 1874 and 1888 and which earned the author an impressive $70,000 (French 242, 252).

To both Micawber and Sellers, language is a tool, an indispensable device which enables them to deny the existence of harsh reality. In the language of each man, the word triumphs over the fact. In one instance, the facts are that the Micawbers' water supply has just been cut off and that Micawber has unwillingly sunk to the level of convincing a naive friend to co-sign and thus guarantee not just one but a second of his worthless IOU's. Despite this crisis, Micawber turns his attention to the preparation of a bowl of punch and "it was wonderful to see his face shining at us …, as he stirred, and mixed, and tasted, and looked as if he were making, instead of punch, a fortune for his family …" "Punch, my dear Copperfield," says Mr. Micawber, tasting it, "like time and tide, waits for no man. Ah! it is at the present moment in high flavour" (*DC* 318, 321, 331, ch. 28). Later, when Micawber publicly exposes the corruption of his employer, Uriah Heep, he knowingly loses for himself the only paying job he ever has had. Although his act once more impoverishes his family, he feels rich with the thought that, in denouncing Heep, he can regain his selfrespect and the respect of his wife: "Emma," he calls to his wife, "Mutual confidence, so long preserved between us once, is restored, … Now welcome poverty! … Welcome misery, welcome houselessness, welcome hunger, rags, tempest, and beggary! Mutual confidence will sustain us to the end" (*DC* 581, ch. 52).

Colonel Sellers, also subject to the misery of poverty, has likewise become expert at using his aptitude for language as a means of obliterating his awareness of the misery; he can even turn the source of the misery into a positive virtue. When the Colonel's protégé, numb with the cold in Sellers' home, snuggles so close to the stove's glowing door that the stove door flies open, all can see that "there was nothing in the stove but a lighted tallow-candle!" Rather than acknowledging his humiliating poverty, the Colonel relies on language to make his poverty seem like a blessing. The Academy of France, he explains, has recently discovered that heat is injurious to those with rheumatism:

> Bless you I saw in a moment what was the matter with us, and says I, out goes your fires!—no more slow torture and certain death for me, sir. What you want is the appearance of heat, not the heat itself.... Rheumatism? Why a man can't any more start a case of rheumatism in this house than he can shake an opinion out of a mummy! Stove with a candle in it and a transparent door—that's it—it has been the salvation of this family (*Gilded Age* 64, ch. 7).

As we know, the Colonel extends an elaborate dinner invitation to a friend only to find nothing in his larder but water and cold turnips. Again, words must suffice to make a virtue out of necessity: doctors, he recalls, have recommended the eating of turnips as a means of resisting the plague:

> "...just fill yourself up two or three times a day, and you can snap your fingers at the plague.... Here, let me give you some more of the turnip. No, no, no, now, I insist. There now. Absorb those. They're mighty sustaining—brim full of nutriment ..." (*Gilded Age* 91, ch. 13).

The Colonel also refuses to recognize the worthlessness of his broken chime clock, which, he claims, the governor himself has vainly begged him to sell to him:

> Remarkable clock! ... She can wake the dead! Sleep? Why you might as well try to sleep in a thunder factory. Now just listen to that. She'll strike a hundred and fifty, now, without stopping, you'll see. There ain't another clock like that in Christendom (Gilded Age 62–3, ch. 7).

Language, then, is the weapon, the elixir, that enables both the Micawbers and Sellers to transform a grim existence into fulfilling life. Although none of them considers himself a poet or even a professional writer, all have an instinct for the appropriate metaphor, the effective rhetorical question, the spell-binding periodic sentence. Micawber displays his rhetorical virtuosity in explaining how the tininess of his salary, ironically enough, enabled him to learn enough about Uriah Heep's financial machinations to expose them. He asks four parallel rhetorical questions:

> [After I accepted the low-paying position] Need I say that it soon became necessary for me to solicit from—Heep—pecuniary advances toward the support

of Mrs. Micawber, and our blighted but rising family? Need I say that this necessity had been foreseen by—Heep? That those advances were secured by IOU's and other similar acknowledgments, known to the legal institutions of this country? And that I thus became immeshed in the web he had spun for my reception? (*DC* 573, ch. 52).

Not to be outdone, Colonel Sellers also relies on rhetorical questions and striking metaphors in explaining why he has chosen Asia rather than America as the market for his newest product, the Infallible Imperial Oriental Optic Liniment and Salvation for Sore Eyes:

> Would I go to all that trouble and bother [of creating a new market] for the poor crumbs a body might pick up in this country? Now do I look like a man who— does my history suggest that I am a man who deals in trifles, contents himself with the narrow horizon that hems in the common herd, sees no further than the end of his nose? ... Why what is the republic of America for an eye-water country? Why, ... in the Oriental countries people swarm like the sands of the desert; every square mile of ground upholds its thousands upon thousands of struggling human creatures—and every separate and individual devil of them's got the opthalmia! (*Gilded Age* 70, ch. 8).

Occasionally an ugly fact is so unmanageable that it stymies the efforts even of verbal artists to ignore it. On one occasion, Mr. Micawber runs out of the euphemisms which normally enable him to overlook his poverty: he admits that he is "at present ... engaged in the sale of corn upon commission. It is not an avocation of a remunerative description—in other words, it does not pay ..." (*DC* 316, ch. 27). Similarly, Colonel Sellers would like always to describe the Washington scene with characteristic optimism, but he cannot find words enabling him to circumvent the fact that few of his countrymen are "opposed to—to—bribery" (*Gilded Age* 268, ch. 35).

In short, Micawber and to some extent Mrs. Micawber anticipate the creation of Colonel Sellers in their implicit attack on capitalism, in their ebullient resiliency, in their flair for the dramatic, and in their ability to use language as the means through which to transform a grim world into a joyful one.

Yet it would be misleading to imply that Mark Twain, in creating the character of Colonel Sellers, was merely bringing about an Americanization of Mr. Micawber. Indeed, the two men differ in several significant respects. In the first place, the two attacks on capitalism, though both indirect, differ in tone. Micawber thoroughly enjoys flaunting the very laws of capitalism which, verbally, he claims to respect. Sellers, on the other hand, retains unswervingly his faith that daring and imaginative speculation will inevitably make him and his friends rich—if not today, then tomorrow. The Micawbers put up a pretense that they are just about to spring out for an economic opportunity—but they never spring; they insist verbally that they are models of prudence—but they are never prudent (Kincaid 179).

The Colonel, on the other hand, retains so much faith in capitalism that he is genuinely surprised each time his efforts lead to financial disaster. While Micawber is outside the mainstream of Victorian society, Sellers is the quintessence of his age. To William Dean Howells, he embodied "the sort of Americanism ... characterized in its boundlessly credulous, fearlessly adventurous, unconsciously burlesque excess [which prevailed in the post-Civil War] period of political and economic expansion ..." (Howells 841).

The characters also differ significantly in that Micawber's conscience torments him unremittingly during the brief period when he allows his employer Uriah Heep to make him his accomplice in corruption. Colonel Sellers, however, has a kind of naiveté or lack of moral sensitivity which permits him to acquiesce in Washington, D. C., to the prevailing hypocrisy and greed which he finds everywhere. Although he characteristically fails to earn a dollar for himself through his Washington lobbying, he accepts as inevitable the corrupt practices of his fellow lobbyists, of representatives and of senators:

> I am afraid some of them do buy their seats—yes, I am afraid they do,—but ... it is sinful,—it is very wrong—it is shameful. Heaven protect *me* from such a charge.... And yet when you come to look at it you cannot deny that we would have to go without the services of some of our ablest men, sir, if the country were opposed to—to—bribery. It is a harsh term. I do not like to use it" (*Gilded Age* 268, ch. 35).

Since the naive Colonel lacks the moral sensitivity of Micawber, Mark Twain can put him to uses to which Dickens never puts Micawber. For example, Mark Twain himself supported the gold standard and denounced the issuance of paper money which was only partially redeemable. In actual history, in 1872, the Secretary of the Treasury, George S. Boutwell, had responded to speculators' demands by issuing five million retired greenbacks to stimulate investment in the development of the West (French 131–32). To expose the evils of this practice Mark Twain distances himself from Sellers and has Sellers defend paper money with a flimsy argument:

> What we want is more money. I've told Boutwell so. Talk about basing the currency on gold; you might as well base it on pork. Gold is only one product. Base it on everything! You've got to do something for the West. How am I to move my crops? We must have improvements (*Gilded Age* 326–27, ch. 44).

In a similar ironic way, Mark Twain makes the Colonel provide unconvincing justifications of diplomatic and political practices which Mark Twain himself denounced. Responding to President Grant's attempt in 1870 and again in 1871 to convince Congress to agree to an American annexation of the Dominican Republic, Colonel Sellers voices the essence of American jingoistic imperialism: "I go for putting the old flag on all the vacant lots. I said to the President, says I, 'Grant, why don't you take Santo Domingo, annex the whole thing,.and settle the bill afterwards.' That's my way" (*Gilded Age* 293–94, ch. 40).[1]

Micawber and Sellers differ, in short, in their response to living according to the laws of capitalism and in their degree of tolerating financial corruption in others. They differ also in the level of language which they employ. As we have seen, both have learned to survive in the world of cold facts by creating in the world of words a sanctuary of love and joy. Thus their use of language would seem to have much in common. Yet, there are significant differences. Although Micawber is a failure by any conventional Victorian standard, his selection of words makes him seem to be in command of all. Like Dr. Johnson, the eighteenth-century arbiter of correctness, Micawber relies chiefly on polysyllabic words of Latin origin, such as *falsification, mystification, universal applicability;* he draws his metaphors from the Bible, classical mythology, Shakespeare, Chaucer, Thomas Grey, Dr. Johnson, Pope, Edward Young, Burns. In his dramatic account of his unwilling complicity in Uriah Heep's embezzlement, Micawber names the precise moment when

> I began, if I may so Shakespearingly express myself, to dwindle, peak, and pine. I found that my services were constantly called into requisition for the falsification of business and the mystification of an individual whom I will designate as Mr. W. ... This was bad enough; but, as the philosophic Dane observes, with that universal applicability which distinguishes the illustrious ornament of the Elizabethan Era, worse remains behind (*DC* 573, ch. 52).

But Micawber does not restrict himself to speaking Shakespearingly; at times he recalls Dr. Johnson, as he addresses the ten-year old David Copperfield as "Sir" and "My dear Copperfield." He has the eighteenth-century love for the euphemistic cliché: he is a "foundered bark"; "Hope has sunk beneath the horizon"; "he is under the pressure of pecuniary embarrassment" (Schilling 110–13).

The Colonel's oratory, on the other hand, echoes neither Shakespeare nor the eighteenth-century. It characteristically takes the form of a seemingly endless vernacular monologue reminiscent of those delivered by earlier Mark Twain characters: Simon Wheeler in "The Notorious Jumping Frog of Calaveras County" (1865) and Jim Blaine in "Jim Blaine and His Grandfather's Old Ram" (1872):

I intend to look out for you, ... my boy.... I got some prodigious operations on foot; but I'm keeping quiet; mum's the word; your old hand don't go around pow-wowing and letting everybody see his k'yards and find out his little game.... And then there is the hog speculation—that's bigger still. We've got quiet men at work ... mousing around ... and don't you see, if we can get all the hogs and all the slaughterhouses into our hand on the dead quiet—whew! it would take three ships to carry the money.... but what's the use of talking about it—any man can see that there's whole Atlantic oceans of cash in it, gulfs and bays thrown in (*Gilded Age* 67–68, ch. 8).

The metaphors in Sellers's language derive not from the Bible and Shakespeare but from such favorite Mark Twain sources as American Indians and the game of poker: "your old hand don't go around pow-wowing and letting everybody see his k'yards"; his language also reveals Mark Twain's genius for transforming one part of speech, for example, the noun *mouse,* into another: "We've got a quiet man at work ... mousing around." The word *fat* is conventionally a noun or an adjective; but Sellers assures us that his future railroad will make available enough sassparilla "to fat up all the consumptives in all the hospitals from Halifax to the Holy Land" (*Gilded Age* 202–03, ch. 27).[2] In an earlier encounter with old friends after a long separation, the Colonel uses the word *good* in both standard and non-standard ways:

Now is it you sure enough—turn around: hold up your heads! I want to look at you good! Well, well, well, it does seem most too good to be true, I declare; Lord, I'm so glad to see you! Does a body's whole soul good to look at you! Shake hands again! Keep on shaking hands! Goodness gracious alive (*Gilded Age* 44–45, ch. 5).

Thus, in all cases, Sellers eschews the formal grammar and Latinized vocabulary of Micawber, relying instead on the vernacular of the Mississippi valley.

Despite the differences, there seems little question of Dickens' influence. And when we consider that influence, we are reminded once more of Dickens' endless energy, an energy which could persist even after his death in the suggestion and stimulus which his writing was able to pass on to others. We are also reminded how that influence could stimulate the works of another gifted writer, but works that are fresh and vital, not derivative. In the Micawbers, Dickens created characters who reflect the disruption which prevailed as eighteenth century agrarian England gave way to the industrial capitalism of the nineteenth century. As loving sensitive people, they lack the will to rid themselves of their eighteenth-century civility and embrace nineteenth-century economic competitiveness. The Gilded Age which Colonel Sellers inhabits, on the other hand, reflects the stimulation and wonder evoked by Americans' awareness that they now had the industrial tools needed to subdue and exploit a rich, huge continent. And the extravagant language of Sellers reflects this stimulation and wonder.

Moreover, when we compare such characters, we learn that a measure of any artist's success is his ability to build on the tradition which he has inherited from artists of the past. This means that the writer's success depends on how effectively he has been able to force language to convey human experience in areas overlooked by or unavailable to earlier writers. In order thoroughly to appreciate Mr. Micawber, we must know something of the language of Shakespeare and that of Dr. Johnson's eighteenth century, languages which are put to new and effective uses in the utterances of Mr. Micawber. The pompous Johnsonian language spoken by Mr. Collins, Jane Austen's comic character in *Pride and Prejudice,* serves to make him suitably ridiculous; when we recognize in the statements of Micawber a similar language but tempered by the humane Micawber's ironic attitude toward himself, we are conscious that Dickens has added another dimension to the literary tradition which he inherited.

Likewise, in order thoroughly to appreciate Mark Twain's achievement, we must see that the Micawbers provided Mark Twain with models of the comic spirit as expressed within the context of Victorian England; but that Mark Twain succeeded in re-rendering this same comic spirit within the context of the American Gilded Age. Only then can we recognize that Mark Twain has added to our literary heritage by demonstrating for authors yet to come the power of American vernacular and metaphors derived from the native scene: "There's whole Atlantic oceans of cash in it"; only then can we see that he has wrenched such words as *mouse, good,* and *fat* out of their conventional usage and so used them as to startle the reader into making his own active response.

Finally, an examination of the comic spirit as exemplified in Dickens and Mark Twain offers a further personal reward. One learns that it is sometimes better for one to pay what one might owe not with money but with punch, with joy and with words.

NOTES

1. For further discussion of Mark Twain's criticism of policies of the Grant administration, see Bassett and French.

2. Mark Twain was so amused by the verb *to fat up* that he repeated it when Huck Finn muses on Miss Watson's inability to gain weight.

WORKS CITED

Baetzhold, Howard G. "Mark Twain and Dickens: Why the Denial?" *Dickens Studies Annual* 16 (1987): 189–219.

———. *Mark Twain and John Bull: The British Connection.* Bloomington: Indiana UP, 1970.

Bassett, John E. *"The Gilded Age:* Performance, Power, and Authority." *Studies in the Novel* 18 (1985): 395–405.

Canby, Henry Seidel. *Turn West, Turn East: Mark Twain and Henry James.* Boston: Houghton, 1951.

Dickens, Charles. *David Copperfield.* 1850. Ed. and Intro. by George H. Ford. Boston: Houghton, 1958.

French, Bryant Morey. *Mark Twain and "The Gilded Age" : The Book that Named an Era.* Dallas: Southern Methodist UP, 1965.

Howells, William Dean. "Mark Twain: An Inquiry." *North American Review* 191 (1910): 836–50.

Kaplan, Fred. *Dickens: A Biography.* New York: William Morrow, 1988.

Kincaid, James R. *Dickens and the Rhetoric of Laughter.* Oxford: Oxford UP, 1971.

Mills, Nicholas C. "Social and Moral Vision in *Great Expectations* and *Huckleberry Finn.*" *Journal of American Studies* 4 (1970): 61–72.

———. "Charles Dickens and Mark Twain." *English and American Fiction in the Nineteenth Century: An Antigenre Criticism and Comparison.* Bloomington: Indiana UP, 1973.

Ridland, J. M. "Huck, Pip, and Plot." *Nineteenth Century Fiction* 20 (1965): 286–90.

Schilling, Bernard N. *The Comic Spirit.* Detroit: Wayne UP, 1965.

Twain, Mark and Charles Dudley Warner. *The Gilded Age: A Tale of Today.* 1873. Ed. and Intro. by Bryant Morey French. Indianapolis and New York: Bobbs, 1972.

Twain, Mark. *Mark Twain's Autobiography.* Ed. by Albert Bigelow Paine. 2 vols. New York: Harper, 1924.

Vogelback, Arthur L. "Mark Twain and the Tammany Ring." *PMLA* 70 (1955): 69–75.

"Their Places are a Blank": The Two Narrators in *Bleak House*

Richard T. Gaughan

One striking feature about *Bleak House* is that everything of any consequence seems to happen too late. After her frantic search for her mother, Esther finds Lady Dedlock only when she can no longer help her. The suit of Jarndyce vs. Jarndyce ends only after Richard Carstone has been irretrievably lost in the false hopes and expectations it spawns. Sir Leicester forgives Lady Dedlock her secret past only after she has already set out on her fatal flight. Esther's marriage to Woodcourt seems at first doomed by his profession of love coming too late and is brought about only by the *deus ex machina* intervention of John Jarndyce. Inspector Bucket arrests Hortense and brings her to justice, but as Hortense herself defiantly says, he cannot repair the damage she has already done. Clues seem to be red herrings leading to more questions than answers and when there are answers they seem woefully inadequate to what has happened during the search for them. Even Esther's Bleak House, the place where so many of the novel's conflicts are apparently to be resolved, seems too little too late.

This uncertainty about what, exactly, things mean is unquestionably a way for Dickens to create and maintain suspense in his elaborate plot, but it also indicates something more—that the social and legal worlds of the novel are not as complete and self-sufficient as they pretend to be. Not only are there injustices that go unaddressed (not to mention unredressed) and social problems that are neglected when they are not denied outright, but the very clues that are supposed to dispel the mysteries and restore order to the novel's world are themselves ambiguous. Meaning always seems to exceed intention and expectation, thereby creating a life outside the two prevailing systems of order, Chancery and the world of fashion, and their assumption that meaning and personal identity can be adequately defined in objective and fixed terms. The real mystery of the novel becomes not so much the "who did what to whom" mystery of the plot as the mystery of the life that escapes and is ignored by the systems of social order.

This may seem like the long way round to criticize the injustices and corruption of Chancery and the world of fashion, but it must be kept in mind that in many ways the novel is as much of a closed system in its way as Chancery and the world of fashion are in theirs. If Dickens limited his criticisms of the world he depicts to his thematic criticisms, his novel would be just one more system, however enlightened and humane, in a world where the requirements of systems always seem to prevail over whatever is unique and individual and therefore outside the systems. To avoid repeating the ills of the world he depicts in the very form of his novel, Dickens must analyze not only thematic injustices and corruption, but also what makes the world the way it is, what its imaginative logic and formal structure are and what is wrong with this way of imagining the world. He must not only represent this world but represent the way it represents itself.[1]

To do this, Dickens uses two narrators who not only represent and embody two points of view that go into making up the novel's world but who also represent and embody the two-fold way in which the novel is a response to that world.[2] The third-person narrator is essentially critical. He exposes the unacknowledged conflicts that lie at the heart of the social and legal order. These conflicts constitute a kind of hollowness or blank at the center of a social world that seems to be totally dominated by institutionalized systems of order,[3] a hollowness that is covered over by displays of privilege and the complexities and deferrals of the legal machinery. Esther, who is the intersection of so many of the forces at work in the novel, is the missing center of the third-person narrator's story. She is the individualized imagination, perhaps the imagination of the novel itself, that can contain in her story the conflicts that make up her world but whose identity is the use she makes of her psychological and narrative inheritance and not the sum of those conflicts. In short, the third-person narrator shows that the real mystery in the novel is the life the systems of order must ignore and Esther is the expression of that life.

Since the criticism of the novel's world cannot take place solely on the thematic level, the question remains of how the two narrators can represent the controlling imagination of the novel's world. I believe that one way they do this is by presenting the novel's world and, in Esther's case, herself, in terms of what Bakhtin would call languages. Language, in Bakhtin's view, is an essentially social phenomenon. In this he is following one of the directions suggested by Saussure, but he goes further than Saussure by suggesting that language is not just a cultural inheritance that the individual adapts to but is a diverse collection of highly individual ideological interpretations of the world. Because language is determined so thoroughly by ideological purposes, any national language is composed of many other languages all defined by such influences as social class, profession, education, and age, each of which is an assertion about and a way of creating the world. Since, for Bakhtin, there is no universal language, no comprehensive and authoritative point of view (although there are official languages like the language of Chancery in *Bleak House),* all these languages can, unless an official language is imposed by force, enter into a dialogue about the world and how it can be lived in. The individual does not so much submit to the rules of an antecedent system as find unique ways of entering into a dialogue about the world and society, thereby making the human world a world that is always being revealed as it is defined and interpreted by these many languages and by their intricate relationships to each other.

Because the novel is a hybrid literary form, one that is composed of many other genres or literary languages, it alone among the major genres, for Bakhtin, is suited to representing the historical world in its constant process of becoming through languages. The novel, throughout its history and because of the nature of its form, depicts the simultaneous coexistence of many languages that define experiences of a world that cannot or can no longer be formulated or interpreted in any single or universal language.[4]

The narrative world of *Bleak House* is full of these languages. There are the impersonal and official languages of Chancery and the world of fashion and the more idiosyncratic languages of the many characters. There is even a language that fears or seems to fear language—John Jarndyce's refusal to hear any expression of gratitude from those whom he has helped. This multiplicity of languages, however, is not the problem afflicting the novel's world and Esther's search for an identity, although the often predatory competition among characters may, at times, make it seem so. The problem is that this multiplicity is, in important respects, only superficial. The vacuum created by the absence of a universal order has been filled by Chancery and the world of fashion. By itself, this would not be a problem. The problem arises from the fact that Chancery and the world of fashion usurp the position of a "natural" and universal order and effectively prohibit any other attempt to respond to the world.

To indicate that there is a fuller world that has been usurped and corrupted by this second nature created by the law, Dickens repeatedly contrasts the precincts of the law and the denizens of those precincts, like the Smallweeds, to a natural world that is conspicuous by its virtual absence:

> [T]hese pleasant fields, where the sheep are all made into parchment, the goats into wigs, and the pasture into chaff.[5]

What could be one of many social expressions of the becoming of the world in uniquely human and dynamic ways has become instead an elaborate system or game that objectifies and dehumanizes the human world by defining it exclusively in terms of its own rules and requirements.[6]

In this system or game, power is transferred from one character to another according to how well each can play the game or emulate the system and how effectively each can define other characters in usable and objective terms. There are, ultimately, no winners in this game except the game itself. This is one reason why the conclusion of the Jarndyce lawsuit is not a judgment about justice but the exhaustion of the estate in court costs. As the third-person narrator wryly observes:

> The one great principle of the English law is, to make business for itself. There is no other principle distinctly, certainly, and consistently maintained through all its narrow turnings. Viewed by this light it becomes a coherent scheme, and not the monstrous maze the laity are apt to think it. (603–04)

This social and institutional use of language as a game in which power is circulated is then mimicked by most of the characters in slightly varying forms at various social levels. Instead of the dialogue Bakhtin describes, the languages in *Bleak House* tend to mirror each other or to be variations on a single theme.[7]

Esther, as an individual in this objectified and dehumanized world, must try to escape the relentless repetition of this theme so that she can discover and express what is uniquely her. But, she cannot do this in isolation because she is very much a product of this world. Her search for an identity and a way to express that identity must be coordinated with the story of the world that both produces and threatens to destroy her. Esther is the "nothing" that the individual is in the world the third-person narrator depicts and criticizes. As such, her story is a response and necessary counterpart to the story that the third-person narrator tells. The two narrators, then, represent not only two kinds of experience of the world (objective and personal) but also two ways of imagining the world that constantly call forth and depend on each other as a necessary partner in the dialogue about the world. In this way, the dialogue among languages that is repressed or missing at the thematic level is restored on the narrative level as the third-person narrator reveals the terms of the conflict and Esther creates an identity out of them.

From the beginning of the novel, the third-person narrator pierces the obscuring fog of Chancery to get to the "heart" of the matter, or, more precisely, to show the place where Esther will provide the heart. He not only reveals the mysteries of the plot, he uncovers the deeper mystery of the kind of world the ordering systems of the social world unintentionally create. He begins with a world apparently divided by social classes and fragmented by contending self-interests. In this world secrets abound because so many of the characters try to survive solely in terms of the overriding systems of order. Whatever is personal or spontaneous, because it cannot be assimilated to the systems, must become a secret. This secrecy, in turn, creates the opportunity for personal variations on the official game of getting and circulating power. Secrets can be used by one character against another to define the character with the secret in terms of the detecting character's desire for power. This kind of relationship between characters is best represented by the relationship between Tulkinghorn and Lady Dedlock, but it also characterizes most of the other relationships, including Mrs. Snagsby's suspicions about her husband, Guppy's schemes to win Esther, Mrs. Woodcourt's plan to discourage Esther, John Jarndyce's plan to marry Esther, and, more playfully, Skimpole's whimsical willingness to play any number of parts in other characters' versions of the world.

It is not only the characters who have secrets, however. Society as a whole has a secret life in Tom-All-Alone's. By closing itself off from anything that does not conform to its two dominating systems of order, the social world in Bleak House creates a negative shadow world filled with the physical suffering and degradation that is the direct though unacknowledged result of its objectifying and dehumanizing system of order. The fact that the consequences of this use of languages are physical is important. For Dickens, as for Bakhtin, language is a social act. The way language is used not only defines the world explicitly in systematic terms, it also defines that world in what is not asserted directly and openly. Language always opens an horizon on the world that then calls forth other responses. For this reason, languages and the ordering systems they generate are not, in Dickens' novel, abstract texts; they are embodied parts of the human world that both dialectically and fatally create consequences far beyond the order they institute.

This often denied relationship between what society systematically asserts as real or meaningful and what it, in fact, creates as the unintentional and uncontrollable result of these assertions is the secret behind all the other secrets and is the one secret the third-person narrator is always detecting and disclosing. His detective work, unlike that of the other detectives in the novel, is not circumscribed by the closed system of exchanging power. He detects and exposes the secret, if destructive, life created on the outskirts of this elaborate language game, the kind of life Esther will give a more specific and less destructive form to in her narrative.

The two best examples of this secret life created by Chancery and the world of fashion, the two official languages of the novel, are Jo and Lady Dedlock. Jo, whose very name is a minimal use of language, lives entirely outside the sanctioned languages of his society. He is not only illiterate in the sense that he cannot read or write, he is excluded by the languages his society uses to confer social meaning. He cannot, for example, understand either Chadband's hypocritical preaching or, except in the most rudimentary way, the Lord's Prayer that Woodcourt tries to teach him as he is dying. In fact, Jo dies before he can get to the last word in, "Hallowed be thy Name." Jo's illiteracy is quite clearly a social problem in the ordinary sense of the term, but it is also a social problem in the sense that any society that defines itself entirely in terms of its systems will inevitably create Jo and his cosufferers in Tom-All-Alone's and so undermine its ability to meet the human needs of its members. Jo is not only the most powerful symbol in the novel of the excluded individual, he also embodies the consequences of this exclusion. He is thoroughly dehumanized and utterly powerless. Like the refuse he sweeps at the crossroads, he is simply moved on by his society. But he cannot be moved on far enough. He unintentionally plagues his society in a quite literal sense. He spreads the diseases incubated in Tom-All-Alone's—diseases that are the physical consequences created by a society that conceives of and uses language as nothing more than as an exclusive and mechanistic system.

Those who are entirely excluded from society, however, are not its only victims. Even those at the top of society, like Lady Dedlock, are victimized by the requirements of the game that preserves their privileged station. At first glance, Lady Dedlock seems to be Jo's antithesis. She is an expert user of her language and one who enjoys the highest privileges of social rank. She should be as powerful as Jo is powerless, but she is not. Her very aptitude in using her language requires a self-annihilation that results in powerlessness. Lady Dedlock cannot afford a personal identity. That she once had a life apart from the one she lives in the world of fashion and that she once "impulsively" asked Tulkinghorn about the handwriting on a document are her undoing. To succeed she must so completely identify herself with the "language" of social conventions that she loses her freedom and, eventually, herself.

Between Jo's exclusion from language and Lady Dedlock's imprisonment in it is Skimpole's whimsical, or perhaps cynical, reshaping of his life into literature. Skimpole seems to reject the terms offered to him by his world and to have found escape and refuge in his ability to transform just about anything into something artistic or beautiful. He understands that perspective is an important influence on meaning and he manipulates perspective to escape the tyranny of socially defined meaning, in particular personal responsibility. To manage this escape, however, Skimpole artificially, as it were, denies that there is any moral or ethical dimension of life other than the narrow pieties of the social world. He expressly renounces principle for the sake of poetry and in so doing denies that there is a relatedness in human life that is an important source of the richness and beauty he uses to protect himself from the coarse touch of the ordinary.

Far from acting contrary to the values of the social world, Skimpole actually extends those values into the realm of art and literature. He, like Chancery, is simply there to be supported and his whimsical stories are a personal version of the endless smoke-screens of the legal system. He does not subvert or offer an alternative to the social world; rather, he is its poet laureate. He makes beauty and art into yet one more system whose evil, like that of the world of fashion, is that it is "a world that is wrapped up in too much jeweler's cotton and fine wool, and cannot hear the rushing of the larger worlds, and cannot see them as they circle round the sun" (55)—cotton doubtless provided by the charming slaves on plantations in America. Nevertheless, by living and narrating his life as if it were the life of someone else, as if, in other words, he were a third-person narrator living a first person life, Skimpole shows the dangers inherent in both Esther's attempt at self-creation and the third-person narrator's objective and detached view.

What is required is a way to encompass both the diversity of possible meanings and the need for order and stability, a way to incorporate the many perspectives that go into making up the novel's world into a unifying wholeness. The third-person narrator sets the stage for this synthesis. In many ways, he closely resembles Skimpole in his understanding that meaning is more indefinite than the social systems imply and has something of Skimpole's chameleon quality as well. He flies about the novel's world like the crow he uses as a metaphor for the interconnectedness of the world and he presents each part of the world as a separate but related perspective on the world. But, if the third-person narrator is like a less self-serving Skimpole, he is also like Skimpole's spiritual antithesis—Inspector Bucket. Bucket is as devoted to maintaining the public order as Skimpole is to escaping its incon-

venient demands.[8] Bucket's primary concern is to bring to justice those who
threaten the public order by acting outside it. The third-person narrator, too,
has a conception of the public order, one that is more comprehensive than
Bucket's, and he seeks to bring to justice all those, including institutions, who
act against its interests. Skimpole and Bucket, in other words, symbolically
embody the limits at which the third-person narrator's story becomes what it
criticizes. Although he combines the awareness of the multiplicity of meaning with an urge to order he nevertheless cannot escape these shadow figures
who serve as constant reminders that this combination is always only
momentary and can be achieved only as the result of the imagination finding
that even its own creations are beyond its control and not as a result of either
a mental calculus or a carefully managed dialectical synthesis of ideas.
Skimpole and Bucket together define the area within which a unification of
order and multiplicity can take place by showing how neither by itself effectively responds to the corruption of the novel's world.

The need for such a unification is perhaps most vividly presented when
Inspector Bucket and Esther set out to try to find Lady Dedlock. At this point,
the two narratives become, for a while, simultaneous. It is as if Bucket is the
emissary of the third-person narrator who, with Esther's help, draws all the
essentials of the novel's world together. Their frantic search for Lady
Dedlock repeats schematically the third-person's narrative. Bucket takes
Esther back through all the major scenes of the novel and through all social
levels. This search is not just the culmination of the central plot, it is a final
drawing together of the social world into the destructive whole it has always
been.

When Bucket and Esther finally find Lady Dedlock dressed in Jenny's
clothes, lying dead at the gate to the pestilential graveyard in Tom-All-
Alone's, the secret of the social world is disclosed in its fullness. The apparent divisions in the social world, divisions that protect those in power from
the consequences of the world they are creating, are, as Sir Leicester feared in
a very different context, washed away. The jumbling together of the novel's
world in the novel's opening chapter is here repeated and fulfilled. The medium, however, is no longer fog but death. Lady Dedlock and Jo, the antitheses
of how language is used as a way of ordering the world in the novel, are here
symbolically joined together in this final image of a world destroyed by the
kind of language accepted by society as exclusively real.

But, of course, all of this does not really resolve the problem. Bucket and
Esther arrive too late. If there seems to be a kind of poetic justice in everything that happens, it is nonetheless a justice that leaves unaddressed the

problem of what can be done in the kind of world where even retribution has almost no meaning. If anything constructive can be done it must be done through Esther's narrative since she is not only an important survivor of all this destruction, but also represents the voice of the individual who must make sense of herself out of the materials provided to her by her world. She must, in other words, interpret the same story the third-person narrator is telling from the point of view of personal identity. It is at this level, the level of the uniquely personal, where the conflicting but mutually dependent demands of multiplicity and order must be met if any alternative to the systems and their languages is to be found in the novel.

Esther, as the voice of the individual trying to define a language of her own out of the languages or stories she inherits from others, is deeply implicated in virtually all of the novel's action but is also in the unusual position of being dispossessed. She is, to the best of her early knowledge, an orphan who is barely tolerated by her godmother and who bears the guilt of some unexplained shame. Like many of Dickens' heroes, she is as close to being utterly excluded from the social world as it is possible to be without becoming a powerless or irrelevant outsider. This gives her the rare opportunity to improvise rather than merely accept her identity and, more importantly, to improvise a narrative suitable to this identity. Esther is in the position to devise a narrative that both formally and thematically expresses the complexities of an identity that is partly the product of the social order (and its various failures) and partly exempt from all forms of public order. Esther, in fact, has more than just a conventional identity as the narrator of and character in a novel; she is, in effect, the name Dickens gives to the novel's attempt to create a new form of expression out of the languages born of systems that, taken by themselves, seek to formalize and therefore destroy identity.

Esther's early life at Windsor epitomizes the dilemma she will face throughout the novel and already suggests the kind of strategy, both personal and narrative, that Esther will use. Esther's godmother and aunt, Miss Barbary, treats Esther the way Esther will be treated by so many of the other characters, even those who are benevolent towards her: as the illustration of a text or story. In this case the text is literally a text, the Bible (or, more exactly, those parts of the Bible having to do with retribution), but many of the characters with whom Esther comes into contact have similar "texts" or narratives of their own lives they want Esther to become a part of. One reason for this is that Esther is, in some respects, a relatively free agent in a world where most characters are bound by their social and legal roles. She doesn't exactly fit any of the roles of the elaborate plot produced by Chancery and the world of fashion. She is certainly involved in these plots but, because of her uncertain legal status, she does not have an officially prescribed role. She is in important ways that which is not defined; that is, she is the negation (and, I would suggest, the decomposing negation) of the systems of order and their languages. This makes Esther something of a wild card in a game otherwise determined by its own rules. As such, Esther is from the very start a threat who must be isolated from the game she threatens or neutralized by being made a part of it.

Miss Barbary tries to do a little of both to Esther. Miss Barbary tries to isolate Esther as much as possible from the society of others. She has good reason to do this since Esther's very existence is a constant threat to let the cat of scandal out of the bag of secrecy. But Miss Barbary goes even further. By telling Esther she is responsible for some unexplained shame, she wants Esther to feel unworthy of having the kind of life Esther sees her friends enjoying. In other words, she wants Esther to internalize the isolation Miss Barbary is able to impose in external ways. If Esther can be made to internalize her isolation, Miss Barbary can make Esther an accomplice in her story of guilt and punishment and be assured that her work will be continued long after her death.

Esther accepts her confused sense of being guilty and unworthy, but she does so in a curious way. She translates her guilt into a feeling of being somehow outside the ordinary, of needing to deserve and to earn what should be given freely. As a result, she never quite allows herself to feel that she is what others want her to think she is. She ascribes their approval to their good nature and generosity rather than to what she has done or who she is. She accepts their opinion of her not as a description but as a goal she has not yet reached. By doing this, Esther always remains somewhere outside or beside what everyone says about her, thereby fulfilling Miss Barbary's prophetic, "You are set apart," but in a way unimagined by her.[9] She is, in her own mind, a nothing around which others organize their desires or a mirror in which others are reflected. She establishes this role even in relation to her beloved Dolly:

> And so she used to sit propped up in a great arm-chair, with her beautiful complexion and rosy lips, staring at me—or not so much at me, I think, as at nothing—while I busily stitched away, and told her every one of my secrets. (62)

This is to say, Esther presents herself and her story in terms directly contrary to those of the social world: she presents herself as a becoming rather than as a fixed whole. When Esther buries her beloved Dolly just before she leaves Windsor for Greenleaf she seems to hint at this symbolically. She not only renounces having any dolls of her own (that is, repeating in her treatment of others the treatment she received at the hands of her godmother), she renounces being a doll for others as well.

All of this adds up to the kind of coyness and self-deprecation that readers often find so irritating and troubling. But, Esther has a good reason for acting in this way. Like Jo, who is her symbolic brother, she is all but powerless in the social world. Her particular form of self-effacement, which is later given such literal form, is a necessary method for someone who is not only an orphan, and therefore dependent on others, but also an illegitimate child. Esther has no legal basis for any demand she may wish to make of the social world. She must exist, since she was born, but she must do so in the least conspicuous way possible. Esther seizes on this necessity and converts it into the very form of her identity and into the way she tells her story. Esther's story is a story of discovery, even if it is deflected and indirect, and not, as is the case with Tulkinghorn, with whom Esther is symbolically linked,[10] a narrative of concealment.

Because Esther is, from the start, the object of the interest and of the narratives of others, she must, to survive at all, decline the temptations to define herself in the terms offered to her by her parents, her guardian, and her world. She must define an identity somewhere between these demands and not in a fixed role, an identity composed of the various narratives Esther inherits but one that cannot be summed up in any of these languages. Esther must use the conventions of the story she tells as self-consciously as she receives the good opinion of others. Since her identity is somewhere outside the roles she is asked to play, the way she tells her story will be as "coy" as Esther herself must be and will be a reflection of her role as the decomposing negation of the stories of others.

One of the ways Esther makes her story her own is by undermining the usual expectations of a first-person narrative, especially one that is being told in retrospect. She does not pretend that her discovery of an identity can take place independently of the effects of the parts others want her to play or that it can be fully explicit, let alone sequentially disclosed. This makes her narrative method indirect and oblique, like the tacking maneuvers of Phil Squod, who, like Esther, has had his share of disastrous head-on contacts with the world, and allows Esther to represent her experience of herself as one that is, initially, an experience of self that takes place through the eyes and narratives of others and only later becomes the creation of a self out of this experience:

I don't know how it is, I seem to be always writing about myself. I mean all the time to write about other people, and I try to think about myself as little as possible, and I am sure, when I find myself coming into the story again, I am really vexed and say, "Dear, dear, you tiresome little creature, I wish you wouldn't!" but it is all of no use. I hope any one who may read what I write, will understand that if these pages contain a great deal about me, I can only suppose it must be because I have really something to do with them, and can't be kept out. (162–63)

The only way Esther can escape her entanglement in the languages of others and use her renunciations to create and express her identity is to suffer a radical alienation from the person everyone wants her to be and, consequently, also a clear alienation from the conventional expectation that a first-person narrator is an integral whole. This cannot be simply a change of roles. Esther must become radically different from the roles assigned her by the plots and by the various interests and narratives of others so that she can find her own language, tell her own story, and find her own identity. The source of this alienation is, of course, her illness.

Esther's fever, delirium, and disfigurement simultaneously free Esther from a life largely defined by the expectations of others and make her the only character (and the only narrator) who must incorporate the divisions and deformations of the world at large into her experience of herself and into her story of that experience. Her illness and the resulting disorientation and alienation, in other words, allows Esther to incorporate the multiplicity of who she is into the very form of her identity. That Esther is infected by Jo is a way of fulfilling Miss Barbary's prophecy but it is a fulfillment with the usual unexpected consequences. Like Jo, Esther pays the price of the denials of her parents and of society, but by both fulfilling and surviving the destiny that has been set for her by the past and by society, she is freed to institute her own identity and her own vision of the world.

Esther's fever does more than change her looks; it effectively makes her a new person. All the things she tried to be for others are now irrevocably changed. She can perform the same duties, but their meaning will be different because Esther is different. Esther has lost in her disfigurement the only sure source of her identity—her face. When she looks into a mirror she sees a stranger. For this reason, what Esther says is never more than an image reflected in a mirror and Esther is always outside the image she projects. It is as if Esther allows us to look over her shoulder at her reflection in a mirror but never allows us to see her face directly. This is more than coyness. Esther is permanently alienated from any fixed image and her indirect narrative embodies that alienation in its hesitancies. Esther's disfigurement puts her outside the stories of other characters and even outside the story she was developing for herself in terms of the other characters. From this point on in her story, Esther can no longer find herself partly reflected in the other characters surrounding her; she finds her identity in the midst of their failure as possible ways to express and explain the world.

All of the characters most closely associated with Esther are, to one extent or another, damaged by the parts they play in the world, in Esther's story, and in the novel. Richard, Ada, John Jarndyce, Miss Flite, Caddy Jellyby, and Prince Turveydrop all bear some marks of having been defeated in their contact with their world. More importantly, all these characters represent possible alternatives to the novel's world that, for one reason or another, are no longer workable or no longer workable by themselves. Richard's romantic heroism, Miss Flite's apocalyptic imagination, Ada's romantic devotion, John Jarndyce's quixotism, Caddy and Prince's attempt to rescue the romance of the family, all represent possible stories or genres that can no longer succeed by themselves. They are the debris of a whole history of attempts to interpret and express the world, possible embodiments of the imagination that Esther might have assumed.[11] But, Esther, like the novel as a genre, is on the other side of their failures. The story of her identity is the story of how these stories are only partial perspectives on the world and of the resulting revelation of a sense of self and world that is a becoming and not a product.

This relationship between Esther and instances of other failed expressions of the imagination is especially pronounced in Esther's relationship to her mother. Lady Dedlock is, or should be, a tragic figure who resolutely follows her fate. As a tragic figure, Lady Dedlock should embody a paradox that is central to the human condition, like Oedipus' suffering a fate that is, at the same time, of his making and not of his making. Lady Dedlock, however, fails in this respect because her fate is entirely the result of her refusal to imagine herself apart from the roles assigned to her by her society and her own ambition. She is not confronted by contradictory and universal forces, all of which are fully justified;[12] she is simply caught in the switches of her own pride. That her end is more melodramatic than tragic is the result of the fact that her suffering takes place in a world and in a literary form in which there are no universals to support and explain her suffering. Her tragic suffering cannot purify the novel's world, restore it to a wholeness or even indicate where that wholeness may lie, and so cannot produce the catharsis proper to tragedy. Nevertheless, Lady Dedlock's tragic suffering can provide another type of catharsis: the negative catharsis of freeing Esther, as both a character and narrator, from the tragic imagination and the self-destructive forms tragedy is forced to assume in this world. Where tragedy fails, however, the novel begins and Lady Dedlock's failure as a tragic figure allows Esther to become the imagination that survives the disappearance of tragedy, the imagination of the novel itself.

Esther's narrative, then, her voice, is the voice of the novelistic imagination faced with the inadequacy of all previous literary languages, to return to Bakhtin's term, to its purpose and its world. Esther is the product of these other languages, just as the novel itself is, but, like the novel, Esther cannot fully believe in any of them. Her language is the language of alienation, but it is the alienation produced by a multiplicity that cannot be resolved into simple confrontations or choices. Esther, like the characters associated with her, is damaged by the conflicting claims of the many languages that go into making her up. She bears the scars of this damage on her face and incorporates her alienation into the very fabric of her narrative, but her experience of their failure itself depicts an identity and an experience of the world that lies always just beyond these languages, in the intervals of their dialogue. Esther's story is, in other words, the story of the novel itself as it attempts to create a world born out of multiplicity, even a repressed multiplicity, without falsifying that multiplicity. Esther is the name Dickens gives to the novelistic imagination, to its own distinctive but happily mongrel imagination, and the task it sets itself.

Esther's dialogue with the third-person narrator is, at bottom, the novel reading itself aloud. It is up to Esther to define an identity out of the failures and denials of social languages. The forces at work in the novel's world are, for Esther, possible selves and possible forms of self-expression. When she defines her identity out of all the possible selves, both personal and narrative, that she is offered she is also operating as the mind of the novel itself discovering a way of defining a relationship to the world apart from but not outside of the power struggle of the social world. The third-person narrator needs Esther to find a resolution to the problem of the objective and detached use of language he both poses and represents. But, Esther needs the third-person narrator's narrative as ballast so that her story does not become as monolithic as the world she struggles to overcome. In this way, the two narrators are, in effect, Dickens' way of telling the story of the novel's attempt to represent its world as the subject of many stories and not the closed domain of just one.

NOTES

1. D. A. Miller, in *The Novel and the Police* (Berkeley: U of California P, 1988), pp. 58–106, persuasively shows that, as much as he might want to, Dickens cannot, once and for all, establish his novel as an alternative to the abuses and dangers of Chancery or, its companion institution, the police. As careful as Dickens is to distance his novel from these institutions, he cannot change the fact that the novel is historically and formally linked to the delays and deferrals of Chancery (and the bureaucratic world at large), on the one hand, and the consoling but never quite satisfying closure of the police, on the other. Instead, Dickens' novel, like the two Bleak Houses, is in an "exposed" and anxious state, momentarily achieving alternatives that, as soon as they are realized, are lost again.

   I agree with much of Miller's reading of the novel, especially his idea that the novel is in a constantly exposed and anxious state, but it also seems important to remember that this anxious state is, at least partly, the result of the way Dickens' novel subjects all forms, including itself, to critical questioning. After all, Chancery and the police can be regarded as possible narrative (or nonnarratable narrative) forms because Dickens treats them as such. Left to their own devices, the representatives of these institutions do not admit that or act as if these institutions are only possible expressions or interpretations of the social world. Dickens, on the other hand, does not just present his novel as a representation and interpretation of social or private life but also as a way of thinking about representations and interpretations, including its own. Whatever thematic or formal alternatives he might have to offer are, it is true, only momentary and, like Esther's narrative, dispersed throughout the novel, but this is because the alternative is not here or there *in* the novel but *is* the novel itself as a form of thought. The exposed and anxious state of the novel, its frequent self-examination and concern with the play of perspectives that, by defining a world, also discovers something unexpected and new, is the alternative to the institutions the novel presents and sometimes resembles. There may, in fact, be no escape in the sense of any final resolution or alternative, but escape may not matter if the terms of confinement are always also the first shape of a larger world they can't help but reveal.

2. Peter Garrett, in *The Victorian Multiplot Novel: Studies in Dialogical Form* (New Haven: Yale UP, 1980), also discusses *Bleak House* in terms of the dialogue between the two narrators and he, too, uses some of Bakhtin's ideas to explain the nature of this "dialogue," but he sees the dialogue primarily as one between the general, largely spatial, perspective and the individual and temporal perspective. Garrett argues that these perspectives are incompatible and create a decentering of meaning in the novel. I want to argue that these two narrators are two moments of the same search for an alternative to the oppressiveness of systems, whether they are large and institutional or small and private.

3. I say this hollowness is at the center of the social world but examples of the failure of the social world, like Tom-All-Alone's, are usually depicted as being on the fringe of the respectable social world. That these fringe realities seep into the center of the social world is characteristic of the direction of Dickens' anatomy of what ails the body politic and culminates in the metaphor of infection.

4. M. M. Bakhtin, "Discourse in the Novel," in *The Dialogic Imagination,* Ed. Michael Holquist, trans. Caryl Emerson and Michael Holquist (Austin: U of

Texas P, 1981), pp. 262–63. Bakhtin's ideas about language are an attempt to overcome what he sees as the needless abstraction of languages into systems in traditional linguistics. Bakhtin wants, instead, to locate the study of language and the novel in the ways languages are used in concrete situations by individuals with more on their minds than conforming to grammatical norms. In many ways Bakhtin's ideas about language and the novel resemble, in their attempt to redirect the discussion away from abstract systems and make the individual the central consideration, what Dickens is doing in the novel. See also M. M. Bakhtin, "The Problem of Speech Genres," in *Speech Genres & Other Late Essays,* trans. Vern W. McGee, eds. Caryl Emerson and Michael Holquist (Austin: U of Texas P, 1986) and V. N. Volosinov, *Marxism and the Philosophy of Language,* trans. Ladislav Matejka and I. R. Titunik (Cambridge: Harvard UP, 1986).

5. Charles Dickens, *Bleak House* (New York: Penguin Books, 1971), p. 639. All future reference will be from this edition and will be cited in parentheses.

6. I want to distinguish what I call the idea of systems from the kind of interconnectedness Robert Alan Donovan discusses in his essay "Structure and Idea in *Bleak House,"* in *The Victorian Novel: Modern Essays in Criticism,* ed. Ian Watt (Oxford: Oxford UP, 1971), pp. 83–109. The interconnectedness of the novel's world is, as interconnectedness always is, ambiguous. It can be reassuring, as Donovan explains, or it can be oppressive, as Esther's story shows. What tips the scales at any given moment is, as Blake might say, how it is imagined. For both the third-person narrator and Esther, interconnectedness, or, less abstractly, brotherhood, is a reason for openness to what can never be fully expected. It is a reason for seeing the world as likely, at any given moment, to change its entire shape and meaning. For Chancery and the world of fashion, on the other hand, it is proof of a closed and finite world that need never be given a second thought.

7. I do not want to suggest that all the characters in the novel are thoroughly defined by the official languages. Much of the novel's appeal is its variety of singular characters. But, the characters act and react towards each other primarily in the terms defined by Chancery and the world of fashion. A good, if comic, example of this identification with the powers that be, even when this identification is not particularly appropriate, is Tony Jobling's cherished collection of copper-plate impressions of "The Divinities of Albion, or Galaxy Galary of British Beauty" (340). The appeal of characters like Tony Jobling is that their unique perspective on the world is irrepressible *in spite of* their attempts to conform to the values they believe they need to embrace to survive.

8. This may be one reason why the third-person narrator so closely resembles Inspector Bucket. Bucket, like the narrator, has a comprehensive knowledge of the social world and is the only character, except for Esther, who traverses the entire social spectrum. He also shares with the narrator the ability to enter into apparently sympathetic relations with other characters and to tailor his manner to the circumstances he finds himself in.

It is interesting in this connection that both Skimpole and Bucket share a kind of amorality. Skimpole is simply unconcerned with what might be the personal sufferings of others, except insofar as they might be aesthetically interesting while Bucket, although at times sympathetic to others, is usually consumed by the whist game he plays with his adversaries. For another view of Bucket's purpose in the novel, see J. Hillis Miller, *Charles Dickens: The World of his Novels* (Cambridge: Harvard UP, 1959), p. 176.

9. This is an early instance of the way in which Esther fulfills the stories she inherits from others but in unexpected ways. This is one indication that the multiplicity of meaning denied on the social level is restored on the personal level even if this restoration carries a heavy price.

10. Perhaps the most conspicuous image uniting Esther and Tulkinghorn are the keys Esther carries around with her. In what must be a muted pun, Esther not only is the key to the central plot, she is the bearer of all the keys to Bleak House. Tulkinghorn, on the other hand, has everything in his residence locked up but there is no key visible.

11. Charley, too, is a form Esther could have assumed had she resigned herself to the role she initially defined for herself. As such, Charley is a constant reminder that Esther is more than even she sometimes thinks she is.
    In this connection it may also be worth noting that Allan Woodcourt is also the product of a "literary" heritage he is supposed to follow and redeem. In his case, he is the product of Welsh (ap Kerrig) and Scottish Highlander (MacCoorts) nobility and is expected by his mother to restore the faded glory of the past in his choice of a wife. As the descendent of these two families, Woodcourt is also the product of two literary traditions: Welsh epic and Highlander romance. But, just as he has pedigree but no money, these two literary traditions are of limited value and have only a dimished part to play in the world of a novel. By choosing Esther, who is disfigured by the stories of her own family, and a life of service and self-sacrifice, Woodcourt repeats the same decision Esther makes in her narrative.

12. I have in mind here Camus's definition of tragedy in "On the Future of Tragedy," in *Lyrical and Critical Essays,* ed. Philip Thody, trans. Ellen Conroy Kennedy (New York: Vintage Books, 1970), p. 301.

WORKS CITED

Adorno, Theodor. *Aesthetic Theory.* Trans. C. Lenhardt. Eds. Gretel Adorno and Rolf Tiedemann. London: Routledge & Kegan Paul, 1984.

———. *Minima Moralia.* Trans. E. F. N. Jephcott. London: Verso, 1978.

Bakhtin, M. M. *The Dialogic Imagination: Four Essays.* Trans. Caryl Emerson and Michael Holquist. Ed. Michael Holquist. Austin: U of Texas P, 1981.

———. "The Problem of Speech Genres." In *Speech Genres & Other Late Essays.* Trans. Vern W. McGee. Eds. Caryl Emerson and Michael Holquist. Austin: U of Texas P, 1986.

Camus, Albert. "On the Future of Tragedy." In *Lyrical and Critical Essays.* Ed. Philip Thody. Trans. Ellen Conroy Kennedy. New York: Vintage Books, 1970. 295–310.

Donovan, Robert Alan. "Structure and Idea in *Bleak House.*" In *The Victorian Novel: Modern Essays in Criticism.* Ed. Ian Watt. Oxford: Oxford UP, 1971. 83–109.

Frank, Lawrence. "'Through a Glass Darkly:' Esther Summerson and *Bleak House.*" *Dickens Studies Annual* 4 (1975), 91–112.

Garrett, Peter K. *The Victorian Multiplot Novel: Studies in Dialogical Form.* New Haven: Yale UP, 1980.

Kucick, John. "Action in the Dickens's Ending: *Bleak House* and *Great Expectations.*" *Nineteenth-Century Fiction,* 33 (1978), 88–109.

———. *Excess and Restraint in the Novels of Charles Dickens.* Athens: U of Georgia P, 1981.

———. "Repression and Representation: Dickens's General Economy." *Nineteenth-Century Fiction* 38 (1983), 62–77.

Miller, D. A. *The Novel and the Police.* Berkeley: U of California P, 1988.

Miller, J. Hillis. *Charles Dickens: The World of his Novels.* Cambridge: Harvard UP, 1959.

Ragussis, Michael. "The Ghostly Signs of *Bleak House.*" *Nineteenth-Century Fiction,* 34 (1979), 253–80.

Sawicki, Joseph. "'The Mere Truth Won't Do': Esther as Narrator in *Bleak House.*" *The Journal of Narrative Technique,* 17 (1987), 209–24.

Senf, Carol A. "*Bleak House:* Dickens, Esther, and the Androgynous Mind." *The Victorian Newsletter,* 64 (1983), 21–27.

Volosinov, V. N. *Marxism and the Philosophy of Language.* Trans. Ladislav Matejka and I. R. Titunik. Cambridge: Harvard UP, 1986.

Wilt, Judith. "Confusion and Consciousness in Dickens's Esther." *Nineteenth-Century Fiction,* 32 (1977), 285–309.

Winslow, Joan D. "Esther Summerson: The Betrayal of the Imagination." *The Journal of Narrative Technique,* 6 (1976), 1–11.

Young, Saundra K. "Uneasy Relations: Possibilities for Eloquence in *Bleak House.*" *Dickens Studies Annual,* 9 (1981), 67–85.

Zwerdling, Alex. "Esther Summerson Rehabilitated." In *Charles Dickens: New Perspectives.* Ed. Wendell Stacy Johnson. Englewood Cliffs, NJ: Prentice-Hall, Inc., 1982. 94–113.

The Grotesque and Urban Chaos in *Bleak House*

Kay Hetherly Wright

When Miss Flite describes her "dreadful attraction" to the court of Chancery in Dickens' *Bleak House* (553), she is voicing the classic response to the grotesque: an uneasy mixture of attraction and repulsion. But while she sees only the court itself as the incomprehensible "monster" (554), almost everything in the novel is actually connected in some way to Chancery, from the obvious Krook and his rag and bottle shop to Chesney Wold and Tom-all-Alone's, to disease, poverty, and the all-pervading fog.[1] Clearly, Chancery serves as some kind of model around which various elements of the novel organize themselves, but we still must ask, just what is Chancery and how does it function in itself and in relation to the rest of the novel?

One way to explore these questions is by analyzing Dickens' use of the grotesque throughout the novel. The term "grotesque" is slippery, however, and as Geoffrey Harpham emphasizes in his book *On the Grotesque*, critical confusion rather than consensus over the term prevails. Harpham cites what he calls the two most important books of this century on the subject, both of which are "prodigiously well informed, carefully argued, persuasive accounts," which, nevertheless, "manage to contradict each other utterly on the most basic premises" (xvii–xviii). These are Wolfgang Kayser's *The Grotesque in Art and Literature* (1963) and Mikhail Bakhtin's *Rabelais and His World* (1971). Both see in the grotesque elements of the comic and the fearful, but while Kayser emphasizes the terror of the grotesque and sees the response of laughter as the most difficult and troubling aspect, Bakhtin delights in the grotesque as an expression of primordial energy, an "exuberant acceptance of all life," including death (Harpham 207, n. 77). Harpham juxtaposes Bakhtin and Kayser to stress that the essential quality of the grotesque is its indefinability.

In describing rather than defining the phenomenon, Harpham emphasizes the process of trying to classify and interpret that which we sense as grotesque:

> When we use the word "grotesque" we record, among other things, the sense that though our attention has been arrested, our understanding is unsatisfied. Grotesqueries both require and defeat definition: they are not so regular and rhythmical that they settle easily into our categories, nor so unprecedented that we do not recognize them at all. They stand at a margin of consciousness between the known and the unknown, the perceived and the unperceived, calling into question the adequacy of our ways of organizing the world, of dividing the continuum of experience into knowable particles. (3)

For Harpham, the grotesque can be described according to different forms it may take and according to how these forms affect the interpretive process, but there is no essence which is the grotesque. What makes something grotesque in appearance is the fact that it somehow eludes our usual ways of classifying information. Thus grotesque forms may occupy multiple categories at once or fall between categories altogether, but there is always something familiar about these forms which is what makes them confusing or unsettling.[2]

The world of *Bleak House* cannot be read, by either the characters or the reader, as one that is simply knowable. Rather, like Harpham's model of the grotesque, it is a world where categories are constantly crossing, where what seems familiar becomes strangely unfamiliar as we look more closely, and where the inhabitants are sometimes so baffled by the world around them that they can no longer survive in it.[3] At the heart of this world is Chancery, which both acts and refuses to act as the organizing principle of the novel, and it is here that an analysis of the grotesque in *Bleak House* must begin.

On the level of realism, Chancery is familiar enough as an inefficient and corrupt court system, but recognizing this does not explain much. Similarly, Chancery cannot be adequately explained by seeing it in simple moral terms, as one critic does when he argues that the court represents "evil" that "will end by poisoning itself" (Blount 191). Nor does it fit a logical context of simple cause and effect as the "main cause" of the social problems in the novel (Steig 326). Rather, Chancery is much more important as an emblem representing the principle of chaos that Dickens associates with modern urban life and which, as an embodiment of the grotesque, can be recognized on the level of realism or in terms of cause and effect, but can never be fully understood in those or any other contexts.[4]

In Jarndyce and Jarndyce we have a close-up view of Chancery as it typically operates, and, as the narrator tells us, it is "so complicated that no man alive knows what it means ... no two Chancery lawyers can talk about it for five minutes without coming to a total disagreement as to all the premises" (52). Just as the grotesque cannot ultimately be defined, Chancery cannot be pinned down, and those who insist they understand it are operating under an illusion. Sir Leicester is just such a person whose whole way of thinking depends on the strict classification of all things, whether it be justice and injustice, the class system, or meaning itself. Leicester's view of the court is in direct opposition to the narrator's and ours:

> he regards the Court of Chancery, even if it should involve an occasional delay of justice and a trifling amount of confusion, as something devised in conjunction with a variety of other somethings, by the perfection of human wisdom, for the eternal settlement (humanly speaking) of everything. And he is upon the whole of a fixed opinion, that to give the sanction of his countenance to any complaints respecting it, would be to encourage some person in the lower classes to rise up somewhere—like Wat Tyler. (60–61)

Leicester, with his "fixed opinion," his confidence in "the perfection of human wisdom for the settlement of everything," and his belief in a rigid class system, sees a world that he has carefully constructed in his mind rather than the shifting one that is there.

Contrary to Leicester's perceptions, Chancery undermines any effort to explain its workings in clear-cut terms. Most obviously, it is a court of law which impedes justice rather than championing it. The documents related to various cases serve more to block communication than to foster it, and the more one studies those documents, the less he or she understands them. Whatever Chancery is, in other words, is beyond grasping through language or logic. It cannot be grasped emotionally either since it evokes a powerful ambivalence, as Miss Flite, in her mad wisdom, recognizes. For her, "There's a cruel attraction in the place. You *can't* leave it" (553). Like other suitors, she watches Chancery destroy one after another of its clients, but continues to go there daily, hoping for a settlement she knows will never come. The court for her is not so much a place as a horrible, but fascinating creature which has somehow gotten her and the others under its power. "I went to look at the Monster," she explains, "And then I found out how it was, and I was drawn to stay there" (554). Ironically, in accepting that Chancery operates outside of any recognizable logic, the "mad" Miss Flite is much closer to understanding it than the methodical Sir Leicester.

Even as the novel opens, we see the world of Chancery as one in which normal divisions of time, space, and species seem to have collapsed into each other. Thus, though we are in the midst of nineteenth-century London, it would not be unusual to see a Megalosaurus "waddling like an elephantine lizard up Holburn Hill" (49). Not only has the Mesozoic age crossed over into the modern, but the Megalosaurus itself, if we met it, would be a cross between a mammal and a reptile.[5] In addition, on this day that seems never to have actually broken, dogs cannot be distinguished from the mud that surrounds them, and the people standing on bridges feel as if they were actually in balloons, hanging in the sky. The fog pinches toes and fingers cruelly, and the gas knows, with "a haggard and unwilling look" (50), that the shop lights, like the day itself, are out of whack, having been turned on two hours early. Michael Goldberg's description of Dickens' method is especially appropriate here and even more so for Dickens' use of the grotesque as Harpham describes the term: "The things related by metaphor are not simply like each other, they display a tendency to overleap the restraints of metaphor and to become each other" (221). In short, as the novel begins, Dickens shows us a foggy, fluid world, and "at the very heart of the fog" *(BH* 50) is the High Chancellor.

The court, at the center of this strange world, is no more stable as the novel begins. Like the dogs outside, the Chancellor himself is indistinguishable from the mud, or so it seems since Mr. Tangle repeatedly addresses him as "Mlud."[6] As for the court, it has a dark "owlish aspect," and its suitors become like animals as they battle abstract legal concepts which seem to take on concrete form; thus the men are "tripping one another up on the slippery precedents, groping knee-deep in technicalities, running their goat-hair and horsehair warded heads against walls of word ..." (50). At times the court resembles a grotesque carnival where documents "grimly writhed into many shapes," and lawyers are transformed into absurd marionettes who, with their summaries "of eighteen hundred sheets, bob up like eighteen hammers in a pianoforte, make eighteen bows, and drop into their eighteen places of obscurity" (54).

Associated with all this carnivalesque confusion is a cruel and irrational laughter, for though Jarndyce and Jarndyce "has been death to many ... it is a joke in the profession" (52). Even as the case closes and Richard Carstone's mouth fills with blood, the court is a scene of senseless, hysterical laughter:

> the people came streaming out looking flushed and hot.... Still they were exceedingly amused, and were more like people coming out from a Farce or a Juggler than from a court of Justice ... presently great bundles of paper began to be carried out ... which the bearers staggered under.... Even these clerks were laughing. We glanced at the papers, and seeing Jarndyce and Jarndyce everywhere, asked an official-looking person who was standing in the midst of them, whether the cause was over. "Yes," he said; "it was all up with it at last,"

and burst out laughing too. (922)

After seeing the tremendous "sorrow and ruin" (374) that has come out of Jarndyce and Jarndyce, we cannot help but see the laughter associated with it as the uneasy laughter of the grotesque.

The closest human parallel to Chancery is Krook who shares and reinforces the grotesque characteristics of the more abstract court system.[7] Krook is important as a human embodiment of the vague "monster" underlying the modern city rather than as its victim or as a realistic character. Even in appearance Krook, like Chancery and its surroundings, belongs to multiple categories at once as the initial description of him makes clear:

> [He's] short, cadaverous, and withered; with his head sunk sideways between his shoulders and the breath issuing in visible smoke from his mouth, as if he were on fire within. His throat, chin and eyebrows were so frosted with white hairs and so gnarled with veins and puckered skin, that he looked from his breast upward, like some old root in a fall of snow. (99–100)

Krook seems to simultaneously occupy the world of the dead and the living, a nightmarish realm of fire-breathing men, and the vegetable world. His character is no less simple than his appearance, as Miss Flite attests: "He is a very eccentric person. He is very odd. Oh I assure you he is very odd!" (100). While Flite attributes his eccentricity to madness, elsewhere Krook is identified with the demonic, as in his relationship to the black cat, Lady Jane, as his "diabolical familiar" (Blount 196), and when we see him "with his lean hands spread out above the body like a vampire's wings" *(BH* 189). All these associations—death, madness, and the demonic—suggest that Krook inhabits some realm bordering the known and the unknown so that his existence teases logical thought and potentially threatens our ability to comprehend the world. Krook's death is a final example of such teasing when, as many critics note, the man spontaneously combusts rather than the room which is "so stuffed with inflammable rubbish that it constitutes a fire hazard" (Goldberg 221).

Like Krook himself, a human monster who parallels the institutional monster of Chancery, Krook's shop mirrors the court. Thus, as the court undermines justice, in Krook's shop, out of which one would expect him to make a living, "Everything seemed to be bought, and nothing sold there" (99). Language is divorced from communication in both places, and this failure suggests one of the strongest connections between the two. As one critic argues, Krook's copying of letters on the wall that he cannot read represents a "death of meaning ... so closely paralleled in Chancery by the reams of rhetoric and trivia produced in each endless court case that the kinship between Krook and the Lord Chancellor is never clearer than it is here" (Kelley 263–64). Finally, as in Chancery, Krook's shop evokes the disturbing response of attraction/repulsion. This is most clear in the case of Snagsby who associates the shop with secret dealings he is involved in but does not understand:

> Impelled by the mystery of which he is a partaker, and yet in which he is not a sharer, Mr. Snagsby haunts what seems to be its fountain-head—the rag and bottle shop in the court. It has an irresistible attraction for him. (500)

At the same time he is attracted to this imagined source of mysteries, Snagsby is "ill at ease ... he always is so, more or less, under the oppressive influence of the secret that is upon him" (499–500). Yet, like Miss Flite, Snagsby is drawn to this uncomfortable place by a "dreadful attraction" (553).

Ambivalence is also manifested in Krook, as in Chancery, through the yoking together of horror and laughter. Krook, after all, is essentially a comic figure, and any uneasiness we may feel about his crossing over of categories will probably be mixed with a good portion of amusement. However, in the context of the novel he is a sinister figure, and in the most obviously grotesque incident of *Bleak House,* Krook's spontaneous combustion, the mixture of the comic with the horrible is potentially a very disturbing one.

There can be no doubt that Dickens himself saw the potential for horror in this strange kind of human burning which he went to great lengths to prove as an actual possibility.[8] Perhaps his efforts to ground the phenomena in reality were made, in part, to insure the horror of the incident, and certainly his descriptions are horrible, or at least disgusting. Most readers are bound to feel these emotions when they realize, for example, that the soot that "smears like black fat" (505), "the thick yellow liquor" that "defiles" Guppy's fingers (509), and the "greasy" air that "Mr. Snagsby sniffs and tastes again, and then spits and wipes his mouth" (500) are all by-products of the burned Krook. "I find it gives me the horrors" (500), says Weevle of the greasy air, and he has no idea yet of the source. At the same time, however, throughout Dickens' melodramatic rendering of the buildup and realization of Krook's death, there is a strong sense of the comic, as in the climactic discovery by Guppy and Tony:

> Here is a small burnt patch of flooring: here is the tinder from a little bundle of burnt paper, but not so light as usual, seeming to be steeped in something; and here is—is it the cinder of a small, charred and broken log of wood sprinkled with white ashes, or is it cool? O Horror, he *is* here! and this from which we

run away, striking out the light and overturning one another into the street, is all that represents him. (511)

To feel both repulsed and humored by Krook's bizarre fate is in keeping with the ambivalence of his character and with the sensation of the grotesque.

Interestingly though, critical response to Krook's death reveals an unwillingness to allow for this sensation and, instead, some readers seem determined to place the incident firmly into a single context. One critic, for example, emphasizes the horror of the incident and ties it to what he sees as the moral of *Bleak House*. Practically ignoring the comic, he asserts, "Obviously Dickens was using the horror to horrify," and in recognition of the grotesque quality of horror, he adds that "it is more than possible he was indulging a personal attraction towards the gruesome" (Blount 86). He insists that this is a serious incident which serves to illustrate the novel's moral stance:

> The Krook travesty has a generalized relevance ... and it represents in its extreme form the moral affirmation the novel makes in the face of evil. Thus the assertion that the self-engendered poisons of evil *will* eventually work their own destruction is given positive yea-saying authority. (Blount 211)

In direct contrast, another critic argues that the scene is incapable of carrying any "grave weight," and as a contribution to the theme of corruption destroying itself, Dickens' rendering of spontaneous combustion "is all of no avail" (Harvey 36). Instead, he sees the incident as a "farcical anticlimax" with an "intrinsic quality of humor" which disarms the horrible: "A description of the stages of human disintegration or of recognizable human remains may awaken horror, but the sudden evaporation of a man into soot and effluvium is not serious" (Harvey 36). Seeing the incident as almost exclusively comic or horrible, as these two do, illustrates the confusion that naturally results from ambivalence, but it also misses the point that Krook's spontaneous combustion, like the workings of Chancery, propels us into the unstable realm of the grotesque, where understanding is always incomplete.[9]

While Krook's spontaneous combustion is the novel's most sensational instance of the grotesque, more ordinary manifestations also add to the sense of an ungraspable world that defies classification. One of the most important of these is uncertainty about origins, a motif which recurs throughout the novel. In his short discussion of *Bleak House*, Harpham notes the centrality of this motif:

> In [*Bleak House*] the law is so intertwined with evil that the authority and legitimacy of law itself are brought into question, with the result that [the novel is] obsessed with questions of bastardy, legitimacy, and confusion over origins.

(103)

Once suitors enter Chancery, they become engulfed in a system incapable of recognizing their humanity. Here there is no viable source of authority or meaning, no coherent center, but only a void filled with bogus documents and posturing lawyers. As an emblem, the court signifies, as well, a more generalized failure of any system to humanize the urban landscape or provide meaningful structures. And as products of such a society, the people of *Bleak House* also lack coherent identities, which we see in the many orphans and illegitimate children of the novel. Thus, just as Chancery and its fog envelop practically the entire world of the novel, questions of legitimacy, bastardy, and confused origins are everywhere.

Dickens' treatment of these questions intensifies the grotesque quality of his vision. As Harpham explains, incest, bastardy, deformation and other taboo subjects are potentially in the realm of the grotesque because of the way we are trained to think about them in childhood. Young children develop "discriminatory grids," and impose them on the world as a way of making sense of their experiences. Those things which are excluded from their grids appear, then, as "non-things," and so are suppressed, only to inevitably resurface from time to time as sources of "anxiety, horror, astonishment, laughter or revulsion" (4)[10] Harpham also sees illegitimate birth as a metaphor for the grotesque in general:

> Grotesque figures ... seem to be singular events, appearing in the world by virtue of an illegitimate act of creation, manifesting no coherent, and certainly no divine intention. (5)

Bleak House raises questions of illegitimacy and origins from a variety of angles, whether it be in Chancery, the many orphans of the novel, or language itself.

In Chancery, Jarndyce and Jarndyce illustrates confusion over loss of origins. Besides the fact that no two lawyers can ever agree about the premises of the case, they "have twisted it into such a state of bedevilment that the original merits of the case have long disappeared from the face of the earth" (145). It seems that there is no original source for Jarndyce and Jarndyce, but that it's simply always been. However, the determined suitors insist on understanding the case and bringing it to a close, at least where they are concerned, through studying documents and attending sessions tirelessly. But of course understanding and closure always eludes them; besides the apparent lack of a relationship between words and their meanings, when the case does finally close, the surviving suitors are no better off than before. At one point, Richard thinks he has gotten to the "core" through diligent studying of the documents, but the reader and Esther know better:

> He had got at the core of that mystery now, he told us; and nothing could be plainer than that the will under which he and Ada were to take, I don't know how many pounds, must be finally established if there were any sense or justice in the Court of Chancery—but O what a great *if* that sounded in my ears.... (374)

The fact is, the "sense" of Chancery will always be beyond Richard's and everyone's reach. Although the central document is eventually found, the case is dissolved because there is no more money, and as a result, the original intentions of the case become irrelevant.

At the same time, Chancery, with its countless cases like Jarndyce and Jarndyce, continues on, its workings as obscure as ever, like the mud Dickens sees as one of its closest kin. At one point, the narrator moves us from the court to another place with the following transition: "diving through law and equity, and through that kindred mystery the street mud, which is made of nobody knows what, and collects about us nobody knows whence or how" (186). Significantly, this dive takes us to the court's near relation, Krook's rag and bottle shop.

Like the court, characters in *Bleak House* also demonstrate confusion over origins or problems with identity which indicate their participation in the world of Chancery. The novel shows that any relationship to a system like Chancery will inevitably have a crippling effect. This it is not simply because Chancery is a corrupt court, but because of the institutionalized quality itself that characterizes modern society and de-centers those who identify themselves with it.[11] As J. H. Miller explains,

> As soon as a man becomes in one way or another a part of such a system, born into it or made a party to it, he enters into a strange kind of time. He loses any possibility of having a present self, or a present satisfaction, loses any possibility of ever going back to find the origins of his present plight.... (27)

All the characters of *Bleak House* suffer, to a greater or less degree, as a result of being part of a systemized society. Because their suffering often takes the form of a lack of focus or center, the members of such a society resemble the grotesque quality of the society itself.

Problems with identity and purpose are especially common among the more important figures of *Bleak House*. Esther is an orphan as well as an illegitimate child, and her problems with self-definition stem from a troubled uncertainty over her origins. As a child, she is traumatized when her guardian convinces her that "Your mother, Esther, is your disgrace, and you were hers" (65). As a result, she represses her romantic desires out of guilt over her illegitimacy even before she completely understands it.[12] This inability to accept aspects of herself results in Esther's fragmentation, or her state of being "orphaned, having no center" (Creevey 64). Esther's shame intensifies when she does learn who her mother is, for then her illegitimacy is made clear, and her subsequent illness is closely related to this shame.

Esther's self-condemnation reveals her own participation in a society that systematizes human relationships. She, like her parents, Lady Dedlock and Nemo, accept the social taboos attached to illegitimacy and sexual relationships across class boundaries. The result of this acceptance for all three is loss of self. Lady Dedlock represses her sexuality, as Esther does, and lives a sterile life totally at odds with her earlier relationship with Hawdon. As Christopher Herbert puts it, "Her suppression of her original identity" leads her into a "state of death-in-life" (113), so that she becomes a kind of nonperson. That Nemo does the same is even more obvious. His existence is no existence at all, as Tulkinghorn makes clear: "Nemo is Latin for no one" (185).[13] Lady Dedlock also represses her love for her illegitimate daughter, even after acknowledging her, and allows herself a reunion with the man she had loved only as she is dying. In the clothes and identity of a destitute woman, she falls on her lover's grave, accepting the disgrace and non-existence society imposes on those who fail to fit its accepted patterns.

Unlike her parents, Esther emerges from her illness, but as a kind of grotesque in appearance with a face unlike its original. Esther's repression has erupted, freeing her from some of her anxiety and uncertainty over origins, but at the same time implicating her in the system that upholds the taboos which have totally destroyed her parents, and countless nameless others.

As a participant in this system, epitomized in the monstrous visions of Chancery and Krook, whose spontaneous combustion is a more complete eruption, Esther cannot avoid being scarred. One critic argues that "Esther's rebirth" is "in every way [the] antithesis [of] Krook's death from spontaneous combustion" and that the two events are "dramatically juxtaposed" to bring out the contrast (Pikrel 88). Certainly, in many ways Esther is the antithesis of Krook and of what Chancery represents, particularly in her generosity and willingness to sacrifice herself for others. And she does experience a "rebirth" by partially regaining her past and eventually allowing herself a romantic involvement with Allan Woodcourt. However, as a participant in the world of Chancery, her fever, erupting into temporary blindness and disfigurement, connects her with Krook, as well as with Vholes, whose face is scarred by "a red eruption here and there" (589), and even with Phil Squod, "a little man with a face all crushed together, who appears, from a certain blue and speckled appearance that one of his cheeks presents, to have been blown up, in the way of business, at some odd time or times" (357). While the nature of each of these people's participation in the *Bleak House* society varies greatly, from Phil's willingness to be a passive victim to Vholes' sinister victimization of the helpless, all contribute to the continuation of the system that scars them.

Besides being peopled with physical grotesques who have lost some crucial part of their selves, *Bleak House* further explores confusion over origins and loss of identity in its many host/parasite relationships. Harpham puts this relationship in the context of the grotesque when he writes that identities

> are not necessarily discontinuous, but could flow into each other. This sense of flowing-into is a consistent quality of the grotesque, in which not only identities, but codes, systems, and distinctions of any kind are thrown together with no dominant principle that could enable us to determine what the entity is by itself, what is properly the inside and what the invader outside. (106)

In the kind of relationship Harpham describes here, the parasite so takes over the host that the original characteristics of the host become barely recognizable.

The central parasite of *Bleak House* is Chancery, and its most obvious hosts are the suitors like Richard, Flite, and Gridley, whose absorption in their cases proves deadly. In each case, the suitor loses the sense of his or her separate identity to the point of madness or death. Chancery and its lawyers are characterized as sucking the life out of their clients until they disintegrate. Miss Flite explains to Esther, for example, that the Mace and Seal, emblems of Chancery justice, "Draw people on, my dear. Draw peace out of them. Good looks out of them. Good qualities out of them. I have felt them even drawing my rest away, in the night" (554). Later, referring to the same emblems, Miss Flite tells Esther that Richard has been drawn by them as she has so that now, "next to myself he is the most constant suitor in court" (874). But while Flite loses mainly her senses through an obsession with Chancery, Richard loses everything. His debilitation is dramatized through his relationship with Vholes, clearly a parasite intent on sucking the life from his host in the name of Jarndyce and Jarndyce. Vholes has "something of the Vampire in him" *(BH* 876) which is clear when he comes to Richard's house for dinner, and we see that the real dinner is Richard himself. During the meal, Vholes not "once removed his eyes from his host's face" (878). This parasite's "host," once a young, enthusiastic man has degenerated so that he now appears "thin and languid, slovenly in his dress, abstracted in his manner..." (878). After Richard's breakdown in court, Vholes's look is described as "slowly devouring" and he gasps "as if he had swallowed the last morsel of his client" (924). In the end, Richard has lost so much of his former self that he, like Lady Dedlock and Nemo before him, becomes nothing, leaving Vholes and Chancery nourished and ready for the next victim.

Gridley is another suitor sucked lifeless by his absorption into Chancery. He insists on demanding justice aggressively, convinced that otherwise he "should be driven mad" (266) as Miss Flite has been. Instead, less deluded but still like Richard, he's driven to the point of total exhaustion. When Esther sees him in this state he is

> so changed that at first I recognized no likeness in his colorless face to what I recollected.... His voice had faded, with the old expression of his face, with his strength, with his anger, with his resistance to the wrongs that had at last subdued him. The faintest shadow of an object full of form and colour, is such a picture of it, as he was of the man from Shropshire whom we had spoken with before. (406)

Once again, Chancery, like a tremendous parasite, has sucked the life out of its host until the original man is barely recognizable.

Bleak House abounds with parasites and hosts engendered by systems whose external operations, like Chancery's, "conceal a sucking void into which the weak ... fall to their ruin" (Harpham 103). For individuals, participation in such systems may lead to madness, death, disease, or disfigurement, while for the lowest classes, it may result in abject poverty as well. For what is Tom-all-Alone's but an entire neighborhood sucked dry through hunger, disease, and neglect until buildings as well as people are only vaguely recognizable as what they once were.[14]

In *Bleak House* Dickens does not offer simple solutions to deinstitutionalize modern life or to transform the urban chaos into a coherent world, though some critics claim unconvincingly that he does.[15] In fact, Dickens' own response to the city was complex: it was the classic response to the grotesque. Writing in an 1846 letter to the *Daily News* about the "horrible fascination" of public hangings, Dickens claims that "the attraction of repulsion [is] as much a law of our moral nature, as gravitation is in the structure of the visible world..." (qtd. in Collins 248). This kind of ambivalence often surfaces in his novels with the city as its source.[16] In *Bleak House* Dickens seems particularly fascinated by the profound sense of dislocation he associates with London, and he never suggests a cure for it within the city. Rather, he shows through the novel's central characters, those who survive that is, that the only solution is to escape the urban labyrinth, as do Jarndyce and Ada in their ironically named Bleak House and Esther and Woodcourt in theirs. Bleak House becomes, then, a kind of "pastoral alternative to the hellish urban situation Dickens' novels increasingly explore" (Goldberg 208).

While I have argued for the complexity of Dickens' vision of the modern city as intrinsically grotesque, his retreat into pastoralism, where life is made simple through Christ-like self-sacrifice, is disappointing.[17] Equally disappointing is Esther's total lack of involvement in the decision to marry Woodcourt. While she certainly understands or accepts her past more fully than she did earlier in the novel, she finally submits to complete passivity and self-abnegation. If Esther begins the novel de-centered by repression and confusion over her origins, she ends it by finding her center in Woodcourt rather than herself. Yet, the tension created by Dickens' juxtaposition of the complex urban nightmare with the simple realm of pastoral is not resolved by this neat ending.[18] It is likely, in fact, that Dickens' placement of Esther in an idyllic world stems from his own uneasiness with his grotesque vision. Newsom claims that in Dickens' inability to explain exactly what he meant by "the romantic side of familiar things," he reveals that he is "profoundly at odds with himself whenever he touches upon the larger scheme of things in his journalistic and private writings, and that it is only in the novels that he achieves anything like a resolution of his own conflicting views" (5). In *Bleak House* however, Dickens also seems to be at odds with himself when he concludes an otherwise profound novel with a simple ending. He has shown only what is "substantially true, and within the truth" *(BH* 41) about the modern city, and part of that truth is that we can never fully grasp how it works. He even warns us that a total comprehension is undermined at every turn by showing us a vision of the city as grotesque. But perhaps unable to leave his readers and himself with such a disturbing vision, he leaves us instead with a world that is just as unreal as the other was "true."[19]

The novel closes with the hint that even Esther's original beauty may have been restored in this Edenic world. In other words, in this setting her complicity with the city as grotesque, and the grotesque itself, is disarmed. Even this suggestion, however, does not render Dickens' treatment of the grotesque less effective. *Bleak House* remains a powerful depiction of modern urban life as a grotesque landscape which lacks any kind of coherent center.

NOTES

1. A number of critics note this connection. See for example Steig's article (326–27), Kelley, and Blount (esp. 194–95).

2. As examples, Harpham uses a series of engravings and paintings from the 15th-19th centuries, explaining how their skewing of recognizable categories—logical, ontological, and hierarchical—creates a sense of the grotesque in which "something is [perceived as] illegitimately in something else" (10–11).

3. Harpham deals briefly with *Bleak House* in his book (103–4), comparing it to *Wuthering Heights,* one of his chief models of grotesque narrative. Focusing on Heathcliff as his central grotesque figure, Harpham writes, "The nearest thing to Heathcliff in narrative is not another character, but the court of Chancery in Dickens' *Bleak House"* (103).

4. See Ousby (382–83) and Herbert (107) for similar views.

5. Harpham writes of an "abbreviation" or "shortcut" as a form of grotesque in which an older form merges with a more recent one. One example of this is what he calls "abridged evolution" in which a creature is attached "to another phase of its own being, with the intervening temporal gaps so great that it appears that species boundaries, and not mere time, has been overleaped" (11).

6. Robert Baker, at the University of Wisconsin-Madison, brought this word play (my lord—mud) to my attention.

7. The connection between Krook and Chancery is made explicit in the novel on pages 100–101, where we learn from Flite that Krook is actually "called among the neighbors the Lord Chancellor."

8. In addition to Dickens' comments in the Preface to *Bleak House* (42), see Blount, Haight, and Gaskell.

9. As Harpham points out, "All grotesque art threatens the notion of a center, by implying coherencies just out of reach, metaphors or analogies just beyond our grasp" (43). Thus concepts of perfect unity, clarity, or closure do not easily allow for the grotesque since its form and the interpretation of that form are based on that which refuses to be contained.

10. Harpham draws from the work of anthropologist Edmund Leach in making this connection between the grotesque and taboo.

11. This view is very close to Miller's, who, in his introduction to the novel, attributes the characters suffering to "the systematic quality of organized society" (27).

12. See also Herbert's discussion of Esther's illegitimacy which "fills her ... with the sensation, as mysterious as the appeal of Chancery, of causeless guilt." This sensation, he argues, is like a state of "uncanniness" (110–11). Zwerdling discusses the impact of Esther's repressed guilt as well (430–31, 436).

13. See Herbert (1984) for an excellent discussion of Nemo's role as "the very image of that total unravelling of the self that is so often witnessed in *Bleak House"* (112–13).

14. See Herbert for an illuminating discussion of Tom-all-Alone and poverty in *Bleak House*. He argues that "social disorders epitomized by Tom's ... take on a ghostly and terrifying aspect ... because they are habitually *repressed"* by society in general. Their reemergence into consciousness, then, creates the sensation of the uncanny (or the grotesque), as Freud describes it (105–6).

15. Blount argues, for example, that Dickens' "remedy ... was brutally simple. If paper was the problem, burn it; put an end to the superstructure of administration; and in its place establish a personal, direct form of philanthropy that can never forget the human issues at stake" (187). Arac claims that Dickens offers an "understanding of [his] physical, moral, and historical environments that will allow the English to avoid the frenzy of revolution by avoiding the decay of conservatism" (7), and further, that in *Bleak House* the individual can have complete "power over his environment" and fully "comprehend his world" (70, 72).

16. A number of critics have identified Dickens' ambivalence toward London as a source of his fiction and a few note his use of the grotesque or related techniques as appropriate for portraying the city. See, for example, Collins (14, 248), Clayborough (219), Fanger (65), and Goldberg (195, 214).

17. I count five references to self-sacrifice in the last chapter of the novel which is only four pages long (932–35).

18. Claims that Esther finally achieves clear-sightedness seem especially unconvincing, as the following do: "Esther moves from fog and shadow to clarity and sunshine, from isolation and estrangement to affiliation, from randomness to order, from low esteem to the highest valuation" (Pikrel 95); Esther becomes "a testament to the power of the individual to achieve a clear sightedness which is at once literal and metaphorical" (Ousby 389).

19. Zwerdling's final analysis states the problem well: "The institution of Chancery goes on. The government remains in the same incompetent hands. The church and the charitable organizations are as corrupt as ever.... Yet the book ends not in London but in Eden, where a small group of good and permanently innocent people transform the new Bleak House into a community of love existing outside the blighted world described in the rest of the novel. As Dickens' satire becomes more savage, his need to invent an escape from the world he satirizes becomes more desperate and increasingly forces him to resort to fantasy." (438)

WORKS CITED

Arac, Jonathan. "Narrative Form and Social Sense in *Bleak House* and *The French Revolution." Nineteenth-Century Fiction* 32 (1977): 54–72.

Bakhtin, Mikhail. *Rabelais and His World.* Tr. by Helene Iswolsky. Cambridge: MIT Press, 1971.

Blount, Trevor. "Dickens and Mr. Krook's Spontaneous Combustion." *Dickens Studies Annual* 1. Carbondale: S. Illinois UP, 1972. 183–211.

Clayborough, Arthur. *The Grotesque in English Literature*. Oxford: Clarendon, 1965.

Collins, Philip. *Dickens and Crime.* NY: St. Martin's Press, 1962.

Dickens, Charles. *Bleak House.* NY: Penguin, 1971.

Fanger, Donald. *Dostoyevsky and Romantic Realism: A Study of Dostoyevsky in Relation to Balzac, Dickens, and Gogol.* Cambridge: Harvard UP, 1965.

Gaskell, E. "More About Spontaneous Combustion." *The Dickensian* 69 (Jan. 1973): 25–35.

Goldberg, Michael. *Carlyle and Dickens.* Athens: U of Georgia P, 1972.

Haight, Gordon S. "Dickens and Lewes on Spontaneous Combustion." *Nineteenth-Century Fiction* 10 (1955–1956): 53–63.

Harpham, Geoffrey Galt. *On the Grotesque.* Princeton: Princeton UP, 1982.

Herbert, Christopher. "The Occult in *Bleak House." Novel* 17 (1984): 101–15.

Kayser, Wolfgang. *The Grotesque in Art and Literature.* Tr. Ulrich Weisstein. NY: McGraw-Hill, 1963.

Kelley, Alice Van Buren. "The Bleak Houses of *Bleak House." Nineteenth Century Fiction* 25 (1970): 253–68.

Miller, J. Hillis. Introduction. *Bleak House.* By Charles Dickens. NY: Penguin, 1971. 11–34.

Newsom, Robert. *Dickens on the Romantic Side of Familiar Things: "Bleak House" and the Novel Tradition.* NY: Columbia UP, 1977.

Ousby, Ian. "The Broken Glass: Vision and Comprehension in *Bleak House." Nineteenth Century Fiction* 29 (1975) 381–92.

Pikrel, Paul. *"Bleak House:* The Emergence of Theme." *Nineteenth Century Literature* 42 (1987): 73–96.

Steig, Michael. "Structure and the Grotesque in Dickens: *Dombey and Son; Bleak House." Centennial Review* 14 (1970): 313–31.

Sucksmith, Harvey Peter. *The Narrative Art of Charles Dickens: The Rhetoric of Sympathy and Irony in his Novels.* Oxford: Clarendon, 1970.

Zwerdling, Alex. *"Esther Summerson Rehabilitated."* PMLA 88 (1973) 429–39.

Doubles, Self-Attack, and Murderous Rage in Florence Dombey

Richard Currie

Recent criticism of Dickens' Florence Dombey has suggested that there is more than sentimentality to her characterization. Linda Zwinger's important feminist essay discovers ground for viewing Florence as an erotic heroine. Catherine Bernard argues that Dickens provides credible psychological defenses with which Florence handles her father's hatred of her. Harry Stone detects the portrayal of genuine sexuality in Florence's relationship with Walter Gay.[1] In regard to the psychological complexity of Florence's characterization, I suggest that Florence Dombey represents one of Dickens' most effective depictions of the power of repressed anger, which plays a crucial role in the father-daughter relationship central to an understanding of *Dombey and Son.*

Florence's repressed anger is presented throughout the stages of her life. When Florence is a young girl her rage is expressed through Susan Nipper, her maid, who functions as Florence's double or alter-ego. In that capacity Susan verbalizes the anger that Florence does not speak for fear of offending her father. When Florence passes puberty and becomes a young woman, the narrator accompanies her while she "muses" steadfastly about her relationship with her father (*Dombey and Son* 315). The narrator reports that in her musing Florence attacks herself for inadequacy and insufficiency, blaming herself for the fact that Mr. Dombey does not love her. Repressed anger fuels Florence's attack upon herself. As an adult, Florence dreams that her father and step-mother, Edith Granger, are dead. The fulfillment of the wish in the dream reveals that Florence's anger has the intensity of murderous rage.

Alienation from the self occurs after Mr. Dombey strikes his daughter producing a suicidal wish.

113

The portrayal of Florence's anger deepens her characterization. With anger an element of her characterization Florence can no longer be regarded as a sentimental figure who lacks psychological reality. A woman whose rage is silenced by love and displaced to another is not a character devoid of feeling. A woman who blames herself for her father's failure to love her displays the signs of psychological abuse. And a woman who dreams that an abusing father is dead harbors anger and resentment for his mistreatment of her. The view that Florence embodies only "love, sacrifice, purity [and] grace" must be revised.[2]

Apprehension of Florence's repressed anger rests upon three bases. The expression of Florence's anger through Susan Nipper is a variation of the doubling technique that scholars have long noted in Dickens and other writers. Otto Rank, Robert Rogers, and Izvetan Todorov have pointed out that use of a literary double is a way for writers to express the feelings or aspirations of another character. Rank argues that destructive impulses are often associated with a double, while Rogers analyzes doubling that involves the splitting up "of a recognizable, unified entity [such as anger] into separate parts" (*The Double in Literature* 5). Izvetan Todorov in *The Fantastic* suggests that "themes of the other" or doubles involve "the relation of man with his desire" (139). Fred Kaplan and Albert Hutter have demonstrated that Dickens employs doubling as a literary method in his fiction. Kaplan argues in *Dickens and Mesmerism* that the doubling of characters or the splitting of psychological states into two characters (such as Pip expressing his anger through Orlick) is characteristic of Dickens' fiction. Hutter analyzes *A Tale of Two Cities* for how doubling functions in individuals (Sydney Carton and Charles Darnay) and nations (England and France) ("Nation and Generation in *A Tale of Two Cities*" 449). The pattern of self-attack that Florence experiences as a young woman follows the dynamics set forth by twentieth-century psychologists such as Freud, Klein, Winnicott, Kernberg, Kohut, and Spotnitz. These writers claim that individuals direct anger at themselves that is really meant for others, often employing love in order to protect a loved or revered object from their anger. Specifically, Freud, in "On Mourning and Melancholy," concludes that rage against another is behind the melancholiac's self-deprecating laments. In "Narcissism: An Introduction" Freud argues that aggressive elements of a psychological nature are found in hypochondriacs (*Collected Papers* IV 155, 42). Klein locates hidden anger in the infant's splitting of the mother into two in "Notes on Some Schizoid Mechanisms" (*Envy and Gratitude and Other Works* 42). Winnicott discusses rage directed onto the self in order to protect another in "Primitive Emotional

Development," while Kohut notes that rage, "when ... blocked from being directed toward [the parent] self-object," can turn against the self (*Through Pediatrics to Psychoanalysis* 156; "Thoughts on Narcissism and Narcissistic Rage" 657). Otto Kernberg suggests that narcissistic character disorders prevent the patient from feeling his rage, and Hyman Spotnitz provides clinical evidence that attacking the self is a way to protect the parent ("Further Contributions to the Treatment of Narcissistic Personalities" 257; *Psychotherapy of Pre-Oedipal Conditions* 93–100; 101–116). It is also possible, as John Kucich suggests in *Repression in Victorian Fiction,* that repression functions in order to increase the experience of subjectivity rather than to ward off feeling. If so, Dickens' depiction of Florence's isolated musing increases her experience of anger. For within the thoughts that the narrator attributes to her is the rage that Florence does not show the world. Florence's repression of her anger increases the fury with which, as we shall see, she attacks herself for not having the love of her father. Dickens' understanding that dreams have autobiographical meaning, lastly, enables us to see that Florence's dream in chapter 35 of the novel is one of repressed anger. Dickens wrote, in his *Household Words* article "Lying Awake," that "we have all ... committed murder and hidden the bodies" in our dreams (161). Catherine Bernard, moreover, has demonstrated that Dickens considered dreams to be mental episodes that revealed information about the dreamer ("Dickens and Victorian Dream Theory").

In his July 1846 letter outlining his plans for *Dombey and Son,* Dickens told John Forster that he intended to create a hostile environment for Florence. She is to experience indifference and her father's growing antipathy after Paul Dombey, Mr. Dombey's favorite, dies (*Letters* IV 489–90). Since Mr. Dombey prefers boys to girls for dynastic reasons, his dislike of Florence is, while cruel, not motiveless. Florence's hidden anger therefore results from neglect and rejection. Each is established early in the novel. When Paul is born, the narrator indicates that Florence has been ignored for six years: "What was a girl to Dombey and Son [but] a piece of base coin that could not be invested—a bad boy nothing more" (*Dombey and Son* 3). Mr. Dombey shows no concern for his daughter after she is abducted by Mrs. Brown and he commits a revealing slip of the pen when he instructs a monument maker to write "beloved and only child" rather than "beloved and only son" as Paul's epitaph (237).

In an environment where the child's sex and very nature win her nothing but hostility, the expression of any feeling, let alone an angry one, will scarcely be encouraged. It is not surprising that Florence does not believe that she has a right to verbalize feelings, or even to conceive them. As her father has hidden his dislike of her, she has learned to hide her feelings. For while Dickens says Dombey is secretly troubled by his daughter, he expresses no disapproval except for an icy indifference to her welfare. Dombey's indifference masks feelings of hostility which are revealed when he tells Polly Toodle, Paul and Florence's nurse, that Florence can "come and go without regarding me" (35). But while Dombey hides his hostility under a facade, fear of offending the father characterizes Florence's attitude towards her father when she is a child. Evidence that Florence is fearful of offending Mr. Dombey is abundant. When Polly Toodle prevails upon Dombey to let his daughter play with Little Paul and Florence presents herself for the occasion, the narrator notes that had Dombey looked "with a father's eye he might have read" Florence's "passionate desire" and "fear of [her] being too bold and of offending him" … (32). Dickens places particular emphasis on her reluctance even to approach her father. Answering her father's summons to play with Paul, Florence enters the room "timidly" (32). Among the "impulses and fears [that made] her waver" is "the pitiable need in which she stood of some assurance and encouragement" (32). Florence habitually desires to hide from her father, justifiably fearing that he will "repulse" her. When Polly urges Florence to say good-night to her father, she resists by "spreading her hands before her eyes, as if to shut out her unworthiness and cries out, "'Oh No, he don't want me, he don't want me'" (35).

Florence's fear of offending her father is a sign that protection of the object (her father) will be a major concern of her life and a major theme of the novel. Protecting the object from anger, Freud argues in "Mourning and Melancholia," is undertaken in order to maintain a relationship with an object. Winnicott, in "Primitive Emotional Development," and Spotnitz, in "The Narcissistic Defense," follow Freud in asserting that an individual will direct anger against the self for fear of alienating the loved object. What Arlene Jackson calls guilt is actually anger meant for Mr. Dombey.[3] As a child, Florence hides from her father because she knows that she is not wanted. Later, as a young woman, Florence attacks herself and makes excuses in order to exonerate her father for his neglect of her that has made her an orphan in her own home. But it is the fear of offending the father, the timidity and "fear of being too bold," which suggest that Florence is inclined to defer to her father and bear the burden of neglect that his cold, unfeeling nature dictate. In chapter 6, that mental condition is made explicit when the narrator remarks that Florence has "the habit, unusual to a child, but almost natural to Florence now, of being quiet and repressing what she felt" (74).

John Kucich suggests that Charlotte Brontë "cultivates withdrawal … as the preferred field for a turbulent kind of emotional experience" (*Repression in Victorian Fiction* 5). The young Florence Dombey also withdraws feelings. But the nature of her "turbulent" emotions are conveyed to the reader through Susan Nipper. Called "Young Spitfire" by Dickens, Susan speaks the angry feelings that Florence does not verbalize. The "illegitimate" status, under-lined by Susan, that Florence occupies in her home provides the fuel for her anger before she reaches womanhood. As Freud suggests in his essay "Family Romances," the child is always certain of a mother's maternity but uncertain of a father's paternity" (SE 239). Before dying, Mrs. Dombey looks at her daughter and provides the emotional security that Winnicott argues is essential for a child's well-being in "Mirror-Role of Mother and Family in Child Development." The child, knowing that it is seen, draws the conclusion that it exists. The child also comprehends that she "can now afford to look and see" as well as creatively understand her environment. The child also learns "not to see what is not there to be seen" (134).[5] The eye contact between Florence and her mother establishes a connection between Susan and Florence and demonstrates how Susan functions to verbalize the anger that Florence has repressed. As we shall see, Susan has seen the neglect and psychological abuse that Florence cannot see and does not hesitate to speak the anger that Florence has repressed. Florence has learned who she is by looking into her mother's face, but she has also learned how not to see the hostility that Mr. Dombey has surrounded her with.

Yet the feeling that Florence does not belong in the Dombey home results from her uncertain status, and that uncertain feeling surfaces in the young Florence as outcast. The motif extends to Florence's aunt, Mrs. Chick, and Miss Tox when Susan expresses her strong disapproval of the patronizing way that they treat Florence. Susan understands what Florence suffers and will not tolerate it. Later Susan excoriates the two women when Mrs. Chick disparagingly comments that Florence "don't gain on her father in the least" and that "Florence will never, never, be a Dombey, not if she lives to be a thousand years old" (50). Susan explodes, "Oh you beauties … never be a Dombey won't she, its to be hoped she won't, we don't want any more such, one's enough" (53). Susan's anger on behalf of Florence extends to other peo-ple associated with Mr. Dombey. When Susan rebukes Polly for telling her not to wake the children, Polly recognizes that Susan has verbalized her mis-tress's angry thoughts and says, "There now … you're angry because you're a good little thing and fond of Miss Florence … and yet you turn round on me, because there's nobody else" (53). After Susan criticizes Major

Bagstock, Carker, and Mrs. Pipchin, Florence implores her maid not to and says that her father has a right to his friends and housekeeper. Love, as it will when Florence attacks herself, functions here to silence the expression of anger. Florence permits no criticism of her father; she acts always to defend his prerogative.

The silencing of Mr. Dombey is what Susan achieves when she confronts him after Florence has been told not to bother her father as he lies injured in his bed. Mr. Dombey's prone position not only foreshadows the grave where he will lie in the dream that Florence will have about her father but also his financial ruin, partially achieved by another angry woman, Edith Granger. While Mr. Dombey vainly seeks to rouse someone in the house, Susan angrily tells him that "he'd rather lose his greatness, and his fortune piece by piece and beg his way in rags from door to door ..." (589).

Prominent in Susan's angry discourse is the image of the eyes. Susan's reference to what she has seen reminds us of the link between Florence and Susan, and that she functions as Florence's alter-ego. "... I have seen her grief ... and I have seen her in loneliness," she tells Mr. Dombey. Susan has "seen her sitting nights" to help Paul with his learning. She has seen Florence "with no encouragement and no help, grow up to be a lady" and she has "seen her cruelly neglected and keenly feeling of it ... and never [saying] one word, but ordering one's self lowly and reverently towards one's betters" (589). None of this, of course, has Mr. Dombey, who has never looked at Florence with "a father's eyes," seen. He has been wrapped up in grief over the loss of little Paul and repressed the feelings he does have for Florence. The identity that Florence drew from her mother Mr. Dombey undermines. Nor has he been aware of his daughter's love and rage until Susan has pinned him to his bed and confronted him with it. Finally, Susan says that she has seen Florence steal guiltily up to the door of Mr. Dombey's sickroom and then steal down into "the lonely drawing rooms" crying for her father. Susan says it is not the first time that she has heard and seen Florence cry for her father and that "its a sinful shame" (589–90).

Though the scene above occurs late in Florence's childhood, her rage as a child has been communicated primarily through Susan Nipper. When Florence passes puberty, Dickens presents her anger through a series of attacks upon the self. Evident in the attacks upon the self are protection of the object from any criticism as well as a sexual yearning for her father. At age 14, Florence presses her lips upon her father's closed door when no one is around and desires to be admitted in order to show him some affection (244). She places flowers in his room when he is away and removes them lest he disapprove of her love. Mr. Dombey's indifference to his daughter as a child has been replaced by active dislike which Florence discovers when she accidentally comes into his room while he works at his desk one evening. "There was not one touch of tenderness or pity ... not one gleam of interest, parental recognition, or relenting in [his] face" (252). The incident casts "a shadow on her head," and the shadow will later seem to Florence to be lodged in her bosom after Mr. Dombey strikes her when she sees it in a mirror. The image of the shadow follows Freud's idea of how "the shadow of the object [falls] upon the ego" in a melancholiac's self-reproaches (SE 249).

But the process in which that shadow will come to be reflected back to Florence in Sol Gill's mirror has its origins in the fantasies that Florence weaves about herself and her father. Called "The Study of a Loving Heart," the pattern in which Florence attacks herself and defends her father begins in chapter 23 where the words "solitary" and "mysterious" in the title "Florence Solitary, the Midshipman Mysterious" emphasize how isolated Florence is when she conducts her musings as well as the fantasy-like quality of those musings. "As if her life were an enchanted vision," the narrator says, "there arose out of [Florence's] solitude ministering thoughts, that made it fanciful and unreal" (313). Idealization of the object occurs when Florence fantasizes that she and her father had shared the love of little Paul while he was alive (313).

But love has another function in Florence's thoughts. Part of the unguarded and unrestrained feelings loosened by the fantasy are Florence's critical thoughts about herself. In fantasizing a happy life for her dead mother and brother in an after-life, Florence imagines that her concern for her father will damage him. "... [The] fancy came upon her, that, in weeping for his alienated heart she might stir the spirits of the dead against him" (314). Moreover, Dickens says that Florence employs her "loving nature" in order to defend and protect her father. The "sentimental" daughter inspired by "the impulse of her loving nature ... strove against the cruel wound in her breast, and tried to think of him whose hand had made it only with hope" (314). Love has silenced the expression of anger that will later grow into the intensity of murderous rage. Examples of self-attack and protection of the object continue. Her faults, Florence believes, are the reason that her father does not love her. She is too young and lacks a mother. Misfortune has kept her from learning "how to express to him that she loved him" (314). Knowing how to gain his affection has become an "art" that if she will just be "patient enough will win him to a better knowledge of his only child" (314). Florence's feelings of love exonerate Mr. Dombey's cold neglect and dislike of her. The anger

Florence should feel toward her father, and which a Susan Nipper would verbalize in no uncertain voice is turned against the self.

The dynamics of self-attack and object protection displayed in "The Study of a Loving Heart" establish that Florence is not, as Lawrence Frank contends, a figure of grace who saves her father at the end of the novel (*Dickens and the Romantic Self*). What Dickens depicts, rather, is how Florence's repressed anger causes her to appear as a sentient, all-suffering heroine. But the quiet, withdrawn way Florence behaves when she is with other people that Frank and other critics take to be a psychologically unreal love is not the whole of her personality. It is a defense against the expression of anger. Examining the narrator's accounts of Florence's private musings reveals that beneath the passive exterior that Florence presents to the world lives an angry woman. The psychological reality to be found in Dickens's characterization of Florence Dombey is hidden anger. The redirection of anger intended for another but directed at the self is a process learned in childhood that, unless ameliorated, lasts a lifetime. For Florence, hiding her anger begins at age six. But the pattern of self-attack, of which the examples discussed here are merely the first instances, can be found in Florence's need to abase herself before her father and to plead for his forgiveness when she is an adult.[6] After Florence is a happily married woman, after Mr. Dombey has struck her and blamed her for his second wife's estrangement, Florence is compelled to search for her father's love and to gain his approval. The demands of Victorian culture upon a woman certainly contribute to Florence's cry "Don't cast me off, or I shall die," but the underlying forces belong to an infantile yearning born from emotional neglect (801).

The pattern of self-attack evident in Florence's musings in her puberty involves not only her thoughts about Mr. Dombey but also the people associated with him. Neighboring families where fathers are loved by daughters and fathers who love their orphan daughters also produce the fantasies where love of her father wards off Florence's angry thoughts about Mr. Dombey. Invited to spend time in the villa of Sir Barnet and Lady Skettles so that their son can make love to her, Florence ignores "young Barnet" and spends her time observing children staying in the house at Fulham who enjoy the love of their father and mother. As she did with the children near her home in London, Florence seeks to "be taught by them to show her father that she loved him" (334). Thinking of how Mrs. Brown, who robbed her when she was a child, spoke fondly of her daughter, Florence reflects, that her own mother, "who had loved her well," would have come to dislike her (335). Blighting the smile that her mother gave her before she died, Florence imagines her mother alive and actively hating her "because of her wanting the unknown grace that should conciliate that father naturally [but] had never done so from her cradle" (335). In the phrase "and yet she tried so hard to justify him, and find the whole blame in herself," the attack upon the self is not only severe but also bound up with defending and protecting Mr. Dombey from her anger, which is murderous in intent. Florence would rather falsify her experience that she had with her mother than admit to the anger that she bears for her father. Protecting Mr. Dombey's good name and reputation motivates Florence's thought that "she must be careful in no thoughtless word, or look, or burst of feeling awakened by any chance circumstances to complain against him, or to give occasion for these whispers to her prejudice" (337). Similar to Esther Summerson in Bleak House who, as D. A. Miller points out in *The Novel and the Police,* is always on guard against saying or admitting anything good about herself, Florence polices her thoughts. Nothing negative can be said about Mr. Dombey and Florence will take pains to insure that no behavior of hers will produce negative comment. The criticism of her father causes Florence to reflect that she, not Mr. Dombey, must be patient for "however long the time in coming, and however slow the interval, she must try to bring [the] knowledge [that she loves him] to her father's heart one day" (337).

Nor is controlling the world's opinion about her father the extent to which Florence's super-ego will go in disciplining her thoughts. Dickens points out that "if a book were read, and there were anything in the story that pointed at an unkind father, [Florence] *was in pain for their application of it to him; not for herself* (emphasis mine 338). Florence empathizes with the pain that her father has caused her and it brings to mind the "shadow" that was cast upon her by Mr. Dombey earlier in the novel. She is now persuaded that his pain has been caused by her existence in his life. Moreover, the injured fathers that Florence fantasizes in "any trifle of an interlude that was asked, or picture that was shown, or game that was played" stand for Mr. Dombey. Florence's thoughts exhibit the murderous rage that she feels for her father. Applying Freud's explanation of the dynamics of the situation in "Mourning and Melancholia," Florence desires her father's injury but turns the aggression back onto her self by identifying with Dombey's pain.

As Florence matures and her father remarries, self-attack and the use of love to silence anger are employed in Florence's musing about James Carker and Edith Dombey. Unsettled by Carker's assuming a kind of power and authority over her, Florence wonders if her dislike of Carker is "part of that misfortune" that "had turned her father's love adrift" (385). She resolves "to conquer this wrong feeling" and fantasizes that the notice of someone who, as Lawrence Frank argues, is a virtual double for Mr. Dombey, confers honor upon her (*Charles Dickens and the Romantic Self*). The entrance of Edith into Florence's life produces another series of attacks upon the self as well as a thinly veiled attack upon Mr. Dombey. The desire to attack her father now lies behind Florence's attack upon herself. This development is revealed when Dickens creates the scene in which Florence finds herself in her father's company alone as his companion for the first time in her life. It prepares us for Florence's murderous dream. The narrator reports that Florence "... [has] prayed to die young, so she might die in his arms" (482). Psychoanalytically speaking, suicide is the ultimate form of self-attack. But, as Freud argues in "Mourning and Melancholia," behind the attack upon the self in melancholiacs is an attack upon the object, i.e., Florence's father. Beneath Florence's suicidal wish is the desire to kill Mr. Dombey. Yet Florence in her musing prefers her own death rather than complain about her father. The desire for acceptance and affection from the unyielding Mr. Dombey has ensured that any negative thought that she has will be denied. In its place, Florence gives her father "a tearful blessing" in her prayers. Not once has she "breathed his name to God at night" but with forgiveness on her mind. She has "repaid the agony of slight and coldness, and dislike, with patient, unexacting love, excusing him, and pleading for him like her better angel" (482). Florence's conscious thoughts exclude the idea that in rejecting the love of his daughter Dombey has been wrong. This behavior is an example of turning the other cheek with a vengeance. So unacceptable in her father's eyes does Florence clearly believe she is, that only total forgiveness and a nearly total self-abnegation are conceived as possible avenues of thought for her. Yet the eagerness to forgive Mr. Dombey that Florence displays should not lead us to think that Dickens's artistic vision has failed him. Florence's characterization has been designed and executed as a psychologically abused individual. An unmistakable sign of the abuse is the attack upon the self motivated by repressed anger.

Repressed anger also fires Florence's dream. Now a young woman who has suffered the emotional abuse of a father who finds her very presence repulsive and threatening, and whose singing and grace are admired, the focus of her life is still gaining her father's love. Men do not really interest her. In prepration for the dream Dickens provides an incident of self-attack in which Florence's pleas to Edith for help in learning how to love her father is a litany of her perceived failings and shortcomings. She has not been "a favourite child" and has not known how to be. She missed the way "and had no one to show it to [her]" (486). But Edith, a victim of the Victorian sexual system that produced her unhappy marriage to Mr. Dombey, is no help to Florence, and her refusal is the catalyzing event for a dream of unbridled aggression. Florence dreams of "seeking her father in wildernesses" which suggests that she feels that she will go anywhere to find him as well as the futility of that quest. Feelings of anguish and failure as well as erotic feelings for her father are suggested by "fearful heights" that she climbs and "the deep mines and caverns" that she enters in the dream. Anger is revealed in the part of the dream specifying that Florence is "charged with something that would release [Mr. Dombey] from [some vague] extraordinary suffering … yet never being able to attain the goal and set him free" (487). For failing to pay attention to her in her waking moments, Florence punishes her father with imprisonment. Yet other parts of the dream suggest that Florence would set him free if she could and indicate that Florence, despite neglect and mistreatment, has a feeling of compassion for her father. Such a feeling agrees with the way that she has exonerated Dombey in her fantasies of self-attack. Nevertheless, the desire to imprison the father expresses Florence's anger and the second part of the dream continues the angry thoughts. Death appears when Florence sees her father dead "upon that very bed, and in that very room" (488). At the end of Florence's search for her father she finds a wish fulfilled. It is a murderous wish and the feeling revealed is the wish to kill. Dickens here employs his belief that dreams are autobiographical in nature ("Lying Awake"). But Florence also finds Edith "in every vision" of her dead brother as well as the one with Walter Gay whom she believes has been lost at sea. Finally, Florence encounters Edith at the bottom of "a dark grave" (488). Considering the fact that Edith has just denied Florence's cries for help, it is not surprising to see that Florence has angry feelings for her new mother. What Florence desired most from Edith—help in learning how to gain Mr. Dombey's love—Edith denies. Nor is it surprising that Florence associates Edith with her dead brother and Walter, for Dickens wants to suggest in the dream a contrast between what Florence feels for the people who have loved her and those who have spurned her. Paul and Walter are not found dead by Florence in her search for her father. Paul lives and the dream shows that Florence still retains fond feelings for him. But Mr. Dombey and Edith are killed in Florence's thoughts.

The "terror" of the dream awakens Florence and Edith consoles her (488). A kind of death now envelops Florence. Totally alone, her hopes that her new mother could help her in her quest to gain her father's regard dashed, Florence's musings show an increasingly hopeless feeling that seems to recognize the futility of her aspiration. Alienation from the self is the final stage of Florence's psychology that Dickens presents in *Dombey and Son*. The feelings of love that silence or distort the criticism of her father into an attack upon the self seem to be more fantastical, more hopeless, more painful. Florence fantasizes that she sees the "shadow" that has been in her mind appear on her bosom in the mirror of Sol Gills's house where she has sought refuge after her father has struck her. Dickens prepares the reader for these climatic scenes by presenting a series of attacks upon the self that are characterized by Florence's self-abasement.

Florence's thoughts concern Edith and the growing estrangement between Mr. Dombey and his new wife. She observes the "greater bitterness between them every day" and that "knowledge deepened the shade upon her love and hope." The "shade" upon Florence's love and hopes is the shadow that Florence has felt heavily upon her life since her brother died and which Dickens has invoked in order to designate how Florence's life has been blighted. Because of it Florence is "compelled ... to think of her love for [Mr. Dombey and Edith] with fear [and] distrust" (579). Seeing "her father cold and obdurate to Edith, as to her ... hard, inflexible, unyielding" Florence wonders "... could it be that her own dear mother had been made unhappy by such treatment, and had pined away and died?" (579). But this question which raises the possibility that Florence will think, if not speak, something sharply negative about Mr. Dombey is silenced by her thought that in loving Edith she is committing "a crime" (580). Florence thinks that the love she bears Edith is affection that her father will dislike, and that he will consider her an "unnatural child" because she has willfully "added" the "wrong" of loving Edith "to the old fault of never pleasing him" (580). Edith's "next kind word or glance" inspires Florence's negative thoughts that Mr. Dombey's "cold manner" towards her and Edith played a role in her mother's death. Quickly, she considers the thoughts "black ingratitude." Behind the self-abasing thoughts is Florence's desire to attack Mr. Dombey, but Florence silences them with love and so protects Mr. Dombey from her anger.

A sign of self-abasement, the shadow appears again to thwart Florence's anger when, stealing into her father's bedroom where he lies injured, she prays to God "to bless her father and to soften him towards her ... and if not, to forgive him if he was wrong, and pardon [her] prayer which almost seemed impiety" (584). Always the shadow is upon Florence's ego so that even her prayers are somehow wrong. Prayers are considered impious when the person who prays is actually guilty. Claudius's prayer in *Hamlet* is an an example of an impious prayer which he recognizes when he says "My words fly up, my thoughts remain below?/Words without thoughts never to heaven go" (Act III, iii). But unlike Claudius, the only sin Florence has committed is to love her father in the face of his implacable hostility. Nevertheless, she considers her prayer "impiety" because it might be interpreted as questioning and implicitly criticizing Mr. Dombey's behavior towards her. And Florence feels that she has no right to complain about her father's treatment of her.

The shadow is transferred to Edith as she falls away from Florence. Dickens indicates that Florence has internalized the shadow and repressed her anger when she muses that Edith becomes "like the image of her father … a mere abstraction … growing paler in the distance, every day" (623). The loss of Edith, Florence reflects, has the consolation that no longer divided between her affection and duty to the two, Florence could love both and do no injustice to either" (624). Now "shadows of her fond imagination, she could give equal place in her own bosom, and wrong them with no doubts" (624). Loss of love seems like no comfort, but for Florence it is. The intensity of her feeling that she has wronged Mr. Dombey and Edith by thinking negative, angry (and murderous) thoughts about them is a dominating one. Any relief from such rage is welcome.

The shadow of guilt analyzed in these scenes that has shaped Florence's behavior achieves a kind of bodily expression after Mr. Dombey strikes her with his hand. The long estrangement between Edith and Florence's father ends when Edith runs away with Carker. Hearing of this calamity, Florence is full of "compassion for her father" and runs to him "as if she would have clasped him round the neck" (637). But Dombey, in a "frenzy," turns on his daughter and [strikes] her crosswise, with that heaviness, that she tottered on the marble floor" (637). Prominent in Florence's reaction to Mr. Dombey's violence is her recognition that while she has "no father upon earth" and that her father has murdered "that fond idea to which she had held in spite of him," Florence also forgives him. The shadow of the object upon the ego lodges itself in Florence's bosom when she looks at herself in the mirror. Florence is effectively alienated from herself. "Homeless and fatherless [Florence] forgave him everything", Dickens comments. "[H]ardly thought she had need to forgive him, or that she did" (649). While dismissing her father, Florence's willingness to forgive him indicates a well of affection for him. That affection silences any anger that she might direct at him. Instead, Florence attacks herself by fantasizing a gloomy future in which she would find "some little sisters whom she could instruct" and who would "intrust her, in time, with the education of their own daughters" (649). Florence Dombey could then carry the "secret" of her alienation from her father, shortly to be called wickedness, to the grave (650). The "secret" is the mark that her father's hand made when he hit her as well as that old "unworthiness" that Florence has faced since her birth. Recuperating at Sol Gills's house, Florence muses sadly about Walter Gay, whom she thinks is dead, and then thinks of her father. Shame and self-attack characterize her thoughts. Dickens indicates that Mr. Dombey has been torn out of her heart, but Florence is so appalled by the wrenching she has suffered that she hides her eyes and shakes "trembling from the least remembrance" of her father's assault upon her (655). Florence will not look into the mirror "for the sight of the darkening mark upon her bosom" frightens her "as if she bore about her something wicked" (655). Most of her life Florence has interpreted her father's dislike of her as something that was wrong with her. She fantasized a loving relationship with her father and criticized herself for shortcomings. Mr. Dombey's violence, however, has shattered her illusion. She recognizes the feeling of shame in herself and feels that there is something deeply wrong with her. Florence covers up the mark of Mr. Dombey's brutality "with a hasty, faltering hand [hiding it] in the dark" and weeps (656). That mark is the shadow that has covered her life in the Dombey household and indicates that her rage will only be directed at herself, not the person who deserves it.

A portrait of hidden anger through a double, a pattern of self-attack in which love is used to quiet rage and a murderous dream constitute the rage buried in Florence Dombey. She is far from being the sentimental creature whose forgiveness of Mr. Dombey is simply a question of grace and purity. Florence's quiet exterior is a defense against aggression and Dickens's artistry has captured the delicate psychological dynamics in which a person will hide rage in order to hope for love.

NOTES

1. Research for this article was completed at the National Endowment for Humanities Summer Seminar "Political and Religious Romance in the English Novel" directed by Judith Wilt at Boston College in Summer, 1991.

2. Lynda Zwinger argued in 1985 that "sexual desire, ambivalence, fear and anxiety are written in *Dombey and Son* ... transforming the sentimental heroine into a desirable one" ("The Fear of the Father: Dombey and Daughter" 432). Catherine Bernard's discussion is in her doctoral dissertation, "Dickens and Dreams: A Study of the Dream Theories of Charles Dickens." Harry Stone's account of sexuality in Florence is in *Dickens and the Invisible World: Fairy Tales, Fantasy and Novel Making*. Florence may yet receive positive feminist critical assessment accorded other Dickensian heroines. Marcia Goodman ("I'll Follow the Other: Tracing the (M)other in *Bleak House*" *Dickens Studies Annual* 19 (1990):

147–68) and Suzanne Graver ("Writing in a 'Womanly Way' and the Double Vision of *Bleak House." Dickens Quarterly* 4: 3–13). Jean Ferguson Carr ("Writing as A Woman: Dickens, *Hard Times,* and Feminine Discourse" *Dickens Studies Annual* 18 (1989): 161–79) has brillantly explored how Dickens is often. "… empathethic with oppressed women" such as Louisa Gradgrind and her mother.

3. Among critics of Florence's characterization, Harry Stone and Jonathan Arac have noticed the attack upon the self (*Dickens and the Invisible World: Fairy Tales, Fantasy and Novel Making* 149); *Commissioned Spirits: The Shaping of Social Motion in Dickens, Carlyle, Melville and Hawthorne* 104–5). But Stone and Arac deal with the issue briefly and do not discuss the significance of the pattern nor the way Florence shields her father from her anger. Typical of the critical response to Florence that sees no representation of rage in her characterization are the remarks of Steven Marcus (Florence "has a totally passive grace" *Dickens: From Pickwick to Dombey* 146; Françoise Basch ("a creature of love, sacrifice and purity," *Relative Creatures: Victorian Women in Society and the Novel* 219); Alexander Welsh ("a power against death as a destructive force," *City of Dickens* 185; and Michael Slater ("What strains our credulity is the stasis of her passionate yearning for her father's love," *Dickens and Women* 255). Susan Horton suggests that Florence is an angel designed by Dickens to appeal to Victorian taste (*Interpreting Interpreting: Interpreting Dickens's Dombey* 67) while Nina Auerbach argues that Florence is part of that world known as feminine as opposed to the masculine world that Mr. Dombey inhabits ("Dickens and Dombey: A Daughter After All." *Dickens Studies Annual* 5 [1976]: 95–114).

4. Bernard cites the autobiographical fragment where Dickens notes that he often dreamed of the time he spent working in Warren's Blacking Factory. Fred Kaplan provides additional evidence of the explicit connection between Freud and Dickens when he notes that after his work with mesmerism Dickens concluded that physical diseases often displayed psychological symptoms (*Dickens and Mesmerism: The Hidden Springs of Fiction*). Myron Magnet (*Dickens and the Social Order*) suggests that Dickens' account of aggression is similar to Freud's in his reading of *Nicholas Nickleby.*

5. Arlene M. Jackson suggests that Mr. Dombey is "swallowed up" by sentimental Florence [who is] obsessed with the "need to be loved" ("Reward, Punishment, and the Conclusion of *Dombey and Son," DSA* 7: 103–127).

6. Winnicott's essay is found in *Playing and Reality,* 130–38.

7. The pattern of self-attack appears in nine chapters and six of the twenty monthly numbers of the novel. Chapter 24, "The Study of A Loving Heart," contains five examples. Chapters 23, 26, 28, 36, 43, 47, and 48 each contain at least one example, while chapter 35 has two.

WORKS CITED

Arac, Jonathan. *Commissioned Spirits: The Shaping of Social Motion in Dickens,*

Carlyle, Melville and Hawthorne. New Brunswick, NJ: Rutgers UP, 1979.

Auerbach, Nina. "Dickens and Dombey: A Daughter After All." *Dickens Studies Annual* 5 (1976): 95–114.

Basch, Francoise. *Relative Creatures: Victorian Women in Society and the Novel.* New York: Schocken, 1974.

Bernard, Catherine. "Dickens and Dreams: A Study of the Dream Theories of Charles Dickens." NYU Diss. 1977.

———. "Dickens and Victorian Dream Theory" *Victorian Science and Victorian Values: Literary Perspectives.* Ed. James Paradis and Thomas Postlewait. New Brunswick, NJ: Rutgers UP, 1985: 197–216.

Carr, Jean Ferguson. "Writing as A Woman: Dickens, *Hard Times,* and Feminine Discourse" *Dickens Studies Annual* 18 (1989): 161–78.

Dickens, Charles. *Dombey and Son.* Ed. Alan Horsman New York: Oxford UP, 1974.

———. "Lying Awake." *Plays, Poems and Miscellanies.* Boston: Houghton Mifflin, 1894.

———. *The Letters of Charles Dickens.* The Pilgrim Edition. Ed. Kathleen Tillotson. Vol. IV New York: Oxford UP, 1977.

Frank, Lawrence. *Charles Dickens and the Romantic Self.* Lincoln, Nebraska: U of Nebraska P, 1984.

Freud, Sigmund. "Mourning and Melancholia." *Collected Papers.* 4 New York: Basic, 1959: 152–70.

———. "Family Romances." *Standard Edition of the Complete Psychological Works of Sigmund Freud.* IX Tr. James Strachey. London: Hogarth, 1959: 235–44.

———. "Narcissism: An Introduction." *Collected Papers.* New York: Basic, 1959. Vol. 4 : 30–39.

Goodman, Marcia. "I'll Follow the Other: Tracing the (M)other in *Bleak House.*" *Dickens Studies Annual* 19 (1990): 147–167.

Graver, Suzanne. "Writing in a 'Womanly Way' and the Double Vision of *Bleak House.*" *Dickens Quarterly* 4: 3–31.

Horton, Susan. *Interpreting Interpreting: Interpreting Dickens's Dombey.* Baltimore: Johns Hopkins UP, 1979.

Hutter, Albert. "Nation and Generation in *A Tale of Two Cities.*" *PMLA* 93 (1978): 448–62.

Jackson, Arlene. "Reward, Punishment, and the Conclusion o*f Dombey and Son.*" *Dickens Studies Annual* 7 (1978): 103–27.

Kaplan, Fred. *Dickens and Mesmerism: The Hidden Springs of Fiction.* Princton, NJ: Princeton UP, 1975.

Kernberg, Otto. "Further Contributions to the Treatment of Narcissistic Personalities." *Essential Papers on Narcissism.* Ed. Andrew P. Morrison New York: New York UP, 1986: 245–292.

Klein, Melanie. "Notes on Some Schizoid Mechanisms." *Envy and Gratitude and Other Works, 1946–1963.* New York: Dell, 1977: 1–24.

Kucich, John. *Repression in Victorian Fiction: Charlotte Bronte, George Eliot and Charles Dickens.* Berkeley: U of California P, 1987.

Miller, D. A. *The Novel and the Police.* Berkeley: U of California P, 1988.

Magnet, Myron. *Dickens and the Social Order.* Philadelphia: U of Pennsylvania P, 1985.

Rank, Otto. *The Double: A Psychoanalytic Study.* Tr. and Edited Harry Tucker, Jr. Chapel Hill: U of North Carolina P, 1971.

Rogers, Robert. *The Double in Literature: A Psychoanalytic Study.* Detroit: Wayne State UP, 1970.

Slater, Michael. *Dickens and Women.* Stanford, CA: Stanford UP, 1983.

Spotnitz, Hyman. *The Psychotherapy of Pre-Oedipal Conditions.* New York: Jason Aronson, 1976.

Stone, Harry. *Dickens and the Invisible World: Fairy Tales, Fantasy and Novel Making.* Bloomington: Indiana UP, 1979.

Winnicott, D. W. "Aggression in Relation to Emotional Development." *Through Pediatrics to Psychoanalysis.* New York: Basic, 1975: 204–18.

———. "Primitive Emotional Development." *Through Pediatrics to Psychoanalysis.* New York: Basic, 1975: 145–56.

———. "Mirror-role of Mother and Family in Child Development" *Playing and Reality.* (1971) Harmondsworth, UK: Penguin, 1980: 130–38.

Zwinger, Lynda. "The Fear of the Father: Dombey and Daughter." *Nineteenth Century Fiction.* 39 (1985): 420–40.

Large Loose Baggy Monsters and *Little Dorrit*

H. M. Daleski

What, then, does one do with a "large loose baggy monster" such as *Little Dorrit?* If one is filled with a jaundiced Jamesian sense of its lack of an "indispensable centre" and its flaunting of "the accidental and the arbitrary," the only way to save it from itself would be to shoot it and have done. But of course there are other less drastic ways of approaching it. One could, for instance, try to make a virtue of the monstrous fact of its many tongues; but in getting close enough to see how these work both apart and in unison, one would run the risk of being badly bitten. Or one could try, more adventurously, to ascertain its sex and let that determine one's appraisal of it; but what if it's androgynous? Or by means of careful and skilful measurement, one could show that the trunk-like protuberance at its front moves in an opposite direction from that of the tail-like protuberance at its back; but in seizing hold of these extremities at the same time and pulling them towards oneself in order, most daringly of all, to oscillate between them, one might cause the collapse of even so sturdy a beast. Or one might opt for discretion as the better part of valor, and, keeping one's distance, choose merely and cautiously to try to observe the monster as a whole. One would then be relieved to see that it is less monstrous than might have appeared, rather large than loose or baggy, and when it moves its slow bulk, hanging together smoothly, even beautifully.

Many critical accounts of *Little Dorrit* have viewed it as hanging together tightly enough—some might feel even too tightly—in terms of its presentation of its manifold prisons, actual and metaphorical. This was how I approached it when I wrote about the novel some twenty years ago. I envisaged its structure as a series of concentric circles cohering in the Marshalsea prison at its center; and I posited the idea of arrest, evoking stoppage as well as custody, as the link between the central symbol of the prison and the circular manifestations of metaphorical imprisonment. Individual instances of arrest multiplied into a vision of England itself as subject to a paralysing stagnation, a condition revealed not only in the functioning of its government but in the nature of its social relations, its high finance, its religion, its art, its love and sex. The general paralysis was seen to be attributable to an inner corruption stemming from a widespread recourse to patronage, jobbery, deception, and false appearance. In my analysis I concentrated on the presentation of this cluster of ideas in the depiction of the Circumlocution Office; of Society (as represented by those formidable ladies Mrs. Merdle, Mrs. Gowan, and Mrs. General); of William Dorrit and the Marshalsea; of Mr. Merdle; of Mrs. Clennam; of Gowan; and of Miss Wade.

Coming to the novel again twenty years later, I still think this can stand as an account of its organizing principles and of its remarkable artistic coherence. But I am aware now of challenges to those principles and to that coherence that I previously ignored. What are we to make, for instance, of the suggestion that a state of imprisonment is a consequence not only of the specific and characteristic features already referred to but of the human condition itself? The narrator insists on this idea both towards the beginning and again towards the end of the narrative. When William Dorrit is admitted to the Marshalsea, he establishes a special relationship with the turnkey. After a time the two men are "the oldest inhabitants" of the prison, but Dorrit outlasts the turnkey. When the latter sickens and dies, he is said to "[go] off the lock of this world" (105).[1] And when Clennam in his turn is imprisoned in the Marshalsea, the "iron stripes" of the prison gate are portrayed as being "turned by the early-glowing sun into stripes of gold. Far aslant across the city, over its jumbled roofs, and through the open tracery of its church towers, struck the long bright rays, bars of the prison of this lower world" (831). If, therefore, all the world's a prison, what are we to make of those characters who are manifestly shown to be free? Is this the kind of inner contradiction that effectively subverts any idea of a unifying coherence? And even if we decide to downplay what are after all only two passing references in a novel of nearly nine-hundred pages and so ignore the seeming contradiction, what are we to do in more general terms with those characters who are free? Must they not be seen as disruptive of the novel's unity, spinning off at a tangent from all those characters who are imprisoned in one way or another?—and the imprisoned are the major figures in the narrative. What, indeed, in claiming overall coherence, do we do with the marginal characters, the ones who rate hardly a mention in critical discussions such as the one I undertook twenty years ago? And what of Clennam and (especially) Little Dorrit, characters who have major billing but do not seem to be at the thematic center of interest? It is questions such as these that I wish to explore in revisiting the novel.

II

If the Marshalsea stands firmly at the center of the narrative, the prison in turn stands on the implacable fact of imprisonment for debt, though the Marshalsea itself and imprisonment for small debt had both been abolished by the time Dickens wrote the novel. It is the idea of debt—the payment or non-payment of what is owed—that mediates between the free and the imprisoned in *Little Dorrit.* It is, moreover, a rich concept, evoking diverse forms of payment. The Oxford English Dictionary lists two main kinds of debt and a subsidiary usage. The primary meaning is "that which is owed or due; anything ([such] as money, goods, or service) which one person is under obligation to pay or render to another." The figurative meaning of debt is "as the type of an offence requiring expiation, a sin." And the subsidiary usage stems from the Latin *debitum naturae,* meaning "the debt of (or to) nature, the necessity of dying [or] death."

The subsidiary usage, the debt to nature, enables us to resolve the seeming contradiction of our being asked to view characters as at once free and in prison. When the turnkey "[goes] off the lock of this world," he pays his debt to nature, and so, like a debtor in the Marshalsea who gains his freedom by paying what he owes, the turnkey is released from life. It is his life that has been in pawn, as it were, and is now redeemed; but in his personal relations he has not owed anything, and so he has always been a free man. His being both free and unfree is thus a paradox, a master trope, not a Jamesian confusion or a poststructuralist contradiction.

William Dorrit's story runs in tandem to the turnkey's. With his debt unpaid prior to his coming into his legacy, it seems as if death alone will get him out of the Marshalsea; and indeed, at one stage Clennam thinks the only possibility of his release from prison will be "by the unbarring hand of death—the only change of circumstance he [can] foresee …" (231). Ironically, the legacy frees Dorrit physically, but psychologically he can never put a lifetime's imprisonment behind him; and when he pays his final debt, it is from the Marshalsea that he in effect departs, having returned there in his disordered mind. Similarly, Mr. Merdle, the greatest debtor of them all, who is always taking himself into custody, dies as "the greatest Forger and the greatest Thief that ever cheated the gallows" (777), not to mention all those, like Clennam, whom he has also cheated and ruined; but he too may be seen—since he takes his own life—as in his own way undertaking a final settlement.

The two other forms of debt are given a more vivid definition than the dictionary offers when Clennam early on in the narrative informs his mother that he has decided "to abandon the [family] business," but asks her to remember that he has always previously submitted to her wishes:

> Woe to the suppliant, if such a one there were or ever had been, who had any concession to look for in the inexorable face at the cabinet. Woe to the defaulter whose appeal lay to the tribunal where those severe eyes presided. Great need had the rigid woman of her mystical religion, veiled in gloom and darkness, with lightnings of cursing, vengeance, and destruction, flashing through the sable clouds. Forgive us our debts as we forgive our debtors, was a prayer too poor in spirit for her. Smite Thou my debtors, Lord, wither them, crush them... (86).

The debt Clennam owes his mother is the obligation to play his part in the family business, but his refusal to do this makes him not only a "defaulter," like any other debtor who fails to make good what he owes, but, as she sees it, a sinner, one whose debt or trespass is beyond the heavenly Father's forgiveness and requires nothing less than divine retribution. Which she thinks of herself as enduring, for when Clennam asks her whether it is possible that his father has "unhappily wronged any one, and made no reparation" (87), she savagely applies this to her own case:

> "Reparation! ... It is easy for him to talk of reparation, fresh from journeying and junketing in foreign lands ... But let him look at me, in prison, and in bonds here. I endure without murmuring, because it is appointed that I shall so make reparation for my sins...." (89)

It is because Clennam guiltily regards himself as owing two debts that he cannot pay—the debt to his mother, and the mysterious family debt that he intuits and wishes to make restitution for but does not know to whom or for what—that he is shackled, or, at any rate, feels he has lost his freedom of movement, being liable, as he tells Mr. Meagles, "to be drifted where any current may set" (59). His condition is strikingly epitomized when, on his first visit to the Marshalsea, he is locked in, along with all the other debtors.

Clennam's condition is contrasted with that of Little Dorrit, who has drawn him to the Marshalsea on this occasion. She has been born in the prison, lives in it, and yet—in a variation of the master paradox—is free to come and go as she pleases. Her freedom, both physical and psychological, is a mark of her status in the narrative, a status that is linked to the central idea of debt, for in general it is the payment of debt that sets off those who are free from those who are imprisoned, actually or metaphorically. It is from the age of eight, when her mother dies, that she becomes the protector of her father, "impelled by love and self-devotion": "From that time the protection that her wondering eyes had expressed towards him, became embodied in action, and the Child of the Marshalsea took upon herself a new relation towards the Father" (111). What she freely "takes upon herself" here is an obligation, the loving service and protection of her father, that she unremittingly pays to him from then until his death. This kind of protection, like the loving selflessness that sustains it, is set against the self-serving patronage that is one of the attributes of states of imprisonment in the novel. From this time on she also exhibits the qualities of "self-reliance and self-helpfulness" that her father has speedily lost in prison, qualities, Clennam supposes, that her brother Tip likewise does not possess (181–82). The way in which Little Dorrit meets her obligations, initially self-imposed but then greedily enforced by her father, is repeatedly stressed: "She pays twice as much for [a lodging at the turnkey's] as she would for one twice as good outside," says Tip. "But she stands by the governor, poor dear girl, day and night" (127). Frederick Dorrit states that they all would "have been lost" without her: "She is a very good girl, Amy," he says. "She does her duty" (134); and Clennam, unwittingly echoing him, says to her, "I know that all your devotion centres in this room, and that nothing to the last will ever tempt you away from the duties you discharge here" (434). The debt she discharges is paid for from the heart, as is specifically indicated on the day Clennam informs her father of his coming release from prison:

> his daughter, laying her face against his, encircled him in the hour of his prosperity with her arms, as she had in the long years of his adversity encircled him with her love and toil and truth; and poured out her full heart in gratitude, hope, joy, blissful ecstasy, and all for him. (468–69)

Little Dorrit is thus the most striking example of an organizing principle which diversifies a narrative that is heavily overshadowed by its prisons and prisoners; but at the same time her meeting of her obligations through her self-sacrificial love is not presented as an unmixed blessing, for it makes her a party to continued lies and deception, and serves to entrench her father in falsity, establishing her to all intents as an accessory after the fact in his corruption. Enforcing a similar complexity of view, the novel also indicates that not all those who pay their debts are free. Pet Meagles, for instance, pays all she owes—and more—to Gowan, but far from being liberating, this has the effect of locking her into a bad marriage. This exception to the rule, however, is enriching, not disabling.

Allowing for the sort of qualification and exception just noted, the organizing principle also serves to integrate free and active characters with those more prominently subject to arrest. There is, for example, the group of characters associated with Bleeding Heart Yard, most notably, Doyce, Plornish, and Pancks. At first sight it might appear that these characters exist primarily and merely to fulfil functions in the plot: Doyce takes Clennam into partnership in his firm, and then brings about his release from the Marshalsea; Plornish serves to connect Little Dorrit and Mrs. Clennam, and then mediates between Clennam and the Dorrits; and Pancks establishes William Dorrit's claim to the legacy that he unearths for him, thus freeing him from prison. But they play a more significant part in the narrative economy than that.

Doyce is an inventor, an "ingenious" one, as Mr. Meagles says, and, when he meets Clennam, he has twelve years previously perfected an invention that is of "great importance to his country and his fellow-creatures." When he tries "to turn his ingenuity to his country's service," however, he falls foul of the Circumlocution Office, and so becomes, Meagles declares, "a man to be shirked, put off, brow-beaten ... a man to be worn out by all possible means" (160–61). After "a dozen years of constant suit and service," all he has accomplished is to become one of "the Legion of the Rebuffed of the Circumlocution Office," being "decorated with the Great British Order of Merit, the Order of the Disorder of the Barnacles and Stiltstalkings," a distinction that leads Clennam to commiserate with him:

> "It is much to be regretted," said Clennam, "that you ever turned your thoughts that way, Mr. Doyce."
> "True, sir, true to a certain extent. But what is a man to do? If he has the misfortune to strike out something serviceable to the nation, he must follow where it leads him."
> "Hadn't he better let it go?" said Clennam.
> "He can't do it," said Doyce, shaking his head with a thoughtful smile. "It's not put into his head to be buried. It's put into his head to be made useful. You hold your life on the condition that to the last you shall struggle hard for it. Every man holds a discovery on the same terms."
> "That is to say," said Arthur, with a growing admiration of his quiet companion, "you are not finally discouraged even now?"
> "I have no right to be, if I am," returned the other. "The thing is as true as it ever was." (233)

Clennam takes a commonsense view of Doyce's predicament when he suggests it would perhaps be best for him to drop the matter, but that would be to bring all his efforts to a stop—to accept arrest, that is to say. This, however, is a submission Doyce will not make, for in opposition to the history of Circumlocutionary paralysis, he implicitly poses the parable of the talents. He believes life is not given to be squandered because it is not given at all: it is "held"—like a loan that has to be paid for; and "to the last"—before, that is, the final debt of nature has to be met—the "condition" of life's tenure is continued and hard "struggle." And a discovery, he maintains, is "[held] … on the same terms," standing to a man's credit but stemming from the same inscrutable source and demanding its own form of payment. Doyce, furthermore, has a profound sense of both professional and personal obligation, of the need to render what is owing to one's work and to one's self. Consequently he insists that he has to make the most of his talents, not bury them, and to persist with his unfortunate invention, not let it go. Willingly paying everything that is required of him, Doyce is set off from all the miserable debtors in the Marshalsea. It is thus fitting that he should be the one to liberate Clennam by agreeing to make the guilty, shackled man his partner and so "[opening] to him an active and promising career" (p. 312); though it should be noted that Clennam himself helps to throw off his shackles, for it is he who initiates the idea of the partnership. Doyce liberates Clennam for a second time when he literally frees him from prison at the end of the narrative.

The case of Plornish makes for an interesting comparison with that of Doyce. A plasterer, one of the really poor people living in Bleeding Heart Yard, he finds it hard to make ends meet, so hard that he has been forced to do time in the Marshalsea—"I have been on the wrong side of the Lock myself," he tells Clennam (180)—and when he subsequently visits the prison, he looks on at activities there "with the mixed feelings of an old inhabitant who [has] his private reasons for believing that it [may] be his destiny to come back again" (327). Yet, unlike Tip, for instance, Plornish is not corrupted by his experience in the Marshalsea, and he remains a truly free spirit outside it. The condition of his freedom is not an unshakeable personal integrity of the kind manifested by Doyce, a determination to stand by what is due to one's own abilities, but a readiness to pay what is due to others, even when he has little enough to draw on. This aligns him with Little Dorrit, and indeed this capacity is most strikingly exemplified in relation to his father-in-law, as it is in her case in relation to her father. His indigent father-in-law, Old Nandy—the "livery" with whom Dorrit on a memorable occasion is appalled to see his daughter enter the Marshalsea, arm in arm and smiling—is reduced to living in the Workhouse, but Plornish repeatedly begs him to move in with his family. The speech he regularly makes at such times is wonderfully lack-

ing in lucidity, but the freely undertaken sense of obligation to the old man
shines through:

> "John Edward Nandy. Sir. While there's a ounce of wittles or drink of any sort
> in this present roof, you're fully welcome to your share on it. While there's a
> handful of fire or a mouthful of bed in this present roof, you're fully welcome
> to your share on it. If so be as there should be nothing in this present roof, you
> should be as welcome to your share on it as if it was something, much or little.
> And this is what I mean and so I don't deceive you, and consequently which is
> to stand out is to entreat of you, and therefore why not do it?" (416)

Old Nandy, who is virtually a prisoner in the Workhouse, for he is "kept in"
there and only "let out" on special occasions (416), remains as free a soul as
his son-in-law, and for the same reason. Nor, as his answer to Plornish indicates, is he to be outdone in terms of lucidity (Dickens being quite inimitable
in such matters):

> "I thank you kindly, Thomas, and I know your intentions well, which is the
> same I thank you kindly for. But no, Thomas. Until such times as it's not to
> take it out of your children's mouths, which take it is, and call it by what name
> you will it do remain and equally deprive, though may they come, and too soon
> they can not come, no Thomas, no!" (417)

At first sight Pancks seems the odd man out in this Bleeding Heart Yard
group since it is his occupation to make others pay what they owe as he
squeezes rentals out of the poor of the Yard in the interest of the benevolent
Mr. Casby. But his main function in the plot—his establishing of William
Dorrit's right to his fortune—is also made the means of placing him in the
thematic pattern. He undertakes the work involved in connection with the
Dorrit money without promise of either success or reward. Indeed since he
has to borrow money in order to pursue his activities—and from whom if not
the patriarchal Casby?—he risks mortgaging himself in doing so, but this is a
price he was willing and ready to pay in full, as he later indicates to Clennam:

> "I said to that boiling-over old Christian," Mr. Pancks pursued, appearing great-
> ly to relish this descriptive epithet, "that I had got a little project on hand; a
> hopeful one; I told him a hopeful one; which wanted a certain small capital. I
> proposed to him to lend me the money on my note. Which he did, at twenty;
> sticking the twenty on in a business-like way, and putting it into the note, to
> look like a part of the principal. If I had broken down after that, I should have
> been his grubber for the next seven years at half wages and double grind...."
> (461–62)

In a glorious scene, Pancks finally reveals what he truly is by breaking free
from Casby, denouncing him to the inhabitants of the Yard—"this mound of

meekness, this lump of love, this bottle-green smiler" are among the more vivid of the epithets he uses (869)—snipping off "the sacred locks that [flow] upon his shoulders" and cutting his broad-brimmed hat down "into a mere stewpan" (872). Pancks thus not only "discharges" himself from Casby's service (869) but discharges a long-festering debt, choosing this way of settling accounts with the Patriarch.

Dickens's portrayal of Flora Finching may be regarded as his way of settling accounts with Maria Beadnell, the sweetheart of his youth, with whom he over-expectantly renewed acquaintance in middle age and in whom he was speedily disillusioned. Flora has no essential function in the plot, seeming to have forced her way into the novel under the pressure of direct personal experience on the part of the author. As such we might expect her to epitomize the defect that Henry James specifically objected to in baggy monsters—their accommodation of "the accidental and the arbitrary"—and Dickens's presentation of her may serve as a convenient test of the way marginal and apparently redundant characters are handled in a large narrative such as *Little Dorrit.*

We may take Flora's initial appearance as representative. When Clennam first meets her, he tells her he is happy to find that neither of them has "forgotten the old foolish dreams," at a time when they saw all before them "in the light of [their] youth and hope":

> "You don't seem so," pouted Flora, "you take it very coolly, but however I know you are disappointed in me, I suppose the Chinese ladies— Mandarinesses if you call them so—are the cause or perhaps I am the cause myself, it's just as likely."
> "No, no," Clennam entreated, "don't say that."
> "Oh I must you know," said Flora, in a positive tone, "what nonsense not to, I know I am not what you expected, I know that very well."
> In the midst of her rapidity, she had found that out with the quick perception of a cleverer woman. The inconsistent and profoundly unreasonable way in which she instantly went on, nevertheless, to interweave their long-abandoned boy and girl relations with their present interview, made Clennam feel as if he were lightheaded.
> "One remark," said Flora … "I wish to make, one explanation I wish to offer, when your Mama came and made a scene of it with my Papa and when I was called down into the little breakfast-room where they were looking at one another with your Mama's parasol between them seated on two chairs like mad bulls what was I to do?"
> "My dear Mrs. Finching," urged Clennam—"all so long ago…"
> "I can't Arthur," returned Flora, "be denounced as heartless by the whole society of China without setting myself right when I have the opportunity of doing so, and you must be very well aware that there was Paul and Virginia which had to be returned and which was returned without note or comment, not that I mean to say you could have written to me watched as I was but if it had only

come back with a red wafer on the cover I should have known that it meant
Come to Pekin Nankeen and What's the third place, barefoot." (194–95)

I have quoted Flora at length for two reasons. First, I hope this makes palpa-
ble the glorious exuberance with which she is conceived—she is surely one
of the triumphs of the novel. It is an exuberance which places her beyond the
reach of simple satire, and it imbues her with a characteristically Dickensian
vitality. She is imbued too with a wild creativity of her own; and it is notable
that the quality which is attributed to her as she "interweaves" the past and
the present is one that the novelist specifies as a mark of his own art, for in
the Preface to the 1857 edition of the novel, Dickens wrote: "[A]s it is not
unreasonable to suppose that I may have held [the] threads [of this story] with
a more continuous attention than anyone else can have given them during its
desultory publication, it is not unreasonable to ask that the weaving may be
looked at in its completed state, and with the pattern finished" (35). Second,
the quotation also catches, I trust, the wonderfully free flow of Flora's speech.
A very Molly Bloom in the making, offering a stream of speech not to be outdone by a collateral stream of consciousness, Flora, we are told, "whatever
she [says], never once [comes] to a full stop" (192). "Running on" (193) as
she does, even though she is stuck in the past, she bursts through constraints;
and this indeed points to her place in the overall pattern. By no means accidental or arbitrary, Flora too is one of the free characters ranged against those
who are imprisoned. Nor is this a matter merely of freedom of speech. Flora
may easily float off to China, to Pekin Nankeen and What's the third place,
but she renders unto Caesar the things which are Caesar's. She pays her dues
in the world in which she lives, that is to say, paying what is owed to truth
and reality not only with "quick perception" but with an open admission of
them, no matter how damaging to herself. "I know you are disappointed in
me," she says to Clennam; "I know I am not what you expected, I know that
very well." And when Clennam begs her not to say that, she insists she
"must," impelled, it would seem, by the same kind of imperative that ani-
mates Daniel Doyce. She has "a decided tendency," we are subsequently told,
"to be always honest when she [gives] herself time to think about it" (333);
and where deception and false appearance are manifest on all sides, this is a
quality that gives her more than incidental standing in the narrative.

Questions of standing of a different kind preoccupy Fanny Dorrit, who is
filled with a sense of her "father's standing, even in the Society in which he
now [moves]" as "eminently superior" (287); accordingly, and like him, she
feels Little Dorrit is "disgracing" the family when she associates with Old

Nandy, "coming along the open streets," as Fanny puts it, "in the broad light of day, with a Pauper!" (418). Similarly, she can never forgive or forget Mrs. Merdle's initial elimination of her from the life and hopes of the bright young Sparkler because she is no more than "a dancer." Her encounters with Mrs. Merdle after William Dorrit has come into his money are not only delightful but also illustrative of the final twist given the motif of debt. Fanny's free and indomitable spirit is evoked in scene after scene with Mrs. Merdle, in which she boldly takes on that redoubtable lady, but hers is a freedom that is compromised. "The shadow of the Marshalsea wall" is viewed as "a real darkening influence," and we are told that it can be seen "on the Dorrit Family at any stage of the sun's course" (300). The Marshalsea, that is, is morally contaminating, and taints the Dorrit children as well as Mr. Dorrit. Tip's love for his sister Amy, for instance, is said to have the "Marshalsea taint upon it" (277); and even Little Dorrit is held to be not altogether immune to it. When she is told of her father's coming release and says, "It seems to me hard that he should pay in life and money both," her comment is taken to reveal the taint, though only a "speck" of it (472). We may feel, given the debt of nature, that her remark is not injudicious; but the narrative establishes a firm moral standard, insisting that debts must be paid even while condemning imprisonment as a penalty for the failure to pay.

The nature of Fanny's taint is revealed when Little Dorrit asks her whether she intends to marry Mrs. Merdle's son:

> "Why, perhaps," said Fanny, with a triumphant smile. "There may be many less promising ways of arriving at an end than that, my dear. That piece of insolence may think, now, that it would be a great success to get her son off upon me, and shelve me. But, perhaps, she little thinks how I would retort upon her if I married her son. I would oppose her in everything, and compete with her. I would make it the business of my life....
> "And the dancer, Amy, that she has quite forgotten—the dancer who bore no sort of resemblance to me, and of whom I never remind her, oh dear no!— should dance through her life, and dance in her way, to such a tune as would disturb her insolent placidity a little. Just a little, my dear Amy, just a little!" (649–51)

In her desire to triumph over the woman who once scorned her, Fanny, making the end justify the means, commits herself to a loveless marriage in order to pay Mrs. Merdle back, declaring it to be "the business of [her] life" to pay her back. She may thus hope to settle accounts with Mrs. Merdle to her satisfaction, but, stemming from a sense of what is owed her rather than what she owes, this is not the kind of paying that is the mark of an unblemished freedom in the novel. And since Fanny's way of paying Mrs. Merdle back results in her binding herself to Mr. Sparkler—results, that is, in a life sentence—it should be distinguished too from the way in which Pancks arranges for his final reckoning with Mr. Casby, for he makes that a means of true liberation.

Fanny's marriage, of course, is contrasted with that of Little Dorrit and Clennam. Their stories, it is asserted, are subject to a "destined interweaving" (140), but for a protracted period Clennam's love for her is blocked—locked in, as it were—because he does not recognize what he owes her:

> He heard the thrill in her voice, he saw her earnest face, he saw her clear true eyes, he saw the quickened bosom that would have joyfully thrown itself before him to receive a mortal wound directed at his breast, with the dying cry, "I love him!" and the remotest suspicion of the truth never dawned upon his mind. (433)

The turning point comes when Clennam is imprisoned in the Marshalsea and, brooding on his circumstances, realizes how much Little Dorrit has "influenced his better resolutions": "None of us clearly know to whom or what we are indebted in this wise," says the narrator, "until some marked stop in the whirling wheel of life brings the right perception with it" (787). When Little Dorrit returns to England and visits Clennam in the prison, he responds to his sense of her devotion being "turned to him in his adversity" by admitting to himself how much he loves her; but he finds it impossible to accept her offer of financial help even though she begs him to give her the joy of knowing she will thus "have paid some little of the great debt of [her] affection and gratitude" (828–29). It is only when he knows she has lost everything that they are free—though she is "locked in his arms" (886)—to write off their debts to each other.

There remains for us to acknowledge our debt to the large beast with which we started. Some looseness! Some bagginess! Some monster!

NOTES

1. References are to the *Penguin English Library* edition of the novel, ed. John Holloway (1967).

Repetitions During Pip's Closure

Robert A. Stein

Many repetitive notes occur while Pip brings his narrative to a halt—and this is my basic interest: to explore possible distinctions about a rather teasing fact of life and of aesthetic form, iteration, under conditions likely to accentuate its uses; and to speculate about the relationships among its varieties. By Pip's closure, I mean his final three chapters, although I see those as inextricable from the one event that enables Pip's eventually stopping, Magwitch's death: in a dynamic sense, its ambiguities seem to me to lead to various closing repetitions.

Stopping is never as easy as starting. What I will be doing might fall under rubrics as anciently new critical, vaguely Freudian, and warily homologous, yet I also think I am looking where everything is in Dickens, marvelously on the surface.

II

That Freud construed analysis as story-telling, at least for the analysand if not so evidently for the analyst, helps to keep psychoanalysis within our critical canons. He believed termination should occur when the analysand's anxieties dissipate and all the potentials of his story are explored. But here are Freud's terms: "the analyst must have formed the opinion that so much repressed material has been brought into consciousness, so much that was inexplicable elucidated, and so much inner resistance overcome that no repetition of the patient's specific pathological processes is to be feared" (182).[1] The especially hard measure is "no repetition."

The difficulty lies in the relationship between repetition and change. Moreover, Freud's phrase "no repetition" implies (or allows) that there may be varieties of repetition. The sheer absence of repetition seems as unthinkable as a textless void, or a person with no past.

Another difficulty in Freud's making repetition a measure for his analytic closure entails eros and thanatos, for repetition can indiscriminately serve both; and this "confused" (according to LaPlanche and Pontalis) point persists in his middle- and late-period theorizing. The dual subservience occurs because repetition always entails "binding" (a key word especially for Peter Brooks's Freudian "masterplot"); and there are "two types" of binding (again, LaPlanche and Pontalis), explicable either by "the laws governing unconscious desire and the organization of phantasy ..., the laws ... of the primary process," or on the other hand by the laws of the ego (51–52, 78). If we accept "where id was, ego shall be" as a shorthand outline for personal freedom, its dialectic, wherein repetition shuttles between conscious and unconscious poles and carries the impulses of either eros or thanatos, loads repetition with ambiguities that psychoanalytic readings of Pip's fate cannot ignore.

Nor is this only a matter of theory. By plotting his life, Pip masters, or attempts to master, his painful past. The consequence of repetition during Pip's closure, it seems to me, is not so clear—not in determining a particular judgment about what he seems to have mastered and how he has changed but, rather, in determining the fact that he has been read persuasively as wishing to change. Moreover, if, in effect, his wishes are denied (and there are many variations of this judgment, ranging from regarding him as mature but dull, having become another "pale young man," to regarding him as thoroughly regressive in the final three chapters following Magwitch's death), it may be because only one form of repetition is recognized during closure, as Pip assiduously matches past and present moralistically to remind himself about what he hopes his namesake need never experience himself.

I would like to explore two rather different possibilities regarding types of repetition. The first, which is epistemological, disturbed Freud for a while. Distinguish *repetition* along the lines of its content—*something* is repeated—or as the very fact of repetition itself, that is, as *process*. Repetition as *process,* which may be implicit in theorizing or in "going through the motions," can "color" the *content* of repetition, thereby creating the uncanny. (The "moor eeffoc" lettering captures a familiar "uncanniness" in Dickens' autobiographical fragment.) I suspect the distinction between *process* and *content* may be useful because it fits Pip's manner, the fluctuating distance his narrative adopts with regard to his past and hence to his sense of himself. Sometimes he seems aware only of the *content* of his recollections, recreating his experiences as if unmediated by time and thought, and sometimes the very *process* of recurrence seems paramount. The distinction between repetition as content and as process breaks down, of course, ultimately.[2] But it is also uncannily real, like the wavering line between the dancer and the dance.

Or perhaps I should have said sock and shoe, because another distinction I would like to explore can be designated as the sock turned inside out, or, on the other hand, the sock and the shoe. It is hard to name these without stumbling into yet more difficulties, so the figurative designations may be helpful. It is also hard to say just what is at the basis of the distinction between repetition in the form of a sock and shoe, and a sock turned inside out. Two differences occur to me as suggestive. Either repetition invokes grounding that enables mimesis—namely, the sock and the shoe—or repetition demands exclusively internal referentiality that enables poesis—namely, the sock turned inside out. The other difference elaborates the first but may be more important. If repetition invokes grounding it can stop; if repetition is hermetic, obviously it also can stop, but the point is its potential endlessness. The sock can be turned forever inside out. Once molded to fit the shoe, however, the sock forever bears that stamp—turn it inside out how you will—and this perfect match, however replicable, need occur just once.[3]

In brief, repetition either invokes or ignores a ground; and repetition leads either to something singularly absolute or to endless replications of something. Endlessness seems dependent on groundlessness, and this is perhaps the price of change. No form of repetition is free from history, but history has moved Pip's analysis to the interesting juncture that it is so seriously stalled it looks like it may stop.

III

To enable closure to even begin, the one indispensable event is the death of Magwitch, which is also "a significant retrospect, a summing up" (Brooks 95–96). It is a conventional scene (Reed 156–71) that allows Pip to preserve what he has learned yet also requires, because of the potent ambiguities it contains, the mastery that stopping affords. In order to consider what varieties of repetition are exposed by closure, and what their relationships may be, it is necessary first to clarify just what ambiguities are caught up in the death of Magwitch. This requires putting to the side expectations Pip sanctions and allowing for other expectations derived from his narrative yet clearly unsanctioned by him—indeed, hardly plausible to him after years of analysis.

"You had a child once," Pip says to the silent Magwitch,
"whom you loved and lost." A stronger pressure on my hand.

"She lived and found powerful friends. She is living now. She is a lady and very beautiful. And I love her." (494)

Magwitch's sentencing and jailing have been depicted to notice disjunctions between worldly justice and divine ends, making his death plangent and, in turn, underscoring Pip's equivocal allusion to Luke 18 (which concludes the death scene).[4] Yet Pip reinvests great expectations with the significance he has seemed to discard. What prompts this repetition of the past and thus seems to throw things out of kilter?

1. Magwitch never said he "loved and lost." This is Pip's sentimental emendation or, if you will, a sort of fiction-within-the-fiction, perhaps something like a screen. It is drawn while Magwitch tells Pip and Herbert about Compeyson and interrupts himself to abort a tangent that would have to become Molly and Estella. After that, Pip's detective work discloses the history his patron omits. (The most sensational detail is Jaggers's memorable logic during the trial of the mother of Magwitch's child, namely, the supposition that the child [Estella, ca. 3 years old] clawed her mother [Molly] in defense against the mother's murdering her.) In brief, what Pip is able to say to his dying patron is as transparently a tactful pretense as Joe's telling young Pip that Joe's father "were ... good in his hart, don't you see."

2. Magwitch's fate and Pip's are synonymous on the most telling mysteries, the nature of the initial crime (to the extent that one is primal), and the culpable parties. Once the plotting dispenses with Pip's delusions about the origin of his fortune it reasserts paternity as an (unresolvable) issue, so that (I would argue) Magwitch upon dying is above all a quasi-brother. Again, many details conspire to establish the synonymity of Magwitch's and Pip's fate. The most powerful come out during Magwitch's account of himself, counterpointing Pip's initial discovery of "the identity of things" by being forced to thieve. Magwitch silently assaults us, saying he never had

"more notion where I was born than you have—if so much. I first became aware of myself down in Essex, a-thieving turnips for my living. Summun had run away from me—a man—a tinker—and he took the fire with him, and left me very cold." (371)

The qualifying locution marvelously pins down what is hypothetical. We can have only a "notion" about our births. (About his birth, Milton's Adam says, "who himself beginning knew?") The "Summun" is scathing because of its potential. The nameless torchbearer could be a father or a fellow-wanderer. And the tie with Pip's story is close, verbally and in substance.[5] The common bond among the quasi-family of *Great Expectations,* Joe, Biddy, Estella,

Magwitch, Pip—"We are all orphans," Carlyle had declared—is abandonment and loss, a curious bond, incidentally, because it works out so there is no difference between a parent's sense of loss and a child's of abandonment. The melodrama of Magwitch's dying is invested with a knowledge of the unordained start of the "universal struggle" that disputes its ordained outcome, and that also disputes any expectations about its worldly progress.

3. Other hand gestures complicate Magwitch's last one: "he raised my hand to his lips. Then he gently let it sink on his breast again, with his own hands lying on it." Thus Magwitch's response to hearing of his daughter's fate and protegé's love for her. A blessing? A pardon? Pip's own gesture of releasing his clasped hands—that is, withdrawing his from Magwitch's— becomes a motif for outlining Pip's altered feelings about Magwitch. (During the trial, Pip remains "holding the hand he stretched forth to me.") A further complication comes in through the hand Pip burns during the decidedly ambivalent (angrily punitive *and* rescuing), flaming end of Miss Havisham. Then there is Jaggers's admonition that Pip ought to cut off his unscarred hand because of his meddlesome detective work about the spoils of past, "poor dreams" (445); Jaggers's admonition complains about Pip's probing his role in Estella's fate. On this score Magwitch's silent, last gesture becomes a reversal (admonition-approval) of Jaggers's violent, verbal gesture. Perhaps most similar to Magwitch's final gesture is Pip's parting from Estella, when he fails to dissuade her from marrying Drummle. Having performed his futile "rhapsody" (Out of my thoughts! … O God bless you, God forgive you!"), Pip then recalls he "held her hand to my lips some lingering moments, and so I left her" (391).

4. If the hand gestures during Magwitch's dying assimilate others that signal conflictual passions, the final gesture helps keep the final scene from fulfilling the expectations its narrator would sanction. Actually, till the allusion to Luke, Pip's narrative presence is indistinct. Distancing has fallen away, the past (re)happens now. This immediacy is important, it seems to me, because it permits Magwitch's final hand gesture to be apprehended theatrically, a spectacle entailing both the painful myth of gentility as delusory and the implied blessing of the "gentleman" by his expiring "second father." Both those implications—paradoxically, what is delusion authenticates the blessing—are melodramatically effective. And from that viewpoint, Pip's speech is disquieting, especially as he elides Estella's life between Magwitch's loss and Miss Havisham's gain, and then stops to create a silence wherein all the old, great expectations can glide: "She is a lady and very beautiful. And I love her."

IV

Performing his "superimposition of ... [his Freudian] model of the functioning of the psychic apparatus on the functioning of the text," Peter Brooks
infers that Magwitch's dying "leads straight to" the Bulwer-Lytton inspired
ending's most "troublesome" implication, namely, that Pip's "experience of
Satis House has never really been mastered" (112, 137–38). Though Brooks
finally rejects this inference and instead explicates how Pip achieves "mastery" over his past, it seems to me much to the point that his analysis permits
ambiguities in Pip's speech like those I have tried to explain. However, the
connection between Pip's speech during Magwitch's dying and the revised
ending seems to me to be more difficult, and provocative, than just Pip's feelings about Estella. Pip frequently notices that Estella's unlovable nature cannot cancel his love; in a sense, that is the whole point. His infatuation transcends its genesis, which it so happens crystallized his daily discontent with
his lot in life. Now that his fortunes are altered again, knowing the impossi-
bility of his desire regarding Estella is easier for Pip than integrating what her
father represents.

The ambiguities of Pip's final moments with his dying patron are not con-
travened by the events and tones of either the initial or the Bulwer-Lytton
prompted endings: baldly restated, Pip seems both to discard the myth of gentility and to reinvest in it. Thus, some of what Pip has already learned seems
to be unlearned, the self created by his own narrative unraveled—to say nothing of what may subsequently transpire as a result of Magwitch's dying.

That "summing up" scene is also, of course, a major act in Pip's oedipal
drama, but Freudian readings that keenly note his ambivalence towards
Magwitch oddly reduce the ambiguities loosened by Pip's reenactment of his
"second father's" death. A long critical tradition affirms the value of Pip's
anguish, as he himself does, and this thematic can be readily reconciled with
psychoanalytic considerations.[6] Brooks's interpretation favors Pip's "working
through" to achieve "binding"—that is, to the narrative necessities Brooks's
"masterplot" model defines. One problem with this has already been noted:
that "binding" itself, and by the same token repetition, are truly tangled within Freudian theory, so that both liberating and inhibiting implications are
implicit and undecidable as mutually exclusive alternatives.

I do not see why the theoretic tangle has to be a knot—why, in other
words, an either/or choice about whether Magwitch's dying establishes
"binding" of salutary or other sorts must be argued (in effect, then, reaffirm-
ing or rejecting readings of Pip's growth). The supposedly soothing truths Pip

shares only when Magwitch's response must be mute revive possibilities (for reasons I hope I have suggested) defined by Pip's history that preempt unequivocal interpretation. It will be apparent from Magwitch's death till the very end that "in essence, closure is an act of 'make-believe,' a postulation that closure is possible" (Miller 267).

Pip is seriously stalled but he is not a modernist endgamer. Stopping, he still has to fight off the arbitrary, and to win. That he reinvests *great expectations* with all their old power during Magwitch's dying may be stretching a point, yet between Pip's ambiguities then and his last words foreseeing "no shadow of another parting from" Estella there are perhaps more significant developments—in brief, more repetitions, perhaps of distinguishable kinds.

V

Repetition as *content* is so strong, hardly any distancing sense of *process* occurs in the hallucinatory phase of Pip's illness. The pressure of financial debt blends into a feverish "vapour of limekiln" that, by strongly established associations, recalls the threatening figures met in the distant past, and the lurid criminality Orlick represents (and which Pip recently [re]confronted). The "vapour of limekiln" also recalls the damp and chilly mists that rise and fall marking the changes in Pip's fortunes (the abandoned kiln is out on the marshes edging the familiar shore flats). Prepositions show Pip's losing control: "But the vapour of a lime-kiln would come between me and them [i.e., the snatches from memory], disordering them all, and it was through the vapour at last that I saw two men looking at me."

The shift from designating the "vapour" as "between me" and recent events to "through the vapour at last I saw..." charts an assertion of will and then submission. In other words, at first Pip may wish to use the recent past to impose control, not just of that past, which is being "disordered" by the "vapour," but of the demanding, present fact of indebtedness. Then past and present entirely merge, as if seen "through" each other; they are no longer "between" one another controlled by a person self-consciously recollecting. (This movement to "through" is also apt because a smell is sometimes felt to surround the feverish person, who may dissociate himself from it to affirm a "healthful" or "realistic" perception.) Everything is only now: Pip awake and in dialogue with the men pressing him into a debt repayment scheme. The synonymity of past and present remains unspoken, all *content* as it were. Pip is back where he began, at the marshes, unmonied and smelling, coarse, abandoned, helpless.

All our great expectations are defined by chaining together supposition and fact, wish and deed, shameful secret and public corroboration. The links in the chain pull apart according to time's steam-engined pace. Marriage and death—traditionally and perhaps even sacramentally the novel's unshackled new beginnings—of course help Pip's establishing closure. Forgiveness, which is much discussed when Pip is with Joe and Biddy and also with Estella at the very end, helps too, even if Pip's narrative as a whole gleams more with the wish to forgive than the peace of having done so. Finally, the links in the chain may be broken by the perceptions formed as if newly during the narrative process itself. (That Pip calls the metaphoric chain to his analysts' attention ["Pause you who read this ..."] first upon his meeting Estella hardly excludes from its links his very first recollections about "the identity of things.") Judging Pip's efforts to free himself from his past is difficult because our therapies differ. It may also be that the kind of repetitions required or accentuated by closure make it impossible to represent historically defined and yet undetermined—that is to say, epiphanic—perceptions.

By illness he goes backwards on purpose, to hear "the dear old home-voice" again. Pip thus "fancied I was little Pip again," poignantly trying to resume healthful growth "as if I were the small helpless creature to whom he had so abundantly given the wealth of his quiet nature (501)." This repetition of Pip's dependence on Joe entails a question of thematic emphasis; I hear it as tendentious, in effect lightening a darker motif—on the admonitory use of private myth, for Joe told Pip about "how small and flabby and mean you was" in order to reproach Pip's punctuating Joe's tactful lies about his first wife (57). In any case, the repetition exhibited here (I shall momentarily argue) is the sock-turned-inside-out variety, which also occurs when Pip, his illness entirely cured, has to pass by "the fingerpost" marking the village boundary again (515–176), accompanied this time by Joe and his new wife. And both these repetitions, the "fingerpost" and the dependence on Joe, are more significant as *process* than as *content*.

The "vapour of lime-kiln," on the other hand, as well as Pip's final exchanges with Magwitch, entail repetition of content. These are also instances of a grounded repetition, invoking the horror of primeval and unordained beginnings. If this appears to verge on saying that these aspects of repetition occur necessarily *together—content* and grounding—I should add that I cannot make this claim. I am still trying to work out what repetition signifies, what its varieties are, and how they come into play during closure.

If it is true that the *content* of the past recurs during Magwitch's dying and Pip's illness, to the extent that past and present are shown as synonymous, it would appear that the myth of gentility is a reversal of the horror of primeval and unordained beginnings. Hence there are alternate pasts, as reversible as a sock turned inside out. Hence also, these alternate pasts can provide a grounding for a sock shaped by its shoe. It would appear that in fighting off the arbitrary in order to stop, it is necessary to come to the elusive edge of repetitions, exhibiting various kinds in various relationships, in order to vivify the (illusory) nature of change.

VI

Pip says, "but I did not rumple" his namesake's hair when "I took another stool by the child's side." This is another amidst numerous details like the fingerpost and Joe's literacy and love showing how "everything is the same as in the opening scenes, but in everything there is a difference" (Meisel 329).[7] And I doubt any analyst, of Freudian or Lacanian persuasion, would want Pip to bother explaining what he did not do or, for that matter, the (re)use of the singular Pip-stool "fenced into the corner with Joe's leg." Even though a ground is readily available (Pumblechook used to rumple Pip's hair, much to his distress; Joe's leg used to "fence" off Pip a corner by the hearth), Pip's reporting what he does not do is much like turning the sock inside out, boring and a little willfully solipsistic—especially since repetition and its sometimes paradoxical relation to change is reduced to "I again" in Pip's marvelously timed announcement of Joe and Biddy's progeny. Although all these repetitions may be "grounded" by Pip's past, their deliberateness and meanings make them function as if they were essentially *process;* they stress moral notes and the illusion of change, by their polarization of past and present.

Another instance of such repetition occurs when Pip decides asking Biddy to marry him and to help define his future work as well. However, perhaps this material should be considered in a bit more detail, for it illustrates how tentative distinctions among forms of repetition necessarily are, and how those forms may interact. In a sense, the meaning of Pip's decision becomes clear upon his discovering her married to Joe. Biddy (and of course Joe himself) is pristenely free from "great expectations." Pip's wanting to (re) turn to her smacks of atonement. This can be underlined by repetition in the form of process, yet it has the effect of also underlining the possibility that Pip recently reinvested (during Magwitch's death) in the very myth his impossible bride has perpetually denied, and that he himself also had rejected, or been forced to reject, during previously narrated choices and events. To the extent that Pip

is reenacting the old choice between Biddy and Estella, this is change moral-
ized or repetition as process, turning the sock inside out. Yet it also reinforces
the sort of repetition that denies change, the comforting, tactful, and perhaps
more deeply provocative affirmations Pip makes when he tells Magwitch
what he has discovered about his daughter's fate and his own unchangeable
devotion to her.

To repeat, the one juncture indispensable for closure, Magwitch's dying, is
narrated so that Pip's possible reinvestment in the myth of gentility—even
though the conclusive aspects of the scene mute such worldly concerns—
entails a form of repetition that is mimetic—that is, grounded in the (living)
past; and the consequential potency of this past is reasserted during Pip's hallucinatory illness. Past and present are not polarized.

The relationships among the repetitions exhibited during the closure of
Great Expectations occur so that once a mimetic possibility is achieved, poesis is inevitably reasserted. Or to say the same thing differently: once the
ground is (re)exposed, the potential endlessness of repetitions also becomes
apparent. And this kind of repetition entails predominantly *process.*

Whether the confluence of repetitions during Pip's closure can be attributed in a causal way to the requirements of closure itself remains an open
question. I suspect that the discontinuities of narrative codes (the proairectic
and hermeneutic)[8] become especially apparent during closure, leaving gaps or
ambiguities of meaning that repetitions in effect seal. Yet if indeed various
forms of repetition exist, they must occur throughout Dickensian narrative,
especially because of his proclivity for anagogic elaborations.

The kind of repetition figuratively described as sock and shoe encourages
mimesis. In theory it is Platonic, achieving perfection whenever the shoe fits.
By the same token, this form need not be enacted again; it can represent the
end. The variety of repetition figured as a sock turned inside out is insepara-
ble from its absolutist yarn. If Pip's performance of closure begins with him
"grounded," back where he started, during his recollection of Magwitch's
death and the illness and indebtedness he subsequently faced, it is as urgently
true that change rather than recurrence is his obvious wish. Only the fact of
progeny "follows" (according to *proairetic* logic) from Pip's (re) visiting Joe
and Biddy after eleven years away, underlining the already apparent significance of their marriage, but the abundant implications of their progeny's
name include realizing that since one plot is possible, another is, also.
Essentially the same point is made by dating Pip's absence from England.
Starting yet another eleven years later, his account would be different again.
It is a marvelously teasing, intellectual irony (for us, if not for Dickens) that

almost everything is subject to revised or new plotting, only the tombstone beginning is not.

VII

Closure cannot occur without repetition, yet sometimes repetition is employed more lightly than during Pip's establishing closure, the lines among the possible iterative varieties blurred for the sake of a halt.

Revising psychoanalysis, Lacan lightened the weights repetition had assumed amidst Freud's evolving formulations. Now repetition seems to occur like a shadow made by mysterious psychic agencies, straddling their functions however the signs and signifiers that sustain everything in the flux of language allow. According to Ellie Ragland-Sullivan's suggestive summary: Lacanian "repetitions" display "the effort to place 'something' unified and familiar between a Real void in being and intimations of their own Imaginary nature. Repetition, therefore, is a normal mode of the subject, unaware that its curious structure makes it live the dialectical unconscious at the level of conscious life" (112).

These auspices let us discard the sock and shoe. The crux is how the past comes to be construed as a living past. If there no reason for postulating regression and growth held in the sway of thanatos and eros, and enacted by repetition promiscuously tangled amidst psychic strata, then the only form of repetition that remains seems to be that of the sock turned inside out. What Freud left equivocal, Lacan has simplified. The same result is accomplished by presuming that everything, in effect, exists only as a linguistic construct, a world only of language, to be shaped, and reshaped, according to its hermetic dynamics. Content may be distinguishable from process during repetition, but there seems no reason for trying to tell. Lacanian repetition is, to repeat, "normal," not perceived as such, and an expression of "the dialectical unconscious." It cannot be "grounded," though it contributes to the illusion of a ground ("'something' unified and familiar"); and perhaps most tellingly, Lacan does not turn repetition into a measure for when analysis should terminate.[9]

Yet the transitions we unhappily manage are not left altogether unpredictable, nor unavailable. For Pip tells his story so poignantly and precisely that when our critical canons again change, his analysis will resume its inexhaustible course. Moreover, he has been quite sufficiently understood all along. He would be discomforted to realize—if not exactly led back into analysis—how, upon achieving closure at last, the various repetitions he employs embody truths contrary to the changes he expects.

NOTES

1. I select these dicta to acknowledge, by their contrast to my interpolated terms about the completion of a story, the gap between the Freud of literary and of psychoanalytic traditions; the currently literary Freud-cum-Lacan is wittily challenged by Janet Malcolm's "J'Appelle Un Chat Un Chat," which discusses among other studies that claim Freudian debts Peter Brooks's *Reading for the Plot: Design and Interaction in Narrative*. Brooks analyzes *Great Expectations* according to a "masterplot" he bases on Freud as well as Barthes, Lacan, and Todorov.

2. I take the process/content distinction from Neil Hertz's explication of Freud's essay, "The Uncanny" (esp. 100–2).

3. I take the distinction between repetition as "grounded" or dependent on exclusively internal referentiality from J. Hillis Miller's introductory chapter, "Two Forms of Repetition," *Fiction and Repetition: Seven English Novelists*. I also adapt one of the figurative descriptions Miller employs; his explanation is ample and complex. Miller briefly employed the same "two forms of repetition" in one of his major contributions to Dickens criticism, *"Sketches by Boz, Oliver Twist*, and Cruikshank's Illustrations," *Charles Dickens and George Cruikshank*, esp. p. 29. There the "two forms" are named after Plato and Nietzsche and called "authentic" and "inauthentic"; the "dark" possibility is that they are identical. Another cautionary note—whether correct in tacitly dismissing the "two forms" or not I cannot judge—occurs in a review of Miller's *Fiction and Repetition* by Robert Scholes: "The whole distinction, when taken seriously, reduces itself to that between obvious similarity and not-so-obvious similarity" (100). *If* it were possible to calibrate how "obvious" a repetition is, Scholes's idea would seem to invite some paradigms, some ahistoric, structuralist scheme; and in effect shift the ground away from Miller's more traditional (and historical) ones.

4. I have discussed this material, from a viewpoint quite different from my interest here, in "Pip's Poisoning Magwitch, Supposedly: The Historical Context and Its Implications for Pip's Guilt and Shame."

5. That Magwitch's earliest remembrances echo Pip's is also noted by Max Byrd, "'Reading' in *Great Expectations*" (264); Pearl Chesler Solomon observes more links equating Pip's and Magwitch's lives (169).

6. The immense amount of criticism devoted to *Great Expectations* is cogently reviewed, with an eye especially on the issues of Pip's moral and psychological growth, esp. in notes #1 & 7, Christopher D. Morris, "The Bad Faith of Pip's Bad Faith: Deconstructing *Great Expectations*," *ELH*, 953–54.

7. Meisel provides an extensive array of the systematic recapitulations; his reading is characteristic of those performed under the sway of New Criticism that stressed Pip's rebirth. More reflective of the recent decades' broader interests in the text's riddles and irresolutions—much to our advantage in continuing to read Dickens— is Dianne F. Sadoff's comment: "Pip's equivocal rebirth demands the retelling [by

Joe and Biddy's Pip; by the tombstone (re) visited by Pip and his namesake] of the lost link between fatherhood and origin. While the story initiates little Pip into the mysterious metaphysics of identity and self-naming, its status as repetition means rebirth as a figure for self-engendering remains problematic" (41). Sadoff's reading is Lacanian.

8. Barthes's codes are conveniently reviewed in Brooks's *Reading ...* (18).

9. A good sense of analysis as practiced by Lacan is given by Stuart Schneiderman's *Jacques Lacan: The Death of an Intellectual Hero.*

WORKS CITED

Brooks, Peter. *Reading for the Plot: Design and Interaction in Narrative.* New York: Alfred A. Knopf, 1984.

Byrd, Max. "'Reading' in *Great Expectations.*" *PMLA* 91 (1976), 259–65.

Dickens, Charles. *Great Expectations.* New York: Signet NAL, 1980.

Freud, Sigmund. "Analysis Terminable and Interminable. *"Collected Papers,* V, ed. James Strachey. New York: Basic Books, 1959.

Hertz, Neil. *The End of the Line: Essays on Psychoanalysis and the Sublime.* New York: Columbia UP, 1985.

Laplanche, J., and J.-B. Pontalis. *The Language of Psychoanalysis.* Trans. Donald Nicholson-Smith. New York: W.W. Norton, 1973.

Malcolm, Janet. "J'Appelle Un Chat Un Chat." *The New Yorker,* April 20, 1987: 84–102.

Meisel, Martin. "The Ending of *Great Expectations.*" *Essays in Criticism* 23 (1965), 326–31.

Miller, J. Hillis. *Fiction and Repetition: Seven English Novelists.* Cambridge: Harvard UP, 1982.

———— and David Borowitz. *Charles Dickens and George Cruikshank.* Los Angeles: William Andrews Clark Memorial Library: U of California, 1971.

Miller, D.A. *Narrative and Its Discontents: Problems of Closure in the Traditional Novel.* Princeton: Princeton UP, 1981.

Morris, Christopher D. "The Bad Faith of Pip's Bad Faith: Deconstructing *Great Expectations.*" *English Literary History* 54 (1987), 941–55.

Ragland-Sullivan, Ellie. *Jacques Lacan and the Philosophy of Psychoanalysis.* Urbana: U of Illinois P, 1986.

Reed, John R. *Victorian Conventions*. Athens: Ohio UP, 1975.

Sadoff, Dianne F. *Monsters of Affection: Dickens, Eliot & Bronte on Fatherhood.* Baltimore: Johns Hopkins UP, 1982.

Schneiderman, Stuart. *Jacques Lacan: The Death of an Intellectual Hero.* Cambridge: Harvard UP, 1983.

Scholes, Robert. Rev. of *Fiction and Repetition,* by J. Hillis Miller. *Nineteenth-Century Fiction* 38 (1983): 97–101.

Solomon, Pearl Chesler. *Dickens and Melville in Their Time.* New York: Columbia UP, 1975.

Stein, Robert A. "Pip's Poisoning Magwitch, Supposedly: The Historical Context and Its Implications for Pip's Guilt and Shame." *Philological Quarterly* 67 (1988): 103–16.

Dating The Action In *Great Expectations*: A New Chronology

Jerome Meckier

"It has been my sad experience," Albert Guerard lamented, "each time I have tried to disentangle the time-scheme of *Nostromo,* to come up with a different result" (211). Dickens wanted no such difficulty plaguing daters of the action in *Great Expectations.* Before commencing chapter 48, he compiled a list of "Dates" to recheck the timetable for his story's major events and determine how old the characters should be at the crucial points.[1] Never before or afterward did he plant so many clues in his narrative to help readers keep track of time passing.

Nevertheless, no consensus has emerged. If one confines the novel's main action between 1807 and 1810 and 1823 to 1826 as Mary Edminson did, the time-frame is too elastic: either 13 or 16 or 19 years (35). Similarly, Anny Sadrin assigned the opening scenes to 1807 at the latest, but feared that the story must stop by 1824, possibly by 1820, in which case the time-scheme becomes "narrower" toward the end—that is, Dickens apparently set aside insufficient room for Pip's London experiences, some of which overlap. "All that can be asserted," Sadrin concluded, "is that Pip must have been born with the century or slightly earlier." Nearly as flexible as Edminson, she suggested a time-frame of 13 to 17 years: circa 1807 to 1820–24 (42).[2]

Previous daters have overlooked an essential clue. On "a Saturday night" in the "fourth year" of Pip's apprenticeship to Joe, Jaggers astounds the group in the Three Jolly Bargemen with news of Pip's "great expectations" (ch. 18). Next morning (ch. 19), Pip frets because "six days" must elapse before his departure for London. After breakfast, Joe burns Pip's indentures and the pair proceed to church, Pip exulting in the "novelty" of his "emancipation" from the forge. This mood would have lasted longer, he recalls, if "the clergyman wouldn't have read that about the rich man and the kingdom of heaven." (Pip refers to the story of the wealthy man who asked Jesus what one must do to secure eternal life [Matthew, 19:16–24; Mark, 10:17–25; Luke, 18:18–25]. He is instructed to sell all, give the proceeds to the poor, and follow Christ— an invitation he declines. Afterward, Jesus warns the disciples that a camel will pass through a needle's eye more easily than a rich man can enter the kingdom of heaven.) This ironically appropriate reading dismays the newly endowed Pip, who considers it untimely; for the dater of the action, however, it unlocks the novel's time-scheme, which turns out to be impressively consistent. Internally, *Great Expectations* is tighter and more self-corroborating than previous daters have granted.

Before revision in 1867, the Lectionary printed at the beginning of the Book of Common Prayer appointed three days (not two, as now) on which each of the New Testament lessons was to be read. This means that there are nine days from which to choose the Sunday morning in chapter 19 of *Great Expectations*. For a plethora of reasons to be enumerated shortly, the main action of the novel—the time from Pip's churchyard encounter with Magwitch to his flight to Egypt—must take place between 1805 and 1830. Pip leaves for London in the summer: in chapter 18, he refers to "summer evenings" and reports that the kitchen door "stood open ... to air the room." The dates prescribed in the Lectionary can thus be narrowed to three: 21 May (Matthew), 9 June (Mark), 6 July (Luke). The second is automatically out— no June 9 fell on a Sunday between 1805 and 1833; Matthew would fix the year as 1815, while for Luke, 6 July fell on a Sunday in 1823.[3]

Using these two possibilities, one can infer some other dates. If Pip is "in the fourth year" of his apprenticeship in chapter 18, he is presumably 17, for apprenticeship normally lasted seven years from age 14 to 21. In chapter 36, Pip reveals that his birthday comes in November; therefore, he has just turned seven when the novel opens. Accordingly, if one prefers 21 May 1815, Pip departs for London on 27 May; he was born in 1797; and the novel commences on Christmas Eve 1804. If one accepts the later Sunday, Pip leaves his village on Saturday 12 July 1823 at age 17; he was born in November 1805; and the novel begins on Thursday, 24 December 1812, late in the year of Dickens' birth. Since the date from Matthew seems much too early, Pip and Joe probably hear the reading about the perils of great wealth on 6 July 1823. The critical London section of *Great Expectations* commences at a time when previous daters thought Pip's adventures were already over.

Dates

Herbert Pocket speaks of Miss Havisham's matter having happened "five and twenty years ago." At that time, Pip is—say 18 or 19. Consequently it happened 6 or 7 years before Pip, and Estella—who is about his age—were born.

But say that the matter was a year or so in hand—which it would be—that would reduce it to 4 or 5 years 5 or 6 years before they were born.

Magwitch tells his story in the Temple, when Pip is 23. Magwitch is then about 60.
Say Pip was about 7 at the opening of the story. Magwitch's escape would then be about 10 years ago. If Magwitch says he first knew Compey about 20 years ago, that would leave about 4 years for his knowledge of Compey and whole association with him up to the time of the escape. That would also make him about 40 when he knew Compey, and Compey was younger than he.

When Magwitch knew Comp became known to Compey the end of Miss Havisham's matter would thus have taken place about 7 or 8 years before.

Estella, as Magwitch's child, must have been born about 3 years before he knew Compey.

The ages in the last stage of Pip's Expectations, stand thus:
Pip about 23
Estella " 23
Herbert " 23
Magwitch " 60
Compey " 52 or 53
Miss Havisham " 56 (I judge her to have been
　　　　　　　　the elder in the love time)
Biddy " 24 or 25
Joe " 45
Jaggers 55, Wemmick near 50, and so forth.

In the novel's Third Stage, Dickens noted, Pip, Estella, and Herbert are all twenty-three, and Pip claims that he and Estella "were nearly the same age" (ch. 29). If Pip was born in 1805 and the novel opens in 1812, it must be 1828–29 in the final chapters—that is, Magwitch returns shortly after 11:00 P.M. on a "wet and stormy" night in November or early December 1828 and tries to flee the country on a cold morning in March 1829; Pip sails for Egypt later that spring. Since Magwitch is 60, he was born in 1768; the 52 or 53-year-old Compeyson was born in 1775–76. Miss Havisham, who lives to be 56, has to have been born in 1772, while the 24 or 25-year-old Biddy was born in 1803–4. Joe Gargery, 45, was born in 1783; Jaggers, 55, in 1773; and Wemmick, 50, in 1778. Although Orlick was omitted from the "Dates" memorandum, Pip reckons the journeyman's age at "about five-and-twenty." If it is 1819–20 in chapter 15 when Pip, who is 14 or 15, makes this observation, Orlick was born in 1794–95.

"More than twenty years older" than the 7-year-old Pip in chapter 2, Mrs. Joe must be at least 27 when *Great Expectations* begins in 1812; therefore, she was born in 1785. Orlick cripples her in chapter 15 when Pip is 14 or 15, which would make Mrs. Joe 34 or 35. At her death in chapter 34, Pip has not yet come of age but is close to doing so: if he is 18 or 19, Mrs. Joe is about 40 when she dies. Joe is 56 when Pip returns from Egypt. This means that in his early fifties he has fathered a son and a daughter—assuming that little Pip, whom the narrator calls "I again,"[4] is no older than seven in chapter 59 and that the little girl sleeping in Biddy's lap is younger.

Estella, Dickens figured, was born "3 years" before Magwitch became Compeyson's accomplice. If chapter 58 transpires in 1828, when Estella is 23 and she was born in 1805, Magwitch and Compeyson began their disastrous association in 1808, when the former was 40 and the latter 33 or 34, which confirms Dickens' calculation that Magwitch was "about 40" when he met Compeyson. "Miss Havisham's matter," her victimization by Compeyson and Arthur Havisham (her stepbrother), took place "about 7 or 8 years" before Magwitch and Compeyson joined forces. If they teamed in 1808, then Miss Havisham's wedding did not take place in 1800 or 1801, when she was already 28 or 29 and Compeyson 25 or 26.

If, however, one uses 21 May 1815 as the date for Pip and Joe to hear the Lectionary reading, chapter 58 takes place in 1820 and the criminal relationship between Magwitch and Compeyson dates from 1800. But a 1797 birthdate for Pip not only prevents Dickens and Mr. Pirrip from being roughly co-eval (in 1860, Mr. Pirrip would be 63 instead of 55 to Dickens' 48); it also relegates Miss Havisham's non-wedding to the eighteenth century (1793–94), thereby lessening the impact of this seminal non-occasion, the earliest event in the novel's satiric critique of the nineteenth century's distorted values. Consequently, when Magwitch relates his lifestory in the Temple (ch. 42), it seems wisest to postulate that Pip and Herbert are both 23, the convict 60, and the year 1828; Pip has been a cosmopolite, living on Magwitch's money, for about five years: 1823–28. These calculations all point to the mid-1820s as the time for Pip's London experiences.

To put the illegally returned convict on a steamer bound for Europe, Pip, Herbert, and Startop must row down the Thames past the customs checkpoint. Preparing for this trip, Pip has learned to "shoot" London Bridge (ch. 46)—he can time his approach so that the rapid current of the outgoing tide will sweep his boat straight through the bridge's dangerously narrow arches. The point to emphasize is his observation that "it was Old London Bridge in those days."

New London Bridge opened on 1 August 1831. Although the first pile was driven on 15 March 1824, Pip never mentions its construction. But the omission cannot be taken as proof that Magwitch must try to escape before 1824, as both Edminson and Sadrin maintain (E, 29; S, 42). Evidently, the incomplete bridge created no obstacle for Pip's boat. If it is no later than March 1823 in Chapter 54 when Pip is 23, he would only be about 15 if he and Joe heard the reading on 21 May 1815; this is too early for Pip to be in his "fourth year" as an apprentice unless he began at the unripe age of 10 or 11. If Pip and Joe listen to the reading on 6 July 1823, a Pip born around 1800 would have to be 23 *before* leaving for London, which is absurd because he comes of age there in chapter 36.

When Pip and Wemmick converse in chapter 36, the former has just turned 21. Wemmick relays his official sentiments—not his "Walworth sentiments"—about loaning money: he advises Pip that pitching one's fortune into the Thames is wiser than loaning it to a friend. He even lists the six Thames bridges from which Pip can choose to do the deed—London (built 1176), Southwark (1819), Blackfriars (1769), Waterloo (1817), Westminster (1750), and Vauxhall (1816). If it is 1826 here rather than 1821 or earlier as it would be according to Sadrin, Wemmick's failure to include New London Bridge is not surprising: Pip could hardly discard his money from a bridge still at least five years short of completion. Similarly, Wemmick omits Hammersmith Suspension Bridge across the Thames in West London; it was not finished until 1827. If Pip and Joe heard the reading from Matthew in 1815 instead of from Luke in 1823, it would only be 1818 in chapter 36; two of the bridges that Wemmick mentions would be brand new, and one would not yet exist.

Admittedly, Wemmick's bridge list is "an almost undisguised means of helping us date the events" (Sadrin 41), but not without help from the Lectionary. The 21-year-old Pip has been a Londoner for three or four years by chapter 36; he arrived 16 chapters earlier. During this period, he has studied languages with Mr. Pocket, traveled to Richmond escorting Estella, gone home for Mrs. Joe's funeral, and run himself into debt. Most likely, Pip arrived in London *after* all six of Wemmick's bridges were standing, for none is described as a recent development. Wemmick's list sets Pip's London experiences within brackets, thereby confirming the century's third decade as the time for them. A 21-year-old Pip, in London for several years by chapter 36, cannot have taken up residence prior to 1819, when Southwark Bridge was completed; nor can he have tried to smuggle Magwitch out of England later than 1831, when Old London Bridge was demolished.

An escape in 1823 would occur less than two years after regular steamship service across the English Channel began—too soon, in other words, for the thriving passenger trade that the novel's waterway sequence implies. Not more than half a dozen steamships were plying the Thames in 1815, the first having appeared the year before, and cross-Channel operations did not commence until 1822.[5] Escape to the continent by commercial steamboat prior to that date—in 1819 or 1820, for example—is out of the question. By 1827, however, over 200 steamships were registered as of British ports. The expansion of steamboat usage on the Thames thus came in three waves: 1. experiments during the century's second decade; 2. a boom between 1820 and 1830, which saw trafficking grow from a coastal phenomenon to a cross-Channel enterprise; 3. internationalization throughout the 1830s as transatlantic routes were opened. In 1826, the leviathan, the *United Kingdom,* ran between London and Leith; two years later, the steamship *Atlas* was launched at Rotterdam. Magwitch's escape attempt clearly belongs to the final years of the second wave: departure-times, routes, and destinations—not to mention the number of hours for the steamers to navigate from London to Gravesend—seem well-established. The first steamer that Startop spies, to which Pip hopes to transfer Magwitch, is bound for Hamburg, the second for Rotterdam—destinations that suggest a steamship operation not yet transatlantic but already capable of carrying passengers to North Sea ports beyond the English Channel.

The escape, Dickens instructed himself, was "about 10 years ago." This cannot refer to the escape from the prison ship in the novel's opening chapter. If Magwitch first knew Compeyson "about twenty years ago," it was then 1808, and their four-year association would have lasted until 1812, "the time of the escape," when Pip was 7 if born in 1805. Assuming the escape from the hulks took place in two phases on 23 and 24 December 1812,[6] one finds that it was closer to 16 years ago—that is, at the time of their first confrontation, Pip was 7, Magwitch 44, and Compeyson 36 or 37, and the gap between the abortive escape from the prison ship and Magwitch's unwelcome return from Australia is almost exactly 16 years. Magwitch materializes a week after Pip's November birthday, so he astonishes his reluctant host in late November or early December, and chapters 39–46 focus on the 10-day period from the return to the sequestering of Magwitch (alias Mr. Campbell) in the house on Mill Pond Bank.

Dickens may have meant "10 years ago" to refer to Magwitch's *second* escape attempt, the one by rowboat down the Thames. Although Pip and Herbert await Wemmick's signal at the start of chapter 47, "some weeks" passed before word comes that Compeyson is allegedly out of the way and cannot interfere. Since the escape in chapter 54 takes place in March 1829, "some weeks" actually refers to the eight or more weeks following the convict's late-night apparition. When Dickens wrote his "Dates," he still had the original ending in mind, in which Pip's Egyptian sojourn was to last eight years, and it was then to be "two years more" before the Piccadilly reunion with Estella—thus the escape down the Thames was "10 years ago" if one subtracts first two and then eight years from the date of Pip's final interview with Estella in the original ending.

On the other hand, the section of the "Dates" memorandum that places Magwitch's escape "about 10 years ago" mentions "the escape" again four lines later, this time clearly meaning the one from the hulks because it follows an allusion to the transported felon's "whole association" with Compeyson. So perhaps both references refer to the opening chapters and Dickens miscounted. Such an obvious mistake is hard to posit, however, since Dickens had just listed Pip's current age as "23" and his age as "about 7 at the opening of the story": one cannot subtract 10 from 23 to get 7. Dickens may have realized his error almost immediately, adding "about," which is clearly an afterthought, to cover it. Or he may have been thinking of the time between Pip's first encounter with Magwitch and Jaggers's announcement of Pip's enhanced prospects, a period that runs approximately 10½ years. The passing of this decade, much of it spent visiting Satis House, explains why Pip, upon learning that he was a benefactor, thinks automatically of Miss Havisham rather than Magwitch, although the choice is also wishful thinking.

In chapter 22, when Pip and Herbert are about "18 or 19" and it is therefore 1823 or 1824, Herbert, as helpful a dater of the action as Wemmick,

places Miss Havisham's non-wedding a quarter of a century in the past—
"five-and-twenty years ago, before you and I were," he tells Pip. The year
would have been around 1798 or 1799, which squares almost perfectly with
the estimate given above of 1800 or 1801, "7 or 8" years before Magwitch
met Compeyson. If the jilting of Miss Havisham happened "6 or 7" years
before Pip and Estella were born, the date for it would again be 1798 or 1799,
close enough to the 1800 arrived at above. Finally, if Pip leaves England in
late spring or early summer 1829, when he is 23, and stays away for eleven
years clerking for Clarriker's, it must be late in 1840 when he returns for his
chance meeting with Estella in the ruined garden of Satis House. If one adds
11 to 23, Pip and Estella would both be 34. But since Pip's birthday is in
November and he re-enters Joe's kitchen "upon an evening in December, an
hour or two after dark" (ch. 59), he has probably just turned 35.[7]

Technically, if Pip departs for Egypt in June/July 1829 and returns to his
village in December 1840, he has been away eleven and a half years. If Pip
was abroad for precisely the "eleven years" he stipulates in chapter 59, he
would return to England by June 1840; the six months until his December
visit to the forge would constitute an inexplicable lacuna. On the other hand,
Pip never specifies how long he has been back before he goes to see Joe and
Biddy; he merely states that he has not seen them for "eleven years" and thus
need not have been out of England the entire period, although that is his
implication. Whatever the interval between departure and return, Dickens
chose to enclose his revised novel between two magnificent apparitions:
Magwitch's in the deserted churchyard on 24 December 1812, and Estella's
in its equivalent, the "desolate" garden, twenty-eight years later in December
1840.

The core time-frame, the period required for the novel's main action, is
about sixteen years, six months, and seven days—from 24 December 1812 to
late June 1829, when Pip last visits his village before sailing for Egypt. Pip's
life at the forge, "The First Stage," is three times as long by the calendar as
his London experiences in the next two stages: from 1805 through 1823 for
the initial stage, and from 1823 to 1829 for the second and third, although the
years from 1805 to 1812 are only covered in retrospect and Pip is born a second time in 1812 when Magwitch, holding him upside down, virtually tears
him from the womb of self-pity.

If one enlarges the core to embrace prior causes and include an aftermath,
the novel begins with the courting and jilting of Miss Havisham around
1799–1800, the earliest and most consequential event in *Great Expectations,*
and concludes with Pip's reunion with Estella late in 1840. 8 The resulting

super-frame of forty years or so is distinctly but ironically marital: the novel looks back to a non-wedding and closes, in the revised ending, with the prospect of belated wedding bells for a couple who have been living far apart for over a decade.

Throughout *Great Expectations,* more than in other Dickens novels, good plotting depends on accurate dating. Dickens' apotheosis in both regards came during the seven or eight-month period following Magwitch's unexpected return. Although the dating in chapters 40 through 50 was done with exceptional care, this stretch typifies a novel in which it is generally possible—in fact, advisable—to specify not just the year and month for major developments, but also the day of the week and the time of day. Dickens told Forster that the "Third Stage" was so compact it deserved to be read in one piece (*Letters* III: 216–17). He was proud of the ever-quickening pace; the build-up to the river journey and the escape attempt itself sustain the reader's interest, avoiding what could otherwise have been an anticlimax after the discovery of Magwitch as Pip's secret benefactor.

As much as two years pass between chapters 38 and 39 at the conclusion of the "Second Stage." In the former chapter, Pip enumerates the agonies he suffered while courting Estella during her stay in Richmond with Mrs. Brandley. It is 1826 and Pip, who is 21 and unhappily in love, declares that his Richmond sufferings "lasted ... for what I then thought a long time." During this period, Pip several times escorts Estella back to Satis House to see Miss Havisham. On the sample visit recounted in chapter 38, Estella and Miss Havisham quarrel; Pip spends his first night ever at Satis House, sleeping in the separate building across the yard. If these four or five visits—the one described was repeated, says Pip, "on four similar occasions"—were made quarterly, they carry the action well into 1827; if semi-annual, which seems more likely, the year is 1828 by the start of chapter 39.

"I was three-and-twenty years of age," Pip declares in chapter 39 when updating the action, a statement which confirms that about two years have just passed. Because he adds that "my twenty-third birthday was a week gone," it must be November or early December 1828. "We had left Barnard's Inn more than a year," Pip continues, "and lived in the Temple. Our chambers were in Garden Court down by the river." So Pip and Herbert moved out of Barnard's no later than 1827, having lived there about four years, beginning in 1823.

But Herbert is in Marseilles on business; Pip is therefore alone when his "dreaded visitor" suddenly appears. This happens shortly after 11 P.M., the bells of St. Paul's having just sounded. Magwitch's return triggers a night of soul-searching for Pip that continues until 5:00 A.M. next morning, when he awakens from a short sleep. In chapter 40, as Pip is going to get a light from the watchman, he stumbles over a man crouching on the staircase (i.e., Orlick). Alarmed, he disguises Magwitch, his "second father," as Uncle Provis, but must spend "about five" excruciating days alone with the returned convict before Herbert comes back.

In chapter 41, Herbert recommends spiriting Magwitch out of England. When Magwitch, upon request, tells his lifestory in chapter 42, he recalls meeting Compeyson at the Epsom races "over twenty year ago," which conforms with earlier estimates that Miss Havisham was jilted around 1800—"7 or 8" years before Magwitch and Compeyson met in 1807–8. In chapter 43, which transpires "next day," Pip goes to Richmond seeking Estella but learns of her return to Satis House. Again "next day" but doubtless still no later than December 1828, he proceeds to Satis House, having first encountered a hostile Bentley Drummle at the Blue Boar.

Pip's woeful visit takes up chapter 44: confronting the false patron who misled him, Pip reports his discovery that Magwitch is his secret benefactor but does not identify him by name; he asks Miss Havisham for the rest of the money to purchase Herbert's partnership. When he tells Estella of his love, she responds that she plans to marry Drummle. As Pip is entering the Temple after walking back to London in an effort to exhaust himself, he is given Wemmick's note, "Don't go home." Consequently, Pip spends the night at the Hummums in chapter 45 and the following day at Walworth; Herbert, meanwhile, moves Provis from the latter's Essex Street hideout to Mrs. Whimple's house with the bow-window, where Clara and her father also live. Pip visits Magwitch there in chapter 46; he also takes Herbert's advice and begins keeping a boat at Temple stairs, ostensibly just for exercise despite the snow and sleet of winter ("Never mind the season," counsels Herbert). From this point on, as Pip resumes the rowing he did regularly while studying at Mr. Pocket's, preparations for the escape attempt increasingly come to the fore.

In chapter 47, Pip reports that "some weeks passed" without a signal from Wemmick saying it is safe to try the escape. Thus it is already "February" when Pip rows down to Greenwich with the ebbtide, a relatively short outing compared to the all-day row coming up. That evening, Pip attends the theater and Wopsle, from on stage, spies the other convict from the marshes, i.e., Compeyson, sitting behind Pip. When Pip dines with Wemmick at Jaggers's house in Gerrard Street in chapter 48, the lawyer delivers a note from Miss

Havisham asking Pip to come to her. "Next day," in chapter 49, Miss Havisham supplies £900 for the rest of Herbert's partnership money, then asks Pip's forgiveness. The chapter ends dramatically with Pip rescuing her when she accidentally sets herself on fire. Although chapter 50 reveals that Pip was in his "seventh year" when he helped Magwitch, it deals primarily with Estella's parentage, as does chapter 51, about both of which more later.

"We had now got into the month of March," Pip announces at the start of chapter 52. Wemmick's note suggesting a "Wednesday" escape arrives on a "Monday," and Startop is recruited for the upcoming adventure. Herbert explains the plan to Magwitch on the same Monday, but neither he nor Pip is to see the convict until the escape commences. That evening, Pip receives Orlick's letter, presumably written by Compeyson; it decoys Pip to the sluice-house near the lime kiln on the marshes, the pretense being that the writer knows Pip's plans for saving Magwitch.

Although the appointment is set for 9:00 P.M. tomorrow (Tuesday), Pip decides to keep it immediately. As a result, when the badly shaken Pip, already severely burned in rescuing Miss Havisham, is saved from Orlick by Herbert, Startop, and Trabb's boy, it is still Monday night; he has a whole day's rest before the escape attempt. Fortunately, Herbert found Orlick's note, which Pip, in haste, had dropped in their rooms. But Orlick cannot be pursued without endangering Magwitch.

Pip, Herbert, and Startop set out to pick up Magwitch from Mill Pond stairs on a Wednesday in March 1829; it is half-past eight or "high-water"— just in time to catch the tide as it begins to turn (or ebb) out to sea at 9:00 A.M. "Old London Bridge was soon passed," Pip recalls (ch. 54), but he fails to mention its replacement, which was already under construction. The party reaches Gravesend about 3:00 P.M.; the ebb tide carries them the entire way, but once they pass this customs checkpoint, it slackens and turns. By 5:00 P.M., shortly before sunset, Pip and his companions have pushed off from the spit of "slippery stones" near Mucking Flats and must row in the dark against the incoming tide for another two hours until they reach the "Ship Inn" at Hole Haven, where they spend the night. After breakfast on Thursday, Pip and Magwitch conceal themselves at a "distant point" east of the inn, where Herbert and Startop pick them up by boat "about noon." An hour and a half later, at 1:30 P.M., they see the Hamburg steamer's smoke and row out, only to be intercepted by the police galley.

Besides describing the river journey with a guidebook's precision, Dickens wanted to be chronologically exact as well: he assigned each phase of the trip the amount of time it would actually have taken, a feat made possible by first-hand knowledge of the incoming and outgoing tides. Dickens required 14 chapters (10 weeks) to set the escape in motion, but he quickened the pace steadily, the action reaching a chapter-long peak between 9:00 A.M. on a Wednesday in March 1829 and 1:30 P.M. on a Thursday, about 30 hours later.

Magwitch is arraigned "next day" (Friday), and positively identified three days later, on a Monday, by an old officer from the prison ship.[9] He is scheduled to be brought to trial "at the next session, which [according to Pip] would come on in a month" (ch. 55). On Saturday "in that same week" (i.e., following the official identification of Magwitch), Herbert sails for Cairo, having invited Pip to join him later, and on Monday, having been asked to "take a walk" with Wemmick, Pip attends the latter's wedding.

When the April session comes round, Jaggers requests a postponement to the following one, Trinity term, 22 May—12 June, in hopes that the seriously ill Magwitch will be allowed to die without having to stand trial. Postponement being refused, the trial "came on at once" and, Pip reports, was "very short and clear" (ch. 56). Magwitch is sentenced on a spring day when the "sun was striking ... through the drops of April rain" on "the great windows of the court"; he expires in the prison infirmary when the "number of days [since sentencing] had risen to ten," so it is probably still April 1829. Pip's arrest for debt is almost simultaneous with his physical collapse two or three days after Magwitch's death, and Joe's stint as his nurse then uses up most of May: when Pip's fever finally abates in chapter 57, Joe informs him that "It's the end of May, Pip. To-morrow is the first of June."

Most of that month passes before Pip has recovered. On a Sunday in June, Joe hires a carriage to drive the convalescent into the country, where "summer scents filled all the air" (ch. 57). Several weeks later, still in June, Joe departs on a Monday, having paid the debt of £123, 15s, 6p, for which Pip was arrested. Three days later, a Thursday, Pip returns to his village to thank Joe and propose to Biddy. In chapter 58, he finds "the June weather ... delicious"; he also finds Biddy just married to Joe. "Within a month" he has "quitted England, and within two months" he is "clerk to Clarriker & Company," so he departed in July and is already in Egypt later that month or early in August 1829. "Within four months" (i.e., before Christmas), Bill Barley dies, and Herbert returns to wed Clara and bring her east. "Many a year went round," Pip adds, "before I was a partner in the house," but surely no more than four or five years pass because in the original ending, Pip returned to England after eight years.

Although Dickens deserves high marks for internal consistency and a special commendation for chapters 40–59, several trouble spots stand in the way of a perfect score. Confusion persists regarding 1. Pip's exact age in the churchyard opening scene, 2. the date of Estella's arrival at Satis House, 3. the amount of time required for Pip's visits to Miss Havisham, 4. the duration of his apprenticeship to Joe, and 5. the length of his stay in London.

Pip tells Herbert that he was in his "seventh year" when Magwitch seized him in the churchyard (ch. 50). Has he just turned seven that November, or was he six on his recent birthday? That he was fully seven seems probable, but this judgment is not incontrovertible.[10] Herbert then estimates that Pip's encounter with the convict took place "three or four years" after Magwitch "tragically lost" a daughter. On the same night that she throttled her rival for Magwitch's affections, Estella's mother also punished Magwitch: she had their child "in her possession" and swore that "he should never see it again." Consequently, during Molly's trial for murder, Magwitch "kept himself dark" lest the defendant also be accused of destroying their daughter. Magwitch tells Herbert that this trial happened "a round score o'year ago, and a'most directly after [he] took up wi' Compeyson."[11] It was Jaggers's successful defense of Molly, Herbert adds, that first "made his name known to Provis," whom he did not actually represent until "some four years" after Molly's trial (ch. 51).

If Magwitch teamed with Compeyson about 1808—twenty years (a "score") before his interview with Herbert—then the murder trial and Magwitch's loss of his daughter did indeed take place "some three or four years" before his churchyard meeting with seven-year-old Pip on 24 December 1812. To the best of Magwitch's knowledge, his daughter perished in 1808–9, when she was no more than three or four. The convict may have spared Pip for the simple reason that the lad reminded the hardened criminal of his lost child, who would have been about Pip's age. Playing amateur detective, another facet of the dater's role, Pip combines what he has learned from Miss Havisham in the previous chapter with Herbert's disclosures; from dating several related actions, he concludes that Magwitch must be Estella's father.

In chapter 49, after Miss Havisham has begged for and received Pip's forgiveness, he asks her how it came about that Mr. Jaggers brought Estella to Satis House. She replies that, having "been shut up in these rooms a long time," she "wanted a little girl to rear and love, and save from my fate." Previously, she had read about Jaggers "in the newspapers"—doubtless before her withdrawal from the world—and had "sent for him to lay this place waste for me." So she recalled the lawyer who had helped her seclude herself and commissioned him to find her a girl-child companion. Jaggers apparently had no scruples about taking Molly's child as part of his fee for representing her. Estella was "two or three" and asleep when Jaggers brought her. If Miss Havisham was jilted in 1800, she must have buried herself in Satis House sometime between that date and 1808–9, when Molly hid Estella from Magwitch. Herbert's estimate of Estella's age at "three or four" when Magwitch last saw her fits well enough with Miss Havisham's recollection of Jaggers bringing a girl who was "two or three": in 1808, Estella, like Pip, was three years old.

Since Miss Havisham's "matter," her non-wedding, happened "6 or 7 years" before Pip and Estella were born, Jaggers may first have worked for Dickens' woman in white around the turn of the century, when he was only twenty-seven to her twenty-eight. When he undertook Molly's case some eight or nine years later, he was probably thirty-five or thirty-six. But two possible contradictions surface here: 1, If Molly's defense, according to Wemmick, "may almost be said to have made" Jaggers's reputation (ch. 48), how was he prominent enough for Miss Havisham to read newspaper accounts of his exploits nearly a decade earlier? 2, If Miss Havisham shut herself up for "a long time" before seeking a child, what does she mean in chapter 38 when she claims to have taken Estella to her "wretched breast when it was first bleeding from its stabs?"[12]

In the first instance, Wemmick and Miss Havisham are surely both correct. Although defending Molly was Jaggers's landmark case, he could have been praised in print many times earlier; he would not have needed a national reputation to secure Miss Havisham the privacy of a recluse. In the second instance, the difference in occasions can be used to establish the true version of events. A grateful Miss Havisham does Pip a favor by reciting Estella's history in chapter 49: she repays him for having just forgiven her. One assumes that her recollections are truthful, for she is virtually testifying to Pip, who is playing at being Jaggers. Her earlier statement in chapter 38 was uttered "wildly" under stress. With Pip present, Estella and Miss Havisham exchanged "sharp words"; the latter accused the former of being cold-hearted to her adopted mother and the former retorted that she is merely the woman her adopted parent created. It was for Pip's benefit and to make Estella feel guilty that Miss Havisham exaggerated. She wanted to prove that she had "lavished years of tenderness" upon Estella; therefore, she encouraged Pip and Estella to think that she had adopted the girl in 1800, not as much as eight years later when, increasingly embittered, she devised a plan "to wreak [her] revenge on men." In 1800, when Jaggers first served Miss Havisham,

Estella was not yet born. If she joined the recluse around 1808, she had been at Satis House about five years when Pip's visits commence.

Pip's discovery that Magwitch has been his secret patron prompts him to establish Estella's parentage.[13] As early as chapter 29 and again in 32, Pip, having been startled by Estella's eyes and the movement of her "white hand," subconsciously recalls Molly's intense eyes and powerful hands. But not until chapter 48, while dining with Wemmick and Jaggers in Gerrard Street, when Molly's fingers move as if knitting just as Estella sat knitting at Miss Havisham's, does he feel "absolutely certain that [Molly] was Estella's mother." He then asks Wemmick for Molly's history, queries Miss Havisham "next day" in chapter 49, and in chapter 50, where it is again "next day," learns from Herbert about Magwitch's missing child. In chapter 51, Pip surprises Jaggers with the results of his investigation, but they agree to keep Estella's parentage a secret.

The search for Estella's antecedents nicely fills the interval between Herbert's insistence that Magwitch be smuggled out of England and the receipt of Wemmick's note signaling the start of the river journey. But Pip's motives for inquiring may be mixed: arguably, he cannot fully comprehend his own identity without learning Estella's, yet his demotion from fairy prince to convict's creature drives him to demote the fairy princess as well. Ultimately, however, his research proves that one cannot escape one's origins, for the woman he idolizes and the money for the genteel habits he has acquired originate from the same unhappy source. Pip's inquiries about Estella deserve to run parallel with the preparations for Magwitch's escape for two reasons: 1, Pip ironically bridges what struck him in chapter 43 as an "abyss between Estella in her pride and beauty, and the returned transport whom [he] harboured"; 2, when the convict lies on his deathbed in chapter 56, Pip is able to tell him that his daughter still lives, a consolation that amounts to the final softening in Dickens' attitude toward Magwitch.[14]

It is easier to decide when Pip's visits to Satis House begin than to determine how many there were or how long they continued. At the start of chapter 7, just before Mrs. Joe and Uncle Pumblechook deliver Miss Havisham's request for a boy to "go and play," Pip dates the action himself: "It must have been a full year after our hunt upon the marshes, for it was a long time after, and it was winter and a hard frost." So Pip is first summoned to Satis House one year after Magwitch's recapture—i.e., in winter 1813–14, when he is about eight. He spends the preceding night at Pumblechook's and does running sums for him throughout breakfast next morning. At Satis House, having twice been beggared at cards, he is told to "come again after six days." Since his first visit takes place on Wednesday, his next is scheduled for the following Tuesday or Wednesday, more likely the latter.

Thus the first six chapters occur on 24 and 25 December 1812; chapter 7 opens a year later; and chapter 8 transpires a week later in winter 1813–14. It is still Wednesday night in chapter 9 when Pip lies about his Satis House adventures. Dickens says that chapter 10 begins only "a morning or two later" than Pip's visit to Miss Havisham, but it turns out to be "Saturday," Joe's night to linger at the pub. After school at Mr. Wopsle's great-aunt's, Pip collects Joe at the Three Jolly Bargemen and is given a shilling wrapped in "two fat sweltering one-pound notes" by the stranger who stirs his drink with a file.

In chapter 11, as Pip visits Satis House for the second time, he is scrutinized by a departing Jaggers. He observes the "toadies and humbugs" (Miss Havisham's relatives, who have come to commemorate her 41st birthday), and fights Herbert, "the pale young gentleman." On this long and busy visit, he also plays cards with Estella, who lets him kiss her upon his leaving. The second visit marks the first time that Miss Havisham sends Pip across the staircase landing into the room containing her moldering wedding feast. One of Pip's duties will be to walk Miss Havisham around this room.

On Pip's third visit (ch. 12), he inaugurates the ritual of pushing Miss Havisham around her rooms in a garden-chair on wheels, often for "three hours at a stretch." Assuming the first three visits occur at identical intervals, the third visit probably takes place a week or so after the second, but this time it is settled that Pip is to come at noon on alternate days, which means as many as three visits a week—many more than Dickens describes. Then Pip declares: "I am now going to sum up a period of at least eight or ten months." Were this period to cover the remainder of the chapter, the Pip whom Miss Havisham then notices is "growing tall" and "had better be apprenticed at once" would still be only about nine—five years short of the customary age. Yet if Pip on his second visit was shorter than Herbert, he cannot have increased in stature so noticeably within less than a year. The "eight or ten months" probably refer to the elapsed time between this paragraph and the next, at which point, says Pip, he and Miss Havisham "began to be more used to one another." As an indication of this new intimacy, she asks him a number of personal questions and elicits the information that he expects someday "to be apprenticed to Joe."

The seven paragraphs following Pip's reference to apprenticeship describe through conflation the years of his visits to Satis House, most likely the five or six-year period from his introduction at age eight in 1813 to the start of his apprenticeship. In chapter 12, Pip declares himself "fully old enough now, to be apprenticed to Joe," which sounds as if he has reached the required age.

During this five or six-year period, Miss Havisham often asks Pip to confess that Estella grows "prettier and prettier," and she exhorts Estella to break men's hearts mercilessly, two related proceedings that suggest a prolonged conditioning inflicted alike on Pip and Estella. Consequently, Pip asks, "What could I become with these surroundings? How could my character fail to be influenced by them?" This suggests years rather than months, as does Pip's statement, just before Miss Havisham notes his growth: "We went on in this way for a long time." Pip refers not only to his visits but also to the bickering about them in Mrs. Joe's kitchen, where Joe opposes Pip's absences from the forge while Mrs. Joe and Pumblechook take turns speculating about Miss Havisham's generous intentions.

After deciding that Pip should be apprenticed immediately now that he and Estella are on the verge of adulthood, Miss Havisham instructs him to return with Joe "on the next day but one." This is Pip's last regularly scheduled childhood visit to Satis House (ch. 13). But at Pip's apprenticeship dinner that evening in the Blue Boar, Pumblechook places him "on a chair beside him to illustrate his remarks" about the dangers to apprentices from late hours and bad company. Being elevated on a chair seems unnecessary for a growing boy of fourteen but might suit one who was only nine or ten, as does Pip's reference to "my little bedroom" at chapter's end. Conceivably, Dickens wanted it two ways: a Pip who has outgrown his usefulness as Estella's first victim but who is still easily intimidated. Pumblechook's method of issuing warnings makes Pip childish and pitiable even though the strictures are against such grown-up vices as gambling at cards and drinking "strong liquors."

The articles of apprenticeship are signed in chapter 13, when Pip is about 14 and the year is 1819. He goes to bed "truly wretched" after the celebration dinner, convinced that he "should never like Joe's trade"; he "had liked it once, but once was not now," for the visits to Satis House have ruined his perspective. At the start of chapter 14, Pip states that his hopes of being "distinguished and happy" as "Joe's 'prentice" have evaporated "within a single year"—that is, by 1820 or so, when he is fourteen or fifteen, he has ceased to believe in the forge "as the glowing road to manhood and independence." Pip complains: "Now, it was all coarse and common."

Daters have accused Dickens of being "indefinite" (Deneau 27) concerning Pip's adolescence—his development between ages eight and seventeen.

The "single year," Deneau and Sadrin allege, refers to Pip's visits to Satis House, the "eight to ten months" Pip summed up in chapter 12. Unlike T. W. Hill, who thought Pip's visits continue for "at least five years," Deneau is left with a protagonist who, if apprenticed at nine or ten, is only thirteen or fourteen when he leaves for London in his "fourth year" of apprenticeship (Deneau 27–28); since he is twenty-three when he goes to Egypt, Deneau's Pip must spend nine or ten years in London, which is impossible. According to Sadrin, several years of Pip's life—between thirteen and seventeen—"have been lost" (33) because the spate of visits to Miss Havisham begin when Pip is about eight and only last about a year, yet Pip is more likely seventeen or eighteen than twelve or thirteen when he starts for London four years later.

Pip's growing-up years can be fruitfully reconstructed without prejudice to the novel's time-scheme provided one does not conflate the conclusion of chapter 13 and the start of chapter 14, as if Pip's statements at the end of weekly installment 8 and the beginning of installment 9 formed an uninterrupted observation. The "single year" in question is surely one that passes *between* chapters 13 and 14. The Pip who expresses a "strong conviction" in chapter 13 that he "will never like Joe's trade" is a prognosticator voicing a dread; the retrospective Pip in chapter 14 is not just looking back down "the newly entered road of apprenticeship" but also summarizing his years as a blacksmith; in particular, he divulges that he soon saw his worst fears realized—all in less than twelve months. Until he actually entered the forge in his shirt-sleeves and got himself "dusty with the dust of the small coal," Pip did not fully comprehend how menial his future would be. "Now the reality was in my hold," he recalls (ch. 14), as if a sentence has finally been carried out. It is this Pip, roughly fourteen or fifteen, who has grown "too big" for Mr. Wopsle's great-aunt's school in chapter 15.

As early as chapter 14, a Pip who is fourteen or fifteen confesses that he is "restless aspiring discontented" with his lot and, whenever he thinks of Estella, "more ashamed of home than ever." But his moody confidences to Biddy in chapters 16 and 17 would sound oddly precocious for a ten or eleven-year-old boy; they suit a Pip who is at least old enough for Orlick to hate as a rival for Biddy's attentions. In chapter 17, as they walk along the river on a Sunday in 1822—"It was summertime and lovely weather"— Orlick's interest becomes a problem: Biddy stammers, "I—I am afraid he likes me" and Pip is surprised to find that Orlick's "daring to admire" Biddy has made him "as hot as if it were an outrage to myself." This "very hot" Pip has a man's feelings, not a twelve-year-old boy's.

Chapter 17 depicts the mental and sexual torments of a young snob who realizes that his mind and heart are at odds; he is in love with the wrong woman, and the part of him that is genuinely attracted to Biddy knows it. Since Biddy is about a year older than the 17-year-old Pip, she is old enough to attract Orlick. If Pip were no more than 12 here and Biddy just 13, the 25-year-old journeyman's intentions would resemble a prurient interest in Little Nell.

That the "single year" at the outset of chapter 14 refers to the first year of Pip's apprenticeship, not to his visits to Satis House, becomes clear later in chapter 15, when Pip decides to pay Miss Havisham a visit of gratitude: "But, Joe," says Pip on a Sunday when they are relaxing at the battery on the marshes. "Here am I, getting on *in the first year of my time* [italics added], and, since the day of my being bound I have never thanked Miss Havisham...." When Pip pays this visit, the first in a year, Miss Havisham is displeased until she realizes that he does not want money; then she tells him to "come now and then; come on your birthday," so it is self-evident that Pip pays his respects annually until he leaves for London.

He makes one of these birthday visits ("an annual custom") in chapter 17. Although it is probably the first of its kind, it need not be, for the chapter's opening line—"I now fell into a regular routine of apprenticeship"—suggests that Pip, after a year or so on the job, has resolved to go through the motions of being a blacksmith, no matter how unhappily. This visit is best considered a representative of the several calls Pip paid during his years working for Joe. He has surely just turned sixteen or seventeen and it is November of 1821 or '22. Estella is away being educated, so Pip does not see her on any of his birthdays, nor when dressed in his new clothes on his goodbye visit to his "fairy godmother" in chapter 19, the day before he travels to London.

Ironically, Orlick attacks Mrs. Joe on the evening of the half-holiday that Joe, over his wife's objections, granted Pip and Orlick in order that the former could pay his visit of gratitude to Miss Havisham (ch. 15). Presumably, it is 1819 or 1820 and the fourteen or fifteen-year-old Pip is "in the first year" of apprenticeship. A considerable but unspecified amount of time now passes. First, the Bow Street constables are "about the house for a week or two," pretending to solve the crime; then Pip's sister lies "very ill in bed" for a long period. Thus the phrase "at last" in Pip's statement beginning "When, at last, she came round so far as to be helped downstairs" (ch. 16), could refer to several months. "It may have been about a month after my sister's reappearance in the kitchen," Pip recalls, "when Biddy came to us." In short, when Pip falls into his "regular routine" in chapter 17 and makes his November birthday visit to Miss Havisham, he is probably well into his second (or third) year at the forge and at least sixteen or seventeen.

Considerable periods of time also pass within chapter 17, just as they did in 15 and 16. Although the birthday visit to an "unchanging" Satis House momentarily convinces Pip that time has stood still, he reports becoming "conscious of a change in Biddy." He remembers that she "had not been with us more than a year" when he began to appreciate her womanly virtues. Clearly, one must allow several months for Mrs. Joe's convalescence; then a year passes since Biddy came to live at the forge following the attack on Mrs. Joe. Then Pip's patronizing conversation with Biddy on their summer walk takes up most of chapter 17, which means that seven or eight months have elapsed since the November birthday visit at its start.

In chapter 18, when Jaggers arrives at the Three Jolly Bargemen on 5 July, it is either the same summer of Pip and Biddy's walk or possibly the year following: as chapter 18 opens, Pip's determination to fix the day and year suggests a jump forward. Time seems to have passed since chapter 17, which concluded with Pip's statement that he "kept an eye on Orlick" after that night when he accosted Pip and Biddy. Pip also states that he passed through numerous "states and seasons" when he would resolve to marry Biddy and become partners with Joe only to have "some confounding remembrance of the Havisham days" scatter his wits again. This process of collecting his wits and having them scattered anew went on for "a long time"—long enough for Pip's hope that Miss Havisham will resolve his confusion by making his fortune "when [his] time was out" to imply that the first four years of it are about up by the end of chapter 17.

Although Dickens is not always as precise as a dater would like, he provides enough indications of time's passage between chapters 13 and 17 to account for several years of apprenticeship; similarly, chapters 7 through 12 contained enough indicators of time passing to justify several years of visits to Satis House. Together, these two sequences amply chronicle Pip's metamorphosis from boy to man. When Jaggers arrives on Saturday, 5 July 1823, Pip is at least seventeen as of the previous November. Significantly, the lawyer fails to recognize Pip as the boy he had scrutinized on Pip's second visit to Satis House in chapter 11. Having seen Pip at eight, Jaggers ought surely to recognize him at eleven or twelve; if, however, nine or ten years have gone by since their staircase encounter and Pip is seventeen or eighteen instead of eight, Jaggers cannot be expected to connect the "Boy of the neighbourhood" (ch. 11) with "a young fellow of great expectations" (ch. 18).

On Monday, 7 July 1823, Pip outfits himself at Mr. Trabb's shop in Rochester, secures his place for London at the coach-office, and enjoys being fawned upon by Pumblechook, who gives him an impromptu lunch. "So Tuesday, Wednesday, and Thursday passed" (ch. 19), and on Friday, 11 July 1823, Pip dons his London clothes at Pumblechook's to pay a farewell visit to Miss Havisham. He sets out for London early next morning, having bungled his parting from Biddy and Joe.

In chapter 20, Pip arrives at "the Cross Keys, Wood Street, Cheapside, London"; it is "a little past midday." He becomes a Londoner on Saturday, 12 July 1823, but will not learn his benefactor's identity for another five years and four months (11 weekly installments for Dickens' readers). In November, after just four months in the capital, Pip, according to Dickens' "Dates," will be "18 or 19."

Chapters 20–24, all taking place in July, depict Pip settling in: he visits Jaggers's office; Wemmick accompanies him to Barnard's Inn; there he recognizes Herbert as the "pale young gentleman" (chs. 20–21). Pip and his new roommate attend services at Westminster Abbey on Sunday, 13 July; Pip feels as if "many months" have passed since he left Joe and Biddy. On Monday, 14 July, Pip goes to the Exchange with Herbert and then on to Matthew Pocket's residence at Hammersmith. By chapters 23–24, Pip is already boarding with the Pockets and rowing on the Thames with Drummle and Startop, his fellow-boarders, even though he retains his room in Barnard's. When Pip's future rowing coach remarks that he has "the arm of a blacksmith" (ch. 23), the embarrassing compliment to the would-be gentleman points to a man of seventeen or eighteen, not to a boy of eleven or twelve.

When Pip joins Wemmick for dinner at Walworth in chapter 25, it is his second visit, and he has been in the Pocket family "a month or two." It is probably September 1823, so Pip is practically eighteen, or nearly nineteen if his four years with Joe took him past his eighteenth birthday. In chapter 26, which is also of a prandial nature, Pip and his cohorts—Drummle, Startop, and Herbert—dine with Jaggers at his house in Gerrard Street, Soho. Joe and Mr. Wopsle, the latter having abandoned the church for the stage, come to London on Tuesday in chapter 27; the former brings Pip a message from Miss Havisham: Estella has come home and would like to see him. Presumably, it is still the first year of Pip's London life, yet Joe finds him "growed," "swelled," and "gentle-folked," a remarkable improvement in only five or six months.

Pip returns to Rochester for the first time "next day," a Wednesday. He informs us that "winter had now come round" (ch. 28), so it must be at least January or February 1824, and Pip, who has had a birthday in November, is at least eighteen, possibly nineteen, having been in London for eight chapters. As Pip travels homeward by the afternoon coach, two convicts, one of whom presented him with the two one-pound notes in chapter 10, wish they had Magwitch's gift for themselves. If the year is 1824, their cupidity is awkward: this denomination, as will be discussed in detail later, was discontinued in 1821. If, however, this were Pip's second London winter, a possibility given Joe's awe of his attainments, Dickens would not be off the mark: an isolated issue of the one-pound note took place in 1825–26.

Chapter 29 transpires on a Thursday in either 1824 or '25, probably the former; it contains two indications of time's passage since Pip left his village. First, he is astonished to meet a "much more womanly" Estella, whom he has not seen for several years, perhaps not since the visit to Satis House in chapter 13, when he was about fourteen. Second, he encounters Orlick as Miss Havisham's porter, although it remains uncertain how long it has been since the latter left the forge for Satis House. Pip has an interview with Estella in the ruined garden; dines with her, Jaggers, and Sarah Pocket; and agrees to chaperone her when she comes to London. Next day, Friday, after arranging with Jaggers to have Orlick dismissed, Pip is hooted out of town by Trabb's boy (ch. 30). Back in London, Pip discusses his prospects with Herbert, who predicts: "You'll be one-and-twenty before you know where you are." Pip is definitely not yet of age and apparently some distance from it if one takes Herbert's remark to imply that a clarification of Pip's status is not imminent. In chapter 31, still in the same winter, Pip and Herbert watch Wopsle portray Hamlet.

En route to Richmond, Estella reaches London in chapter 32. Pip meets her coach in Wood Street but, having just toured Newgate with Wemmick, feels "contaminated" by criminal associations. In chapter 33, apparently still in the winter of 1824–25, Pip escorts Estella to Mrs. Brandley's. Pip and Herbert are rapidly running into debt by chapter 34; both have joined a club called "the Finches of the Grove," but Pip cannot become a full-fledged Finch until he comes of age. Therefore, he is still not twenty-one but must be approaching that milestone if the club grants him conditional membership.

"I am now generalizing a period of my life," says Pip in a passage nearly as problematic for chapter 34 as his statement about summing up "eight or ten months" was in chapter 12. The "period" is doubtless Pip's life with Herbert in Barnard's Inn. Inasmuch as Pip and Herbert have been living in the Temple for "more than a year" when Pip turns twenty-three in 1828 (ch. 39), the life-period Pip describes in general terms, a time of repeated attempts to reduce expenditure simply by tabulating debts, probably covers the span from 1824–25 to late 1826 or early 1827. Since Pip turns 21 in chapter 36, the period in question may reach only from 1824–25 to 1826. In sum, Pip probably turns nineteen late in 1824, sometime during the period summarized in chapter 34; he is then twenty-one in 1826 (ch. 36) and has just turned twenty-three in 1828 (ch. 39).

"One evening" during the period of recurrent but fruitless economizing that Pip telescopes, he receives a letter stating that Mrs. Joe died "Monday last" and will be buried "on Monday next" (ch. 34). In chapter 35, as Pip walks from the Blue Boar to the forge for the funeral, he comments: "It was fine summer weather again," which means that at least one full year has passed since he arrived in London; consequently, Pip is almost nineteen—or almost twenty if two years have gone by. Conceivably, chapters 20 through 35 chronicle only the first year of Pip's London life, in which case, having gone into detail and established the pattern, Dickens skips ahead two years *twice:* once between chapters 35 and 36 and again, as noted previously, between chapters 38 and 39.

Pip is twenty-one in both chapters 36 and 37. "I came of age," he declares in the former, "in fulfillment of Herbert's prediction, that I should do so before I knew where I was"—that is, before ascertaining either his benefactor's name or if he is destined to marry Estella. "It was November," says Pip, revealing his birth-month for the first time. (Since Herbert came of age eight months earlier, we can fix his birth-date as March 1805.)

It is Sunday in "winter-time" 1825–26 when Pip visits Wemmick's castle in chapter 37. His purpose is to secure Wemmick's help in purchasing a position for Herbert with some of the £500 he received from Jaggers in chapter 36, the occasion on which Wemmick named London's six bridges. As chapter 37 concludes, the "great event" in Pip's life, the novel's "turning point" or pivotal moment, looms into view. But chapter 38, installment 23, intervenes; it is mostly about Pip's unsuccessful courting of Estella at Richmond but includes an account of one of several visits he pays with her to Miss Havisham in 1826 or '27. Serial readers had to wait two more weeks before Magwitch materialized in chapter 39, one week after Pip's twenty-third birthday and thus in late November or early December 1828, more than five years since "The Second Stage" began.

With no memorandum on "Dates" in front of them, Dickens' original readers had to rely on clues to the time scheme inserted in the text expressly for their benefit. Dickens supplied at least a dozen reasons for stopping the narrative of the main story prior to 1830. A Parliamentary committee condemned transportation and the use of convict ships in 1837; therefore, the novel begins and ends prior to the public outcry that prompted a government inquiry.[15] Returning illegally from transportation ceased to be a capital offense after 1834. Inasmuch as Herbert and Pip share Magwitch's anxieties, his return in chapter 39 must occur considerably earlier: no move is yet underway to lessen this penalty. After 1834, prisoners were sentenced individually, not all at once on the last day of the session.

Pip has no visual recollections of his parents because they lived "long before the days of photographs" (ch. 1). Since Pip has been an orphan for most of his seven years, the novel must begin before 1831 and the Pirrips must have lived much of their lives earlier than that because in 1838 L. J. M. Daguerre (1789–1851) made the first daguerretype, a picture on a chemically treated metal or glass plate. In 1839, he published his *History of the Daguerrotype and Diorama* and submitted his invention to the French Academy; that same year, William Henry Fox Talbot (1800–1877) announced the first photographic print on paper (the calotype) to the Royal Society. Gibbeting fell out of favor after 1832, when the last known instance was recorded; young Pip's fear of meeting such a fate would be unfounded if the novel commenced in the 1830s instead of ending by then.

If it were already 1827, when lucifer matches came into use, and not 1812, Pip could more easily get a light by which to steal food in chapter 2. An English apothecary, John Walker, invented the first successful friction match in 1826; one struck this match by drawing it through sandpaper. Although Walker sold his matches in 1827 at Stockton-on-Tees, similar matches, the ones actually called "lucifers," were first made and sold in London by Samuel Jones in 1829. (Matches using phosphorus instead of sulphur were not mass produced before 1839, and safety matches [strike-on-the-box] were not available for commercial use until 1855). On the other hand, Orlick's use of flint and steel in chapter 53, when it is 1829, places the former journeyman slightly behind the times. Pip probably owes his life not just to Orlick's proverbial slowness ("The man was in no hurry."), but also to his old-fashioned ways: in this case, his dependence on tinder bound to be "damp" in a sluice-house on the "mud and ooze" of the marshes. The match Orlick employs dates from the sixteenth century; it is a piece of cord, cloth, paper or wood that has been dipped in sulphur in order to be easily ignited with sparks from a tinder box. Orlick first gropes about in the dark for flint and steel, just as Mr. Pirrip suggests the boy Pip would have had to do in Mrs. Joe's pantry. Then, says Pip, "sparks fell among the tinder," which was slow to catch fire; then Pip observed "the blue point of the match"; finally, the tinder ignited the match, showing Pip the face of his captor, who then "lighted the candle from the flaring match with great deliberation."

Chapter 16 must take place before 1829. In that year, Robert Peele's Metropolitan Police replaced the Bow Street Runners who come from London to investigate the attack on Mrs. Joe. The soldiers chase Magwitch "in the name of the King," which means the recapturing takes place before 1820, when George III died; indeed, it is probably closer to 1812 because the king's health worsened after 1811, making toasts to his welfare futile. Thanks to such events as the demise of the Runners and George III's death, the 1820s steadily emerge as the period for 1. most of Pip's apprenticeship, 2. the announcement of his expectations, and 3. his consequent London experiences. Pip's confrontation with the convict and his crueler apprenticeship as Miss Havisham's pawn and Estella's plaything occupy the decade prior to 1820.

Repeatedly, either by omission or inclusion. Dickens pointed to 1830 as his terminus. Thus no omnibuses operate in London's streets because the first one did not appear until 1829. The widespread appearance of suburbs for England's largest cities was a phenomenon of the 1830s and '40s; thanks to places like Walworth, the suburbanization process is well under way in the late 1820s. Inasmuch as the old buildings of the Temple were destroyed by fire in 1830, Pip and Herbert's tenancy, which began about 1827, fortunately lasted less than three years. After a fire burned down the old Hummums, the baths were reopened as a hotel in 1821—in plenty of time for Pip to spend the night there in 1828 (ch. 45).

In chapter 40, Pip contemplates Magwitch with abhorrence, "loading him with all the crimes in the calendar." This was still a plausible hyperbole in 1828. Although Newgate calendars, compilations of the recent notorious crimes, were issued from the 1770s only until 1820, Andrew Knapp and William Baldwin, attorneys-at-law, kept alive this tradition with periodic updatings: *The Newgate Calendar* (1824–26) and *The New Newgate Calendar* (1826). When Pip repairs to his village in chapter 28, he must travel with two unwanted companions because "at that time it was customary to carry convicts down to the dockyards by stage-coach." Clearly, the age of railways has yet to arrive, so again it must be earlier than 1830, when the first important passenger service began (Liverpool to Manchester).

Pip refers to paddle steamers on the Thames in chapters 52 and 54. Because these are either headed for Rotterdam and Hamburg or arriving from Leith, Aberdeen, and Glasgow, it must be prior to the upsurge of transatlantic steam navigation in the 1840s, which carried Dickens to America in 1842.

But it cannot be earlier than 1814, when paddle steamships first appeared on the Thames; instead, it must be after 1821, when, as was mentioned above, regular service across the English Channel commenced. At the time of Magwitch's escape attempt, Mr. Pirrip recalls, "steam-traffic on the Thames was far below its present extent" (ch. 54). Therefore, three things have happened, the first two prior to chapter 54: 1. many years have elapsed since the boy Pip watched white-sailed vessels standing out to sea; 2. enough time has passed since 1821 for paddle steamers destined for Europe not to be considered a novelty; 3. in the years since the escape attempt, steam traffic has increased so greatly that it would be far riskier now to intercept a specific steamer in the crowded waterway.

Conversely, although gas was introduced in London as early as 1807, it was not in general use before 1820, and Pip's allusions to this phenomenon in chapters 33 and 48 suggest that its adoption was still not widespread later in the decade. Three other kinds of lighting are used in *Great Expectations:* the "rushlight" or nightlight in the Hummums (ch. 45), Miss Havisham's candle-light, and Pip's reading lamp (ch. 39). A conversion to gas from one form of lighting or another is under way throughout *Great Expectations* (Edminson, 34), but this post-1807 transition is hardly an accomplished fact even in the later chapters. After London's streets were lighted by "flaring open jets" set up "at long intervals," gas was still considered too dangerous for interior use; many shops and houses continued to rely on candles and oil lamps,[16] even though Pip notices the lamplighters busy outdoors and the lights that were "springing up brilliantly in the shop windows" (ch. 48).

In chapter 13, Miss Havisham gives Pip a bag which she says contains "five-and-twenty guineas" to pay the premium when he is apprenticed to Joe. If Pip is about 14, the year should be 1819. Yet guineas, which ceased to be minted in 1813, went out of circulation in 1817. Could Pip have been apprenticed to Joe in either of these years—that is, in 1813 at the early age of eight, or in 1817 at age twelve? Possibly, but not if one emphasizes that Miss Havisham, a recluse, is the donor. She may still think in terms of guineas and could have quantities stored away; although no longer in general use, they would still be legal tender in 1819. When Joe reports the gift to Mrs. Joe later in the chapter, he calls it "five-and-twenty pound." Either Dickens corrected himself or Joe updates Miss Havisham's monetary archaism. If the latter, then Pip reinstates it: the apprenticeship dinner in the Blue Boar comes about, he recalls, because his sister was "so excited by the twenty-five guineas" (ch. 13).

Miss Havisham's is not the first gift of money Pip receives. The shilling that "the strange man" who stirs his drink with a file bestowed on him in the Jolly Bargemen (ch. 10), Pip subsequently discovers, is wrapped in "two fat sweltering one-pound notes." When Pip makes his second visit to Satis House in chapter 11, he is eight and the year is 1813. An eight-year-old Pip who receives two one-pound notes in 1813 presents no difficulty because the government did not cease issuing the easily forged one-pound note until 1821.[17] The problem is that one-pound notes seem to remain current throughout Pip's London experiences, which circumstance tempted Anny Sadrin to halt the main action prior to 1821 (Sadrin 38, 41).

When Pip travels back to his village by stagecoach in chapter 28, a journey already mentioned above in both the discussion of Pip's London experiences and in connection with railways, he is eighteen or nineteen and it is the winter of 1824 or '25. One of the two convicts whose conversation he overhears turns out to have been the deliverer of Magwitch's present in the Jolly Bargemen. Since the other convict wishes they still had the money bestowed on Pip, Sadrin placed the action here in 1820 or earlier, for the one-pound note appears to be circulating freely. Pip's eighteenth birthday, it followed, must also fall before 1820–21 because he was already about that age when he traveled to London eight chapters previously.

In chapter 39, however, when Pip gives back two one-pound notes to the newly returned Magwitch, Sadrin suspected that this event should also predate 1821, which would truncate Dickens' time-scheme for the London chapters even more severely. Born about 1800, Sadrin's Pip is about eighteen on arrival around 1818; but Pip's coach trip home in chapter 28, his twenty-first birthday in chapter 36, and the restitution of the two pounds in chapter 39, when Dickens says Pip is twenty-three, must all take place before 1820–21. Pip cannot age five years while events only move from 1818 to 1820–21. If on the other hand, Pip was born no later than 1797, he would be twenty-three in chapter 39 when it is still prior to 1821. But when Pip turned 21 in chapter 36, the year would have to have been 1818, possibly earlier, and thus at least one of the bridges Wemmick catalogues would not have been built yet (new bridges were completed in 1819, 1817, and 1816).

The solution is to realize that the government merely ceased *issuing* one-pound notes in 1821, which is different from having all those in circulation recalled and destroyed—an impossible task. The goal was to decrease their use immediately and eventually to phase them out. Like our modern two-dollar bill and Susan B. Anthony one-dollar coin, the one-pound note remained legal tender even after the government discontinued printing it in order to discourage forgers. Moreover, as was suggested earlier, it was not untimely or impractical for the convicts to wish that they still had Pip's present in chapter 28, which takes place around 1825, for an isolated issue of the one-pound note took place in 1825–26 during a period of financial crisis.[18]

The notes Pip returns to Magwitch in 1828 are tokens in a ceremonial restitution, not the ridiculous gesture of repaying a sixteen-year loan. Both notes are "clean and new," characteristics Dickens emphasizes, so Pip may have procured these crisp bills purposely after coming into his expectations in chapter 18 or, more likely, in 1825–26. The gift he received in the Jolly Bargemen and the convict who served as Magwitch's emissary have seldom been out of his mind; conceivably, he has carried the notes for repayment purposes at least since he saw the convict again on the coach and wondered whether he "ought to restore a couple of pounds sterling to this creature before losing sight of him" (ch. 28). The notes' cleanness and newness symbolize Pip's futile desire to inherit respectability as well as money, hence to return not only an unwanted gift but all the guilt-by-association, all the dirty complicity, that their "fat sweltering" condition signified in chapter 10. As Magwitch burns the notes, indicating that he is too wealthy to need them and thus reveals himself as the real architect of Pip's fortunes, ceremonial restitution becomes a parody of purification: instead of cleansing himself of Magwitch, Pip sees his illusion that Miss Havisham intends him for Estella go up in smoke.

Compeyson and Magwitch were arrested for passing stolen bank notes. If these were also forgeries, the pair may have helped to undermine confidence in the one-pound bank note first put into circulation around 1797. If chapter 39 takes place prior to 1820 and if, according to Dickens' "Dates," Magwitch first knew Compeyson about twenty years ago, their criminal association would have begun a year or more before the turn of the century, a bit too close to the one-pound note's introduction. Compeyson had been in the "swindling, hand-writing forging, stolen bank-note passing" business (ch. 42) for some time before recruiting Magwitch, who is then "took up on suspicion" (i.e., arrested but not prosecuted) "twice or three times" during their association. If he and Compeyson became "pardners" around 1808, the date suggested above, they began their short-lived schemes at about the right time for mounting public outcries for better currency supervision to lead to their capture some four years later.

Although everyone concedes that Dickens remains the novelist of record, Mr. Pirrip (technically, Mr. Philip Pip) can be designated the penultimate author of *Great Expectations*. If born in 1805, he begins publishing his life story in weekly installments in *All the Year Round* at age fifty-five; he is seven years older than the journal's proprietor, not Dickens' senior by "about ten years" (Sadrin 42). But several questions remain virtually unanswerable: how long did it take Pip to decide on writing his memoirs, and why does he wax autobiographical two decades after the last event in the novel?[19]

K. J. Fielding stated that it was "twelve years or more later when [Pip] was telling the story," but he offered no proof for 1851 as the year of authorship (2). If the year is 1860–61, as seems more likely, one must assume that Pip and Estella were married in December 1840 or early in the new year. Otherwise, it would be dishonest for Mr. Pirrip to conclude that Pip "saw no shadow of another parting" from Estella if he knew in 1860 that they had long since parted—that this final expectation was also wrong. One may theorize that three of the major figures in Pip's maturation process—Estella, Biddy, and Joe—are now deceased, Estella perhaps most recently, and this parting has freed Mr. Pirrip to write.

Unless Estella has died, Mr. Pirrip breaks the promise Pip gave Jaggers and Wemmick not to reveal the "secret" of Estella's parentage (ch. 51). If Estella still lives, Pip has surely confided in her at some point between their marriage and June 1861. Otherwise, an unenlightened Estella was in for a double shock when installments 30 and 31 appeared on the 15th and 22nd of that month: she would learn from chapter 50 that her father was an ex-convict, a transported felon; as Compeyson's murderer, he had been under sentence of death when he expired from injuries sustained in an escape attempt. The next week she would discover from chapter 51 that her mother had stood trial for murder and, although acquitted, had killed another woman in a fight. Molly is probably dead by 1861, so Mr. Pirrip would also have to tell Mrs. Pirrip that he prevented her from meeting both of her real parents. Had Dickens not altered in proof the final line of the revised ending, canceling "but one" in "the shadow of no parting from her, but one,"[20] it would be easier to infer that Estella had recently passed away.

In the cases of Biddy and Joe, the mortality issue is even more ambiguous. If Biddy was still living as of 3 August 1861, she would only be fifty-seven or fifty-eight; more important, she would learn from chapter 58 the real reason that Pip fainted in June 1829: having come to the forge to propose marriage, he had discovered that it was Joe and Biddy's wedding-day. At the time, Pip's collapse was attributed to his recent illness. Pip records his thankfulness that he "never breathed this last baffled hope to Joe" while the latter nursed him through his delirium. If the blacksmith is still alive, he would be seventy-eight, and on 3 August 1861 he would learn that he had unwittingly crushed Pip's last hope. Yet, if marriage to Biddy can stand as Pip's "last" frustration, then his subsequent prediction of no further separation from Estella must be accurate.

Two problematic passages, one canceled in manuscript, can be interpreted to mean that Biddy and Joe are both dead before Mr. Pirrip turns novelist. Recalling the scene in which Jaggers announced that Pip is to leave the forge in order to "be brought up as a gentleman," Mr. Pirrip contrasts his childish elation with Joe's dignified sense of loss: "Oh, dear good faithful tender Joe, I feel the loving tremble of your hand upon my arm, as solemnly this day as if it had been the rustle of an angel's wing!" (ch. 18) Pip seems to be commemorating Joe's protective touch, which he claims he can still feel thirty-eight years later, but the exclamation suggests that by "this day"—9 February 1861 when chapter 18 appeared—Joe has literally become Pip's guardian angel.

In chapter 12, Pip describes the bad influence his visits to Miss Havisham and Estella began to exert on his character. But he concealed his misgivings from Joe and "reposed complete confidence in no one but Biddy," who must have found Pip's expressions of longing for Estella painful because she herself was in love with Pip. As to why he confided in her, Mr. Pirrip writes, "I did not know then, though I think I know now," a confession that he regrets having taken advantage of her sympathy. In the manuscript Dickens added: "Shade of poor Biddy, forgive me!" That Dickens removed this exclamation could mean that he had changed his mind about Biddy's life-span, or else he felt that Mr. Pirrip was already sufficiently remorseful in the chapter's ninth paragraph without this outburst.

A plethora of anachronisms in the text suggests a sizeable gap between events themselves and Mr. Pirrip's recording of them. These anachronisms are things no one in the story could know at the time. In chapter 1, for example, Pip cannot be alluding to Darwin's concept of natural selection; the chapter unfolds forty-seven years too early for the boy to be conscious of "that universal struggle," but Mr. Pirrip is being quite timely if he begins writing in 1859, the year not just for for *The Origin of Species,* but also for Samuel Smiles's *Self-Help,* which maintained that "all life is a struggle." [21] Nor could Mrs. Joe, in chapter 13, where Pip is about fourteen and the year is 1819, allude to Napoleon III when she calls Pip a "young Rantipole." Yet Mr. Pirrip would surely be conversant with this nickname for the French Emperor, whose contradictory and unethical foreign policy upset Queen Victoria throughout the 1850s.

Although Mr. Pirrip's retrospective is ironic rather than nostalgic, he frequently reminds readers how greatly things have changed since he was Pip—that is, "since that time, which is far enough away now" (ch. 2). This phrasing could mean that events in the story are now "far enough" in the past to be talked about because most of the principal actors have passed away. Besides references to "those days" or "that time" and expressions such as "I have often asked myself the question since" (ch. 11), the implication always being that events being recounted took place long ago, Mr. Pirrip specifically refers to changes along the road from Hammersmith to London, a road formerly much pleasanter (ch. 25). He reports major "alterations" in the Temple since he and Herbert moved there from Barnard's Inn (ch. 39). Joe's house, he recalls, was wooden, "as many of the dwellings in our country were—most of them, at that time" (ch. 2). In the same vein, Wopsle performs in a theater whose waterside neighborhood, says Mr. Pirrip, "is nowhere now" (ch. 47).

In chapter 18, Pip compares Joe to the steamhammer, not invented until 1839, as Mr. Pirrip knows but not Pip. In chapter 32, published on 30 April 1861, Mr. Pirrip, not Pip, refers to a time when prisoners "seldom set fire to their prisons" just because they disliked "the flavour of their soup." Apparently no coddler of inmates despite Pip's softening experiences with Magwitch, Mr. Pirrip alludes to the Chatham riots of 8 February 1861, which erupted when the Chatham prisoners objected to a reduction in their diet.[22] (Mr. Pirrip is evidently writing installments of *Great Expectations* about two months ahead of the printer, the exact advantage that Sadrin notes Dickens also maintained [Sadrin 10].) Pip's tour of Newgate with Wemmick as his guide thus evokes a critique of both the former neglect of prisons and of fresh injustices resulting from an "exaggerated reaction" to that neglect. The horrors of Newgate prove that jails were deplorable in the 1820s when felons "were not lodged and fed better than soldiers," which preferential treatment is the form "public wrong-doing" has since taken. Mr. Pirrip seems familiar with Florence Nightingale's complaints about the terrible conditions British soldiers endured during the Crimean War (1854–56).

Surely no snob like his younger self, Mr. Pirrip nevertheless evinces scant respect for either mediums or dentists. In chapter 40, Pip and Magwitch discuss the sort of outfit the latter should adopt as a "disguise." Provis, Mr. Pirrip recalls, "sketched a dress for himself that would have made him something between a dean and a dentist"—that is, it would have been difficult to tell whether he was an antiquated clergyman or an unskilled treater of teeth. Throughout the eighteenth century, dentists were pathetically undereducated, but in 1859, theirs was an up-and-coming profession because the Royal College of Surgeons began awarding certificates of fitness to practice dentistry. Perhaps

Mr. Pirrip merely desired an alliteration; more likely, he wanted to portray the genteel Pip, an apprentice disguised as a gentleman, scoffing at Magwitch's admittedly comical plans for concealing his felonious self in an upstart's attire.

In chapter 4, Pumblechook inadvertently drinks the tar-water that Pip used to replace the brandy given to Magwitch.[23] As the corn-chandler executes a "whooping-cough dance," a terrified Pip, grasping the tableleg under the cloth, "moved the table, like a medium of the present day, by the vigour of [his] unseen hold upon it." Mr. Pirrip shares Dickens' contempt for such trickery and presumably had enjoyed the criticism of clairvoyants in *Punch* from July through September 1860. Inasmuch as "a medium of the present day" is singular, however, the specific target may have been Daniel Dunglas Home (1833–86), the most celebrated mid-nineteenth-century spiritualist. His performances in 1859, including table-tipping, had been favorably reported in the *Cornhill Magazine* for August 1860, but two articles attacking him had appeared in *All the Year Round* that same summer.

Topographers and historians of the drama do not always make reliable daters. If Wemmick weds Miss Skiffins in St. George's Church (ch. 55), the realization that this church was not built until 1822–24 should cause no difficulty; the Wemmick nuptials take place in spring 1829. But W. Laurence Gadd, an authority on the actual buildings and places Dickens used in *Great Expectations,* identified the church as St. Giles's, Camberwell, on grounds that the "period of the story ... was prior to 1823" (113). "The period of *Great Expectations,*" Gadd decided, "corresponds very nearly with the years of Dickens's own boyhood—perhaps a little earlier ... the action of the whole story (except the events of the last chapter and of the latter part of the penultimate one) took place prior to 1830, and probably before 1825" (Gadd 159). Dating the action "prior to 1830" is absolutely correct, provided one includes the "latter part" of the penultimate chapter (Pip's preparations for departure from England). Unfortunately, the retreat to "before 1825," which coincides with the choice of 1823 as the date for the Wemmick wedding, suggests that Gadd, for unspecified reasons, preferred the early 1820s as Dickens's cut-off point. Gadd allowed Herbert and Pip to remove to the Temple from Barnard's Inn when the latter is twenty-two, which is accurate enough, but his view that the "river journey," Magwitch's escape attempt, may be "as late as 1819" is a grievous understatement (116, 119). Pip is just beginning his apprenticeship in 1819; besides, Magwitch could not have expected regular steamer service to Hamburg until the 1820s.

Before the reform of the theater laws through the Theatre Regulation Act of 1843, legitimate drama, especially Shakespeare, was licensed only in the privileged houses—Drury Lane and Covent Garden. What then of Wopsle's *Hamlet?* When did the former parish clerk perform it, and how long is the interval between his attempt to resurrect serious drama (ch. 31) and his decline into minor roles in nautical melodramas (ch. 47)?

Technically, Wopsle's *Hamlet* ought not to have been produced in a small metropolitan theater in a "waterside neighbourhood" earlier than 1844, several years after Pip's return from Egypt. Conceding as much, V. C. Clinton-Baddeley nevertheless spaced Pip's theatrical evenings a year apart, assigning them to 1835 and 1836—which makes these outings, taken jointly, a troublesome anachronism: not only must 1844 become 1835, but Wopsle's debut and decline also threaten the argument that the main action of *Great Expectations* concludes before 1830.[24]

Several of Clinton-Baddeley's assumptions seem off the mark. A Pip whom she supposes was born in 1812, as was Dickens, would indeed be twenty-three in 1835 (C-B, 151), but Pip and Herbert visit Denmark *before* either is twenty-one (the former's coming of age is announced five chapters later). Therefore, Wopsle's slide takes at least two years, and Pip is truly twenty-three when, without Herbert, he again observes his fellow townsman. Pip states that after the *Hamlet* fiasco, Wopsle "had been ominously heard of, through the playbills" (ch. 47); these advertisements have apparently helped Pip to track the parish clerk's steady deterioration, as if they formed a chart. Also, Herbert has been to see Wopsle at least once since the *Hamlet* production. A theatrical decline over a two- or three-year period, perhaps beginning during Mr. Pip's second year in London, parallels Pip's comedown: from Prince of Denmark to trivial roles in Wopsle's case, from Miss Havisham's adopted god-child to Magwitch's paid-for creature in Pip's.[25]

Dickens did not assign to a "minor theatre" of the mid-1820s the privilege of doing Shakespeare, which privilege it could only have received more than a decade later. Instead, he blurred the sharp distinction Clinton-Baddeley draws between a "public-private theatre," where amateurs purchased their parts, and a "minor theatre," in which Wopsle would buy his way into an otherwise professional cast. The theater company in chapters 31 and 47 is another of Dickens' skilfull composites. The advertisement for Wopsle's *Hamlet,* which Joe hands Pip in chapter 27, describes the erstwhile parish clerk as the "provincial amateur," a characterization that leaves his status ambiguous: is he in London to turn professional or to test himself against metropolitan amateurs? Either way, Wopsle's lack of success depletes his bankroll. After two or more years in the capital, Waldengarver (née Wopsle) can no longer afford leading parts.

One should compare Wopsle and his troupe with the stage-struck "don-keys" whom Dickens satirized in "Private Theatres," an 1835 sketch based on his personal observations—it became chapter 13 of *Sketches by Boz* (1836). Like Wopsle, the pay-for-parts neophytes in this sketch spend money "for permission to exhibit their lamentable ignorance and boobyism on the stage"; they, too, assume glamorous stage names—"Horatio St. Julian, alias Jem Larkins," for instance. Shakespearean roles can be easily hired, Richard III going for £2. As "Private Theatres" ends, the curtain rises on a slapdash pro-duction of *Macbeth,* perhaps the prototype for Wopsle's demolition of *Hamlet.* The theater Pip twice attends has attributes of a "minor theatre" but also resembles the "private" theaters Dickens attended almost nightly between 1828–32, while laboring by day as a shorthand writer in Doctors' Commons and dreaming of an acting career.

When the declining Wopsle appears in a nautical melodrama in the minor role of a "plenipotentiary ... from the Admiralty," Magwitch's escape attempt is imminent and the time is "late in the month of February" 1829. The play supplies another proof of 1830 as Dickens' cut-off point for the main action. Although romantic sailor plays flourished from the late eighteenth century until early in the nineteenth, the most popular instance, *Black-Eyed Susan: or, All in the Downs* (by Dickens' friend Douglas Jerrold) ran for 400 nights in 1829.

Like Wopsle's *Hamlet,* neither Old London Bridge nor the easily forged one-pound bank note constitutes an insurmountable barrier to a syncretic reading of the time scheme in Dickens' thirteenth novel. Nor are topical allu-sions an obstacle.[26] References to Darwin, to the controversy about the nature of gentility sparked by *Self-Help,* to the unpopular Louis Napoleon, rioting prisoners, upwardly mobile dentists, etc. may have been intended to create an "illusion of contemporaneity," thereby strengthening the bonds between read-er and narrator (Sadrin 36). Yet they do so by separating *now* from *then,* Mr. Pirrip the author from Pip, his protagonist and former self. Paradoxically, it is this conscious act of separation that results in greater bonding: that Mr. Pirrip writes about the 1820s in 1860 reveals his conviction that what happened to him still has a moral application, not only forty years later but for all time. Contemporaneity is not an "illusion" to be sustained but a fact to be revealed, making Mr. Pirrip's autobiography a tract for Victorian times.[27]

NOTES

1. Not until chapter 47 in the manuscript does "Compey" firmly appear as "Compeyson." If Dickens composed "Dates" later than he wrote chapter 47, "Compey" should be "Compeyson." In chapter 48, Pip starts to uncover Molly's history, eventually unscrambling her connections to Magwitch, Compeyson, and Estella; it was a good place for Dickens not only to doublecheck the figures he had probably been using throughout chapters 1–47, but also to apply them to the remainder of his tale. The memorandum would have been a pointless exercise had it revealed serious discrepancies in the installments already published, or if events already described refused to jell with those planned for the final twelve chapters: as a serialist, Dickens could not go back over the published portion of his novel to adjust differences. Nevertheless, the most noticeable feature of the "Dates" memorandum is the margin for error Dickens preserved by using *about* persistently: Pip and Estella are "about" Herbert Pocket's age, the returned convict is "about 60," etc. Dickens also revised the manuscript to replace specifics with approximations: "a score or so years ago," for example, replaced "a score of years ago," and "might have been" was substituted for "was"—just in case any of Dickens' calculations were incorrect. The two half-sheets headed "Dates" are bound into the Wisbech Manuscript of *Great Expectations* along with two other memoranda, one titled "General Mems" and the other "Tide." These "Dates" were first printed in John Butt, "Dickens's Plan for the Conclusion of *Great Expectations*," *The Dickensian*, 45 (1949), 78–80.

2. R. D. McMaster confined the main action "roughly between 1807 and 1826"; see his edition of *Great Expectations* (New York: Odyssey, 1965), xxiii.

3. Edgar Rosenberg thought of consulting the Lectionary and supplied the three most likely Sundays.

4. That Pip should call Joe's son "I again," as if noting a physical resemblance, is just as curious as Estella's mistaking Biddy and Joe's child for Pip's in the original ending: Pip is not related by blood to either Joe or Biddy.

5. Information for this paragraph comes from George Henry Preble, *A Chronological History of the Origin and Development of Steam Navigation* (Philadelphia, PA: L.R. Hamersly, 1883), 117; Henry Fry, *The History of North Atlantic Steam Navigation* (London: Sampson Low, Marston and Co., 1896), 29–30; and Rear Admiral P.W. Brock, *Steam and Sail in Britain and North America* (Princeton, NJ: Pyne Press, 1973), 10–13.

6. Having been sentenced to fourteen years, Magwitch escapes from solitary confinement and swims to shore on the 23rd; he is subsequently transported for escaping. Compeyson, who was sentenced to only seven years, escapes a day later, on which Pip and Magwitch meet for the first time. Ironically, Compeyson duplicates Magwitch's physically demanding feat in order to escape from his former confederate. On the 25th, Pip mistakes Compeyson for Magwitch's boy-eating accomplice. Magwitch prospers in Australia from sometime after 1812 to 1828, whereas Compeyson, released from prison, resumes a life of crime by 1819, the year Pip is apprenticed.

7. T. W. Hill set Pip's age at thirty-six "when he married Estella," an accurate fore-cast only if the hypothetical wedding takes place at least a year after the reunion in chapter 59. See "Notes to *Great Expectations,*" *The Dickensian,* 56 (Spring, 1960), 126; cited below as H.

8. Hill overestimated the story's length from opening scene to garden reunion at twenty-nine years (H, 126); Sadrin, albeit indecisive, is more or less correct: "six-teen years or so" for the main action and "about twenty-seven years" from churchyard to garden (S, 33). Less exact is her statement that the meeting of hero and heroine in the original ending "was postponed for another two years." Since Pip originally spends eight years abroad and two at home before his Piccadilly encounter with Estella, their ten-year separation is actually a year shorter than their eleven years apart in the revision.

9. Surely this is a somewhat improbable formality, a positive identification after seventeen years by an officer who has seen hundreds of prisoners.

10. Here and throughout "The First Stage," Daniel P. Deneau opted for a younger Pip; see "Pip's Age and Other Notes on *Great Expectations,*" *The Dickensian,* 60 (Winter, 1964), 27; cited subsequently as D.

11. Compeyson capitalized on Magwitch's silence, holding "the knowledge over his head as a means of keeping him poorer and working him harder," Herbert informs Pip (ch. 50).

12. Deneau faults Dickens for contradicting himself on both counts (D, 29). Oddly, Jaggers works for Miss Havisham, defends both Molly and Magwitch, yet never unravels Estella's parentage.

13. See Stanley Friedman, "Estella's Parentage and Pip's Persistence: The Outcome of *Great Expectations,*" *Studies in the Novel,* 19 (Winter, 1987), 410–21.

14. Cf. Walter Hartright's feats of detection on behalf of Laura Fairlie in Wilkie Collins's *The Woman in White,* which preceded *Great Expectations* in *All the Year Round.*

15. The last hulk was not broken up until Dickens' birthday in 1859 (E, 27); transportation to South Wales ceased in 1840.

16. W. Laurence Gadd, *The Great Expectations Country* (London: Cecil Palmer, 1929), 160; cited again as G.

17. Forgeries of the one-pound note were abundant and unstoppable; in 1819, a committee proposed the use of sovereigns instead; after 1821, the one-pound note did not become current again for ninety-three years.

18. Dickens reviewed the one-pound note's problems in the second of two articles on "Bank note forgeries" in *Household Words,* 7 and 21 September 1850. Before 1793, notes had never been issued for sums of five pounds or less, so replacement of golden guineas by one-pound notes put the humbler orders at a disadvantage:

only the affluent and well-educated recognized true Bank paper. Between 1797 and 1817, there were 870 prosecutions for forgery.

19. Edminson and Sadrin found Mr. Pirrip's 1860–61 publishing date inexplicable: no evidence exists for the manuscript having been shelved or its publication delayed, said the latter (S, 34); the final years of the novel's action "are not those of its composition and publishing," the former noted (E, 35).

20. The manuscript version of the revised ending reads: "I saw the shadow of no parting from her, but one." The final two words are then clearly canceled in proof, leaving a rather awkward sentence that Dickens revised again for the Library Edition (1862).

21. Just as Mr. Pirrip cites providence, not Darwin's natural selection, as the life process's first principle, he challenges the preoccupation with struggling upward in Smiles's bestseller, *Self-Help:* 1. Joe Gargery, the personification of such Smilesian virtues as industry, thrift, and self-improvement, wisely eschews the upward mobility that is their specious reward; 2. Magwitch is a ruthless caricature of bourgeois individualism, a satire on the middle-class ethic of aspiration; 3. Pip's expectations make him a self-tormentor: he daydreams about being elevated above his station regardless of merit, but anguishes anew when elevation fails to come from an unimpeachable source.

22. Convicts set fire to Parkhurst Model Prison in August 1850 and Carlyle denounced the prison system itself in "Model Prisons" *(Latter Day Pamphlets,* 1 March 1850), but neither incident seems sufficiently timely for *Great Expectations.* On the Chatham riots, see Philip Collins, *Dickens and Crime* (London: Macmillan, 1962), 20.

23. A mix of water and pine or fir extract, tar-water was widely used as a cure-all in the eighteenth century. Since it has had time to decline in popularity and be revived, chapter 2 must be set early in the nineteenth century.

24. Citing Wopsle's performance, C. V. Clinton-Baddeley pronounced *Great Expectations* "not quite a unity"; she accepted Edminson's dates for the main action but found "different [i.e., contradictory] time strands" in the novel. See "Wopsle," *The Dickensian,* 57 (Autumn, 1961), 150; cited again as C–B.

25. Dickens may have wanted to obscure Mr. Wopole's exact age in order to have things both ways: although the clerk joins the chorus of adults persecuting young Pip at Christmas dinner, he later doubles as Pip's parallel; his audacity in playing Hamlet matches Pip's pretensions both to gentility and Estella's hand in marriage. If he is close in age to Joe and Mrs. Joe (i.e., between 30 and 40) as his "shining bald forehead" (ch. 4) and subsequent shortness of breath (ch. 6) indicate, he would be rather ancient—perhaps well past 40—when he finally arrives in Denmark. In contrast, Edmund Kean was only twenty-four when he became famous as Shylock in an 1824 production of *The Merchant of Venice.*

26. According to Richard D. Altick, topical allusions are in such short supply that "the milieu of *Great Expectations* is less specific" than that of *Hard Times* (1854)

or *Little Dorrit* (1855–57); nevertheless, he concludes that "most of the evidence ... points to the 1820s"; see *The Presence of the Present: Topics of the Day in the Victorian Novel* (Columbus: Ohio State UP, 1991), 135.

27. As Humphrey House noted, "the mood of the books," especially regarding "what money can do," belongs "to the time in which it was written," not to "the imaginary date of its plot"; see *The Dickens World* (London: Oxford UP, 1941; rpt. 1960), 159.

WORKS CITED

Deneau, Daniel P. "Pip's Age and Other Notes on *Great Expectations.*" *The Dickensian,* 60, (Winter: 1964).

Dickens, Charles. *The Letters of Charles Dickens.* Bloomsbury: Nonesuch, 1938.

Edminson, Mary. "The Date of the Action in *Great Expectations.*" *Nineteenth-Century Fiction,* 13 (June 1958).

Fielding, K. J. "The Critical Autonomy of *Great Expectations.*" *Review of English Literature,* 2 (July 1960).

Gadd, W. Laurence. *The Great Expectations Country.* London: Cecil Palmer, 1929.

Guerard, Albert J. *Conrad the Novelist.* New York: Atheneum, 1967.

Sadrin, Anny. *"Great Expectations."* London: Unwin Hyman, 1988.

Constructing the "Literate Woman": Nineteenth-Century Reviews and Emerging Literacies

Margaret L. Shaw

The development of a genuine mass readership in England in the 1850s is a matter of at least one kind of record. And Richard Altick's work in *The English Common Reader* and elsewhere continues to provide the most respected and useful of such traditional social histories. He demonstrates, for example, how changes in printing practices plus an increase in literacy rates in the early part of the century gave rise to a burgeoning newspaper and periodical business, which, in turn, contributed to the first real mass market for literature in England's history ("English Publishing"). Working class literacy rose, as did the income and leisure of the middle class. By the 1860s, the cheap mass-circulation daily newspaper had appeared (Gross 25). New power machinery for binding made the production of books more efficient, and improved shipping, because of faster travel, increased distribution and sales as well (Sutherland 64). Publishers opened new markets by producing a variety of formats for their literature—some new forms and some old ones revived for a new audience: monthly serials, weekly journals, and penny magazines all helped consolidate a mass public. Changes in publishing practice paralleled or instigated changes in reading. Among the general reading public, the activity became a part of daily life. The 1840s marked this expansion in the quantity and frequency of reading due to the easy access of the cheaper forms and the omnipresence of circulating libraries (Sutherland 24). Likewise, railway reading increased with W. H. Smith's production of cheap reading material in the stations (25).

What is not often discussed in such a record, however, is how the new literacy was being stratified and used for political purposes by linking it with gender as well as class. Since the new technology and changing economic and social conditions made it possible for large numbers of women to publish and for the poor to read—cheaper printing made inexpensive reproductions of all books available, for the first time, outside the circulating libraries, to the poorer classes—imaginative literature and the novel in particular became one of the objects of contention in the control of literacy.[1] In the years between 1847 and the 1860s, novels by Charlotte Brontë, Anne Marsh, Harriet Martineau, Elizabeth Gaskell, and George Eliot were being well-received by the publishers and public alike (Helsinger, Sheets, and Veeder 48). As a result, there was a heightened interest within the literary-critical establishment of the time in how this new group of writers and their readership was to be represented. While the construction of a dominant representation of this new literacy was complex, I would like to highlight one element in that process by looking at early nineteenth-century literary reviews. More specifically, I would like to consider how the writers of those reviews worked, wittingly or unwittingly, to "construct" an image of the "literate woman," of her appropriate habits of reading and writing, and, by guiding an emerging literacy in this manner, contribute to the shaping of literary culture in England. In doing so, I will argue that one of the effects of such activity was an increased stratification of literacy which ultimately solidified and privileged the construction of a new "man" of letters and his forms of literate behavior.

What was at stake for the reviewers in the struggle to define the new literacy varied dependent on the reviewer and—at times—the journal for which he or she was writing. Because of the astounding number of new periodicals— over 100 were founded each decade between 1830 and 1880—an equally large number of men and women were finding their way into print by way of reviewing (Heyck 33). Many of them, both men and women, were novelists themselves and were concerned about how their own activity as writers would be perceived. For many male reviewers, the new literacy meant an opportunity for them to shape an audience for their own material and increase the dignity of their positions as new "men of letters," that is, men who wrote through a market system relationship with the public. It was, after all, the increase in the reading public which called this new man of letters into being in the first place (28). The nature of the periodicals promoted diversity and insured that men of letters would be generalists rather than specialists; therefore, writers like George Lewes, Leigh Hunt, and Bulwer - Lytton were not just reviewers of books, but essayists as well. Furthermore, early periodicals did not recruit people in the professions. Most of the male contributors were middle-class men not connected to the university; as a result, some reviewers were accused of being decidedly shallow or ill-informed in their learning, and the anonymity of most of the reviews did little to discourage flagrant irresponsibility. Other reviewers could do much better, but there was a clear danger in setting oneself up as a jack of all trades, as Lewes knew only too well:

> For the most part ... literary men have no raison d'être, have no justification in their talents for the career they stumble through ... How few men of letters think at all! (qtd. in Gross 74)

While men of letters were lionized by the social set, they still held an ambiguous social status. There was a great deal of discussion about whether they were "gentlemen."[2] The claim was that such writers brought with them decidedly middle-class values into the production of texts with their stress on self-discipline, hard work, and methodical habits; Trollope's 1883 autobiography, and Harriet Martineau's in 1877, only served to confirm such claims. The market relationship between public and writer further aggravated the situation. The pressures of the market required that writers produce rapidly and appeal to a large variety of readers, yet the "dignity of literature" mythos demanded they rise above popular acclaim and project a romantic image of the writer-genius (Heyck 32; Poovey 110–113). The result was a self-consciousness among writers such as Dickens, Lytton, and Lewes. The Guild of Literature and Art, established in 1850 by Forster, Bulwer – Lytton, and Dickens was just one example of the attempt by men of letters to elevate their status. The guild promoted a plan of collective patronage to disassociate writers from the market place, but it had little or no effect on what had already become the dominant orientation of writers to their work and public (Heyck 33). When periodicals finally wooed university men to the press, the new breed of reviewer often objected to such efforts, seeing them as an attempt to create a literary elite. A typical article in *The Saturday Review,* for example, attacked Dickens for taking writing too seriously:

> It [the nobility of writing] is the creation of writers who have written upon writing. It has been suggested by those who have seen a hero in the "Man of Letters" and who have spoken of the higher kind of composition as of something godlike and divine. (qtd. in Gross 65)

For the upper classes, the rise of the man of letters was a threat to the supremacy of the Oxbridge "educated class" (Gross 65); the majority of the reviewers responded by defending their status all the more.

The highly prolific publishing industry was able to support a large number of women reviewers and novelists as well. Many were middle-class women with leisure to write, an activity which could be carried on in the home and therefore essentially invisible to the public as work. Other women were drawn to reviewing out of financial necessity, while a few turned novelist or reviewer out of a professional interest as well. Because so many of the early reviews were anonymous, women could write them without fear of speaking in a public voice; they too were sensitive to charges of crossing the boundaries of their class and to the additional charge of violating the decorum of their sex.[3] For these reviewers, the dignity of novels by women was a particular issue, as one might expect, but their responses to their subject varied widely, as we will see, depending on their class loyalties or pretensions, attitudes towards social roles for women, and the degree of seriousness with which they regarded writing as a profession. For them, how the literate woman was to be represented had a more than passing interest.

At the same time that the "man of letters" and the "woman writer" were being consolidated as categories in the culture, the status of the novel as a genre was likewise in contention. Once it became clear that the popularity of the novel was making it the dominant literary form of the century, those reviewers for whom the genre mattered professionally did what they could under the guise of advice to writers and readers to empower those representations of the novel, the novelist, and the reader of novels which best served their own separate interests. And since a large number of those novels were being written by women, the issue of gender became a focal point of the reviews. This use of gender to mark a difference between types of writing and to regulate who can write, about what, and in what manner became a powerful way to regulate as well the social and economic positioning of women in the culture; it had been used in similar ways before, but, given the need to consolidate a "women's sphere," never with such urgency and range. For many women reviewers (and novelists), regulating women's literacy was one way to promote their own sphere of power; as writers themselves, they could predominate in the representation of domestic life—or even of public life, as long as it was done through the personal—and exert moral influence over the lives of men and women. As reviewers, they could exercise a similar power by promoting such practices in other writers. But for many of the male reviewers, their own identities as men of letters were at stake. Their interest was in separating themselves from the literacy of women and lower classes by maintaining a preserve of "higher learning." It is my argument, then, that these various reviewers, including both men and women, devised constructions of female literacy which, while serving separate ends, had the effect of consolidating and then preserving a politically elite definition of literacy that supported a particular gender and class—an effect which directly impinged on the writing of women.

For the group of reviewers I have described, the temptation was great to help bring order to the chaos created by the popularity of a literary form that had as yet no codified critical standards to guide its production. By defining for themselves the "typical" traits of novels, their readers, and their writers, the review journalist was able to guide, represent, and to some extent constitute the public's thinking about writing by women. Although women had a lengthy history as writers of novels, this was the first time that gender itself became such a consistent marker of difference within the genre; in other words, reviewers felt obliged to characterize the writing of women as something in contrast to writing which was increasingly identified as "masculine" and based on a distinct set of experiences. By 1899, Henry James was able to characterize this bifurcation of literacy in England and America in terms of both sex and class; by far the largest group, the "public," were those readers who frequented the circulating libraries and were drawn to the novel:

> There is an immense public, if public be the name, inarticulate, but abysmally absorbent, for which, at its hours of ease, the printed volume has no other association [than "mere mass and bulk"]. This public, the public that subscribes, borrows, lends, that picks up in one way and another, sometimes even by purchase—grows and grows each year, and nothing is thus more apparent than that of all the recruits it brings to the book the most numerous by far are those that it brings to the "story." *(Future* xi–xii)

This inarticulate reader, in contrast to the professional or "educated" reader, was, at least in the influential opinion of Henry James, decidedly female:

> The larger part of the great multitude that sustains the teller and the publisher of tales is constituted by boys and girls; by girls in especial, if we apply this term to the later stages of the life of the innumerable women who, under modern arrangements, increasingly fail to marry—fail, apparently, even, largely, to desire to. (xii)

Such a readership—"the presence of the ladies and children—by whom I mean, in other words, the reader irreflective and uncritical"—was linked, finally, with "the vulgarization of literature in general" (xiv). By the turn of the century, then, the threat of a mass literacy and what supposedly constituted it—the lower to middle classes, women and children—led to the association of such groups with reading and writing that was instinctive, provincial, without form, and amateurish ("uncritical," "unconscious," and "absorbent"). In contrast, definitions of a superior literacy marked by intelligence, organization, and professionalism was being constituted as metropolitan, middle to upper class, and male.[4]

The appearance of such a split can be identified in the reviews of the mid-century as arguments about masculine and feminine imaginations began to appear with unusual frequency.[5] By claiming that women's imagination was not suited for abstract intellectual study, such reviews had the effect of gendering the concrete, reportorial writing associated with novels as feminine. The writing of poetry, drama, and philosophy were left, then, for the "masculine" imagination. In his 1852 essay, "The Lady Novelists," published in *The Westminster Review,* George Lewes enacts what was the standard critical move of the early reviews: begin with a definition of literature as associated with such culturally de-privileged traits as domesticity and sentiment, and philosophy, with the more privileged trait of abstract thought; associate domesticity and sentiment with the "feminine" and abstract thought with the "masculine," and then insist on the equality of the separate "spheres":

> [The] Masculine mind is characterized by the predominance of the intellect, and the Feminine by the predominance of the emotions. According to this rough division the regions of philosophy would be assigned to men, those of literature to women. (175)

Lewes admits, of course, that "no such absolute distinction exists in mankind" and, interestingly enough, abstracts the category of the feminine from the physical body so he might apply it to all literary minds:

> In poets, artists, and men of letters, *par excellence,* we observe this feminine trait, that their intellect habitually moves in alliance with their emotions.... (174)

But within the group of literary minds, he makes further distinctions between poetry and drama, or "high art," and the more "appropriately feminine" pursuit of fiction-writing:

> Of all departments of literature, Fiction is the one to which, by nature and by circumstance, women are best adapted. Exceptional women will of course be found competent to the highest success in other departments, but speaking generally, novels are their forte. The domestic experiences which form the bulk of women's knowledge find an appropriate form in novels; while the very nature of fiction calls for that predominance of sentiment which we already attributed to the feminine mind. Love is the staple of fiction, for it "forms the story of a woman's life." (175)

In order to preserve the realm of poetry and drama as "masculine," Lewes inextricably intertwines the novel with the feminine: thus, the novel itself is positioned as concrete, about the everyday and the domestic, sentimental, and experiential.

In an 1858 essay for *The North British Review,* R. H. Hutton begins his classification of types of imagination by claiming women focus on the visible things of life and men, on the invisible:

> If at any moment, the reveries of all the men and all the women in England could be laid bare to us, there can be little doubt that the latter would be found filled, for the most part, with pictures, memories, or hopes of *visible* human life … But not so with the men: in their minds a curious melee of interests half abstract, and where they were not abstract, often at least less about persons than about things…. And, as are the common thoughts of men and women, so are their imaginative powers. The former have more power to conceive anything, we will not say merely *abstract,* but that requires some withdrawal of the imagination from the human *dress and circumstance* of life; while the latter have more skill in elaborating fresh combinations of human incidents—that flow of event which is one of the greatest necessities of the writer of fiction. (467)

Hutton's stress on the quotidian as feminine and novelistic also allows him to make the implied distinction between high and low art, his sexual and military metaphors underscoring the gendered distinction:

> It is for this reason we conceive that women have not yet succeeded as poets. Poetry is concerned, it is true, mainly with the creation of living and breathing life, yet it certainly requires a power akin to the power of abstraction. The poet must penetrate and battle for a time, nay even *live,* far beneath the surface of life, in order to create fine poetry. (467)

The masculine imagination does more than just report the visible, a clearly elementary function; it must "decypher and interpret it. It requires an effort, something of a spiritual mood, to plunge into the pure beauty of true poetry" (467). According to this division and definition of the imagination, women are forever tied to their concrete, everyday experience: "Their imagination is not *separable,* as it were, in anything like the same degree, from the visible surface and form of human existence; and hence, such poetry as they do usually write, is apt to be mere personal sentiment without any token of true imaginative power at all" (467). Hutton's last comment suggests the kind of privileging of literary forms through gender difference that occurred, regardless of claims to the contrary.

While the author of "On the Treatment of Love in Novels" claims that each genre has its strengths, the novel's association with the commonplace prevents its own expression of love from equaling either the universality of poetry or the intensity of drama:

> Every mode of composition in which love forms a conspicuous element is amenable to laws of its own. While the novel deals with its daily and familiar aspects, poetry idealizes its emotions, and the drama seizes its salient manifestations.... It is not within the compass of the novel or the drama to accomplish this great design with such universality of treatment. They are both more dependent upon extrinsic features, and more limited in their scope and means.... The novel has a wider field for the development of details, but these, unless managed with consummate skill, are more likely to fritter away than enhance the interest.... Thus we may often find that an indifferent play may sometimes be vivid and entertaining, while an indifferent novel is always dull.
> *(Fraser's Magazine* 417–18)

But having made the initial distinction between literary forms, none of these reviewers is content to stop there. Boundaries between male and female writing within the genre were still fluid; therefore, a great deal of energy was devoted to making a difference which would provide for separate spheres for masculine and feminine *novels* as well. In part, the impulse seemed to be to find a way to distinguish good novels from bad. And, the argument goes, since good novels were based on experience, bad novels by women had to be caused by women trying to move into the sphere of male experience. But that argument takes on a more interested cast in essays like Lewes's "The Lady Novelists" in which competition between men and women is put out of play by the insistence on separate literary traditions. One year before Smith, Elder & Company published Charlotte Brontë's *Villette,* Lewes was arguing for the segregation of "women writers" to a sphere of influence separate from man's, an argument based on what he saw as the analogous situation of middle-class women in the larger social arena. According to Lewes, the woman's novel was the "correlate of her position in society," a position marked by its difference from rather than its competition with the male's:

> While it is impossible for men to express life otherwise than as they know it profoundly according to their own experience—the advent of female literature promises woman's view of life, woman's experience: in other words, a new element. (173)

The immediate cause of Lewes's concern, he says, is the large number of women writers who feel they must write like men, a "besetting sin" corrected only when women turn to their strengths and write as women. With their superior *finesse* of detail, their powers of observation, their intimate depiction of pathos and sentiment, women can serve in the aesthetic sphere the same moralizing and humanizing function they are now providing in the domestic. Men, on the other hand, can develop their strengths in plot and characterization and concentrate on the male experience of the public, political world (175).

But clearly, more than concern for the "woman's view" motivated Lewes's plea for a woman's literary sphere. Like other liberal male leaders of a growing literary establishment, Lewes's actions indicate he had a stake in the formation of a new culture for the middle class: The sheer number of essays and reviews he published suggest his determination to establish new standards of excellence in novelistic fiction. To do so meant marking off the liberal humanist limits of the "permanently good and true" from the merely "idiosyncratic" to arrive at a definition of the "literary":

> All poetry, all fiction, all comedy, all *belles lettres,* even to the playful caprices of fancy, are but the expression of experiences and emotions; and these expressions are the avenues through which we reach the sacred adytum of Humanity, and learn better to understand our fellows and ourselves. In proportion as these expressions are the forms of universal truths, of facts common to all nations or appreciable, by all intellects, the literature which sets them forth is permanently good and true.... But in proportion as these expressions are the forms of individual, peculiar truths, such as fleeting fashions or idiosyncracies, the literature is ephemeral.... Nevertheless even idiosyncrasies are valuable as side glances; they are aberrations that bring the natural orbit into more prominent distinctness. (172–73)

Given his commitment to a notion of "universal truth" and his definition of the literary as that which expresses all human experience, Lewes constructs a place for the literate woman in his pantheon of great writers, a position "second only to the first rate men of their day," for writers like Jane Austen, Charlotte Brontë, and George Sand *(Edinburgh Review* 157).

Less consciously, perhaps, Lewes's support of a woman's literary sphere was also an opportunity for him to elevate his own standing as a man of letters. The women writers Lewes privileged as second only to the best men of their age were women whose works best exemplified his own developing literary-critical categories, that is, "realistic" portrayal of human experience, experience that is emotionally "true" (158). This amalgam of romanticism and early realist categories was an important event in the emerging institutionalization of literary realism, but an event dependent as much on the large number of women writers Lewes does not mention as on those men and women he does. Those women who produced fashionable novels only were useful to Lewes and other reviewers since their writing became the "background" against which the features of "great" writing could be made visible. In other words, the sensational features of women's romanticism (the gothic, for example) could be used to establish a difference from the features of realism which Lewes wanted to privilege and naturalize as producing a transcendent vision. Such writing played the questionably serviceable role of the "abberrant" point of view which was to bring the "natural orbit" of the "universal" view into greater relief.

R. H. Hutton's "separate spheres" for "feminine" and "masculine" fiction is based not on experience, but once again on differences, apparently innate, in the imagination. By positing women's imagination as incapable of abstraction or intellectual distance from their material, Hutton constructs their literacy in extremely limiting ways:

> You can always see a kind of intellectual framework, of some sort, in a man's novels, which tells you that the unity is given rather by the mind and conception of the narrator, than by the actual evolution of the story. Feminine novelists never carry you beyond the tale they are telling; they are a great deal too much interested in it. (468)

Thought is always privileged as separate and above fiction; therefore, it is not surprising that the male novelist is the one who provides an "intellectual framework" to the novel; it is the feminine novelists who cannot get outside the narrative. Feminine writers, like feminine readers, "believe" in their own stories, to the point where critical distance and generalization are impossible. The notion of their literacy is that it is more "natural," less learned—cut off from a consciousness about culture and yet immersed within it. Thus, realism and detailed observation are again associated with a woman's particular writing strengths. In terms of the delineation of character, women have a fine perception of surface detail while men are better at imagining "unseen interiors" (473). If women manage to reproduce the interior of any character, it is usually only one and that one based almost always on the writer's own experience (473). But, while lacking abstract intellectual study, women are good with character development because, presumably, they are patient and pliant in their craft (479).

It soon becomes clear, from reading the reviews, that the move to distinguish "masculine" from "feminine" novels has the effect of equating women's writing with domestic realism and all of the problematic features of the novel, while novels by men can claim a scope outside the boundaries of the domestic. Domestic realism was praised for its fine detailing, its ability to teach a moral lesson, and its potential for promoting social reform (Helsinger, Sheets, and Veeder 48–51). Because of its focus on the detail, such novels could vividly portray social evils; they could, literally, control what the reader would look at. As a result, the realistic novel was highly problematic and potentially dangerous. In order to position high art in the realm of the abstract imagination, the art of the novel had to be positioned in the realm of fact. Thus, in an 1853 review of *Ruth*, J. M. Ludlow argues women are better novelists than men because they can add the element of human feeling to close observation and promote social reform; indeed, he defends Ruth's "gloomy" subject matter by appealing to such a reformist function for the novel. Speaking for the novelist, he says:

> I have to paint God's world as I find it, and above all, to shew [sic] others those portions of it on which I think they ought to look; a duty the more incumbent on men, if I am acquainted with holes and crannies which others have not pryed into, and which contain, nevertheless, sights which they should see. (161)

For many reviewers, that a woman is doing the "prying" and pointing makes the practice problematic: since women are supposed to be ignorant of certain evils, it becomes difficult to explain how they can, in fact, write about them in such detail. The defensiveness in reviews such as the one just quoted indicate the extent to which this effect of a realistic style was troublesome for some commentators on the novel.

The solution seemed to be to reassert the association of all writing by women with domestic fiction of a certain sort; by defining novels by women as moralist, sentimental, and suitable for children as well as adults, reviewers were able to reproduce a form of social and institutional control over the power of this particular style. Henry James, in an early comment on the practice of realism with its emphasis on local color, argues that, in contrast to its use in France, "we [in the Anglo-American world] should doubtless be thankful that in our literature it lends its vivifying force only to objects and sensations of the most unquestioned propriety" (Review of *The Schönberg-Cotta Family* 345). Consequently, it is not surprising that the ideal "literate woman" was most often constituted as a writer of tales of moral fortitude, tales such as Anne Marsh's *Emilia Wyndham,* which, according to an 1846 review in *The Examiner,* is an inspiring story of "common and daily" trials (227). The majority of the anonymous review is taken up by lengthy quotations from the novel, selected to illustrate the admirable qualities of the heroine and hero, Emilia's friends, a sensational moment in which the hero nearly kills himself with a "phial" of strange liquid, followed by his rescue and salvation through the devotion of a good servant and Emilia's love. The reviewer then quotes the moral of the novel:

> And so all ends happily: with the lesson that husbands and wives have much to correct in each other, that duty is a better thing than pleasure, and that there is no apparently evil fortune which a cheerful heart, and an honest patience, and a humble reliance in good, may not help us to endure, till even the endurance brings happiness. (228)

By praising the novel for its depiction of domestic scenes, the reviewer suggests what is "improper" for women's writing: passionate excesses, unpleasant scenes, realistic representations of the working class, and so on.

It was novels such as these that led Henry James to claim a growing split between the "cultivated" and the "uncultivated" reader, the latter being "irredeemably inarticulate," "uncritical," and "absorbent" *(Future* xiv). Such a group of readers he referred to, in an 1865 review in *The Nation,* as doing "Sunday reading," a reading which included what he was to call a "special literature" for women and children. The distinction he sets up clearly is designed to make a case for a certain kind of fiction at the expense of another kind. But in the process, all women's writing becomes associated with domestic realism of the weakest sort. The "special literature" by and for women is described by James as being "semi-developed novels" as opposed to "genuine novels." The former are

> books which grown women may read aloud to children without either party being bored; ... they in all cases embody a moral lesson. This latter fact is held to render them incompetent as novels; and doubtless, after all, it does, for a genuine novel the meaning and lesson are infinite; and here they are carefully narrowed down to a special precept. (345)

For the newly literate, then, women's fiction meets a certain need, but, according to James, such works as *The Schönberg-Cotta Family,* the subject of his review, must, to the "impartial reader" as opposed to the "uncritical and absorbent" one, seem repulsive in its "ordinary country-girl jottings" on Methodism.

James's blunt language makes overt what was a similar but more often covert bias in English reviewers' comments on writing by women. He associates their writing, writing he calls "short gaited," with realism, morality, a narrow world-view, ephemeral effects, and the undeveloped mind. In British reviews, an irritating double standard is evident in the polite but hardly serious treatment of writing by women.[6] In an 1849 review of "Noteworthy Novels," Anne Marsh's *Emilia Wyndham* is again the subject of discussion. James Lorimer, the author of the review, clearly finds Marsh tedious and Charlotte Brontë more interesting, preferring Jane Eyre as a character over Emilia. But his criticism, unlike James's, is condescending in its *lack* of directness. After a lengthy paragraph describing his attempt to overlook the "slight" deficiency he finds in Emilia, Lorimer plays the gentleman forced against his will to make a negative judgment:

> There it remains, a fly in our cup, which forbids us to quaff the nectar at our

lips. Such, to a slight—to a very slight—extent, is the case with Emilia Wyndham. Like her author, good, excellent Mrs. Marsh, she is a *wee, wee* bit prosy—the least possible thing "slow." (477)

After several pages of arguing in a similar fashion that the novel is tedious, Lorimer still concludes that this is what the reader, that is, the English gentle-woman, should read:

> She writes as an English gentlewoman should write; and what is better still, she writes what English gentlewomen should read. Her pages are absolutely like green pastures, when we come to them from the barren and terrible scenery of the more ambitious female writers of the day.... We are in no danger with her of falling over a metaphysical precipice into an abyss of unbelief; we feel that her verdure is not indebted for its luxuriance to the heat of a moral volcano. Neither does she belong to those who depend for the interest of their fictions on that which in real life is offensive and disgusting. She seldom paints vicious and degraded characters, or scenes of abject misery; and whilst we remain with her we are pretty safe from having our olfactory nerves regaled by the odours of the workhouse and the dock.... *Emilia Wyndham* is a complete example of the style of novel in which Mrs. Marsh is qualified to succeed, whilst in itself it is also the happiest of her creations. (479)

The value of the book, then, lies in what it keeps invisible: moral volcanoes, vicious or degraded characters, scenes of misery, the working class, crimi-nals, and adultery. What it does offer, we find, is what women "can succeed at"—a simple plot, strong characters, and good detail (481). For Lorimer, reading for women should function as a "tonic" for boredom, a source of moral uplift, and a distraction during times of suffering. Written in 1849, one year after the year of revolutions, Lorimer was arguing for fiction as escape rather than fiction as reform. But in the process, he too associates novels by women with a particular (limited) sphere of influence and style—one which must be so limited as to protect the unsophisticated reader he imagines the novel to have.

For women writers and reviewers like Harriet Martineau and George Eliot, the question of how seriously novels by women would be treated motivated such review essays as Eliot's 1856 "Silly Novels by Lady Novelists" in the *Westminster Review*. She, like Charlotte Brontë, was well aware that male reviewers had a tendency to overpraise writing by women as a double-edged gesture of chivalry which flattered and demeaned at the same time.[7]

> We are aware that our remarks are in a very different tone from that of the reviewers who, with a perennial recurrence of precisely similar emotions, only paralleled, we imagine, in the experience of monthly nurses, tell one lady nov-elist after another that they "hail" her production with delight. (459–60)

Consequently, she herself represented many women writers as "silly," grouping them into the "mind-and-millinery species," novels supposedly about real life but actually hopelessly distorted imitations of upper-class worldliness; the "oracular species," novels in which the writer expounds her unintentionally shallow religious, philosophical, or moral theories; the "white neck-cloth species," novels meant to be Evangelical travesties of the fashionable novel; and the "modern-antique species," novels meant to revive an ancient historical period. Eliot's attack on such novelists was designed to undermine them as "representatives of the feminine intellect" (455). For her, the rush into print by such women empowered the view that "the average nature of women is too shallow and feeble a soil to bear much tillage" and is therefore "only fit for the very lightest crops" (455). And the most "mischievous form of feminine silliness," she argues, appears in the literary form because it is so widely read and tends to confirm "the popular prejudice against the more solid education of women" (454). She concludes with an appeal for a truer representation:

> On this ground, we believe that the average intellect of women is unfairly represented by the mass of feminine literature, and that while the few women who write well are very far above the ordinary intellectual level of their sex, the many women who write ill are very far below it. (460)

Nowhere does Eliot suggest that the general readers of novels are too unsophisticated to appreciate good writers like Gaskell, Brontë, and Martineau; rather, her concern is focused on the reviewers themselves who clearly promote mediocre writing by women as a way of characterizing women's literacy in general. Her review is an attempt to put such representations out of play.

A similar review appearing in the same year in *Fraser's Magazine* discusses the treatment of love in novels and shares Eliot's assessment of current fiction. This reviewer, like Eliot, assumes that the reader is not endangered by reading novels, that, in fact, most readers of the genre are already familiar with its conventions. Consequently, they are not likely to be deceived by the novel's portrayal of human folly or wickedness. The question the reviewer is apparently addressing at first is whether or not knowledge of such aspects of human behavior is desirable for "the rising generation," who read fiction. Such knowledge could, it was argued, help the reader navigate his or her way through the "shoals of life" (405). The question for fiction, then, was whether or not it presented such features of life in a realistic way, that is, based on experience and capable of practical application. Literature is assumed to be a vital instrument of education for the newly literate and rising middle-class and this reviewer, at any rate, argues for their ability to remain unharmed by the novel. As he says, "There is something to be learned even from the discourse of serpents" (405). Whether that may be to learn that some writers were wasting their time and talent or even some lesson in what not to do when composing, the reader would have to be "very shallow and frivolous" indeed to be led astray (405). After all, the readers already know, from the novels their "grandmothers" read, not to be surprised at the timely appearance off a "handsome but ambiguous stranger" since it is from "his avatar the discerning reader, familiar with the shoals' and quicksands of tender woe, sees land afar off" (406). Earlier readers, the argument goes, were more willing to suspend their disbelief and innocently accept contrivances in a plot which contemporary readers, who exist in a more practical world, would not (407).

Although such reviewers denied that the reader was endangered by the novel, they did not deny the link between certain types of novels and gender, nor the notion of separate spheres. Many women reviewers and writers supported such positioning simply because it did, at least, give them some power—power they lacked in other aspects of their lives. Control over representations of women writers and the reading public often meant a chance to contribute to the economic success of an otherwise unempowered group. For some women reviewers, it was a chance to assert some control over literacy for moral reasons. And for others, like Elizabeth Rigby, it meant a way of excluding certain people from the middle and upper classes and protecting themselves from fears of anarchy that reading and writing by the "masses" might bring. For them, as for the majority of the reviewers, male or female, the reviews became a way of policing behavior by establishing notions of propriety in fiction by women. But regardless of the personal motivations of these reviewers, the result was an overdetermined construction of the "literate woman" as a primarily subjective, expressive writer who produced domestic fiction of limited scope, both intellectually and topically. Her readers were gendered as female, lower to middle class, with some to no sophistication about literary conventions, and with few expectations of the novel other than entertainment. Finally, such literacy was eventually expanded to include all "popular" literature, as a split between high and low art developed throughout the century.[8] It was representations of a mass literacy such as this against which women writers found themselves forced to fight in order to enter a literary elite. For the writers who wanted to "speak out of turn," resistance would not be easy. That they did so testifies to their determination and skill; that their effects were less than subversive then, and more so now, testifies as well to the equal power of social and critical representations of writing by women.

NOTES

1. Other sites of contention included educational materials and practices, magazines for working- and middle-class women, and advice books for women and men.

2. I am indebted throughout this section to T.W. Heyck's *The Transformation of Intellectual Life in Victorian England* (London: Croom Helm, 1982, especially pp. 31–33.

3. For a full discussion of this situation for women novelists, see the separate critical work of Sutherland, Showalter, and Kelley.

4. James's comments and how such literacies were being constituted at the turn of the century are part of a larger argument made in "Education: Literacy and Literature" (Batsleer 1985) which examines how political processes within the British educational system instituted literature as the basis of a "national" education and, consequently, of a massive ideological project. The literary reviews I discuss here are an earlier site for such political uses of literature to promote definitions of literacy divided by gender and class.

5. Actually, although there were some notable exceptions among women writers, theories about a female imagination usually split into two types. Theories which associated creativity with passion saw the female imagination as particularly dangerous, leading to immoral conduct or hysteria unless controlled or, failing that, repressed altogether. Other theories, such as the one Lewes advocated, claimed women's imaginations were generally limited and writing was merely compensation for sexual and emotional frustration. In any case, the theories have to be seen against notions of the masculine imagination outlined here which established "artistic creation" as essentially a male activity. For an excellent survey of such theories, see Helsinger, Sheets, and Veeder (1983).

6. For further discussion of such a double standard, see Inga-Stina Ewbanks (1966) and Showalter's *A Literature of Their Own* (1977), 73–98.

7. See, especially, the reference to such a double standard in Brontë's "Biographical Notice" Published in the 1850 edition of E. Brontë's *Wuthering Heights*.

8. Who the readers actually were is still debated, but the definitive study is Richard Altick's *The English Common Reader: A Social History of the Mass Reading Public, 1800–1900* (Chicago: U of Chicago P, 1957.)

WORKS CITED

Altick, Richard. *The English Common Reader: A Social History of the Mass Reading Public, 1800–1900.* Chicago: U of Chicago P, 1957.

————. "English Publishing and the Mass Audience in 1852." *Studies in Bibliography.* VI (1953 for 1954): 3–24.

Batsleer, Janet, Tony Davies, Rebecca O'Rourke, and Chris Weedon. *Rewriting English: Cultural Politics of Gender and Class.* London and New York: Methuen, 1985.

[Eliot, George]. "Silly Novels by Lady Novelists." *Westminster Review.* 66 (1856): 442-61.

[————]. Rev. of *Emilia Wyndham. The Literary Examiner.* April 11 (1846): 227–29.

Ewbank, Inga-Stina. *Their Proper Sphere: A Study of the Brontë Sisters as Early-Victorian Novelists.* Cambridge: Harvard UP, 1966.

Gross, John. *The Rise and Fall of the Man of Letters: A Study of the Idiosyncratic and the Humane in Modern Literature.* New York: Macmillan, 1969.

Helsinger, Elizabeth K., Robin Lauterbach Sheets, and William Veeder. *Literary Issues: 1837-1883.* Vol. III *The Woman Question: Society and Literature in Britain and America, 1837–1883.* New York and London: Garland, 1983.

Heyck, T. W. *The Transformation of Intellectual Life in Victorian England.* London: Croom Helm, 1982.

[Hutton, R. H.] "Novels by the Authoress of 'John Halifax.'" *North British Review.* 29 (1858): 466-81.

James, Henry. *The Future of the Novel: Essays on the Art of Fiction.* Ed. Leon Edel. Vintage, New York, 1956.

————. Rev. of *"The Schönberg-Cotta Family." The Nation.*

Kelley, Mary. *Private Woman, Public Stage: Literary Domesticity in Nineteenth-Century America.* New York: Oxford UP, 1984.

[————]. "The Lady Novelists." *Westminster Review.* 56 (July, 1852): 129–41; rpt. in Elaine Showalter, ed. *Women's Liberation and Literature.* New York: Harcourt Brace Jovanovich, 1971.

[Lorimer, James]. "Noteworthy Novels." *North British Review,* 11 (1849): 475–93.

"On the Treatment of Love in Novels." *Fraser's Magazine.* 53 (1856): 405–18.

Poovey, Mary. *Uneven Developments: The Ideological Work of Gender in Mid-Victorian England.* Chicago: U of Chicago P, 1988.

[Rigby, Elizabeth]. "Vanity Fair, Jane Eyre, and Governesses." *Quarterly Review.* 84 (Dec. 1848): 162, 176.

[————]. Rev. of *"Shirley: A Tale." Edinburgh Review,* 91 (Jan 1850): 153–73.

Showalter, Elaine. *A Literature of Their Own: British Women Novelists from Brontë to Lessing*. Princeton: Princeton UP, 1977.

Sutherland, J. A. *Victorian Novelists and Publishers*. Chicago: U of Chicago P, 1976.

Robinson Crusoe and Friday in Victorian Britain: "Discipline," "Dialogue," and Collins's Critique of Empire in *The Moonstone*

Lillian Nayder

Unlike the majority of Victorian novels, *The Moonstone* is not related by an "omniscient narrator," whose unimpeachable authority imposes itself on the reader. Instead, the story is told in a succession of narratives written by some of the characters and organized through their limited points of view ... however, the "unreliable" and "contradictory" narrative structure of *The Moonstone* works only as a ruse ... To use Mikhail Bakhtin's term, the novel is thoroughly *monological*—always speaking a master-voice that corrects, overrides, subordinates, or sublates all other voices it allows to speak ... the monologism of the narration is exactly analogous to the work of detection in the representation. Just as a common detection transcends the single efforts of various detective figures, a common narration subsumes the individual reports of various narrators. The world resolves its difficulties, and language finds its truth, according to the same principle of quasi-automatic self-regulation.

D. A. Miller, *The Novel and the Police*, 54–56

I

Perhaps more clearly than any other recent study of Victorian fiction, D. A. Miller's *The Novel and the Police* suggests both the pleasures and the pitfalls of reading the English novel through the eyes of Michel Foucault. Like John Bender's *Imagining the Penitentiary*, a study of eighteenth-century English fiction that "sets out from Foucault" (xv), Miller's book uses the concept of "discipline" as it is developed in *Discipline and Punish* to illuminate a variety of novels.[1] Miller calls attention to the subtle yet pervasive modes of social control that operate in a genre traditionally considered lawless, subversive of both social and literary conventions. Although Bender focuses on eighteenth-century novels and Miller on Victorian ones, both critics are engaged in a common revisionary project—to redefine our understanding of a genre commonly described as a mouthpiece of dissent. According to these critics, the ostensibly lawless novel actually performs a "penitential" and a "policing" function.[2]

Miller's work contributes in important ways to the ongoing reassessment of the Victorian novel,[3] and it might serve as a model to those scholars who uncritically accept the self-representations of the novelists about whom they write; it provides us with a timely warning against accepting novels on their own terms. Unlike many of the Victorian scholars who precede him, Miller rejects the "claim ... much advertised in the novel and its literary criticism" that the novel exists in a "critical relation to society"; according to Miller, the very fact that the novel strenuously promotes this view suggests that we should question it (xii, 2).

In *The Novel and the Police,* Miller reveals the inadequacies of a literary criticism that is insufficiently critical, that unwittingly promotes the ideology of the works under study rather than exposing it. But at the same time, Miller's own approach suggests the inadequacies of what has come to be known as "the hermenuetics of suspicion"—of a literary criticism that is *overly* critical, and fails to give writers their due. As Paul Cantor notes in "Stoning the Romance," critics of nineteenth-century literature are, in increasing numbers, demanding "ideological purity" from the writers they study, and expressing dissatisfaction when their demands are not met (707). Describing ideology critique as "a case of one ideology versus another," Cantor asks that nineteenth-century writers "be given credit for the advances they achieved, and not blamed for failing to live up completely to contemporary ideological standards" (709–10, 715).

One of Cantor's main points is that ideology critique emphasizes what writers fail to achieve rather than what they manage to accomplish. In Miller's case, this emphasis is *required* by the Foucauldian premises on which his criticism is based. In the panoptical society that Miller inherits from Foucault, novelists and politicians alike are powerless to achieve much of anything; the possibility of social reform or revolution is precluded by the dissemination of power in the modern state. We are caught in the "intangible networks of productive discipline," Miller asserts (51); "the diffusion of discipline's operations precludes locating them in an attackable center," and hence effective opposition to authority is impossible (17, 62).[4]

The limitations of this approach to the Victorian novel are suggested by the way in which Miller appropriates Bakhtin's theory of the novel, in an attempt to bring it into line with the ideas of Foucault. In *The Dialogic Imagination,* Bakhtin describes the novel as a genre divided by antagonistic forces, which he identifies as "monologic" and "dialogic." The monologic or "centripetal" forces tend toward ideological unity, and the dialogic or "centrifugal" forces toward plurality. According to Bakhtin, the dialogic forces in the novel ultimately win out—the novelist "dethrones" authoritative discourse. In Bakhtin's view, the novel represents a "multi-languaged consciousness"; by means of parody and stylization, it acknowledges the word of "the other" (366–71).

Although Miller often refers to Bakhtin in *The Novel and the Police,* he makes virtually no mention of the dialogic. As the prefatory passage of this essay suggests, readers unfamiliar with Bakhtin are likely to come away from Miller's book with the idea that *The Dialogic Imagination* is entitled *The Monologic Imagination.* Miller distorts Bakhtin's theory of the novel because there is no place for the dialogic in the disciplinary society that he describes; Bakhtin's ideas cannot be neatly squared with those of Foucault. Bender openly addresses his differences with Bakhtin in *Imagining the Penitentiary,* and accuses him of "romanticizing" the novel, but Miller does not. While Bender takes issue with the freedom that Bakhtin ascribes to the novelist, and asserts that the novel cannot evade "the hegemony of official culture" in the manner that Bakhtin suggests (213), Miller simply makes Bakhtin out to be a Russian Jeremy Bentham: "The panopticism of the novel … coincides with what Mikhail Bakhtin has called its 'monologism,'" he asserts (25).

In an attempt to give Collins and his novel their due, this essay makes a case for the dialogism of *The Moonstone.* It provides what we might call a Bakhtinian reading of *The Moonstone* by locating what, in Miller's eyes, appears utopian—an "attackable center" of authority. A number of critics have noted that Collins attacks British imperialism in *The Moonstone*[5]; this essay argues that Defoe's *Robinson Crusoe* is one of Collins's primary targets. In *The Moonstone,* Collins subtly reworks Defoe's novel in order to challenge the authority of this text—to loosen the hold its imperial ideal had on Victorian readers.[6] Collins reformulates Crusoe's relationship to Friday in a number of ways—in various relationships between the British and the Hindus, and between members of the English upper and lower classes. In so doing, he calls into question Defoe's distinction between the savage and the civilized, and exposes what the ideology of imperialism obscures—the connection between racial and social oppression. Although many of the narrators in *The Moonstone* subscribe to the imperial ideology of their day, Collins is himself performing an act of ideology critique in his novel.

II

In October 1856, Collins joined the staff of *Household Words*, the journal that Dickens edited from 1850 until 1859. Collins wrote more than thirty articles for this journal, among them "A Breach of British Privilege." This article consists of a letter ostensibly written by "John Bull," who suspects that Collins is "not English to the back-bone": "I doubt whether you know your Rule Britannia as you ought, and whether you sincerely feel that we are the 'dread and envy' of every foreign community on the face of the earth" (361). Elsewhere in *Household Words*, Collins treats "Rule Britannia" in a way that confirms such suspicions. Both "The Perils of Certain English Prisoners" (1857) and "A Sermon for Sepoys" (1858) address what was probably the most notorious episode in British imperial history—the Indian Mutiny of 1857. They do so in a way that sets Collins apart from the patriotic majority, in whose eyes the Mutiny demonstrated the superiority of the British to the "morally depraved" Oriental.

The Indian Mutiny began in May of 1857. Although the Indian sepoys employed in the British Army had political and economic greviances, the immediate cause of their revolt was religious. Enfield rifles had been introduced into the Army, and the ends of the new, greased cartridges had to be bitten off before they were loaded. The sepoys believed that the cartridges were greased with cow or pig fat, and hence sacrilegious to Hindus or Muslims. Suspecting that the British were forcing them to commit sacrilege, the sepoys rebelled, murdering English women and children. When the British regained control of India later in the year, they committed atrocities of their own—hanging Indians without trial, blowing them from guns, looting and plundering recaptured towns, and massacring civilians. Their actions were generally applauded at home, where the Mutiny had triggered an unprecedented wave of racial hatred.[7]

Dickens, for example, loudly applauded the violence of the British in India, and the "mutilation" of those "wretched Hindoo[s] ... blown from an English gun."[8] "I wish I were Commander in Chief in India," he wrote to Angela Burdett-Coutts on 4 October 1857. "The first thing I would do to strike that Oriental race with amazement ... should be to proclaim to them, in their language, that I considered my holding that appointment by the leave of

God, to mean that I should do my utmost to exterminate the Race upon whom the stain of the late cruelties rested" (Johnson 350).

Dickens decided to "commemorate" what he considered the heroic resistance of the British in India by writing a story based on the Mutiny for the 1857 Christmas number of *Household Words*. He asked Collins to help him write this story, and together they produced "The Perils of Certain English Prisoners."[9] "The Perils" consists of three chapters, the first and third by Dickens, and the second by Collins. It describes an attack in an English colony in Central America; the colony is an island where the silver taken from a mine in Honduras is temporarily stored. English women and children are assaulted and some killed by a heterogenous band of pirates, who raid the island for the silver store. The first chapter portrays the leisurely life on the island before the attack, and ends with the victory of the pirates over the colonists; the second recounts the imprisonment of the British in the jungle; the third describes their escape and eventual victory over their captors.

What is most striking about "The Perils" are its inconsistencies in tone and characterization, which suggest that the intentions of the coauthors are at odds. In the first chapter, for example, Dickens describes the martyrdom of the Englishwomen in the colony, who prefer death to sexual violation: "I want you to make me a promise," Miss Maryon tells Private Davis, "that if we are defeated, and you are absolutely sure of my being taken, you will kill me." "I shall not be alive to do it, Miss," Davis replies. "I shall have died in your defense before it comes to that" (260). In the second chapter, by contrast, Collins portrays the English prisoners struggling to suppress their laughter at the comic antics of the pirate chief, who plays his guitar "in a languishing attitude ... singing foreign songs, with a shrill voice and with his nose conceitedly turned up in the air" (231).

Patrick Brantlinger notes that Victorian writing about the Mutiny generally conforms to a "racist pattern" in which the British are good and the Indians evil: "good and evil, innocence and guilt, justice and injustice, moral restraint and sexual depravity ... are perceived as racially determined attributes in an imperialist allegory that calls for the total subjugation ... and at times for the wholesale extermination of Indians" (200). While Dickens conforms to this pattern in "The Perils," Collins does not. Dickens' chapters are largely melodramatic, and pit the demonic pirates against their innocent British victims. But Collins's chapter is comic, and blurs the stark moral distinctions that Dickens establishes.

Indeed, Collins uses the pirate captain to expose what Dickens obscures— the abuses committed by the British officers in India. Dickens models the

pirate captain on the stereotype of the sadistic sepoy, who "playfully" muti-
lates his English captives with his cutlass (267). Collins models the pirate
captain on the dandified British officers in the Indian Army, known for their
extravagant living and their inhumanity towards their Indian servants.[10]
Collins's pirate parades among his camp followers with stiffened coat-skirts
and lace cravat, like one of "the dandies in the Mall in London" (269). He
abuses the natives under his command, using their backs as writing desks, all
the while complaining of their stench, and covering his nose with "a fine
cambric handkerchief," scented and edged with lace (270–71).

As his biographer Nuel Pharr Davis suggests, Collins makes "a burlesque
out of Dickens' philippic against the sepoys" in "The Perils" (207–8).[11] He
breaks with the racist pattern of Mutiny literature by calling attention to
British rather than Indian excesses. In "A Sermon for Sepoys," similarly, he
suggests that the Indians—portrayed as "mired in changeless patterns of
superstition and violence" in the Mutiny literature (Brantlinger 200)—can be
reformed. Brantlinger observes that British writing about India before 1857
"frequently admitted the possibility that Indians might be helped to progress
in the scale of civilization," but that after the sepoy revolt these "hopeful
though obviously ethnocentric possibilities" were denied (200). Yet Collins
not only believes the mutineers can be reformed; he feels that reformers
should look to Oriental rather than Western ideals in accomplishing this goal.
Instead of preaching to the rebellious Indians from a Christian text, Collins
draws his sermon from one of their own—from the lesson delivered to the
seventeenth-century Muslim Emperor Shah Jehan ("the wise, the bountiful,
the builder of the new city of Delhi") by the wise man Abbas:

> The more gifts you have received, the better use it is expected you will make of
> them. Although the All-Powerful alone can implant virtue in the human heart, it
> is still possible for you, as the dreaded representative of authority, to excite to
> deeds of benevolence, even those who may have no better motive for doing
> good, than the motive of serving their own interests.... Spread the example,
> therefore, of your own benevolence, beyond the circle of those only who are
> wise and good ... and fortify your mind with the blessed conviction that the life
> you will then lead, will be of all lives the most acceptable in the eyes of the
> Supreme Being. (247)

In delivering this lesson, an Oriental parable of the talents, and in representing benevolent and charitable Muslims, Collins dissociates himself from
Dickens, who called for the extermination of "that Oriental race." Collins
suggests that the Indians are as capable of moral goodness as the British
are—a suggestion strikingly out of keeping with the racist sentiments of the
day.

III

Like his chapter in "The Perils" and his "Sermon for Sepoys," *The Moonstone* (1868) breaks with the conventions of Mutiny literature. It does so by depicting Anglo-Indian relations in a way that underscores the criminality of the British imperialists rather than that of the natives. Unlike Henry Kingsley's *Stretton* (1869) and James Grant's *First Love and Last Love: A Tale of the Indian Mutiny* (1868), which promote the stereotype of the sexually violent mutineer, Collins's work portrays the British as lustful and murderous, inverting the standard formula of mutiny novels.[12] Knowing how "John Bull" would respond to an attack on British actions in India ten years before, Collins displaces his critique by describing the more distant Seige of Seringapatam (1799), which established British hegemony in India and stifled the imperial ambitions of the French. The anarchy and destruction wrought by British officers and soldiers during this seige, and described in Collins's prologue, call to mind the way in which the British plundered Delhi and murdered its civilian inhabitants after putting down the revolt.[13]

In *The Moonstone,* eleven different narrators tell the story of a sacred Hindu diamond that is stolen and restolen four times in the course of the narrative. Three of these four thefts are committed by Englishmen. The central plot of the novel is set in 1848–1849. But the "prologue" opens in Seringapatam, shortly before and after the British seige. During the looting that follows, John Herncastle, a British officer, steals the moonstone from its three Brahmin guards and murders them. He then brings the gem to England, bequeathing it to his niece Rachel Verinder. On June 21, 1848, the night that Rachel receives the moonstone, it is stolen by the man she loves, her first cousin Franklin Blake; Blake is acting under the influence of opium, which has been secretly administered to him, and remains ignorant of his crime for much of the novel. On that same night, the Exeter Hall philanthropist Godfrey Ablewhite, another cousin who is pressed for funds, steals the moonstone from Blake. A year later, the three Brahmins who have followed the gem from India to England (and who are descendents of its original guards), steal it from Ablewhite and murder him. The novel ends with a ceremony celebrating the restoration of the moonstone to its Indian shrine, which is observed by Mr. Murthwaite, an English authority on India.

Of the four crimes committed in the novel, Collins mitigates two—those committed by the Brahmins and by Franklin Blake. In the case of the Brahmins, Collins redefines the nature of their crime in his epilogue, explaining its significance in Hindu rather than Christian terms; they have not committed theft and murder, but have forfeited their caste in the service of their god.[14] The epilogue is narrated by Murthwaite, whom Collins consistently represents as a vital and reliable source of information about the Orient. By means of Murthwaite's heightened and lyrical description, Collins encourages us to think of the Brahmins as martyrs rather than murderers; they are purified rather than punished at the conclusion of the novel:

> The god had commanded that their purification should be the purification by pilgrimage. On that night, the three men were to part. In three separate directions, they were to set forth as pilgrims to the shrines of India. Never more were they to rest on their wanderings, from the day which witnessed their separation, to the day which witnessed their death. (526)

Although on entirely different grounds, Franklin Blake also proves to be innocent of the crime he has committed; he steals the diamond unconsciously, out of concern for Rachel Verinder's welfare. But Collins offers no such excuses for Herncastle and Ablewhite, the other two Englishmen who steal the diamond, and who represent the military and the moral might of the British empire. Instead, Collins condemns the hypocrisy and greed of the ostensibly civilized philanthropist and the lawlessness of the ostensibly disciplined military officer, exposing the false pretences upon which the Empire is built.

The Moonstone portrays the injustice of imperial conquest, and it is one of Collins's central ironies that Gabriel Betteredge, a primary narrator, valorizes that idyll of empire building, Defoe's *Robinson Crusoe*. Betteredge, the steward at the Verinder estate, treats *Robinson Crusoe* as if it were his bible; he "believe[s] in *Robinson Crusoe*" (110) in the way that his fellow narrator Miss Clack believes in the divine. Betteredge begins his narrative by quoting from Defoe's, and he consistently acts on its "authority" (45):

> such a book as *Robinson Crusoe* never was written, and never will be written again. I have tried that book for years … and I have found it my friend in need in all the necessities of this mortal life. When my spirits are bad—*Robinson Crusoe*. When I want advice—*Robinson Crusoe*. In past times, when my wife plagued me; in present times, when I have had a drop too much—*Robinson Crusoe*. I have worn out six stout *Robinson Crusoes* with hard work in my service. On my lady's last birthday she gave me a seventh. (41)

The way in which Betteredge describes *Robinson Crusoe* suggests his affinities with Defoe's protagonist. Like Crusoe, Betteredge believes in "hard work" and "Economy" (43). In the manner of his literary prototype, he provides us with the bargain price of his book—four shillings and sixpence (41). He cares little for the company of women, marrying because it is cheaper than hiring a maid (43). And, most importantly, he shares Crusoe's belief in the inherent superiority of the British to the native. Betteredge responds to the Indians who appear at the Verinder estate in much the same way that Crusoe reacts to the cannibals who visit his island—with a mixture of fear and moral self-righteousness. Betteredge refers to Crusoe's terror of the "savage wretches" in describing his own fear of the Brahmins—a set of murdering thieves" who have "invaded" the "quiet English house" he helps to maintain (67, 109).

In his monologic reading of *The Moonstone,* Miller identifies Betteredge as Collins's "spokesman." According to Miller, Betteredge embodies the "collective cognition" of the novel, and expresses the "norms" shared by the community (45). Miller describes what he sees as "the plain dealing" of Gabriel's "self-presentation," and the "unproblematic" nature of his language: "His narrative may not tell us 'the whole truth,' but it can be relied upon to tell us 'nothing but the truth'" (53–54). Although Miller notes that Betteredge "treats *Robinson Crusoe* like an oracle," he dismisses this trait as an "idiosyncracy" that does little or nothing to discredit the authority of the "faithful retainer" (53–54).

Yet we are bound to misconstrue Collins's intentions if we dismiss Betteredge's view of *Robinson Crusoe* in this way. The uses to which Betteredge puts Defoe's novel are central to Collins's conception of this narrator; and they provide the measure of his *un*reliability. Betteredge reads the actions of the Brahmins through the eyes of Robinson Crusoe, but Collins does not. Although the Indians commit murder in the course of the narrative, they do so in order to retrieve their sacred gem and serve their god, not to feast on the bodies of their enemies; unlike the cannibals in *Robinson Crusoe,* the Brahmins are the wronged party in *The Moonstone.* Defoe's Crusoe thwarts the cannibals when they are about to feast on a European victim—"to butcher the poor Christian, and bring him perhaps limb by limb to their fire" (234). Collins's Europeans, by contrast, butcher the Hindus, as the narrator of the prologue observes:

> I got to an open door, and saw the bodies of two Indians (by their dress, as I guessed, officers of the palace) lying across the entrance, dead.
> A cry inside hurried me into a room, which appeared to serve as an armoury. A third Indian, mortally wounded, was sinking at the feet of a man whose back was towards me. The man turned at the instant when I came in, and I saw John Herncastle, with a torch in one hand, and a dagger dripping with blood in the other. A stone, set like a pommel, in the end of the dagger's handle, flashed in the torchlight, as he turned on me, like a gleam of fire. The dying Indian sank to his knees, pointed to the dagger in Herncastle's hand, and said, in his native language:—"The Moonstone will have its vengeance yet on you and yours!" He spoke those words, and fell dead on the floor. (36–37)

Betteredge refers to the Brahmins as "murdering thieves," but Collins suggests that this label applies to the Englishman who initially steals the gem, killing three Brahmins in the process. Unlike Defoe, Collins portrays the "deplorable excesses" (36) of the colonizers rather than the colonized.

Collins not only quotes from *Robinson Crusoe* but redraws its battle lines, subverting Defoe's distinction between the civilized Englishman and the uncivilized native.[15] He treats the Brahmins' faith with the seriousness that Defoe accords solely to Crusoe's Christian evangelicalism. While Defoe ridicules the heathen beliefs of Friday, for whom "old Benamuckee" is god (218), Collins reveals the religious hypocrisy of the evangelical movement, to which his two most corrupt characters, Ablewhite and Clack, belong. He further blurs the distinction between British and native by casting the Brahmins in Crusoe's role, as patrons. In Defoe's novel, the English castaway adopts the young native Friday, saving his life and teaching him Christianity; in *The Moonstone,* the Brahmins adopt an English boy, rescuing him from a life of poverty and teaching him their prophetic powers. The Indians appear at the Verinder estate in the guise of strolling conjurors, accompanied by their young English servant. After the Indians are warned off the premises, Penelope Betteredge and a friend watch their "proceedings," suspecting that the English boy is "ill-used by the foreigners." The Indians put the boy into a claivoiyant trance, but before they can do so they must pour an ink-like substance into the palm of his hand. As Gabriel Betteredge explains, they gain his cooperation in the following way:

> when the Indian said, "Hold out your hand," the boy shrunk back, and shook his head, and said he didn't like it. The Indian, thereupon, asked him (not at all unkindly), whether he would like to be sent back to London, and left where they had found him, sleeping in an empty basket in a market—a hungry, ragged, and forsaken little boy. This, it seems, ended the difficulty. (50)

The Indians use the English boy for their own purposes—to foresee the arrival of the moonstone in Yorkshire; but they do not *ill*-use him. They treat the boy better than do his fellow Englishmen, who allow children like him to live in marketplaces and sleep in baskets. It is left to the ostensibly savage Brahmins to remove the "hungry, ragged, and forsaken" child from the wilds of London. In this portrait of Anglo-Indian relations, Collins exposes the savagery of the English class system rather than that of the Brahmins.

Victorian social reformers often called attention to the barbarism they observed in the London streets. For example, Henry Mayhew, in *London Labour and the London Poor* (1851), describes the London costermongers, "as little developed in their intellects ... and religious state" as the "savages on the other side of the globe" (Brantlinger 116). Like Mayhew, Collins acknowledges the demoralized condition of the English poor in his essays and his fiction. But he offers the more radical critique that what is truly savage in England is the social system that has produced these "heathen." In "Laid Up in Lodgings," for instance, first published in *Household Words* in June 1856, Collins portrays a maid he met in a London boarding house, and suggests that her portrait could be used in "a book about a savage country," as "a specimen of the female population." However, the ignorant and voiceless maid is not his target in this essay. His target is the savage social system that has left this "poor creature" hopeless and mute:

> Life means dirty work, small wages, hard words, no holidays, no social station, no future, according to her experience of it. No human being ever was created for this. No state of society which composedly accepts this, in the cases of thousands, as one of the necessary conditions of its selfish comforts, can pass itself off as civilized, except under the most audacious of all false pretenses. (121)

Collins returns to this subject in "Highly Proper," an article that Dickens found too radical for his tastes.[16] Condemning the "barbarism" of "class prejudice," Collins identifies snobbish members of the middle and upper classes as the "English heathen" rather than ignorant maids and costermongers. He argues that those upper class Englishmen who safeguard social barriers are more in need of Dr. Livingstone than the foreign and domestic savages of whom Mayhew speaks (362). For Collins, ostensibly civilized Englishmen prove barbaric not only in their dealings with the so-called subject races, but also in their treatment of the working class at home.

Collins incorporates this social critique in *The Moonstone* by casting Betteredge in the role of Friday. Although readers are likely to categorize Betteredge with the other faithful retainers so often found in Victorian novels, Collins's view of the savage class system suggests that his portrait of the English servant may be more complex than we assume. Indeed, it is one of Collins's ironies that, in identifying with Defoe's European master, Betteredge overlooks his connection to the exploited native servant. At one point in his narrative, Betteredge implicitly equates his services with those of Defoe's native; refusing to assist Sergeant Cuff with his investigation, Betteredge hopes that he has, in effect, left the detective "without a man Friday to keep him company" (207). But Collins's "man Friday" generally likes to think of himself as a Crusoe figure, to compare his experiences with those of the English imperialist.[17] Collins subtly develops the connection that Betteredge ignores, reformulating *Robinson Crusoe* in such a way that the faithful retainer plays the part of both Crusoe *and* Friday. In so doing, Collins reminds us of what the imperial ideology encourages us to forget—that working-class Englishmen may be masters in India, but they remain servants at home.

While Betteredge plays the part of Crusoe in his dealings with the Indians, he plays the part of Friday in his dealings with Lady Verinder. She is the mistress whom he obeys. Like Friday, who gladly learns to call Crusoe "Master," and uncritically accepts the ideology of the man he serves, Betteredge gladly obeys his social superiors and accepts his place in their social scheme. He identifies his interests with those of his Lady; on those rare occasions when he speaks of class differences, he does so only jokingly, in order to express his pity for the members of the idle class rather than resentment toward them:

> Gentlefolks in general have a very awkward rock ahead in life—the rock ahead of their own idleness.... It often falls heavy enough, no doubt, on people who are really obliged to get their living, to be forced to work for the clothes that cover them, the roof that shelters them, and the food that keeps them going. But compare the hardest day's work you ever did with the idleness [of the gentry] ... and thank your stars that your head has got something it *must* think of, and your hands something that they *must* do. (84–85)

Friday will go nowhere without his master: "no wish Friday there, no master there," he tells Crusoe (227). Betteredge expresses the same loyalty, although in better English: "It was all one to me where I went, so long as my mistress and I were together" (42).

In *Robinson Crusoe,* Defoe presents Friday as the ideal native, devoted and grateful to his European master for weaning him from his savage ways. But Collins does not idealize the faithful retainer. Instead, he stages a confrontation between Betteredge and Lucy Yolland, a crippled, working-class woman characterized by her sense of class injury. In *Robinson Crusoe,* Friday's father remains "a pagan and a cannibal" (241), but does not object to his son's conversion to the Protestant faith and the ways of his European master. Lucy, by contrast, treats Betteredge with scorn for his respectful deference to his social superiors. Lucy is the friend of Rosanna Spearman, a housemaid unlucky enough to fall in love with the gentleman Franklin Blake. When Rosanna kills herself out of despair, Lucy expresses her sense of outrage at Blake's cruelty:

> "Where's the man you call Franklin Blake?" says the girl, fixing me with a fierce look, as she rested herself on her crutch.
> "That's not a respectful way to speak of any gentleman," I answered. "If you wish to inquire for my lady's nephew, you will please to mention him as Mr. Franklin Blake."

> She limped a step nearer to me, and looked as if she could have eaten me alive. *"Mr.* Franklin Blake?" she repeated after me. "Murderer Franklin Blake would be a fitter name for him.... Where is he?" cries the girl, lifting her head from the crutch, and flaming out again through her tears. "Where's this gentleman that I mustn't speak of, except with respect? Ha, Mr. Betteredge, the day is not far off when the poor will rise against the rich. I pray Heaven they may begin with *him."* (226–27)

If *The Moonstone* is in some sense a mutiny novel, a representation of imperial affairs, it is also a novel about class resentment and the threat of social rebellion at home. Although Collins endorses neither Lucy's call for revolution nor the Indian Mutiny, he juxtaposes the two rebellions in order to reveal what Betteredge does not see—the connection between the exploitation of the English working class and that of the subject races. As Brantlinger notes, the imperial ideology sought to obscure this connection, and hence to maintain the social status quo. By appealing to the patriotism of the workers, and defining the native as the common enemy of the British, whether rich or poor, imperialism "deflected ... working-class radicalism ... into noncritical paths" (35). In *The Moonstone,* Betteredge is hardly a working-class radical; but Collins has him unwittingly make the connection that his own ideology obscures. He conflates angry workers with hostile primitives when he describes Lucy as a cannibal of sorts, fearing that she wants to "eat him alive."[18] And he lodges the same complaint against the English housemaid that he does against the high-caste Brahmins; in his view, neither Rosanna nor the Indians know their place.[19] The faithful retainer immediately distrusts the Indians because their "manners are superior to [his] own" (49), just as he distrusts Rosanna because she gives herself "airs": "plain as she was, there was just a dash of something that wasn't like a housemaid, and that *was* like a lady, about her" (55).

Rosanna Spearman and Lucy Yolland, like the mutinous Indians, are upstarts who do not accept the place assigned to them by the ruling class. As a result, they are categorized by the gentlefolk and the more complacent workers in much the same way that the Brahmins are—as "unnatural," "monstrous," "criminal," and "mad" (80, 185, 353). Although two English gentlemen have stolen the moonstone from Rachel Verinder, it is the housemaid and the Brahmins, those characters who most blatantly challenge their superiors, who are initially suspected of the crime.[20] Betteredge ridicules his daughter for believing she is "to be forthwith tried, sentenced, and transported for theft" (131) because he fails to comprehend the ideological basis of this punishment, and hence the basis of her fear—the convenient transformation of working-class poverty and resentment into "otherness," "criminality" and "cannibalism" in the eyes of the upper classes.[21] In "Laid Up in Lodgings," Collins exposes the injustice of this transformation, pointing out that servants are accused of theft on the sole grounds that they are impoverished: "a lady ... misses one of a pair of lace cuffs, and feels sure that the servant has taken it. There is not a particle of evidence to support this view of the case; but [the maid] being destitute, is consequently condemned without a trial, and dismissed without a character" (123). Similarly, in *The Woman in White* (1860), Collins suggests that the category of "madness" is a tool of social oppression; the baronet, Sir Percival Glyde, imprisons Anne Catherick in a private asylum because she threatens his authority. Collins reveals the ideological function of imperial as well as social typology in *The Moonstone*. He exposes the injustice of a system in which British gentlemen commit murder and robbery, while those they exploit, both at home and abroad, are labelled "cannibals," "murderers" and "thieves."[22]

IV

Rather than resting secure in the "stable truths" of the British empire, as Miller suggests he does, Collins reveals their ideological purpose. Like Robinson Crusoe on his island, Gabriel Betteredge speaks for these "truths," in what Miller terms a "master voice." But Collins does not. He represents Betteredge as both Crusoe and Friday in order to reveal the ironies of his position as a servant who speaks like a master. Unlike Defoe, Collins makes us aware of what this "master voice" fails to express—the angry tones of those English and Indian "Fridays" who are less than satisfied with their lot. Although both Defoe and Collins portray the relationship between language and power in their novels, they do so for very different ends. Crusoe tells us that, before Friday's arrival, his parrot was the only creature he allowed to speak (157). Like "Poll," Friday unthinkingly repeats what he hears Robinson Crusoe say. "The aptest schollar that ever was," the native gladly learns those English words that Crusoe selectively teaches him: "I ... taught him to say Master ... and made it my business to teach him every thing that was proper to make him useful, handy, and helpful" (211, 213). Lucy Yolland, by contrast, resists the language lesson that Betteredge delivers; although she refers to Blake as a "gentleman," she does so facetiously. She refuses to parrot her masters in the way that Friday does—to become "useful, handy, and helpful." At the same time, the Brahmins, who know English fluently, only speak it when it suits their purposes—when they are interrogating the lawyer,

Matthew Bruff, for example (324). And Collins's English explorer gladly learns what Defoe's does not—the language of the natives among whom he lives: "I know the language [of the Hindus] as well as I know my own," Murthwaite tells us (524).

As these differences suggest, Collins' novel is dialogic rather than disciplinarian, and more closely resembles J. M. Coetzee's *Foe* than it does *Robinson Crusoe*. In *Foe* (1986), the South African novelist and critic of apartheid rewrites *Robinson Crusoe* from the viewpoint of Susan Barton, a female castaway and Crusoe's island companion. Susan provides us with the "authentic" story of Crusoe and Friday; her narrative "precedes" that of Daniel Defoe, and provides him with his material. Coetzee, like Collins, breaks down Defoe's distinction between the savage and the civilized. Collins casts the Brahmins in the role of Crusoe, while Coetzee suggests that Crusoe has cut out Friday's tongue. Collins recognizes that imperial "typology" is a tool of exploitation; so does Coetzee, who altogether refuses to categorize Friday. Coetzee's critique of Defoe is more stark, more direct, and more searching than that of Collins; unlike Betteredge, Susan Barton sees Crusoe's monologue for what it is. But despite these differences, both the Victorian and the postmodern novelist rewrite *Robinson Crusoe* for the same political purpose: to portray what Crusoe's "autobiography" does not—the realities rather than the idealization of imperial conquest.

NOTES

1. Foucault identifies "discipline" as a diffuse and largely invisible mode of power that began to permeate European societies toward the end of the eighteenth century. According to Foucault, "discipline" is not enforced by any particular institution or leader, but rather consists of "instruments," "techniques," and "procedures," and is thus impossible to resist. To illustrate the diffusion of discipline, Foucault describes Jeremy Bentham's plans for the Panopticon, a prison organized around a central watchtower. In this prison, the inmate is permanently visible, but uncertain of when he is being observed; as a result, "he inscribes in himself the power relation" of prisoner and guard, and "becomes the principle of his own subjection." Miller draws from Foucault's discussion of Bentham in describing the "panopticism" of the novel. See *Discipline and Punish: The Birth of the Prison,* tr. Alan Sheridan (New York: Pantheon, 1977), 202–3.

2. Bender argues that "attitudes toward prison which were formulated between 1719 and 1779 ... in prose fiction ... enabled the conception and construction of actual penitentiary prisons later in the eighteenth century." Miller argues that Victorian novels "systematically participate in a general economy of policing power": "the story of the Novel is essentially the story of an active regulation."

3. See, for example, Myron Magnet's *Dickens and the Social Order* (Philadelphia: U

of Pennsylvania P, 1985), which examines the "other" Dickens—the social disciplinarian rather than the social reformer; and Lennard Davis's *Resisting Novels: Ideology and Fiction* (London: Methuen, 1987), which examines "the regularizing and normalizing features of the novel." Davis draws upon various Victorian novels in developing his thesis—that novel reading effectively prevents social change.

4. For an insightful critique of Foucault's concept of discipline and its use by the new historicists, see Frank Lentriccia, "Michel Foucault's Fantasy for Humanists," in *Ariel and the Police: Michel Foucault, William James, Wallace Stevens* (Madison: U of Wisconsin P, 1987), 29–102.

5. John R. Reed was the first critic to discuss Collins's critique of imperialism in *The Moonstone* at any length. Basing his argument on Collins's "unconventional" behavior, and on the "appeal" of the unconventional characters in his novel, Reed asserts that "the Indian priests are heroic figures, while the representatives of Western Culture are plunderers." Reed notes that Collins sets his main narrative in 1849, the year in which the British forcefully annexed the Punjab. See "English Imperialism and the Unacknowledged Crime of *The Moonstone*," *Clio*, 2 (June 1973), 281–90. Sue Lonoff places Collins's critique of empire in *The Moonstone* in the context of the Eyre controversy, a debate over the actions of the Governor of Jamaica, who brutally put down a native insurrection in 1865. See *Wilkie Collins and His Victorian Readers: A Study in the Rhetoric of Authorship* (New York: AMS, 1982), 178–79. Patrick Brantlinger addresses Collins's attitude toward empire very briefly, and is more tentative in his assessment: *"The Moonstone* ... distantly reflects the Mutiny, perhaps in an anti-imperialist way." See *Rule of Darkness: British Literature and Imperialism, 1830–1914* (Ithaca: Cornell UP, 1988), 295, n. 19. The most recent discussion of the subject is that of Tamar Heller, who briefly examines "Collins' relation to Orientalism" in *Dead Secrets: Wilkie Collins and the Female Gothic* (New Haven: Yale UP, 1992), pp. 190–91, n. 8. She contrasts Collins's "reservations about imperialism" with Dickens's support of it, and suggests that Dickens's harsh criticism of *The Moonstone* may stem from the authors' disagreement on imperial issues. Furthermore, she identifies Collins's reference to Henry Mackenzie's *The Man of Feeling* as "an intriguing, though studiously buried, allusion to anti-imperialist discourse...in *The Moonstone*."

6. For a discussion of the popularity of *Robinson Crusoe* in the Victorian age, see Richard Altick, *The English Common Reader* (Chicago: U of Chicago P, 1957); and William J. Palmer, "Dickens and Shipwreck," *Dickens Studies Annual*, 18 (1989), 39–92. Sue Lonoff briefly examines the relationship between *The Moonstone* and *Robinson Crusoe* in her discussion of Collins's treatment of religious faith. Lonoff notes that in Collins's novel, "Providence becomes even more problematic than it was in *Robinson Crusoe*," and that the "nominal creed" of Collins's evangelical characters "is even more divorced from an active faith than that of Robinson Crusoe." See *Wilkie Collins and His Victorian Readers*, 220–22.

7. On the subject of the Indian Mutiny, see Christopher Hibbert, *The Great Mutiny: India 1857* (New York: Penguin, 1980); and Thomas Metcalf, *The Aftermath of Revolt: India, 1857–1870* (Princeton: Princeton UP, 1964).

8. Charles Dickens, Speech delivered at the Prize-giving of the Institutional Association, 3 December 1858, in *The Speeches of Charles Dickens,* ed. K. J. Fielding (Oxford: Clarendon, 1960), 284.

9. On the subject of "The Perils" and its relationship to the Indian Mutiny, see Patrick Brantlinger, *Rule of Darkness,* 206–8; and William Oddie, "Dickens and the Indian Mutiny," *Dickensian,* 68 (January 1972), 3–5. Neither of these critics discusses Collins's contributions to the story at any length.

10. Christopher Hibbert describes the "high life" led by the British officers in India and the various ways in which they mistreated their native servants, beating them, verbally abusing them, and arbitrarily cutting their wages. See *The Great Mutiny,* 30–39.

11. Davis discusses "The Perils" only in passing, noting that Collins was "much less aghast" than Dickens over the Mutiny.

12. Brantlinger discusses *Stretton* and *First Love and Last Love,* along with a host of other novels inspired by the Mutiny, in a chapter entitled "The Well at Cawnpore." See *Rule of Darkness,* 208–24.

13. As a historical source for his description of the Seige, Collins used Theodore Hook's *Life of General, The Right Honourable Sir David Baird, Bart.* (London: Richard Bentley, 1832), which casts the British imperialists in a much more heroic light than the prologue of *The Moonstone* does. Hook contrasts the murderous cruelty of the Muslim ruler Tippoo with "the gallant conduct" of the British troops, "already chronicled in the annals of fame." Collins, by contrast, makes no mention of Tippoo's cruelty, portraying the criminal "excesses" of the British troops instead. Hook notes that the British pillaged the Muslim treasury after the seige, and that a private in the British Army murdered Tippoo and plundered the corpse; but he appends the following qualifier in a footnote: "Let us hope the man was a Sepoy" (vol. 1: 217). Collins leaves no room for such "hopes" in his account of the plundering.

14. Lonoff makes this point in discussing what she feels is the growing sympathy for the Brahmins in *The Moonstone,* noting that their portrait is "emancipated" for its time. In her view, the epilogue and prologue "reverse and correct" the racist view of the Indians provided in the "inner story"; they are "selfless devotees," while the English are "devious and criminal." See *Wilkie Collins and His Victorian Readers,* 223–25.

15. Collins calls this distinction into question in a variety of contexts throughout his career. His first unpublished novel idealized native life in Tahiti before the arrival of Europeans. The play he wrote (with Charles Fechter) immediately after *The Moonstone* was published, *Black and White,* calls attention to the arbitrary foundations of racial prejudice. The play is set in Trinidad, and its hero, an upper-class Frenchman, is mistaken for a native, and sold into slavery.

16. Dickens wrote to W. H. Wills, sub-editor of *Household Words,* asking him to edit "Highly Proper": "I particularly wish you to look well to Wilkie's article, and not

to leave anything in it that may be sweeping, and unnecessarily offensive to the middle class. He has always a tendency to overdo that." See Kenneth Robinson, *Wilkie Collins: A Biography* (New York: Macmillan, 1952), 119.

17. He "reads" his own experiences through Crusoe's on at least five occasions. See 39, 45, 110, 233, and 519.

18. On the subject of cannibalism and its use as a metaphor for social revolution in the nineteenth century, see Lee Sterrenburg, "Psychoanalysis and the Iconography of Revolution," *Victorian Studies*, 19 (December 1975), 241–64.

19. A considerable amount of recent scholarship examines the connections among race, class and gender in the "colonial mentality." See, for example, Sander L. Gilman's analysis of "The Hottentot and the Prostitute," in *Difference and Pathology: Stereotypes of Sexuality, Race, and Madness* (Ithaca: Cornell UP, 1985), 76–108; Gayatri Chakravorty Spivak's critique of *Jane Eyre* in "Three Women's Texts and a Critique of Imperialism," *Critical Inquiry*, 12 (Autumn 1985); and Elaine Hadley's analysis of Victorian social classification in "Natives in a Strange Land: The Philanthropic Discourse of Juvenile Emigration in Mid-Nineteenth-Century England," *Victorian Studies*, 33 (Spring 1990), 411–37.

20. The Brahmins vow to avenge the crimes of John Herncastle: "The Moonstone will have its vengeance on you and yours" (37). Rosanna openly expresses her resentment of Rachel Verinder: "Suppose you put Miss Rachel into a servant's dress, and took her ornaments off—? ... young ladies may behave in a manner which would cost a servant her place ... it does stir one up to hear Miss Rachel called pretty, when one knows all the time that it's her dress does it" (363).

21. While the faithful retainer "diagnoses" Rosanna's social ambition as a case of "madness," Sergeant Cuff does not. Betteredge provides Cuff with what he considers the "necessary explanations" of Rosanna's behavior; in his view, she "had been mad enough to set her heart on Mr. Franklin Blake." But the detective reveals the inadequacy of this diagnosis in his reply: "'Hadn't you better say she's mad enough to be an ugly girl and only a servant?'" (151).

22. On the connection between systems of classification and "English hegemony in colonial territories," see Harriet Ritvo, "The Power of the Word: Scientific Nomenclature and the Spread of Empire," *Victorian Newsletter*, 77 (Spring 1990), 5–8; George Levine's chapter "The Perils of Observation," in *Darwin and the Novelists: Patterns of Science in Victorian Fiction* (Cambridge: Harvard UP, 1988), 210–37; and Sander L. Gilman's "Introduction" to *Difference and Pathology*, 15–35.

WORKS CITED

Bakhtin, "Discourse in the Novel." *The Dialogic Imagination*. Tr. Caryl Emerson and Michael Holquist. Austin: U of Texas P, 1981. 259–422.

Bender, John. *Imagining the Penitentiary: Fiction and the Architecture of Mind in Eighteenth-Century England*. Chicago: U of Chicago P, 1987.

Brantlinger, Patrick. *Rule of Darkness: British Literature and Imperialism, 1830–1914.* Ithaca: Cornell UP, 1988.

Cantor, Paul. "Stoning the Romance: The Ideological Critique of Nineteenth-Century Literature." *South Atlantic Quarterly* 88 (1989): 705–20.

Collins, Wilkie. "A Breach of British Privilege." *Household Words* 19 (19 March 1859): 361–64.

———. "Highly Proper." *Household Words* 18 (2 October 1858): 361–63.

———. "Laid Up in Lodgings." *My Miscellanies.* Vol. 20 of *The Works of Wilkie Collins.* 30 vols. New York: AMS, 1970. 85–125.

———. *The Moonstone.* Ed. J. I. M. Stewart. Harmondsworth: Penguin, 1986.

———. "A Sermon for Sepoys." *Household Words* 17 (27 February 1858): 244–247.

———, and Charles Dickens. "The Perils of Certain English Prisoners." *The Lazy Tour of Two Idle Apprentices and Other Stories.* London: Chapman and Hall, 1890. 237–327.

Davis, Nuel Pharr. *The Life of Wilkie Collins.* Urbana: U of Illinois P, 1956.

Defoe, Daniel. *Robinson Crusoe.* Ed. Angus Ross. Harmondsworth: Penguin, 1985.

Johnson, Edgar. *Letters from Charles Dickens to Angela Burdett-Coutts.* London: Jonathan Cape, 1953.

Miller, D. A. *The Novel and the Police.* Berkeley: U of California P, 1988.

Sentiment, the Highest Attribute of Art: The Socio-Poetics of Feeling[1]

Julie F. Codell

The meaning of the term "sentiment" in Victorian art dictionaries mirrors its rise and fall as an aesthetic criterion and a signifier of the social function of art. James Elmes's *General and Bibliographical Dictionary of the Fine Arts* (1826) defines sentiment with the residue of the eighteenth-century cult of sensibility: "The evidence in his work of feeling and sensibility in the mind and perceptions of the artist. This quality may be almost identified with *Expression.*" Adeline's *Art Dictionary* (1890) defines sentiment as "the general effect by which the artist has expressed his own feelings and sought to inspire the same feelings in the spectator ... a subtle quality," dependent upon "colour, drawing, or any of the means" used in art.[2] Adeline's concern with art's effects on the spectator marks the word as truly Victorian.

Between these two dictionaries which bracket the Victorian period, Fairholt in his *Dictionary of Terms in Art* (1850) takes an entire column to define sentiment in contradistinction to the brevity of the other two dictionaries, an indication of its importance for Victorian art theory. For Fairholt, sentiment was "the leading idea which has governed the general conception of a work of Art, or which makes itself visible to the eye and mind of the spectator through the work of the artist," and art's most valued quality: "In the creation, as well as in the adoption of the artistic form, the feeling remains predominant." Feeling was defined as what the painter "mentally felt when he originally conceived the work and which he embodies to similarly affect the spectator," thus creating what Martin Meisel has termed "affective symbolism."[3]

As Thackeray noted, while sentiment was the highest quality in art, it could not be easily defined.[4] Complex and multivalent, its amorphous meaning, often synonymous with "poetic," encompassed connotations of moral values, social propriety, mere sentimentality and the highest human sympathy, as well as a socializing function—to elicit sympathy from the viewer through an *appropriate* expression of strong feeling stirred by *accurate* visual detail (e.g., Ruskin's belief that sentiment did not require the loss of truthfulness). Between 1840 and 1870 sentiment developed a decidedly Victorian flavor, dependent upon the reciprocity of depicted empirical detail and a curious affective moral edification of the spectator that had social and moral implications. After 1870 the term was denigrated, as art critics privileged painterly and formal matters at the expense of narrative, although sentiment's Victorian associations persist today in popular visual culture.

Comparing the language of the critical receptions of several popular Victorian paintings with the paintings themselves, I will examine the rhetorical use of sentiment in art criticism. The Victorian dialectics of sentiment appear in its two diverse meanings: Romanticism's legacy of the deep, inarticulate, personal feeling (*within* and *of* the artist and the critic) and the Victorian signifier of social norms of expression (*for* the beholder/public). Artists' sincerity was often read back from their paintings. Critics stressed adherence to a decorum of expression and gesture, especially of the most powerful sentiments, grief and love; one critic defined sentiment as "a strong emotional restraint," which caused "aesthetic disgust" when breached.[5] Steadfastly determined to guide the spectator's affective states, critics wove long, complex narratives, detailing multiple emotional states going well beyond their source in the paintings' images (a practice begun by Ruskin's exegeses on Turner's paintings, e.g., *The Slave Ship*). Sentiment, decorum, and social order constructed a "discursive formation," to use Foucault's concept, for the critical reception of paintings, even when interpretations differed. A single painting could engender diverse interpretations, not only in critical reviews, but also in the context of the collection in which it co-existed or for successive collectors.[6]

Adapting some concepts from emotion studies by sociologists and anthropologists (e.g., feeling rules, dramatistic roles) to my examples of art critics' rhetoric, I will explore the critics' use of sentiment in art to examine (1) structures and purposes of critical exegeses as socializing acts that ascribed and privileged certain affective readings, (2) debates within the discursive formation over the nature of sentiment and the appropriateness of images and figures for audience identification and empathy, and (3) broader implications of the rhetoric of sentiment for the Victorians' evangelical project to introduce the arts to the "lower orders" so as to channel social and moral acculturation through the decorum of affect.

The philosopher of the sublime, Edmund Burke, adumbrated many of the uses of sentiment in his description of the function of sympathy as a substitution of ourselves into the "place of another" until we are affected emotionally. According to Burke, the arts "transfuse their passions from one breast to another, and are often capable of grafting a delight in wretchedness, misery and death itself" (44–45). Burke's definition of sympathy relied on tragedy: our emotions were more heightened, the more noble and powerful the hero. He recommended pity, however, as the highest passion "because it arises from love and social affection" (44). Attacking artists and critics for their lack of broad culture to explore "the rationale of our passions," he proposed that the arts appeal, instead, to everyone, rather than to small circle of cognoscenti: "The true standard of the arts is in every man's power; and an easy observation of the most common, sometimes of the meanest things in nature, will find the truest lights" (54). Burke's appeal to the common spectator and his advocacy of an affective mission for the arts foreshadowed the Victorian meaning and use of sentiment, though without the association with tragedy and exceptional, heroic figures. On the eve of the Victorian era, sentiment in art was synonymous with the equally nebulous term, "poetic." One critic writing in the *Athenaeum* associated sentiment with subjects literally taken from poetry.[7] The poet was, after all, according to a *Westminster Review* critic writing on Tennyson's *Enoch Arden,* one who "operates on the emotions of his hearers and readers by the exhibition of such human feeling as is calculated to stir their sympathies or antipathies.[8]

Before Victoria ascended to the throne, critics debated the meaning of sentiment and the causes of its popular appeal. A critic attacking John Martin's operatic illustrations of the Bible (1834) argued that the painter "fails in conveying the sentiment of his subject. He not only does not delineate character nor depict emotion, but his pictures have no human interest." On the other hand, in Rembrandt's *Jacob's Dream,* "It is the feeling of the painter that enters into the picture, which affects the beholder. We view the scene through the medium of his mind and are impressed in proportion to the truth and vividness of his perception." Rembrandt depicted a common burgher type, while Martin's paintings were excessively fantastic: "The more remote a thing is from our habits, the less it affects us. The most powerful way to address the imagination is through the habits, not through the senses.[9]

For Sir Charles Morgan in 1834 the artist represented the middle term between the intellectual lost in thought and the sensualist of low morals; the sensitive artist, both keenly perceptive of the outside world *and* introspective, could "influence the general sentiments of an entire nation."[10] Relying on associationist theories, Morgan argued that art excites memory, experience, poetic illustrations, speculations on cause and effect, and analogues in the physical and mental worlds, transforming facts into ideals. Archibald Alison, the aesthetic philosopher most closely connected with associationism, described the laws of painting as the unities of sentiment, association and emotion.[11]

Sentiment reinforced morality by encouraging empathy and gentleness, signifiers of a high level of civilization. Raphael's work, for example, was great because it "brings home to men's bosoms those universal sentiments in which its morality is based."[12] Of a painting by Murillo, one critic speculated that "it must be a hard heart indeed that will not be softened and made more gentle under its benign influence."[13] For a *Blackwood's* critic, hope for the future of British art, over which many critics agonized, lay in its progress toward more and fuller sentiments as signs of national progress and dominance (anticipating Herbert Spencer's discourse on sympathy):

> still are our artists rapidly progressing in that next best line, the line of human sympathies. When love, pity, fortitude, tenderness, innocence, as well as the greater energies of cultivated worth, engage the genius of the painter, as we see they do, and will do, the British artist is raised to a higher profession; his venture is great; and he will elevate himself, the art and society.[14]

Sentiment was accessible to everyone and its promotion adversely affected respect for connoisseurship which was seen as the residue of an aristocratic, elite culture and as mystifying, the "cabala of connoisseurship," according to one critic (Olmsted 43). Edward Chatfield subordinated connoisseurship to feeling:

> Let the connoisseur rave as he will about what he calls *texture* and *touch*, there is nothing to be compared to the delight afforded to the mind by an elevated style of art, which places all the means used in a subordinate position and produces in the thoughts an ecstasy, associated with the best and loftiest emotions, of which human beings are capable.[15]

Here Chatfield cited in a footnote that an eminent living writer, "neither artist not connoisseur," wept in front of a painting. R. H. Horne praised the criticism of Fuseli, Barry, Opie, Reynolds, and Landseer who "take a similar untechnical tone: directly the inherent power of the subject sublimates the feeling and intellect, and thus places them above their subject, instead of below, in the laboratory." He cited Jonathan Richardson's 1719 formulation of the end of painting as "elevating and improving nature and thus communicating valuable ideas."[16] Another critic in 1838 also argued for sentiment's predominance over composition in Joseph Severn's *First Crusaders in Sight of Jerusalem*. Criticizing the painting for its many figures looking in all directions instead of toward Jerusalem, he dictated that "the monotony which might, in another case, offend the artist's eye, would have added intensity to his embodiments of the sentiment of his subject."[17]

Anna Jameson, taking the side of the connoisseur against the lay audience, modified Sir Walter Scott's statement that a painting should recall natural emotions. She insisted that technical means were crucial to such ends distinguishing the professional from the amateur among critics as well as among painters.[18] She praised Edwin Landseer for his perfect blend of technical skills and sentiment to suggest thoughts "that do often lie too deep for tears." In her opinion, and she was not alone, Landseer was "our *national* painter." William Etty's robust nudes, on the other hand, were coarse in her estimation, probably due to his subject, although she phrased her dislike in terms of "form and colour too often prevailing over the sentiment, the material and sensual over the spiritual and ideal." Another critic cited Etty's "aims to satisfy the judgment rather than to touch the heart ... neither politic nor just...." His nudes "excite no sympathy and rouse no generous emotion."[19]

The most interesting art critic of sentiment was William Thackeray because he both praised and criticized sentiment. In Landseer Thackeray found too little of it, citing Landseer's inability "to do what is the highest quality of an artist, to place a *soul* under the ribs as he draws them." He much preferred Charles Leslie, technically coarser but more charming.[20] His favorite was William Mulready on whom Thackeray lavished the praise of the layman: "I can't say much about the drawing of this picture, for here and there are some queer-looking limbs; but—oh Anatole!—the intention is godlike ... such expressions as a great poet would draw." Thackeray's other favorite was Charles Eastlake whose *Our Lord and the Little Children* went "straight to the heart, and then all criticism and calculating vanishes at once."[21] For Thackeray the end of art was "to strike far deeper than the sight" and therefore criticisms of technique were irrelevant when a painting achieved this empathetic, rather than merely perceptual, end.

Thackeray, however, loathed one artist most closely associated with sentiment and sentimentality, Richard Redgrave. Of Redgrave's *The Sempstress* (1846) based on Thomas Hood's "Song of the Shirt," Thackeray wrote

Mr. Redgrave has illustrated everything except the humor, the manliness, and the bitterness of the song. He has only depicted the tender, good-natured part of it. It is impossible to quarrel with the philanthropy of the painter. His shirtmaker sits by her little neat bed, work, working away. You may see how late it is, for the candle is nearly burnt out, the clock (capital poetic notion!) says what o'clock it is, the grey-streaked dawn is rising over the opposite house seen through the cheerless casement, and there (from a light which it has in its window) you may imagine another poor shirt-maker is toiling too. The one before us is pretty, pale, and wan; she turns up the whites of her fine, fatigued eyes to the little ceiling. She is ill, as the artist has shown us by a fine stroke of genius— a parcel of medicine-bottles on the mantelpiece! ... Mr. Redgrave's other picture, the "Marriage Morning," is also inspired by that milk-and-water of human kindness, the flavour of which is so insipid to the roast-beef intellect.[22]

The more populist *Art-Union* admired Redgrave's *Marriage Morning* because of "its refined sentiment ... from a class of subjects which so few artists can paint without vulgarizing."[23] Thackeray's complaint was that Redgrave's sentiment was too acquiescent, too pretty, too much "in the namby-pamby line." Redgrave's seamstress was an industrial martyr, the lighting and upward eyes reminiscent of paintings of martyred saints. She was depicted as living alone, although in reality she would have shared her dwellings and her rent. Despite the painting's theatricality and lack of realism, *The Art Union* loved *The Sempstress* because she suffered quietly and with decorum presumably the way workers were supposed to suffer in the turbulent, volatile 1840s (Casteras and Parkinson 118–19):

> the story is told in such a way as to approach the best feelings of the human heart: she is not a low-born drudge to proclaim her patient endurance to the vulgar world: her suffering is read only in the shrunken cheek, and the eye feverish and dim with watching.

Most other critics also found the piece moving and affective. The issue here is whether sentiment could be induced if the subject were not pretty or heroic. Sir Egerton Brydges writing in 1837 argued that "We require human character and human affections; but we require them select, and worthy of admiration or love. We are moved by the contemplation of a great man in solitude, when he is sick of the turmoils and disappointments of ambition." For Brydges, sentiment is a feeling combined with "a strong internal consciousness of moral feeling."[24] The Pre-Raphaelite Brotherhood (PBR) was often criticized for thwarting its spectators' empathy by its preference for unlovely women and namby-pamby males as judged by Victorian standards of gender roles, something which painters were expected to maintain if they wanted to touch their audience's collective heart (Codell 255–90).

To touch the heart meant lovely figures in genre subjects instead of historical or grand subjects, as well as a preference for contemporary, preferably British, artists over Old Masters. A critic for *Blackwood's* argued that the most important pictures were of ordinary people; these were pictures of true sentiment: "They are precious to cultivated minds and pure tastes.... and therefore art rather than art history should be the criterion for purchasing pictures."[25] As one critic wrote, "Sympathy must be gained—sensibility must be excited—and the observer be made to identify himself with the subject, which can hardly be expected, when he is called upon to weep with Hecuba, or to rage with Achilles." Nevertheless, painting must not gratify the "taste of tinkers and cobblers" but improve it until they "acquire a relish for what is beyond the usual range of their observation and preference," ultimately for "a sound and healthful revolution in taste and feeling."[26] Art might turn revolutionary political potential into a desire to change taste and feeling, or alter taste through the exercise of proper feeling, and so discourage revolutionary fervor on the part of the workers.

Many critics felt that the purpose of painting was to spread happiness, even in the show of the commonplace, thus eliminating suffering as a desirable subject in art.[27] Several critics attacked sentiment for trivializing subjects and for being the antithesis of philosophic thought; philosophy generalized, while sentiment encouraged attention to details.

> The world, for example, at any rate the English world, is growing excessively curious about little details of the lives of individuals. This description of curiosity is only a species of what Mr. M. Arnold might call provincial sentiment.... The higher, the more general, and the more complex any subject is—the greater, in a word, its human importance,—the less seems to be its human interest. Details alone make an impression on the popular mind.... Curiosity accordingly is but a form of sentiment.... Both are equally opposed to and inconsistent with the philosophic spirit, which cares more for history than for anecdote, and for general laws than particular instances.[28]

Nevertheless, this critic's view was far outweighed by those to whom sentiment extended a vital social role to the critic as cultural empathizer.

The extent of the critics' identification with figures was remarkable. They read entire narratives from the one moment depicted in a painting. Examples of such critical readings, or perhaps over-readings, offer insight into the role of the critic as national empathizer and educator of feelings. In 1853 on John Everett Millais's *Order of Release* a critic wrote:

> We see still in her eye the fear that has harassed her—she is not quite sure of his liberty—we read the whole story of her struggles, and sorrows and heroic endurance, in that hectic flush mounting upon the pallid cheek: we understand at once the fulness of joy to which she does not yet dare to give way, the nervous exultation, the effort at calmness, the resolution that has vanquished all difficulties and that now comes for its own reward, with a show of self-control, which will presently give way to a flood of happy tears.[29]

William Michael Rossetti, perhaps sharing Thackeray's preference for realism, noted more caustically, "The wife's feet are preternaturally delicate and unsoiled for one who has been walking barefoot" (213).

In 1855 a critic writing on Millais's *The Rescue* (fig. 1) became overwrought with imaginative identification:

> A figure booted and helmeted is descending a staircase, laden with a rich prize—none of your knights of chivalry, none of your free lances, but a hero of this nineteenth century—a soldier of the fire brigade. This prize which he has carried off consists of three children ... The little ones are struggling to be free to reach the outstretched arms of the mother, who kneels, all in white nightdress, on a lower step. The thin lip tightly pressed against the half-shown teeth, the hectic crimson of the cheek, the wild eye, show that in her breast, the agony of maternal terror has just changed into the ecstasy of joy over her rescued darlings. But she cannot be sure they are safe till she holds them in her arms ... He holds the children tenderly, for the brave heart is ever kind.... There is a true sense of pathos in this ... The Roman satirist is wrong when he attributes our sympathy for the misfortunes of the rich and great to a spirit of flunkeyism ... It is a sorry sight to see that filthy hose trailing over the woven flowers of the carpet. Through the window you see the earliest light of a cheerless dawn upon wet roofs—there is pathos in that contrast too! ... This is a great picture, the greatest of all the artist's works, greater than "The Release" or "The Huguenot", full of labour and thought, true to nature and human nature.[37]

Here, Rossetti would have agreed with the critic's attribution of heroism to the firefighter. Rossetti said of the figure, "There is the whole battle of Inkerman in that face," making him analogous to Crimean War soldiers (215). He was willing, furthermore, to defend the painting's faulty realism in the way the smoke billows as a "necessary suppression ... a bold conventionality necessary in order not to interfere with the expression of the picture," preferring sentiment to correct depiction (217).

This is a particularly interesting painting in terms of the discursive formation regarding sentiment. The expressions on the faces of the fireman and the mother were much debated. Excessive emotional expression in the case of men was often ambiguously depicted in Victorian paintings, with men usually covering their faces completely to avoid being seen crying (George Elgar Hicks's *Woman's Mission: Companion to Man;* William Windus's *Too Late;* Arthur Hughes's *Home from the Sea*). Though criticized for his unemotional response to the situation by the critic of the *Art Journal,* the fireman was also positively characterized as restrained despite the fire by virtue of his cool English character, or his manliness, or his working-class "stolid indifference," due in any case to his nationality, gender, or class. The mother's curiously reserved expression, unexpected in the case of a woman, was criticized as too calm or her appearance was read in line with conventional expecta-

John Everett Millais, *The Rescue*, 1855. (Permission of the National Gallery of Victoria, Melbourne, Australia.)

Thomas Faed. *Worn Out*, 1868. (Courtesy of the Forbes Magazine Collection, New York.)

tions: she was described variously by critics as "fantastically wild," "ecstatically grateful," filled with "hysterical joy" or "a wild and enthusiastic joy," or as being "wild with tenderness." One critic saw her as expressing "an ecstatic joy that floods every pulse of her being—parts her panting lips, and lights up her azure eyes like cressets," in a highly erotically charged description (Cooper 475–80). Her restraint was read as wild emotion in light of the narrative, her gender and her social role as mother. The connotations of emotion in Western European culture include associations with irrationality, instinct, subjectivity, chaos, and women. In its pejorative implications emotion is usually condemned when it is excessive or when it is absent, signifying estrangement and alienation. Both the fireman and the mother exhibit overly restrained expressions under the circumstances and critics either condemned their lack of feeling or read emotions into them according to the social categories of gender, class, and social role (Lutz 287–309).

One other inherent quality of sentiment was its role as a kind of social glue between the classes. In 1841, a critic described the artist as "a being of love; and what is love if it be not the power of sympathy with the life of another, of making it one's own, of nourishing while purifying it."[31] Reverend St. John Tyrwhitt in 1869 delineated a complicated layering of spectator responses, both working and middle class, to Thomas Faed's 1868 *Worn Out* (fig. 2) to assure the middle-class spectator that workers would be appeased by the painting's evidence of their heartfelt sympathy:

> We wonder if Mr. Faed ever went to see what navvies and workmen thought of his "Worn Out", with its homely and novel sentiment and deep simple pathos, which the roughest man or woman in England might run and read. No easier picture ever was painted which escaped being commonplace; perhaps it was hung too high to benefit the poor students who might have learned their worth from his science, method of work, and clear painting. But only from a notion of the average moral effect of that work on hard-working men and weary mothers of families. It must at least have given them to understand that their long endurance of all the trials of hard life is felt and sympathized with by men; and how much more by God, who made men? The question is not whether the British bricklayer can give a coherent account of the whole show when he comes out of it, but whether one, two, or three pictures have put new thoughts, hopes, ideas into his mind.[32]

Interestingly, middle-class sympathy is reminiscent of God's, no less.

These examples of the social and moral role of the critic in interpreting and valorizing sentiment can perhaps best be understood in the context of the theory of social constructionism currently used by sociologists and anthropologists. The social constructionist view of emotion reconsiders the philosophical history of emotion, rejecting the assumptions that emotions are simply physiological, essentialist, and ineffable experiences. The same physiology can be labeled as different emotions among different individuals and cultures. Instead, constructionists argue that emotions, like thoughts, are created from sociocultural practices, particularly in the case of what philosophers such as Descartes have called the higher emotions, precisely those denoted as sentiments by Victorian art critics, novelists, phrenologists, and sages. Emotions in this context are intentional and cognitive, and their identification always incorporates the local moral order, i.e., the system of rights, obligations, duties and conventions of evaluation (Harre 8). Many sentiments are emotions coupled with moral precepts, e.g., remorse, shame. Therefore, understanding any sentiment requires an understanding of the cultural context to avoid misidentification and projection on the part of the reader, sociologist, anthropologist, or art historian. Furthermore, the assumption of identification is not based simply on introspection for constructionists (Harre 17). The self is not always the last resort in apprehending its own emotion. We can and often do misidentify our own emotions or tell one another that our emotions are inappropriate in a particular situation. Often our discourse of emotion is judicial, rather than informative (Harre 27).

Such a method would not have been alien to the Victorians. One art critic argued that art's origins antedate "the varied modes of life; while in the manner of its announcement of sentiment, it is frequently sequent to them," the very assumption on which constructionists base their assertions.[33] He then pointed out that social experience was, thus, necessary to an appreciation of art, the true test of art being how it approximates these experiences. I would argue that sentiment was formative; it helped the spectator learn how to feel which emotion and in which circumstance. Following the social constructionist method means examining related extra-art sources, as, for example, the popular system of phrenology, in which sentiment played a major role as the mediator between intellect and raw, brute feeling. The sentiments were the higher emotions, according to phrenology books. In this paper I will examine sources close to the art world.

One of the most prominent sentiments was grief, presumably an uncontrollable emotion full of authenticity and candor. In 1851 Lady Eastlake, art critic and wife of Sir Charles Eastlake, the director of the National Gallery (1855–65), however, advised that certain forms of expression, even of grief, were inappropriate in art and in life. For Lady Eastlake, classical art's decline was marked by a propensity to "represent only the extreme paroxysms of sorrow and suffering. There were in point of fact none of those truly human sympathies which daily rejoice us in the commonest walks of life for antique art to expand in" (71). She argued further for ideal types: "every sex and every age of life has a physiognomy proper to itself, and only to be rightly defined by its dissimilarity." This propriety meant that some expressions of emotions were unartistic because "such paroxysms of the countenance are too ugly for the light" (77). She concluded her essay with a warning to women and artists alike (78):

> No woman objects to show her grief while it is confined to the interestingly plaintive expression and gently falling pearly tear; but when the features become agitated and the nose red, she very properly covers them up, knowing intuitively that the chief muscle set in action by such emotions is significantly termed by the anatomists *distortor oris*.

The attractive and moderately grieving mother in Frank Holl's *Her Firstborn* (1877) exemplifies Lady Eastlake's decorum of grieving. Another critic responding to the "furious paroxysm" of Hercules in G. Patton's *The Madness of Hercules* claimed, "The countenance is unworthy of the character, inasmuch as we see there no indication of anything promotive of human good."[34]

Eastlake was only one end of the spectrum, however. The anatomist Charles Bell, a favorite of the Pre-Raphaelite Brotherhood painters, preferred paroxysms and encouraged the candid expression of emotions (88):

> Let us imagine to ourselves the overwhelming influence of grief on woman, the object in her mind has absorbed all the power of the frame, the body is no more regarded, the spirits have left it, it reclines, and the limbs gravities; they are nerveless, and relaxed, and she scarcely breathes; but why comes at the intervals the long-drawn sigh?—why are the neck and throat convulsed?—what causes the swelling and quivering of the lips, and the deadly paleness of the face?—or why is the hand so pale and earthly cold?—and why, at intervals, as the agony returns, does the convulsion spread over the frame like a paroxysm of suffocation.

Bell's language is phenomenological, emphasizing the kinesthetic, visceral, and internal experience through imagination and identification. Lady Eastlake's language is perceptual and social, evaluating the appearance of emotion through layers of the moral order and social self-consciousness. It is Bell's language, however, that is similar to the examples I have given from art criticism, and this implies that the critics served to help the spectator read into, and vicariously experience, the depicted sentiments, to identify with the grieving or joyful subjects in order to learn the proper sentiments by feeling privileged emotions associated with appropriate circumstances depicted in the painting. In general the painters and critics shared Lady Eastlake's socio-moral order. The exceptions, the early paintings of the PRB, were soundly condemned for their aesthetic of intensity displayed in figures of abrasive gawkiness and unlovely faces which foiled their spectator's identification and empathy. Yet, although the critics upheld middle-class propriety, as reflected in the clean wife's feet and the smoke-free children in Millais's paintings, their language is like Bell's, an exercise in intense, imagined identification with a constructed narrative that endorsed heroism, gratitude, appropriate sorrow, the rewards of virtue and middle class hegemony. They also shared Bell's preference for scenes from ordinary life with ordinary people, though most critics preferred prettified people and sanitized situations. Bell advised artists to use friends and family as models and to avoid idealizing figures.

Constructionists argue that our very capacity to experience certain emotions depends upon our learning to interpret and appraise situations and experiences in terms of norms, standards, and principles all judged as appropriate or desirable. In short, this means that we acquire emotions in the context of our comprehension of situations seen through the values of our community: "emotions are a socially prescribed set of responses to be followed by a person in a given situation. The response is a function of shared expectations regarding appropriate behaviour" (James Averill in Harre 33). Emotions, furthermore, serve sociocultural purposes: "the meaning of an emotion—its functional significance is to be found primarily within the sociocultural system" to restrain undesirable emotions and behavior and to sustain and endorse hegemonic values (Lutz in Harre 34–35).

> According to constructionism, moral sentiments such as "guilt" and "pity" are not ontologically prior to moral judgment because a grasp of certain moral rules is a precondition of the capacity to feel the moral sentiment ... it is because the moral sentiments involve moral attitudes such as the evaluation of an act as morally wrong that ... such sentiments can involve agent responsibility and be subjected to rational appraisal and criticism ... moral worth and emotion are not separable, since emotion has a crucial role in conveying the sincerity of moral worth.

The critics' appropriation of Millais's fireman and mother in *The Rescue* is a clear example of the attribution of emotional qualities through the projection of gender, class, and social roles according to which the fireman and mother were condemned or praised.

Constructionists have much to say about the nature of social roles in the construction of emotions. James Averill theorizes that emotions are "transitory social roles—that is, institutionalized ways of interpreting and responding to particular classes of situations" (Harre 100). These roles, furthermore, are open-ended, allowing for improvisation. Theodore Sarbin borrows metaphors from drama and rhetoric to describe the nature of role-playing in emotion construction. For Sarbin, conduct as shaped by one's status or position in society is one determinant of emotion. A more compelling explanation of emotion acculturation is his notion of the "dramatistic" role played according to a set of socialized emotion roles, such as the lover, the fool, or the grieving widow. These are not closely tied to social roles but to varying social circumstances which can affect everyone in a particular culture. Furthermore, according to Sarbin, these emotional roles have a logic which follows the narrative or the social drama and which allows for reflection and criticism of the emotions displayed. Our emotional repertoires are learned through "paradigm scenarios," the prototypes of social situations for life's various plots (Sarbin in Harre 88–92). The implication is that emotional behavior is intentional and rhetorical, to persuade others of our feelings and to act according to the emotion roles we have witnessed as part of the sociocultural order and beliefs.

The rules of emotion which structure these roles are rules of appraisal, or perceiving and evaluating a situation (*The Sempstress; Worn Out*); rules of behavior, the ways an emotion is organized and expressed (*The Rescue*); and rules of prognosis, the appropriate time for an emotion to run its course (*Order of Release* or the public's irritability at Victoria's extra-long grieving over Albert's death; see Averill in Harre, 107). In Augustus Egg's first painting of his three-canvas work *Past and Present* (1858), the excessive emotion of the literally and figuratively fallen wife and the impassive, resigned husband tell the spectator that no pleading will serve to allow such a woman to remain under domestic protection and that the husband's behavior is dictated by duty apart from any emotional bonds or desires he might have. The wife's lack of moral fiber is demonstrated by her excessive display and her appeal to the sentiments of hope and love in such an unredeemable situation. The affect of husband and wife reflect their respective assimilation of the social values and roles against which their emotions are pitted and judged as appropriate or not.

For the Victorians, sentiments were moral and idealized; artists and critics served to naturalize and ideologize the correct feelings in their appropriate situations. In this context, art seemed to be a major channel of moral edification through the depiction of sentiments. Critics had a moral duty to present in their complementary verbal language the means for empathizing and labelling proper sentiments and emotional experiences, just as artists were expected to present the proper narrative and respectable figures. Lord Kames

claimed, "A taste for the Fine Arts goes hand in hand with the moral sense …
rooted in human nature and common to all men."[35]

I am arguing here that artists, whose sincerity was a common critical topic,
had a moral role in painting works we consider sentimental and conventional.
The long exegeses by the critics can also be explained as a moral exercise for
edification and acculturation through the affect of the spectator. I would like
to consider the question of why art served this function. Lady Eastlake is
helpful here. She explained that reading the human face was vital for
Victorians as a way of preserving society "from the most bewildering confu-
sions and fatal mistakes" in a world in which everyone dressed well and
seemed respectable (63). Phrenologists, too, implored their readers to learn to
read faces as signs in order to choose the right business or marriage partners.
Perhaps in an urbanized world in which Victorians had to contend daily with
total strangers, the reading of faces, expressions, and gestures, popularly
semiotized in phrenology and art, replaced traditional education through family life and the tribal knowledge of neighbors in rural districts and small
towns.

Offering a new social and moral epistemology through proper feeling, art
was considered a vital means for controlling and acculturating the lower
orders. Art served as a repository of social and moral propriety, and thus
embodied a valuable pedagogy for the working class, both in terms of main-
streaming and controlling emotions by modelling their emotional education,
and by offering another self-help tool for their upward mobility. The issue of
who should see art exhibitions was much debated among the Victorians,
reflecting the desire to expose workers and artisans to art as a means for control and to inspire self-help, as well as expressing the fear that crowds of
workers might destroy art works and museums. The debate was settled in
favor of exposing the workers to art, and the press expressed surprise at the
well-behaved crowds attending exhibitions. When in 1830 the British
Museum removed the requirement that visitors sign the register for entry,
attendance quadrupled, demonstrating that the working class was interested
in self-improvement (L. King 30). The most successful demonstration was
the creation and prosperity of the London Art Union (formed in 1837) and of
the Mechanics' Institutes. In the 1830s the British, galvanized by the Select
Committee of 1835–36, began to compare English art institutions with those
on the Continent and to address the transformation from aristocratic patronage to public support for art. Hopes were high; one manufacturing engineer
from Manchester recommended casts in factories for workers to see on their
lunch time, instead of going to the pub (L. King 30). For twenty years George

Godwin, a leader of the Art Union, hoped art would be available to the public and that the government would encourage artists "to produce works of high teaching; noble truths set forth so as to awaken noble feelings—which may serve to convey to posterity a worthy idea of the mind and powers of the nineteenth century" (L. King 101–30). The Victorian notion was not that truth and beauty were interchangeable but that beauty and goodness were. The Art Union reports attested to art's role in the spectator's improvement by inspiring proper feelings: "Art gives us nobler loves and nobler cares, furnishing objects by the contemplation of which we are taught and exalted, and so are ultimately led to see beauty in its highest form which is GOODNESS" (L. King 214).

The moral sphere was also tied to the political sphere. In one critic's words, "The more the Arts advance the more sociable do men become. As they extend, the political conditions of a people become more assured, factions are less inveterate, controversy less hateful, revolutions less tragical, authority less severe, and seditions less frequent."[36] As Richard Altick points out, the hope was that art would calm "the fevers of a nation in which political and social bitterness was reaching dangerous levels." He cites the Art Union's faith that cultivating the taste of the public "softens' men's manners and suffers them not to be brutal" (Chapter 33). Yet despite the ambition of progressive manufacturers, of the London Art Union and of the 1853 Act for Encouraging the Establishment of Museums in Large Towns, only the National Gallery was free to all and attended by all the classes. Attendance at the British Museum required a ticket obtained from the trustees for most of the century, and Royal Academy exhibitions cost a shilling and were not open on Sundays until the end of the century, despite the fact that Sunday museum attendance had been the practice on the Continent almost a hundred years earlier.

The Reverend Samuel Barnett and his wife Henrietta held their first of many annual exhibitions in 1881 for the poor of Whitechapel in London's East End, perhaps the poorest district in the city (Borzello). This first show exhibited works by such luminaries as Watts, Leighton, Crane and Burne-Jones, and many of the selections regularly came from R. A. exhibitions. Old Masters and contemporary foreign artists were also shown, and each show contained between 200 and 300 pictures. The Barnetts' intention was to put art in the service of Christian values to create what Frances Borzello describes as the Seamless Society, an image of caring and loving in a world of harsh reality and neglect. Henrietta Barnett noted the effects on two working girls of seeing a painting in which a man assures his dying lover that death shall not part them, that love was eternal. For the Barnetts art served religion and morality through its images of eternal love and mutual caring in which even dogs served as guardians, as in the painting *Left in Charge*. The most repeated image in the Whitechapel paintings was the unified family. Mixing life and art, Ruskin was quoted in several catalogues: "We cannot arrest sunsets nor carve mountains, but we may turn every English home, if we choose, into a picture which shall be 'no counterfeit, but the true and perfect images of life indeed.'" The large attendance at the exhibitions from 1881 to 1898 indicates their popularity, although their moralizing effects are difficult to determine. According to the Barnetts, not the most objective but nevertheless the sole recorders of the responses of the largely artisan attendants, paintings of pathetic subjects were the most popular. The exhibitions were free after the first year, open until 10 p. m. every evening and on Sundays, still a controversial move. Borzello concludes that the Barnetts hoped art would train the mind and emotions of the poor "to encourage the poor's acceptance of the status quo" (30–42). The Barnetts' hopes of encouraging art for the elevation of the poor by means of a permanent series of exhibitions among the working class was to inspire them to acquire the accouterments, including the proper sentiments, of middle-class hegemony.

Burke claimed that our social affection expressed in sympathy allowed us to be "inquisitive without impertinence" (53). Sentiment allowed the spectator to become a voyeur in the most private moments of love and grief, transforming these experiences from the private to the public sphere. While Robin Ironside argues that the emphasis on expression in Victorian art was the result of the excessive restraints on behavior, Michel Foucault presents a contradictory argument, that the Victorians were encouraged, were given an "incitement to discourse" publicly about the most private sexual experiences (Ironside, 13–15; Foucault). I think Foucault's articulation of this deprivatization of sex is a paradigm; not only sex, but the most intense personal emotions were publicly displayed in an attempt to coordinate and associate them with the proper social circumstances of family (Foucault's theory of the increasing naturalization of marital heterosexuality and illegality of other forms of sexual behavior), gender and class roles. Recent scholars of melodrama in films generalize further, arguing that the "pleasure of being touched and giving way to tears" (Diderot) expresses the spectator's powerlessness in the face of loss within the two conventions of melodrama: the occurrence of events happening too late, realizing time's irreversibility (e.g., in titles such as *Past and Present, Worn Out, Too Late, Her Firstborn),* and the exploration of extreme emotional states (Neale 6–23).

The once-held rejection of the study of popular culture by virtue of its transparency has been replaced by analyses of its depth and psychology. The transparent, easy meanings of Victorian paintings of sentiment are the result of the spectators' familiarity with the world of the paintings, a familiarity which made the paintings appear "natural." These art works were "contextual 'homes' for the viewer" who shared the painters' and critics' assumptions and values (Affron).

Victorian sentiment demarcated the changes in Victorian socialization of art from private connoisseurship to public accessibility, in the development of an aesthetics for a mass audience away from technique and handling toward socially redeeming justification. Sentiment carved out a modern role for art in the wake of the evacuation of local or tribal practices for socialization. Writing in 1902 the art critic Claude Phillips argued desperately for the universality of sentiments in a last dying gasp of Victorian faith in art's power to improve and civilize its audience. Writing on the popular sentimental painter Fritz von Uhde, whom he compared favorably with Rembrandt, Phillips assured his readers of the universality and, indeed, imperialism of their own emotional response to von Uhde (13):

> the sincerity of whose art even those who will have none of it cannot deny, at once obtains a hearing, just because the human-divine elements of pity and love awakens at once responsive chords not in the breast of his own fellow-countrymen alone, but in the whole human race.

Art museums and exhibitions became public property with a new social role: to manage the heart and bring it in line with social mores and cultural ambitions. The critic directed socialization through empathy and identification. Victorians hoped their art would assure them an exalted social and moral reputation based on the representation of their collective sympathetic nature.

NOTES

1. I wish to thank the University of Montana for a Research Grant in 1981 which helped me begin my study of sentiment in Victorian art criticism. A version of this paper was read at the August 1989 Dickens Project Conference in Santa Cruz.

2. The quote from Elmes's *Dictionary* has no page number, while the quote from Adeline's *Dictionary* appears on page 360. Both were published in London.

3. P. 187; italics mine. Fairholt considered sentiment one of the three primary elements of composition, along with subject matter and space, in his definition of composition (126). Like sentiment, feeling is as conceptual, "mentally felt" (Meisel, 68), as it is emotional. On sentiment in Victorian literature, see Kaplan.

4. "Strictures on Pictures," *Fraser's* 7 (June, 1838): 758–64; see also Olmsted, 236–37.

5. Review in *Westminster Review* 91 (1869): 82.

6. For an intriguing study of the varied meanings attributed to a single painting, see Arscott.

7. *Athenaeum* 31 March 1832: 209–10; Olmsted, 17–18.

8. *Westminster Review* 82 (October, 1864): 187.

9. *Westminster Review* 20 (April, 1834): 452–65; Olmsted, 44–45.

10. "Of Certainty of Taste," *Athenaeum* 2 November, 1834: 804–7; Olmsted, 92.

11. "The British School of Painting," *Blackwood's Edinburgh Magazine* 40 (July, 1836): 74–85; Olmsted, 126.

12. *Blackwood's* 45 (Jan.–June, 1839): 815.

13. *Blackwood's* 42 (October, 1837): 693.

14. *Blackwood's* 46 (Sept. 1839): 311.

15. "Poetic Painting and Sculpture," *New Monthly Magazine* 55 (Feb. 1839): 196–205; Olmsted, 259.

16. "British Artists and Writers on Art," *British and Foreign Review* 6 (April, 1838): 610–57; Olmsted, 210.

17. "Royal Academy," *Athenaeum* May, 1838: 346–47; Olmsted, 218.

18. "The Exhibitions of the Royal Academy. English Art and Artists," *Monthly Chronicle* June, 1838: 348–55; Olmsted, 227–28.

19. "The Royal Academy. The Seventy-First Exhibition, 1839," *Art Union* 1 (May 1839): 65–71; Olmsted, 278.

20. "Strictures on Pictures," *Fraser's* 17 (June, 1838): 758–64; Olmsted, 236–37. See also Roberts on Thackeray's criticism.

21. "A Second Lecture on the Fine Arts," *Fraser's Magazine* 19 (June, 1839): 743–50; Olmsted, 297.

22. "May Gambols; or, Titmarsh in the Picture-Galleries," *Fraser's Magazine* 29 (June 1844): 700–16; Olmsted, 535.

23. *Art-Union,* June 6, 1844: 153–72; Olmsted, 509.

24. "An Essay on Originality of Mind," *Fraser's* 15 (Jan.-June, 1837): 581–83.

25. *Blackwood's* 75 (Jan.–June, 1854): 429.

26. "Reflections Arising Out of the Late 'Exhibition,'" *Art Union* 2 (August, 1840): 126–27; Olmsted, 334.

27. *Athenaeum,* Jan.-Dec. 1839: 558.

28. *Saturday Review* 24 (Nov. 2, 1867): 561–62.

29. *Fraser's* 47 (1853): 707–08.

30. *Fraser's* 49 (1855): 709–10.

31. *Westminster Review* 35 (1841): 185–86.

32. "Skilled and Literary Art Criticism," *Contemporary Review* 11 (May-Aug. 1869): 116.

33. *Blackwood's* 49 (Jan.-June 1841): 371.

34. "The Royal Academy. The Seventy-Sixth Exhibition," *Art-Union* 6 (June 1844): 153–72; Olmsted, 501.

35. "The Progress and Patronage of British Art," *Art-Union* 7 (Jan. 1845): 5–7; Olmsted, 587.

36. "The Future of British Art," *Art-Union* 7 (Jan. 1845): 5–7; Olmsted, 587.

WORKS CITED

Affron, Charles. *Cinema and Sentiment.* Chicago: U of Chicago P, 1982.

Altick, Richard. *The Shows of London.* Cambridge, MA: Harvard UP, 1978.

Arscott, Catherine. "Employer, Husband, Spectator: Thomas Fairbairn's Commission of *The Awakening Conscience.*" *The Culture of Capital: Art, Power and the Nineteenth-Century Middle Class,* eds. J. Wolff and J. Seed. Manchester: U of Manchester P, 1988: 159–90.

Bell, Charles. *The Anatomy and Philosophy of Expression as Connected with the Fine Arts.* London, 1816.

Borzello, Frances. "Pictures for the People." *Victorian Artists and the City: A Collection of Critical Essays.* Ed. I. Nadel and F. A. Schwarzbach. Oxford and New York: Pergamon 1980: 30–42.

Burke, Edmund. *A Philosophical Enquiry into the Origins of Our Ideas of the Sublime and Beautiful.* Ed. J. T. Boulton. New York: Columbia UP, 1958; org. pub. 1757.

Casteras, Susan and Ronald Parkinson, eds. *Richard Redgrave, 1804–1888.* New Haven and London: Yale UP, 1988.

Codell, Julie. "Expression Over Beauty: Facial Expression, Body Language, and Circumstantiality in the Paintings of the Pre-Raphaelite Brotherhood." *Victorian Studies* 29 (1986): 255–90.

Cooper, Robin. "Millais's *The Rescue:* A Painting of a 'Dreadful Interruption of Domestic Peace.'" *Art History* 9 (1986): 475–80.

Eastlake, Elizabeth. "Physiognomy." *Quarterly Review* 90 (1851): 62–91.

Foucault, Michel. *The History of Sexuality.* Vol. I. Trans. by Robert Hurley. New York: Vintage, 1980.

Harre, Rom, ed. *The Social Construction of Emotion.* London: Basil Blackwell, 1986.

Ironside, Robin. *Pre-Raphaelite Painters.* London: Phaidon, 1948.

Kaplan, Fred. *Sacred Tears: Sentimentality in Victorian Literature.* Princeton: Princeton UP, 1987.

King, Anthony. "George Godwin and the Art Union of London, 1837–1911." *Victorian Studies* 8 (1964): 101–30.

King, Lyndel Saunders. *The Industrialization of Taste: Victorian England and the Art Union of London.* Ann Arbor: UMI Research P, 1982.

Lutz, Catherine. "Emotion, Thought, and Estrangement: Emotion as a Cultural Category." *Cultural Anthropology* 1 (1986): 287–309.

Meisel, Martin. "Seeing it Feelingly: Victorian Symbolism and Narrative Art." *Huntington Library Quarterly* 49 (1986): 67–92.

Neale, Steven. "Melodrama and Tears." *Screen* 27 (1986): 6–23.

Olmsted, John Charles. *Victorian Painting: Essays and Reviews.* Vol. I: 1832–1848. New York and London: Garland, 1980.

Phillips, Claude. *Emotion in Art.* Ed. Maurice Brockwell. New York: Books for Libraries Press, 1968; org. pub. 1925.

Roberts, Helene E. "The Sentiment of 'Reality': Thackeray's Art Criticism." *Studies in the Novel* 13 (Spr-Sum 1981): 21–39.

Rossetti, William Michael. *Fine Arts, Chiefly Contemporary.* London: Macmillan, 1867.

The Year in Dickens Studies: 1990

Chris R. Vanden Bossche

What I have attempted to do in this essay is to identify trends and directions in Dickens criticism. Given the large body of criticism under review, I have not tried to duplicate the work of reviewers who provide detailed critiques of this criticism nor have I attempted to provide an abstract of each critical work. Instead I have focussed on the major critical problems that emerge in this body of criticism, as well as trying to see what is being missed. I have grouped the criticism into two broad overlapping categories, feminist and historical criticism. As we will see, in many cases the difference between these categories is more a matter of subject than of procedure, since both feminist and historical criticism often employ the same critical protocols. However, most of the feminist criticism under review is unified by a concern with the criticism of character and identity. I have therefore followed the discussion of feminist criticism with criticism that deals primarily with identity and character. In discussing historical criticism, I will first deal with literary history and then move through several varieties of historical criticism, including the history of ideas, historicist criticism, and biographical criticism. I begin each of these two sections with criticism that is mainly theoretical in emphasis, employing Dickensian texts and the history of Dickens criticism and scholarship to explore theoretical issues. Of course, not all of the criticism falls neatly within this arrangement, but the fact that the majority of it does already reveals something about trends in Dickens criticism.

The way in which my two categories ultimately overlap is immediately evident in the most theoretical of the feminist writings. Both Judith Newton and Laurie Langbauer are concerned with the way feminist criticism engages with the historical work of Michel Foucault. Because feminist criticism is

concerned with the ways in which gender is constructed at particular historical moments, it has drawn upon various paradigms of historical analysis,
most notably those of Foucault and of Marxian literary criticism. Since much
recent Marxian criticism has been influenced by Foucault, even these paradigms are not easily separable, but, as Newton argues, one key point of difference between them is their treatment of agency and determinism. Marxist
readings of Dickens by Arnold Kettle and David Simpson, Newton argues,
suggest the possibility of agency while the work of David A. Miller suggests
that all apparent resistance only reinforces a social system that has a life of its
own unaffected by author, or critic. Newton has two objections to Miller's
analysis. First, it erases issues of gender, implying that since we are all equally unfree, women are no more restrained by the system than men; Newton
would consequently attempt a more complex reading of the ideological
dynamic of family and public world in *Bleak House* than that provided by
Miller. Second, she feels that feminism, like Marxism, has a stake in seeking
to discover some possibility of agency that can resist forms of power like
Chancery. (For another critique of Miller, see Pendleton.)

Nonetheless, Newton would not be engaging in this critique of Miller if
she did not find his readings powerful and, furthermore, did not find the work
of Foucault useful for feminism. Indeed, much recent feminist work has
found strong support for its attempts to historicize gender in Foucault's
History of Sexuality, which confirms feminist perspectives on the construction of gender. These attractions of Foucauldian history are more fully and
willingly engaged by Laurie Langbauer in *Women and Romance.* Even
though she shares Newton's concern that a Foucauldian criticism risks cir-
cumscribing all possibilities of agency, she finds in it a way of analyzing the
systems of power that control the various possibilities of identity and action
for men and women. She is interested in particular in the function of gender
in the distribution of power, how woman (and romance) functions both as a
locus of rebellion and as a figure of exclusion that enables male empower-
ment. In Dickens' fiction she identifies opposed types, the "homebody" and
the "streetwalker," the woman contained and the transgressive woman, and
explores how each is promoted and disciplined. The figures of the streetwalker and the homebody reappear in Freud, she argues, as the hysteric and the
mother and in contemporary feminist criticism as opposing stances, hysterical
claims of victimization and the desire to control the power that victimizes. In
the end, Langbauer shares Newton's concern that Foucauldian criticism flat-
tens out issues of gender and allows the appropriation of feminist critiques of
power by males seeking to gain power. She concludes that feminism must

remain inconsistent with Foucauldianism even as it employs it, as a resistance to the totalizing tendency of that perspective.

Not surprisingly, the issue of agency underlies most of the feminist essays under review. But raising the theoretical problems is one thing, solving them another. The question in this case is what can be gained from a feminist analysis of Dickens. (The question can also take other parallel forms, for example, what can be gained from a historicist, or Marxian, or deconstructive, or psychoanalytic analysis of Dickens.) This question in turn asks what value does the study of Dickens have for us. The response to this question most frequently posited by recent Dickens criticism relies upon the concept of subtext, the idea that the Dickens text contains within it articulations of alternative points of view not under the control of "Dickens" or his narrative. In response to the Foucault-influenced criticism of John Kucich and Nancy Armstrong, for example, Camille Colatosti argues that Dickens' deeply ambivalent rendering of women makes available a "liberating opening for women who take seriously the rhetoric of female goodness" (5). She argues that in supporting the ideal of feminine self-sacrifice and moral superiority Dickens risks giving women power that he feels necessary to withdraw or conceal. Her conclusion that such moves "reveal the self-contradictions of patriarchy" follows naturally from this analysis, but her critical engagement nowhere establishes how the subtext creates a liberating opening for women, a possibility of agency. Or to put it another way, if women can read the subtext now, why could not Dickens? And if Dickens could read it, then why is it not part of the overt text? Barbara Gottfried shifts the question of agency from reader to character, portraying Summerson as an agent whose narrative overtly acknowledges patriarchy but covertly attacks it, most notably in her relationship to the patriarchal John Jarndyce. Gottfried begins with the claim that the polyphony of the Dickens text "undercuts, questions, subverts the 'givens' of Victorian ideology" (169). But while her arguments for the repression of an underlying anger and resentment in Esther's narration are convincing, she provides little explanation for the existence of this subtext. Precisely because she shifts the issue of agency to Esther, Gottfried risks imputing the subversion to Dickens' own creation.

One way of answering my questions would be to see whether this subtext was legible to Dickens' contemporaries or whether it has only recently become legible owing to feminism. The "trouble" with Esther is that Dickens apparently thought that readers might actually not see any cause for resentment in her situation. The signs of Esther's resentment have now been well established, but most of the criticism still fails to explain why Dickens seems not to have noticed it himself, why he seems to have thought, in other words, that no one would think it offensive that Esther is treated as an old maid who would be happy to marry John Jarndyce. Thus while Gottfried emphasizes Esther's resentment, Chiara Briganti emphasizes the extent to which Esther is a "collaborator" with patriarchy who tries to follow its rules but discovers at moments of crisis that the rules are self-contradictory; hence she also discovers within the text a *"subtext* of madness, illness and ... deep fears" (207; emphasis added). In order to do so, she looks for moments of aporia in Esther's narrative, but argues that one cannot make a case study of Esther since she is always inscribed within the Dickens text. Nonetheless, while this protocol also yields meaningful interpretation, Briganti never manages to explain how the subtexts operates for author and reader. Marcia Goodman, whose reading of *Bleak House* shares much with these, attacks this theoretical problem more directly, arguing that as a construction of Dickens, the figure of Esther Summerson must be read ultimately as a projection of Dickens' (male) desire. Like Gottfried and Briganti, she finds in Esther a self divided between its official and its secret desires, but, she argues, Esther ultimately enacts Dickens' own anxieties about, and desire for, self-revelation. In drawing this figure back into the psyche of Dickens, Goodman does not solve the problem of agency. But her reading does accord with Newton's and Langbauer's concern about how the female figure, and her resistance, can be used for male consolation. (For a non-feminist reading that employs the idea of subtext in similar ways, see the discussion of Baldridge below.)

What is clear from these essays, and from several more discussed below, is that the criticism of character is far from dead in Dickens criticism. Indeed, feminist criticism, with its use and extension of psychoanalytic paradigms, has done a great deal to revitalize criticism of character and the thematics of identity formation. So it is surprising to come upon the argument of Baruch Hochman and Ilja Wachs that postmodernism has "deflected attention from the dramatic struggle, within texts and characters, for selfhood, or personhood, or identity" (392). They take two tacks in making this argument. First, they contend that when postmodernism argues that the novel disintegrates rather than constructs identity, it ignores the historical specificity of the models of identity that operate in the classical novel. Second, they argue that the classical novelist, the Dickens of *David Copperfield* is their principal example, already understands that identity is problematic, that it is something to be strived for, even constructed, and is not yet found at the beginning of a novel. In other words, they want to have it both ways. Postmodernist criticism misunderstands the classical novel; the classical novel already understands postmodernism. But the classical novel, as they demonstrate, does not yet fully understand the radical implications of the postmodernist view of identity. The Victorian novel often posits identity as problematic, but as their own discussion shows, more often in the form of a "buried life" not yet discovered than as a radical lack of center and absence of essence. Furthermore, their argument that postmodernism projects this radical view of identity back into the classical novel is thinly supported; it is certainly not supported by the criticism found here. The Victorian belief in the buried life is nowhere more apparent than in the feminist analyses of *Bleak House* discussed above that employ a distinction between an inner self that exhibits anger, power, and emotion against an outer self that exudes calm, love, and order. Finally, the argument of this essay seems to rest on a misunderstanding of deconstructive approaches to character. The latter would not argue that the novel intends to disintegrate character but that the project of constructing or discovering it, which is fundamental to the Victorian novel, will, by the nature of narrative, deconstruct itself. The claims of Hochman and Wachs might appear to be borne out by Cynthia Malone's essay, which finds that the various veiled women in *Bleak House* "dissolve the boundaries that appear to contain the self," that the truth of identity is not behind the veil but in the veil itself. From this vantage, Malone argues that the novel plots Esther Summerson as "someone else," "no one," and the "mistress of Bleak House" at the same time that it plots her attempt to know herself. But this argument takes place within the explicit assumption that "the detective plot of *Bleak House* suggests that the mystery of identity can be solved" and that Esther can discover her authentic self (108). The problem here is not a postmodernist perspective on identity, but the absence of an explanation for how the "plot itself" undoes the plot of identity. In Malone's reading the plot becomes the agent for deconstructing identity because she brackets the question of how this counterplot can be accounted for.

Rather than being limited by a postmodern reduction of the Victorian treatment of identity, Dickens criticism would benefit from working with other paradigms of character analysis than the psychoanalytic model of identity formation, from, for example, studies of Victorian (i.e., pre-Freudian) theories of identity formation or studies of the semiotics of identity. There is hardly an allusion in these essays to Esther being a governess, yet in the mid-century context the figure of the governess evokes an immense array of connotations that bear directly on her position as a subject and her possibilities for identity formation. While the analysis of textual contradictions may enable us to discover those historical contradictions that underlay or produce

Victorian gender ideology, I think Dickens' novels are asked to do too much work by themselves. It is this absence of attention to historical context that has led me to treat these feminist essays, and the essays dealing with character in the discussion that follows, apart from the historical criticism of Dickens (for an exception, see the discussion of Perera below). As the influence of work like Nancy Armstrong's begins to be felt, there should be more emphasis on the historicity of gender identity. (For other feminist and gender-based criticism, see Feinberg and Roberts.)

Nor is feminist criticism the only kind that keeps alive the criticism of character and identity formation. Richard Gaughan's Marxist analysis of *Our Mutual Friend* explores how an individual, living in a society that orders discourse so as to construct an imprisoning identity, seeks to get clear of those constraints and discover "an authentic identity" (232). Like the feminist critics of *Bleak House,* Gaughan focuses on principal characters who resist a restrictive and dominant order. What gets missed is the differences in the formation of male and female identity discussed by Colatosti, who finds that male and female self-denial function differently in the formation of identity. Similarly Nancy Schaumburger's discussion of the use of time to construct identity in *The Mystery of Edwin Drood* is limited by the assumption that an "integration of personality and capacity for further psychological expansion … only comes on the terms of a positive relation to their past, present, and future" (139). If postmodernist critics tend to overemphasize the undermining of identity, these assumptions from American ego psychology also project twentieth-century conceptions of identity onto Victorian fiction.

Nowhere is the predominance of the paradigms of identity formation more in evidence than in Beth Herst's *The Dickens Hero: Selfhood and Alienation in the Dickens World.* Indeed, these paradigms are apparently so taken for granted that Herst can employ a vocabulary of concepts like alienation, integration, and "true selfhood" without even referring to the theories of identity from which these concepts derive (162). Herst attempts to place Dickens in the context of debates about the nature of literary heroes, but ultimately she provides too little of this context to provide a literary history of character in Dickens and the Victorian novel. Her book provides an account of Dickens's attempt to create a hero, in which the novels up to *Dombey and Son* fail, *David Copperfield* first succeeds, and the later novels shift the emphasis toward the social context. This Whiggish narrative is complicated by the fact that it takes Dickens's comments on the "natural" hero in the 1848 preface to *Nicholas Nickleby* as his standard for characterization rather than as part of the history of his changing conception of human identity and literary characterization; in other words, the earlier novels fail to meet the standard set out in 1848 while the first novel written after the preface, *David Copperfield,* not surprisingly follows the principles outlined there. Herst has some interesting things to say along the way about Dickens' treatment of the coming of age of the young hero, but her analysis of alienation from society is limited by the absence of any analysis of how Dickens presents "society" itself. Furthermore, Herst quite literally limits her study to the Dickens "hero"; heroines are not discussed (Dick Swiveller is the hero of *The Old Curiosity Shop,* Richard Carstone of *Bleak House).* Consequently, character is treated as if the process of identity formation were historically and culturally universal; social alienation is never discussed in terms of gender and class constructs of identity. Ironically, this approach, which is so much at home with issues of character and identity, precisely fails to take into account the historical specificity of models for identity as demanded by Hochman and Wachs.

Nowhere is this absence of historical specificity of character more evident than in another study that seeks to defend the study of character, Jeffrey Berman's *Narcissism and the Novel.* Berman is an adherent of American ego psychology and directs his study against the tendency in literary criticism to prefer Lacan's revisions of psychoanalysis. Citing Peter Brooks's arguments against the traditional uses of psychoanalytic theory to analyze characters, he argues that Brooks reduces psychoanalysis to mere metaphor. Like Hochman and Wachs, he mistakenly assumes that this means that the study of character can no longer take place, rather than that the study of character must be reorientated (as it is in the feminist projects discussed above). He wants to argue, instead for the scientific validity, the empirical verifiability, of ego psychology and its paradigms of identity. Thus he begins with a review of current psychological theories of narcissism, and then proceeds to an analysis of character in the novel in terms of these paradigms, which means ascribing clinically defined narcissism to literary characters. The heroes and heroines of novels from *Frankenstein to Mrs. Dalloway,* he argues, "suffer severe narcissistic injuries" and "then spend the rest of their lives struggling to come to terms with this experience" (49). What is found in the novels is always foreordained by the psychoanalytic paradigms, even though, as is clear from Berman's discussion, there is no final agreement on the etiology of narcissism. Finally, Berman also fails to address the historical specificity of his subject matter. While his survey of the myth of Narcissus from Ovid to Kohut and Kernberg suggests a universal psychology of narcissism, he never explains why his study is confined to novels of the nineteenth and early twentieth centuries, why the novel has any special relationship to this myth.

Ronald Thomas in *Dreams of Authority: Freud and the Fictions of the Unconscious* takes exactly the opposite tack; he attempts to see what the novel contributed to Freud's psychological theories, notably the theory of dreams. Rather than reading psychoanalysis back into the nineteenth-century novel, Thomas argues that the novel forms the prehistory of psychoanalysis. He works forward from dreams of achieving authority in the novel to Freud's fascination with both the novels and dreaming in order to argue that the novel helped shape the discourse of dreaming and the unconscious that Freud took up in his novelistic *Interpretation of Dreams*. Thomas attempts to move beyond the confines of analysis of the subject by investigating how the representation of dreams in gothic, autobiography, and detective fiction encode masterplots that employ the language of medicine, politics, and economics to establish the authority (or identity) of the self. This framework enables him to produce powerful readings, for example, his paired readings of *Jane Eyre* and *Great Expectations*. His fundamental argument is that unlike Jane Eyre, who treats her dreams "as expressions of psychic capital to be put to use in the development of a more authentic, independent self," Pip represses his dreams of a tainted life and depends upon others to construct his identity. Not until he confronts his dreams can he take possession of himself. The result is not only a subtle reading of the novel itself, but an investigation of how Victorian constructions of gender produce differences between these novels and in turn how these novels work to produce gendered identity.

By demonstrating the ways that the discourse on dreaming taken up by psychoanalysis were inflected by Victorian ideas about polity, economy, and medicine, Thomas puts the novel in history as well as writing a history of the novel. In this regard, his book could be placed in the category of historical criticism and literary history to which I now want to turn. There are several types of historical criticism represented here. First, there is literary history, criticism that reads Dickens' works in the diachronic context of the history of literary forms, for example, genre criticism that takes up Dickens within the history of the novel. A parallel and related form of literary history is that which draws upon the history of ideas; the criticism under review includes a number of studies that read Dickens in terms of the history of philosophy and religion. Such histories tend to work from readings of the texts outward to history; thus its paradigmatic form is a series of discrete readings of individual novels presented in chronological order. The books by Langbauer, Berman and Thomas all follow this format (the latter is a slight variant) as do those by Polhemus and Shaw discussed below. In contrast to this diachronic approach to literary history and the history of ideas, another kind of historical criticism treats a particular era synchronically, usually reading a single novel in terms of various contemporary contexts. Some criticism of this sort, like literary history, works from literary texts outward to shed light on historical contexts, but much of it reads from the contexts in, letting the context shed light on the novel. Of this latter kind of criticism, I find two types represented here. First, there is a criticism concerned with reading literature in terms of themes, ideas, events, and other historical developments. Second, there is a criticism that seeks to explore the production of literary texts in relation to immediate biographical and historical determinations. Once again, I begin with a relatively theoretical essay that sheds light on the problematics of this kind of criticism.

Jonathan Loesberg's "Deconstruction, Historicism, and Overdetermination" is concerned with the conflict between deconstruction and Marxism over whether to explain contradictions formally or historically. Loesberg uses readings of *Robert Elsmere* and *Dombey and Son* to argue that precisely because, as both deconstruction and Marxism would argue, contradictions in the treatment of theology, gender, and class are overdetermined, no ultimate cause can be found in either history—the privileged ground of Marxism—or form—the privileged ground of deconstruction. He is concerned with the totalizing tendencies of both forms of criticism, but his analysis finds an answer to this tendency in the principle of overdetermination itself, since it posits multiple causes rather than a single monolithic center of power. Furthermore, he wants to set deconstruction and historicism (or Marxism) against one another so that Marxism can counter deconstruction's tendency to flatten out and thus negate historical specificities and deconstruction can provide an alternative to the tendency in Marxian criticism to privilege economic determinism as the ultimate, totalizing ground of interpretation. In his readings of the novels, Loesberg demonstrates how stopping at the reading produced by either one involves foreclosing the role played by other. These problematics are borne out by the criticism under review that tends either to work from formalist (in Loesberg's terms deconstructive) analysis outward to historical context or from historical contexts inward, in a relatively deterministic reading. I find that, as Loesberg would argue, the richest criticism moves dialectically between the history of the novel and the novel in history.

Patrick O'Donnell's essay on ventriloquism in *Our Mutual Friend,* part of a larger projected study of the figurations of voice in modern narrative, does set a deconstructive reading of voicing in a historical context. Starting from a discussion of the principles of ventriloquism by Dickens's contemporary, George Smith, and Sloppy's well known ability to do the police in different voices, O'Donnell focusses on the way ventriloquism involves the attempt to speak for an other. If Sloppy's ability to disappear into the voices of the police parallels Dickens' disappearance into the novel, a coercive desire to speak for others is more clearly manifested in Podsnap's penchant for sweeping away undesirable, foreign speech and for suppressing his daughter. O'Donnell argues that *Our Mutual Friend* marks a point in Dickens' career when his ability to mimic others was so powerful that it tended to overwhelm his own voice; he thus represents the novel as a struggle between Dickens and his others. O'Donnell's essay is nicely complimented by Wendell Harris's discussion of varieties of double-voicing in the nineteenth-century novel. Through discussion of examples from Eliot and Dickens, Harris clarifies and expands the functions of Bakhtin's polyphony, heteroglossia, hybridization, and other forms of double voicing. He concludes that the apparent emphasis on "telling" rather than "showing" in Victorian novels begins to disappear once one notes the degree to which the narration reflects various voices besides that of the narrator. These two essays are among the very few in this group that treat the history of narrative form in Dickens (for another, see Philip Collins). Even criticism that deals with genre tends to be more concerned with theme than form.

Such is the case with Laurie Langbauer's *Women and Romance* and Ruth Newton and Naomi Lebowitz's *Impossible Romance*. I want to return to Langbauer's book because it is also a study of genre history, moving from Charlotte Lennox's *Female Quixote* to Eliot's *Middlemarch*. Langbauer is concerned with how the culture that produced the novel constructs varying versions of women and romance, consistently construing them as related to one another. In her introductory chapter, she examines how histories of the novel (by Watts and Jameson) have privileged men and novels over women and romance, defining the novel as the exclusion of romance that is further identified with the feminine. In her discussion of Dickens, she finds that his streetwalkers represent the need to escape the strictures of power and his homebodies represent the need to contain the threat of women liberated from power. Streetwalkers provide a locus of rebellion that provides consolation even as its dangers are circumscribed and expelled. While Langbauer works primarily through readings of novels, she seeks to discover in them historical determinations of gender.

By contrast, Newton and Lebowitz's *Impossible Romance* tends to discuss romance in a metacritical fashion as something that exists apart from the culture that produced the novels of Dickens, Zola, James, and Manzoni. They connect the appearance of romance themes in the novel to certain broad cultural situations—particularly the crisis of religious faith—but unlike Langbauer they do not treat it as having a history. Newton and Lebowitz's project is to portray Dickens as a "salvational" novelist, using romance to produce novels that attempt to inscribe the possibilities of a better life in dialectical relation to the realities of his historical moment. While current criticism tends to portray Dickens as a skeptical writer, Newton and Lebowitz argue that he never achieved the skepticism of the twentieth-century novel. But this is hardly grounds for claiming that his liberal humanism should be read as "giv[ing] the Christian spirit its own dominion in an age that sought its dilution" (47). As opposed to reading Dickens from a postmodern perspective, they seem to want to push him into a pre-Victorian framework, reading his novels as "morality plays" (66). It seems to me that their contrast between the "sacred mode" of Dickens' novels and the "secular analysis" of postmodern criticism posits a false duality that fails to explain, in the end, the importance of romance in engaging with the skepticism of Dickens' era. Patrick McCarthy also argues that *Dombey and Son* at least is a "secular Christian version of a *morality play* worked out in particularizing, middle-class art form" (91; emphasis added). McCarthy's analysis, however, focusses not on the thematic deployment of these concerns, but on the use of aggressive language that reflects social anarchy in a Victorian psychomachia that, unlike the later novels, achieves a successful resolution.

Michael Wheeler also feels that recent criticism has too much emphasized Dickens' "more sceptical and 'demythologizing' side" and ignored his engagements with and contributions to Victorian theology (267). In the first half of *Death and the Future Life in Victorian Literature and Theology*, Wheeler provides a masterful survey of the Victorian discourse of consolation and its treatment of the four last things—death, judgment, heaven, and hell. Wheeler is highly attentive not only to the ways in which the Victorians attempted to create a discourse of consolation, but how this discourse inevitably raised questions about language, narrative, and representation, how "it is at the very point of stress or fracture in the discourse of consolation that both the provisional nature of language and communication *and* the grounds of Christian faith are laid bare" (21). In the second half of the book, he brings his study of the four last things to bear on four major Victorian texts, including *Our Mutual Friend*. Whereas Newton and Lebowitz try to trace Dickens' humanism to a source in Christianity, Wheeler more carefully attempts to read his novel as an intertextual engagement with the disputed areas of Christian theology, placing Dickens in the camp of the mainstream broad church. Just as Thomas suggests how Victorian novelists contribute to the development of a psychology of dreams, so Wheeler presents Dickens as a creator of popular and influential images of the four last things. In the end, however, Wheeler does not really settle whether Dickens adapts broad church views of the four last things for a secular perspective on life or whether he adapts his novel to his religious beliefs. By treating Dickens' novel separately he loses the sense of dialogue that he produces in the first part of his study, with the result that the two parts do not entirely mesh. Another attempt to place Dickens in this context, Lewis Horne's reading of *Little Dorrit,* puts him somewhere between the demythologizer and the advocate of Christianity. In reading the novel as a critique of Victorian capitalism, Lewis also argues that Dickens portrays a fallen world, abandoned by God, in which characters must create there own paradise, or hell.

W. David Shaw, like Wheeler, is concerned with the relationships between the history of philosophy, theology, and literature. His *Victorians and Mystery: Crises of Representation* began, he informs us, as an experiment to test the theories of his earlier study of philosophical and theological episte- mology, *The Lucid Veil.* Just as Wheeler moves from a discussion of theologi- cal debates to specific literary texts, Shaw moves in his two books from a dis- cussion of Victorian epistemology to its role in specific literary works. Shaw situates his project in the history of ideas, providing a complex yet intelligible conceptual map of Victorian epistemology, inflected by a sense that it includes "spaces of dissension" (10). While this approach tends to privilege ideas, to suggest that they precede literary form, Shaw's rhetorical analyses of literary texts enables him to move from text to epistemology as well. In order to explore the "Victorian discovery that ... knowledge reveals mystery," he focuses on three areas that manifest an epistemological crisis of knowledge and representation—the unconscious, identity, and theories of knowledge— and three phases of Victorian culture—the authoritarian, agnostic, and exis- tential or pragmatic (322). He places Dickens in his discussion of the uncon- scious, arguing that in *Great Expectations,* an unconscious, secret story is told through figures of repetition and the collapse of apparent differences. As Pip's knowledge of his expectations is both known and unknown to him, knowledge that is really knowledge is discovered to be unknown and unknowable, even when, as in *Great Expectations* and Hardy's *Tess,* the nov- elist evinces a faith that knowledge is recoverable.

Against the objections to the secularizing tendency in Dickens criticism raised by Wheeler and company, the portrait of Dickens as a secularizer is carried forward by Robert Polhemus in his *Erotic Faith,* an extension of the argument in his earlier *Comic Faith.* The difference in these approaches to Dickens and other Victorian writers may not be as great as it seems, however. Increasingly the process of sacralizing religion is being recognized as simultaneously the process of secularizing literature. Certainly, Polhemus's argument is consistent with such a hypothesis. He regards the novel as a means for imagining forms of faith that will replace institutional religious forms and erotic faith as a principle that shaped the nineteenth-century novel. Erotic faith, he writes, is "an emotional conviction, ultimately religious in nature, that meaning, value, hope, and even transcendence can be found through ... erotically focused love" (1). The context for his history of erotic faith and the novel is the history of erotic love as portrayed in Western painting from the Renaissance to the early twentieth century. One would like to see a fuller elaboration of the ideology of eros, but Polhemus prefers to work with the individual novels, and, like other literary historians, works primarily from the novels outward to Victorian culture's faith in eros, rather than from the culture inward, reading these ten novels for signs of a search for faith, for the kind of faith they put in eros. In his reading of *Great Expectations,* he regards Pip as driven by a desire for his lost mother, whom he attempts to discover in Miss Havisham, reading the scene in which her dress catches fire and Pip saves her as a parodic wedding night. Against Wheeler, he asks why Pip should mislead Magwitch about his love for Estella, if "there is eternal life and judgment, according to Christian belief, and if Pip, Magwitch, Dickens and his readers really have faith in God and the afterlife" (137). In other words, why does Pip offer Magwitch the dying consolation of his love for Estella? Taking up a related subject, Jon Reed reads *Great Expectations* as an attack on Petrarchan love conventions, the aristocratic medieval revival of the nineteenth century, and, by extension, demands for platonic aestheticism, as opposed to vulgarity, in art; in other words, *Great Expectations* is Dickens' defense of poesy. At the same time, Reed concludes that, in spite of defending vulgarity, Dickens fears the energies of lower classes as represented by Magwitch, and seeks through Pip's story, not the desire to be a chivalric hero but to divert working class energies into less dangerous channels. With the major discussions of Thomas, Polhemus, and Shaw, one has to wonder if *Great Expectations,* long a classroom favorite, is taking its place at the forefront of the Dickens canon. This place is summed up in Nicola Bradbury's critical overview, which synthesizes much of the strong body of criticism that has grown up around this novel in recent years.

Turning from literary history to historical studies of literature, I want to examine first criticism that focusses on broad historical contexts, contexts that can be regarded as at a distance from the text's immediate circumstances of production. These studies overlap with the criticism of character and thematic criticism when they examine these entities within a larger historical context. In this regard, for example, Richard Gaughan's essay might have been included here. This criticism may also overlap with the history of ideas and literary history just discussed in so far as it examines interrelations among ideas, literature, and material culture. But the difference in the criticism discussed below is that it tends to focus more specifically on social institutions, not just on the ideas that generate and are generated by them; it would be as if Wheeler had focussed on the relationships of Victorian authors to the institution of the church rather than just theological discourse.

Suvendrini Perera's essay on *Dombey and Son,* for example, is concerned both with the institutions and discourses of empire. Perera explores the contradictions within the discourse of imperialism, which adopted the ideology of the feminine sphere so that free trade could portray itself as possessing the feminine virtues of pacifism as against the older, violent, monopolist approach to empire. Drawing on the official *Narrative* of the Niger expedition (1848), Dickens' published critique of it, Thackeray's *The Newcomes,* and other material, Perera argues that in *Dombey and Son* "gender and trade are organized rather as linked operations of a mercantile economy, with Florence's unrelenting and seemingly immutable 'femininity' as much a construct of that economy as Dombey's financial thuggery" (609). While the novel seems to argue for the inclusion of the feminine in commerce—"And so Dombey and Son ... is indeed a daughter ... after all"—it ultimately uses the feminine to reinstate unitary patriarchy; the last word, Perera notes, is that "from his daughter, after all, another Dombey and Son will ascend ... triumphant" (616). Perera's essay not only treats gender in the novel in terms of a contextualizing discourse about men and women, but demonstrates how the discourse of gender is interrelated with the discourse of commerce and empire.

Paul Schacht provides a complimentary reading of the figure of nature in economic discourse as Dickens engaged with it in *Hard Times* and *Dombey and Son.* He argues that, against the utilitarian argument that the laws of nature dictated laissez-faire economics, Dickens countered that nature dictated social responsibility and nurture. In *Dombey and Son,* he contends, culture is feminized by associating nature with nurture through the figure of nursing. But, whereas Perera regards this as a move to coopt the feminine (here her argument is similar to Langbauer's), Schacht argues that, in so far as it under-mines utilitarian economics, it is "subversive" (95). Between them, these two essays show how Dickens' novel attempts to mediate the contradictions in the values of his culture, but they cast his relationship to commerce in contrasting forms. Perera portrays Dickens as more immediately attached to commerce, criticizing it in order to reform and save it, while Schacht has Dickens taking the stance of the outsider, open to more radical social transformation. They take similar stances on the issue of gender, but their conclusions are closer to one another. Schacht acknowledges that Dickens was no feminist but argues that he helped reorient the meaning of paternalism away form traditional masculinity, while Perera finds that the reinstatement of patriarchy in the principal narrative is problematized by narratives like that concerning Alice Marwood. Yet another reading of *Dombey* that focuses on its engagement with the domain of commerce is Murray Baumgarten's exploration of the much discussed symbol of the railway. Baumgarten argues that it should be read not only in relation to the novel's themes but its use of space and time, which were reshaped by the railroad and the attendant forces of industrial capitalism. He notes that novel reading itself became a way of passing time while riding in trains, thus suggesting how novel time and train time interpen-etrate one another.

The essays of Perera and Schacht represent one of two protocols for his-torical criticism represented here. Both deal literally with con-texts, other texts, and patterns of discourse, reading Dickens in dialectical relation with these contexts. The difficulty with this protocol is borne out by the contradic-tory conclusions of Perera and Schacht. Part of the problem may be focussing too narrowly on just one aspect of history, even on just one "con-text," the aspect of historical criticism that Dominick LaCapra has criticized as weak montage. Yet when the scholarship is good, when the procedure is not just the surprising juxtaposition of one con-text with a Dickens text but the reconsti-tution of a discursive field through the careful use of numerous con-texts, then the results can be fruitful. Nancy Metz's essay on *Little Dorrit,* like these, illustrates the advantages and disadvantages of this critical procedure (it is probably no coincidence that all three appeared in *Victorian Studies*). Just as Perera uses the Niger expedition *Narrative* to examine Dickens and empire, Nancy Metz uses Layard's contemporaneous *Ninevah and Its Remains* to examine Dickens and London. Beginning with the ways in which *Little Dorrit* connects a sense of place to a sense of identity, especially Clennam's tenuous identity when he returns to a radically changed London, Metz argues that a concern with vanishing civilizations and the way their remains persist in the present pervades Dickens' representation of London in the novel. While there are risks in focussing on the discourse of vanished empires, Metz demonstrates its breadth through numerous citations of texts and graphic works. Alexander Pettit uses similar procedures to trace a shift in attitudes toward criminal punishment in the nineteenth century, examining the way in which novels by Eliot and Dickens, like contemporary discourse on criminality, treat the criminal as the product of the social order, rather than violator of it, more as victim than as perpetrator. In *Hard Times,* crime breaks down a false social order—Gradgrindian utility—and enables the production of the family.

At the other end of the spectrum are readings that employ a generalized contextual framework, one already established by historical scholarship. Such frameworks range from materialist analyses of social institutions like patriarchy and political economy to histories of ideas, such as solipsism and skepticism. Neither procedure—that of using generalized or specific contexts—necessarily implies a particular relationship between text and context. Generally speaking, there are three possible relationships. First, one can treat literary texts as formative of the context (even if they "deconstruct" it); second, one can treat them as determined, formed by, the context; finally, one can read text and context dialectically, as mutually forming one another. Whether one uses generalized or particular contexts, one can cast the relationship in any of these forms. However, criticism like that just discussed above, which works with particular con-texts, tends to encourage one to read the relationship dialectically in so far as it does not privilege one over the other. However, there are other considerations about critical procedure that must be taken into account. What happens, for example, if you put your discussion of con-texts first, then proceed to Dickens' text? Does this not encourage one to read the con-texts as determining the Dickens text? Lack of attention to such factors can also ultimately obscure the issue of how text and context are related, undermining the critical project.

Critics who use a generalized context often proceed by performing a close reading of the novel and using the context to delimit that reading. Simon Edwards in his essay on "Anorexia Nevrosa vs. the Fleshpots of London" in *Oliver Twist* reads problematics of the novel in terms of the contexts of Victorian consumer culture and recent scholarship on anorexia. Edwards notes that the story begins with the workhouse system that attempts to starve the poor out of poverty, and he goes on to connect this attitude to the anorexic ideal of womanhood. His essay then proceeds to examine how the novel deals with contradictions between this ideal and the evolution of an economic system geared up for increased consumption. Cates Baldridge assumes an even more generalized context in his new analysis of Dickens' oft-noted ambivalence toward revolution as exhibited in *A Tale of Two Cities*. Working from a Marxian perspective, he argues that while Dickens overtly criticizes the revolution for subsuming the individual in the social mass and simultaneously reducing humanity to its lowest level, the novel's subtext reveals a Dickens who, as a critic of commercial culture, is sympathetic with the revolution's anti-individualism. Baldridge finds criticism of individualism in the "Night Shadows" passage as well as in the characterizations of Lorry and Carton; it is ironic, he concludes, that "Carton can only ensure the safety of Liberal society ... by temporarily violating one of its fundamental tenets" (647). If Baldridge tries to find the subtext in which Dickens takes an anti-individualist stance in a historical novel, Alison Case focuses on the antihistorical individualism of his earlier historical novel, *Barnaby Rudge*. Case argues that Dickens, though apparently seeking to emulate Scott's historical novels, actually was writing against Scott and against history, that the popular riot, as Dickens represents it, is not the result of historical causes but simply of individual evil. Case's literary history at least provides some context for Dickens' antihistoricism, but it is too narrowly confined to literary history, as Baldridge's argument suggests. By contrast, Baldridge's strong reading of the novel, like much of the criticism that relies upon a generalized context, tends to treat that context as static and rigid, not changing and not in dialogue with Dickens. He works entirely from the text, not citing any scholarship on the context. Similarly, Edwards uses recent literature on anorexia as well as undocumented assumptions about consumer culture as a wedge to pry into the thematics of food and consumption. These critics can read the text in interesting ways precisely because of their provisional assumptions about context, but ultimately the relationship between text and context, whether it is constructive, determined, or dialectical, remains unexplored. (For other criticism that addresses historical contexts, see Dunlop, Horton, Philpotts, and Schlicke.)

Turning to those studies that focus on the more immediate circumstances of the production of Dickens' novels, I come to Kathryn Chittick's *Dickens and the 1830s* and Jerome Meckier's *Innocent Abroad*. Chittick writes in her preface that what began as a reception history of Dickens' career up through *Barnaby Rudge* ended up as study of the "profession of authorship" (ix). By reading together the first reviews and comments on Dickens' early fiction, Dickens' own comments on his aims and purposes in writing, the novels themselves, and contemporary events, Chittick demonstrates how Dickens' personal history, the history of the publishing industry, the social history of England, and other factors converged in his emergence as a novelist. Her thesis is that while Dickens early on aspired to be a novelist, neither he nor his contemporaries regarded *Pickwick, Oliver Twist, Old Curiosity Shop,* or even *Nickleby,* a novel as that genre was currently understood, that *Barnaby Rudge* was the first work he published in which he set out to write a novel. Through careful reading of reviews, contracts, and letters, she demonstrates the variety of ways in which both Dickens and his readers apprehended his early works as journalism, magazine articles, story-telling, and so on. This argument might seem to be unduly tendentious, but Chittick's point is that this period of experimentation changed the novel and made Dickens a different novelist than he set out to be. She uses frequent complaints about certain qualities of Dickens' early fiction, for example, that he subordinated plot to character, to argue that instead of conforming to existing paradigms for the novel, Dickens reoriented the novel to suit his methods of writing. She shows that the history of his plans for *Rudge,* as well as its content, manifest that he set out to be a novelist in the mold of Scott—it was supposed to be a triple-decker like the novels of Scott—but like all Dickens' fiction it ended up as a serial. She discusses as well the impact of Lockhart's biography, which when it appeared in 1837–1838 led Dickens to see pitfalls in Scott's career. Dickens was remolding the novelistic career and the novel. I only wish Chittick had gone even farther in transforming her reception study—at times it remains primarily that—into a study of how Dickens shaped his early career.

Jerome Meckier's *Innocent Abroad* seeks to challenge and correct certain claims that have been made about Dickens' motivations and behavior during his journeys to America in 1842 and 1867. The only part of this book that bears directly on Dickens' writing is the argument that the effects of the 1842 journey were more wideranging than they are generally thought to be and that the introduction of the American episodes in *Martin Chuzzlewit* was not gratuitous. This, of course, does not solve the question of whether the journey was a cause or an effect of Dickens' shift in perspective. While this aspect of Meckier's argument is productive, much of his book engages in fruitless sparring with critics over whether Dickens was in the right in his strictures against America and in raising the issue of copyright during the first journey and whether the second was motivated by simple greed. Furthermore, Meckier tends to work out minor arguments at a length disproportionate to their importance. For example, Meckier claims that other critics have failed to see that the question "how much did Ticknor and Fields know about Ellen Ternan?" is one of the "really interesting questions" about the 1867 journey, a question he feels important enough to require fifty pages of discussion. To be sure, when interpretations are built upon the construction of biographical events, it is important to settle as definitely as possible such issues of fact. But it seems to me unhealthy to be so immersed in the world of Dickens' studies that this question seems *really interesting;* the contentious tone of the entire book makes it seem ultimately more interested in arguing with other critics rather than in studying Dickens. Meckier does compile exhaustively the evidence on several questions with which Dickens biography has been concerned, and those dealing with these questions will want to consult him, but those seeking enlightenment on the imaginative elements of Dickens' American engagements will be disappointed.

Whereas Chittick's and Meckier's biographical criticism works from biographical material towards generalizations about Dickens' career as a novelist, Peter Ackroyd's new biography resists the tendency to shape the narrative along the lines of general biographical developments. Thus his thirty-five chapters are simply numbered but not titled, as if such labels would be reductive. Ackroyd's narrative appears to take up the facts one at a time, working empirically, accumulating detail, to build a highly circumstantial narrative. Yet his narrative is not as rigorously historicist as Chittick's tries to be. For example, in Chittick's account Dickens somewhat accidentally improvised his way to the serial novel, whereas for Ackroyd it was a stroke of genius showing prophetic insight. In spite of his apparent resistance to generalization, Ackroyd does generalize about how circumstantial details reveal Dickens' character, and he often indicates how a biographical episode was later taken up in the novels. Nor will scholars be able to mine the vast amount of material provided in this long biography, for while Ackroyd has included general bibliographical notes for each chapter, he does not give the sources for his quotations. In his defense, it should be said that Ackroyd is a novelist and this biography has certain literary pretensions and so may not be concerned with the scholarly audience; I will leave the discussion of its literary merits, however, to other reviewers.

Finally, two books take us forward through history, examining what happens when, as Paul Davis characterizes it, the Dickens text becomes a culture text. Davis's book will be appreciated by all who are interested in popular culture and the way Dickens' *Christmas Carol* has been transformed into modern folklore. Davis is not concerned with "fidelity" to Dickens' story, but with the ways that at different moments in its history since 1843 Anglo-American culture has focussed on different aspects of the tale, making it over in its own image—the way the Dickens text could be revised by different cultures at different times while at the same time the text constrained and delimited such revisionings. (It should be mentioned in passing that Davis's book is itself part of the phenomenon it discusses, a large-format, illustrated coffee table book, released in time for Christmas 1990.) Indeed, Davis regards the *Carol* itself a refashioning of pastoral myths for an urban culture. After showing how Dickens' tale rereads Christmas traditions, he traces the movement of the *Carol* from secular scripture to children's literature, from celebration of the "good man of business" to its "greening" for postmodern society. Such a summary hardly does justice to Davis's rich readings, or his survey of stage and film versions, illustrations, and writings on the *Carol*. Just to take one example, he shows that Edwin Meese's defense of Scrooge in the early 1980s (for those who do not recall, Reagan had been called a Scrooge for his comments on homelessness) was not an aberration but part of a trend in the use of the *Carol* that had been developing for some time, the emergence of a "supply-side Scrooge." Davis's general procedure is to reconstruct an era's reading of *Christmas Carol* through his reading of materials from that era. This posits some theoretical difficulties, for the critic's reading tends to merge with that of the past era, which, is itself, of course, only a hypothetical construct. Nonetheless, Davis negotiates these difficulties well, and, in spite of inevitable reductions, manages to keep his portrayals particular through the reading of individual reinterpretations of the story such as Capra's *It's a Wonderful Life*. Whereas Davis rejects the practice of merely comparing stage and film adaptations to the novel but reads them as interpretations of the story, *Screening the Novel* by Robert Giddings et al. does just that in its analysis of David Leans' *Great Expectations* and other film adaptations of Dickens' novels. While the introduction summarizes the theoretical issues involved in screen adaptation, the chapter on Lean's adaptation judges it entirely in terms of the ways it fails, and must fail, to reproduce the novel. Apart from failing to follow the introduction's advice that a film be regarded as an interpretation, not necessarily an imitation (one suspects that the book's three authors did not consult very much here), it tells us little about why film adaptations of Dickens have been on the whole undistinguished and nothing new about Dickens' novels as culture texts.

What makes Davis's study refreshing is that, while it works with a classic text, it has developed new strategies for studying it. Whereas his procedure of recovering different "readings" of the text has its own problematics—as we have seen what interpretative protocol does not?—it at least gives us a new way of apprehending the literary text. Novelty is not the point here, but rather that the aims of some of the criticism under discussion here seem to me at odds with the critical procedures employed. In particular, I think that both feminist and historical criticism would benefit from an attempt to treat the relationship between literary text and social context more dialectically. I do not mean to privilege any particular set of critical procedures, but simply to argue that more attention be given to how the critic represents the relationship between text and context, whatever procedures he or she employs. I emphasize this issue because nearly all of the criticism under review does deal in some way with the contexts of Dickens' novels—the contexts of gender, empire, industrial commerce, class, social order, social change, religion, law, the fine arts, science, and so on. What the criticism of recent years has shown us, as does the criticism under review, is that we cannot regard Dickens' works either as simple reflections or constructions of his culture. If we are to learn more about the relationship between Dickens and his culture, we need not only compare text and context but we must also investigate the inner workings of the relationship between them.

WORKS CITED

Brief articles and introductory works not mentioned in the review are annotated here.

Ackroyd, Peter. *Dickens.* New York: Harper, 1990.

Alexander, Doris. "Dickens and the False True Story." *Dickensian* 86 (1990): 88–92. Discovers that the motives of the woman on whom the Boythorn episode in *Bleak House* is based were not what Dickens and Forster thought they were.

———. "Dickens Speaks Yiddish." *Dickens Quarterly* 7 (1990): 338–39. Notes Dickens's reportage of Yiddish terms that had been absorbed into thieves' cant.

Allingham, Philip V. "The Names of Dickens's American Originals in *Martin Chuzzlewit.*" *Dickens Quarterly* 7 (1990): 329–37. The names of American characters exhibit "an ironic undercutting at work between Christian and surname" (329).

Andrade, Mary Anne. "Wake into Dream." *Dickensian* 86 (1990): 17–28. Alternating waking and dream states in *Oliver Twist.*

Baldridge, Cates. "Alternatives to Bourgeois Individualism in *A Tale of Two Cities.*" *Studies in English Literature* 30 (1990): 634–54.

Baumgarten, Murray. "Dombey and Son and the Industrial World." *Dickens Studies Annual* 19 (1990): 65–89.

Berman, Jeffrey. *Narcissism and the Novel.* New York: New York UP, 1990.

Bradbury, Nicola. *Charles Dickens' Great Expectations.* New York: St. Martin's, 1990. Part of the *Critical Studies of Key Texts* series. Synthesizes much recent criticism of the novel and argues that the novel operates persistently on two levels, specifically of story/secret, structure/suspense, scene/subtext, symbols/signals, and identity/function.

Brattin, Joel J. "Some Old Curiosities from *The Old Curiosity Shop* Manuscript." Dickens *Quarterly* 7 (1990): 218–34. Transcribes and comments on numerous passages that were deleted by Dickens from manuscripts and proofs.

Briganti, Chiara. "The Monstrous Actress: Esther Summerson's Spectral Name." *Dickens Studies Annual* 19 (1990): 205–30.

Butterworth, R. D. "Hoghton Tower and the Picaresque of 'George Silverman's Explanation.'" *Dickensian* 86 (1990): 93–104. Analysis and interpretation via discussion of geographical source and genre.

Case, Alison. "Against Scott: The Antihistory of Dickens's *Barnaby Rudge.*" *Clio* 19 (1990): 127–45.

Cayzer, Elizabeth. "Dickens and his Late Illustrators. A Change in Style: 'Phiz' and *A Tale of Two Cities.*" *Dickensian* 86 (1990): 131–41. Argues for the value of Phiz's final set of illustrations for a Dickens novel.

Chaudhuri, Brahma. "Dickens's Serial Structure in *Bleak House.*" *Dickensian* 86 (1990): 66–84. A reception history of the monthly numbers and a discussion of the use of monthly numbers to structure the novel, both to sustain reader interest and for larger thematic ends.

Chittick, Kathryn. *Dickens and the 1830s.* New York: Cambridge UP, 1990.

Colatosti, Camille. "Male vs. Female Self-Denial: The Subversive Potential of the Feminine Ideal in Dickens." *Dickens Studies Annual* 19 (1990): 1–24.

Collins, Irene. "Charles Dickens and the French Revolution." *Literature and History* 2nd ser. 1 (1990): 40–57. Sources for and influences on *A Tale of Two Cities,* including contemporary events, histories of the revolution, and French theater.

Collins, Philip. "Some Narrative Devices in *Bleak House.*" *Dickens Studies Annual* 19 (1990): 125*f*46. A detailed analysis of the characteristics of the two narrators.

Davis, Paul B. *The Lives & Times of Ebenezer Scrooge.* New Haven: Yale UP, 1990.

Dunlop, C. R. B. "Debtors and Creditors in Dickens' Fiction." *Dickens Studies Annual* 19 (1990): 25–47. Provides an expert overview of creditor and debtor law in Victorian Britain, discusses the pervasiveness of the theme of debt in Dickens' novels, and examines how his ambivalence toward debt reflects his ambivalence toward urban commerce.

Dvorak, Wilfred P. "Dickens and Popular Culture: Silas Wegg's Ballads in *Our Mutual Friend.*" *Dickensian* 86 (1990): 142–57. Dickens used Wegg's ballads "to reveal and refine the nature of Wegg's character and thereby develop ... his major themes in *Our Mutual Friend*" (142).

Edgecombe, Rodney Stenning. "Comic Hypotheses in *The Pickwick Papers.*" *Dickens Quarterly* 7 (1990): 359–70. Enumerates and discusses the satiric uses of comic scientific hypotheses in the novel.

Edwards, Simon. "Anorexia Nervosa vs. the Fleshpots of London: Rose and Nancy in *Oliver Twist.*" *Dickens Studies Annual* 19 (1990): 49–64.

Feinberg, Monica. "Reading *Curiosity:* Does Dick's Shop Deliver?" *Dickens Quarterly* 7 (1990): 200–211. Parallel analysis of how Dickens Swiveller finds integrity through social integration and how Dickens develops a novelistic method that makes that story possible.

Field, Darin E. "'Two Spheres of Action and Suffering': Empire and Decadence in *Little Dorrit.*" *Dickens Quarterly* 7 (1990): 379–83. Argues that empire is as important as the symbol of the prison.

Fleissner, Robert F. "Scrooge's Humbug Dissected." *Word Ways* 23 (1990): 200–204. Connotations of the term humbug.

Friedman, Stanley. "Sad Stephen and Troubled Louisa: Paired Protagonists in *Hard Times.*" *Dickens Quarterly* 7 (1990): 254–61. Parallels between Stephen and Louisa give the narrative "coherence and impetus by inducing us to care about [their] interwoven destinies" (255).

Gaughan, Richard T. "Prospecting for Meaning in *Our Mutual Friend.*" *Dickens Studies Annual* 19 (1990): 231–46.

Giddings, Robert, Keith Selby, Chris Wensley. *Screening the Novel: The Theory and Practice of Literary Dramatization.* New York: St. Martin's, 1990.

Goodman, Marcia Renee. "I'll Follow the Other: Tracing the (M)Other in *Bleak House.*" *Dickens Studies Annual* 19 (1990): 147–67.

Gottfried, Barbara. "Fathers and Suitors in *Bleak House.*" *Dickens Studies Annual* 19 (1990): 169–203.

Greenman, David J. "The Alienation of Dickens's Haunted Businessmen." *Dickens Quarterly* 7 (1990): 384–91. Argues that several of Dickens's middle class figures are marked as alienated, especially through the use of the spirit world. Discusses Tom Smart of "The Bagman's Story," Scrooge, the banker of "To Be Taken With a Grain of Salt," and the businessman of "The Signalman."

Greenstein, Michael. "Liminality in *Little Dorrit.*" *Dickens Quarterly* 7 (1990): 275–83. Draws on anthropological theories of liminality to discuss Dickens' use of threshold situations.

Harris, Wendell V. "Bakhtinian Double Voicing in Dickens and Eliot." *ELH* 57 (1990): 445–58.

Herst, Beth. *The Dickens Hero: Selfhood and Alienation in the Dickens World.* New York: St. Martin's, 1990.

Hochberg, Shifra. "Onomastics, Topicality, and Dickens's Use of Etymology in *Bleak House." Dickensian* 86 (1990): 85–92. Brief discussion of Dickens' naming practices, with specific reference to the naming of Flite.

Hochman, Baruch and Ilja Wachs. "Star People, Hollow Men, and the Postmodernist Hall of Dissipating Mirrors: The Case of *David Copperfield." Style* 24 (1990): 392–407.

Hollington, Michael. "Dickens and Cruikshank as Physiognomers in *Oliver Twist." Dickens Quarterly* 7 (1990): 243–54. Argues that the novels exhibit a hierarchy of capacity for judging physiognomy that in turn reflects the moral character of the judge.

Horne, Lewis. *"Little Dorrit* and the Region of Despair." *Dalhousie Review* 69 (1989–1990): 533–48.

Horton, Susan R. "Swivellers and Snivellers: Competing Epistemologies in *The Old Curiosity Shop." Dickens Quarterly* 7 (1990): 212–17. Finds a conflict between two modes of shopping, older bricolage and emergent consumerism.

Jolly, Diane L. "The Nature of Esther." *Dickensian* 86 (1990): 29–40. Argues that Esther's moral and physical beauty mitigate criticisms that have been made of this character.

Langbauer, Laurie. *Women and Romance: The Consolations of Gender in the English Novel.* Ithica: Cornell UP, 1990.

Levit, Fred. *A Dickens Glossary.* New York: Garland, 1990. A dictionary of words and phrases that might be unfamiliar to a "college freshman" (x). Useful definitions, but one is led to wonder how many freshmen will go all the way to the library (the book costs $50) to discover that "a=bed" means "in bed"?

Loesberg, Jonathan. "Deconstruction, Historicism, and Overdetermination: Dislocations of the Marriage Plot in *Robert Elsmere and Dombey and Son." Victorian Studies* 33 (1990): 441–64.

Malone, Cynthia Northcutt. "Flight and Pursuit: Fugitive Identity in *Bleak House." Dickens Studies Annual* 19 (1990): 107–24.

McCarthy, Patrick. *"Dombey and Son:* Language and the Roots of Meaning." *Dickens Studies Annual* 19 (1990): 91–106.

Meckier, Jerome. "George Dolby to James T. Fields: Two New Letters Concerning Dickens's Reading Tour." *Dickensian* 86 (1990): 171–83. Letters support his argument (detailed in *Innocent Abroad*) that Dickens was not motivated by greed to undertake his reading tour of America.

―――. *Innocent Abroad: Charles Dickens's American Engagements.* Lexington: UP of Kentucky, 1990.

Metz, Nancy Aycock. *"Little Dorrit's* London: Babylon Revisited." *Victorian Studies* 33 (1990): 465–86.

Mooney, Jennifer. "Lost to Liberty: Other Slaves in Charles Dickens's *American Notes." Dickens Quarterly* 7 (1990): 321–28. Finds that Dickens represents not only slaves, but immigrants, Native Americans, and prisoners, as victims of the shortcomings of American society.

Myer, Valerie Grosvenor. *Ten Great English Novelists.* London: Vision; New York: St. Martin's, 1990. Intended as an "introduction to the great names of English literature for those who know little or nothing about them" (7). Contains biographical sketch of Dickens, half of which is devoted to the period before he began writing novels; Myer's readers will still know little about Dickens.

Newton, Ruth and Naomi Lebowitz. *Dickens, Manzoni, Zola, and James: The Impossible Romance.* Columbia: U of Missouri P, 1990.

O'Donnell, Patrick. "'A Speeches of Chaff': Ventriloquy and Expression in *Our Mutual Friend." Dickens Studies Annual* 19 (1990): 247–79.

Page, Norman. *Bleak House: A Novel of Connections.* Boston: G. K. Hall, 1990. Part of *Twayne's Masterwork Studies* series; provides context and interpretation of the novel of an introductory nature.

Pendleton, Robert W. "The Detective's Languishing Forefinger: Narrative Guides in *Bleak House and Little Dorrit." Dickens Quarterly* 7 (1990): 312–20, 371–78. Attempts to recuperate the portrayal of Bucket from David Miller's analysis, arguing that Bucket pulls the narrative together. Treats Clennam and Rigaud as two aspects of the detective as narrative guide.

Perera, Suvendrini. "Wholesale, Retail, and for Exportation: Empire and the Family Business in *Dombey and Son." Victorian Studies* 33 (1990). 603–20.

Petit, Alexander. "Sympathetic Criminality in the Mid-Victorian Novel." *Dickens Studies Annual* 19 (1990): 281–300.

Philpotts, Trey. "'To Working Men' and 'The People': Dickens's View of Class Relations in the Months Preceding *Little Dorrit." Dickens Quarterly* 7 (1990): 262–75. As a context for *Little Dorrit,* discusses Dickens's attempts in his *Household Word* articles to forge an alliance of working and middle classes in order to bring about social change.

Polhemus, Robert. *Erotic Faith: Being in Love from Jane Austen to D. H. Lawrence.* Chicago: U of Chicago P, 1990.

Reed, Jon. B. "Astrophil and Estella: A Defense of Poesy." *Studies in English Literature* 30 (1990): 655–78.

Roberts, Doreen. *"The Pickwick Papers* and the Sex War." *Dickens Quarterly* 7 (1990): 299–311. "There is a sex war going on all through *Pickwick Papers,* and it supplies the impetus for the majority of the book's comic episodes.... The set of postulates and conventions drawn on in the main story is directly inverted in the non-comic group of tales clustered in the first half. And yet the result is not ... thematic sabotage and self-contradiction, but a curious kind of mutual reinforcement" (299).

Rogers, Philip. "A Tolstoyan Reading of *David Copperfield." Comparative Literature* 42 (1990): 1–28. Reads Tolstoy's trilogy *Childhood, Adolescence,* and *Youth* as a revisionary interpretation of *David Copperfield;* finds Copperfield's self-hate revealed in the characterization of Uriah Heep.

Sanders, Andrew. "The Dickens World." *Creditable Warriors.* Ed. Michael Cotsell. London: Ashfield. 131–42. An essay in a volume from the series, *English Literature and the Wider World,* it discusses Dickens' treatment of foreign countries; focusses on *Pictures from Italy* and Dickens' tendency to measure cities by the standard of London and to measure nations by their cities.

Schacht, Paul. "Dickens and the Uses of Nature." *Victorian Studies* 34 (1990): 77–102.

Schaumburger, Nancy E. "The 'Gritty Stages' of Life: Psychological Time in *The Mystery of Edwin Drood." Dickensian* 86 (1990): 158–63 and *University of Mississippi Studies in English* 8 (1990): 137–42.

Schlicke, Paul. "Crummles Once More." *Dickensian* 86 (1990): 3–16. Argues that Dickens had many models for the character of Crummles—not just Davenport—and questions the argument that the novel's theater scenes are central thematically.

———. "The True Pathos of *The Old Curiosity Shop." Dickens Quarterly* 7 (1990): 189–99. Discusses a series of historical factors that combined to "create a context of change and uncertainty" for the novel (196).

Shaw, W. David. *Victorians and Mystery: Crises of Representation.* Ithaca: Cornell UP, 1990.

Smith, David. "'A Little More Play': Cricket in Dickens's Fiction" *Dickensian* 86 (1990): 41–52. Observes that cricket frequently appears in Dickens' novels as an aspect of idealized pastoral.

Smith, Grahame. "'O reason not the need': *King Lear, Hard Times* and Utilitarian Values." *Dickensian* 86 (1990): 164–70. Argues that the influence of *King Lear* can be discerned at the conceptual level in *Hard Times*. Works in particular with the relationship between Lear's "reason not the need" and Dickens's allusion to the Biblical "one thing needful."

Spencer, Jamieson. "Charles Dickens in School: One Teacher's Report Card." *Dickensian* 86 (1990): 105–15. "[A] sketch of specific steps taken by one ardent Dickensian in Missouri to plant the seeds of reverence and respect in one young generation of [high school] students."

Thacker, John. *Edwin Drood: Antichrist in the Cathedral.* London: Vision, New York: St. Martin's, 1990. Thacker argues that Cloisterham cathedral is not just the setting but the central symbol of the novel; in the course of this argument, he joins those who would make Dickens an orthodox Christian (see discussion of Wheeler). Although he attempts to avoid the whodunnit school of *Drood* criticism, Thacker ends up building a good deal of his argument on speculation about what would have been revealed in the unwritten part of the novel.

Thomas, Ronald R. *Dreams of Authority: Freud and the Fictions of the Unconscious.* Ithaca: Cornell UP, 1990.

Ware, Michele S. "'True Legitimacy': The Myth of the Foundling in *Bleak House.*" *Studies in the Novel* 22 (199): 1–9. Using the mythic paradigms of Joseph Campbell and the precedent of the foundling in Fielding, discusses the foundling in Dickens' novels.

Wheeler, Michael. *Death and the Future Life in Victorian Literature and Theology.* Cambridge: Cambridge UP, 1990.

Trollope Studies, 1982–1986

Nancy Aycock Metz

In 1964, Donald Smalley wrote of the glaring disparity between the scant, frequently condescending scholarly work on Trollope and the voluminous attention given to his more highly regarded colleagues, Dickens, Thackeray, and Eliot. "Only a few significant analyses of individual novels have been made," he noted ("Anthony Trollope," in *Victorian Fiction: A Guide to Research,* ed. Lionel Stevenson [Cambridge: Harvard UP, 1964], p. 209), adding "Trollope's particular qualities both as a writer and as a personality continue to evade definition.... He seems still in the process of being discovered" (p. 213). Roughly twenty-five years later the situation is much changed as regards the quantity of Trollope criticism. My computer search turned up a dozen or so titles in hard covers and over seventy journal articles (excluding dissertations and foreign language entries) for the five-year period under review. There is now no dearth of material on individual works (and the range of subjects has extended well beyond the *Barchester* and *Palliser* series). Even the textual side of Trollope scholarship, long an embarrassment in view of the availability of so much manuscript material, has begun to make up for lost time with the publication of two exemplary editions, N. John Hall's *Letters* (Stanford: Stanford UP, 1983) and R. H. Super's *Marion Fay* (Ann Arbor: U of Michigan P, 1982). Although the effort to define Trollope goes on, renewed by the centenary of his death and complicated by recent changes in critical understandings, the scholar of the nineties finds herself differently situated from the voice in the wilderness of a mere generation ago. Indeed, as Bill Overton has remarked in an intelligent re-assessment published during the centennial year (*The Unofficial Trollope,* Sussex: Harvester Press, 1982): "The sheer weight and volume of Trollope's complete works, not to mention the pile of criticism and "Trollopology," perhaps become a labyrinth from which the pioneer critic can emerge, only to blink at what he sees outside"

(p. 155).

BIBLIOGRAPHY

Judith Knelman's "Trollope's Journalism" and her appended "Checklist" (*Library*, 5 [1983], 140–55) provide bibliographical data on Trollope's contributions to journals during the years 1849–1881. Including letters to the editor, 200 such contributions have been identified, a substantial number of them on a variety of political and popular topics written for the *Pall Mall Gazette*. Elizabeth R. Epperly, in "Trollope's Notes on Drama" (*Notes and Queries*, 31 [1984], 491–97) has published a calendar of Trollope's readings in Elizabethan and Jacobean drama from 1866 to 1882, compiled from 86 volumes in the Folger Library. The calendar makes it possible to ascertain which plays Trollope was reading when and how these readings correspond to the publication dates of his novels. This brief essay does not reprint Trollope's often substantial reading notes. More ambitious but less useful is Mary L. Daniels's *Trollope-to-Reader: A Topical Guide to Digressions in the Novels of Anthony Trollope* (Westport, Conn.: Greenwood Press, 1983). Daniels's compilation is flawed by the naiveté of its critical assumptions—assumptions which then become the basis for the book's organization and methodology. For her, the digressions are "pure Trollope—at least of that moment—undiluted by plot, character, theme, or modern exegesis." "By studying these digressions alone, she urges, "we should be able to trace any changes in Trollope's thinking without reference to what we think he meant or to what a particular character said or did" (p. xiii). Daniels's introduction offers no examples of this astonishing claim. Indeed, it would be very difficult to do so, for as many recent critics have pointed out, once one looks at all closely at these asides, their "pure" status dissolves and becomes much more fictional, involved, and problematic. One can find in this compilation fairly straightforward anthologies of Trollope's "official" opinions on such subjects as "Americans," or "Disestablishment," or "Parliament"—though even here context plays an important role. But what the narrator has to say about, for example, gender issues or the way his novels were written, can be positively misleading, and his more abstract musings on the nature of friendship, love, and self-knowledge lose subtlety and point when they are abstracted from their embeddedness in the fiction. It is difficult to imagine the kind of reader Daniels has in mind. An alphabetic arrangement by topic makes a certain kind of sense, but where is the reader who would be likely to search the book using such keywords as "cross-grainedness," "Diana's dart," "double-first," "men butterfly," and "nonfeasance." And what reader would seek out Trollope's reflections on Bill Sikes (much less his strange bedfellow in this volume, Robert Peel) under the heading "rogues"?

EDITIONS

Clearly the most important contribution to Trollope studies during the period covered by this review has been N. John Hall's handsome two-volume edition of *The Letters of Anthony Trollope* (see above). Nearly 2,000 letters are published here, more than double the number appearing in Bradford Booth's 1951 Oxford University Press volume; previously published letters, including those collected by Booth, have been transcribed from a fresh examination of manuscripts or photocopies unless these sources have since disappeared.

The sheer inclusiveness of this edition will prove its greatest asset to scholars. Booth, after all, exercised a high degree of selection over his material, printing in full "only those letters ... which add something to our knowledge of Trollope's character and career, or which ... merit inclusion as independent works of literary art" (*The Letters of Anthony Trollope,* London: Oxford UP, 1951, xxiv). Letters to editors were routinely omitted unless "relevant to some developing situation in his life" (p. xxiv), and summary stood in for full text where the substance of the letter was judged to be only minimally interesting or important. Hall, on the other hand, sets out to produce a text as comprehensive as existing sources will allow. "Quite simply, Trollope's stature today calls for a complete and inclusive edition" (p. xxiii). The extensive "Acknowledgements" chart a research project of massive scale and impressive resourcefulness, drawing on more than 100 libraries, collections, publishing houses, and private archives. The definition of a letter is broadened to include representative postal reports, several of them masterpieces of their kind, though their clarity and shrewdness are frequently expended on mundane issues (e.g., the use of boxes instead of bags on the overland Indian mail route). Letters to the editor are included as a matter of course. The full text of Trollope's wonderfully comic, irate, and self-revealing pair of letters to the *Times* in 1874 appears, even though this traveller's tale of outrage and misfortune en route from London to Luxembourg had no larger repercussions. (A conductor had dropped his book of tickets down a window frame, the company had failed to reimburse him, and *The Saturday Review* had rubbed salt in the wound by tweaking him on his lack of sophistication as a traveller). Often Hall prints both letter and reply, and in some cases both halves of an extended correspondence. Most readers will feel that this violation of strict consistency is well worth the additional depth of insight made possible by juxtaposition. Without it, we would lose (to footnotes, at any rate) gems like George Eliot's compliment to Trollope's organization—his typical novel, she says, is "natty & complete as a nut on its stem" (238). The long sequence of letters to and from John Blackwood especially justifies this treatment; the everyday push and pull between editor and publisher in the production of Victorian novels—the small irritants and accommodations and the mutual respect underlying the whole relationship—are brought vividly into relief by the dual perspective.

The editorial principles of Hall's edition are set forth in his "Introduction"; in an earlier essay for *CUNY English Forum,* "Editing and Annotating the Letters of Anthony Trollope" (1 [1985], 269–73), he explained at greater length how these principles evolved and were tested by the complex demands of the material. While faithful in appearance and detail to their originals, the letters remain generally uncluttered by editorial paraphernalia. Believing that "reading a printed letter should not be like solving little puzzles, puzzles not worth solving" (p. 271), Hall has been conservative with his sics and brackets, and he has chosen not to send readers to footnotes whose only purpose is to append information on duplications and cancellations.

The purposes footnotes do serve in this admirably annotated edition are many and various. Here one finds meticulous research reported with economy, wit, and style. Readers will find in the notes an almost encyclopedic range of knowledge succinctly and selectively presented. When in one letter a price of 3, 200 pounds is set for *Phineas Finn,* the note sets this outright price (Trollope's highest) beside the higher overall payment for *Can You Forgive Her?* and further compares it to the unit price of his fiction generally. Believing that Trollope's letters (unlike Byron's) "need added interest," Hall has fleshed out the context of his subject with interwoven anecdote and reminiscence. Especially useful are the notes that frame and flag the beginning of an extended controversy ("This letter began the troubled publication history of *Rachel Ray*"), providing the context and collecting the cross-references that will make the letter meaningful as part of an episode.

The Trollope who emerges from this major work of scholarship is a rounder, more complex character than we have had access to before, less reducible to the Philistine or the compulsive overachiever—although those aspects of his professional personality are still readable within a more extended and various context. The letters, themselves, however, have received the kind of faint praise and slighting comparisons formerly conceded to Trollope's fictional "appreciation of the usual." In a recent article on "Trollope as Letter-Writer," (*South Atlantic Quarterly,* 84 [1985], 89–98), John Halperin compares the excellence of the new edition to the inherent mediocrity of its raw material: "N. John Hall's impeccably edited two volumes ... must now be regarded as the standard edition. But among the novelists Trollope will never be rated one of the great letter-writers" (p. 89). Everyone, of course, grants Trollope the gift of creating wonderfully complex, revealing letters for his characters. "If only his letters were like *that,*" Hall remarks in his introduction, paraphrasing an earlier comment of Booth's. But, "like life itself they do not always entertain, and they have dull stretches" (p. xxiii). That granted, there is much here that will entertain and reward study. Trollope's artistic *credos,* his parodies of the domestic proprieties, his often iconoclastic assessments of contemporary heroes, his political views and financial jockeying—all are here interwoven with the trivial circumstances of a writer's life in time.

High editorial standards and a handsome finished product are equally the hallmark of R. H. Super's new *Marion Fay* (see above), the first twentieth-century edition of a Trollope novel to derive its text from comparisons between the manuscript and the nineteenth-century printed versions—in this case the one-volume 1884 text, the weekly serial in the *Graphic,* and the three-volume edition of 1882. Scholarly work on the manuscripts is indeed, as Andrew Wright has noted in a recent article, "in its infancy" ("Trollope Revises Trollope," in *Trollope Centenary Essays* [New York: St. Martin's Press, 1982], p. 110). Given the large number of better known Trollope novels awaiting editorial reclamation, Super's choice of the little read *Marion Fay* will seem odd to many readers. The Preface makes an extended case for the ways in which this novel, which others have dismissed as "untypically sentimental and melodramatic" (Overton, *The Unofficial Trollope* [New Jersey: Barnes and Noble, 1982], p. 3) is "vintage Trollope," "the work of a great novelist at the height of his powers, of a masterly and self-confident critic of society (p. xii, xvi). From one perspective *Marion Fay*'s obscurity is exactly the point, for here publication history—with all that is at stake in authorizing a text—becomes hopelessly entangled with questions of critical stature. *Marion Fay*'s history is the story of other "lost" Victorian novels as well: "As copies became harder and harder to procure, scholars found it easier to pronounce upon *Marion Fay* without reading it, or omitted it altogether ... its general fate has been simply oblivion" (p. xx). Super's text reproduces the wonderful illustrations by William Small published with the novel in its original serial form. Trollope's preliminary sketches and *dramatis personae* are also included, along with a detailed account in the Preface of the novel's autobiographical matrix, its composition and publication history, and its contemporary reception. The edition has been meticulously prepared.

The remaining two volumes of Texas Christian University Press's *The Complete Short Stories* have now been published (ed., Betty Jane Slemp Breyer, Fort Worth, 1982, 1983; reviewed in Donald D. Stone, "Trollope Studies, 1976–1981, *Dickens Studies Annual: Essays on Victorian Fiction*, 11, ed. Michael Timko, Fred Kaplan, and Edward Guiliano [New York: AMS, 1983], p. 315). Oxford University Press, in connection with the Trollope centenary, has reissued a paperback series of the Palliser novels set from the 1948 and 1954 Oxford Trollope, edited by Michael Sadleir and Frederick Page, with new introductions and notes.

BIOGRAPHY

Although the full-length biographies-in-progress by Hall and Super, referred to in Donald Stone's review (see above) have not yet appeared, the outlines (and with respect to certain phases, the fine details) of Trollope's professional life have begun to emerge with much greater clarity in a series of journal articles. We know more now about how Trollope worked, and the evidence of the manuscripts, according to John Sutherland, ("Trollope at Work on *The Way We Live Now*," *Nineteenth-Century Fiction* 37 [1982], 472–93) does not support the author's own satirical self-portrait of a novelist "charging at his plot like a horsemen at a fence he cannot see" (p. 493). Sutherland isolates several stages in Trollope's creative process: a period of mental "castle-building" accompanied by some rough note-taking, a "strictly secretarial" writing stage marked by uneven bursts of composition, each devoted to a different strand of the plot, and a proofing phase limited to the correction of errors. The clean appearance of the manuscript tells us more about the way it was used to calculate length than it does about Trollope's creative process, Sutherland argues, and the mutually reinforcing roles of mapping and spontaneity can be seen in the functions of the chapter plans and *dramatis personae*. J. W. Bailey's brief (and it is to be hoped not pre-emptive) look at the manuscript of *The Duke's Children* (*"The Duke's Children:* Rediscovering a Trollope Manuscript," *Yale University Library Gazette*, 57 [1982], 34–38) studies the deletions, a promising subject given that an unheard of one-third of the manuscript was cut by Trollope, without any reweaving of transitional material to reconstitute the whole. Based on a study of twenty percent of the manuscript, Bailey argues that the cuts reduce the complexity of the relationships as originally developed and abridge the full development of the Duke's sensibility. While one may agree with Bailey's conclusion that a new edition restoring these excisions is called for, the essay itself is insufficiently detailed as a study of Trollope's working methods.

An impressive level of original scholarship is achieved in several new studies of Trollope's role in the world of Victorian publishing. Patricia Thomas Srebnik tells the story of "Trollope, James Virtue, and *Saint Paul's Magazine*" (*Nineteenth-Century Fiction,* 37 [1982], 443–63) drawing on a broad understanding of Victorian publishing generally and on specific research into contracts, payment scales, and circulation statistics. Srebnik persuasively rewrites the dismissive, impressionistic portrait of James Sprent Virtue found in Sadleir. The story of Trollope's involvement with Virtue and company as editor of *Saint Paul*'s and of Virtue's disastrous entanglements with Alexander Strahan is told well and clearly. In the process, an indirect picture emerges of Trollope's professional dealings in the marketplace—his concern for giving the public "full measure," his appreciation of the role of "merit and time ... economy and patience" in the success of journalistic enterprises (p. 457).

An interesting sidelight on this general subject is offered in R. H. Super's "Trollope at the Royal Literary Fund" (*Nineteenth-Century Fiction,* 37 [1982], 316–28). Using manuscript material and printed reports, Super summarizes in detail Trollope's role in this organization, which was founded in the late eighteenth century to relieve "persons of genius and learning" or their distressed families. Never humble on behalf of the profession of letters, Trollope urged in his speeches that literary men be awarded compensation equivalent to that enjoyed by other professionals. His own role in the organization was marked by a conscientious attention to detail and by tact and kindliness in his dealings with applicants for charity.

The critical reception of Trollope's fiction has been re-examined from several perspectives. The sharpest debate has centered on the question of whether *The Way We Live Now* was, as John Sutherland claimed in his introduction to the World's Classic edition, "a failure on publication." R. H. Super's rejoinder to Sutherland's "remarkably inaccurate" account of the novel's publication ("Was *The Way We Live Now* a Commercial Success?," *Nineteenth-Century Fiction,* 39 [1984], 202–10) was rebutted in turn by Sutherland ("The Commercial Success of *The Way We Live Now,*"

Nineteenth-Century Literature 40, [1986], 460–67). The whole exchange throws into relief the enormous complexity of the publishing process as it bears on literary evaluation—from the economics of type-setting to market determinants on the timing, appearance, and size of various editions, to the impact of advertising and reviewing. The last of these is K. J. Fielding's subject in "Trollope and the *Saturday Review*" (*Nineteenth-Century Fiction,* 37 [1982], 430–42). In an intelligent essay, Fielding revises twentieth-century judgments about the hostility of the *Saturday Review*'s assessment of Trollope's fiction, arguing that the "willingness to engage in rational argument"—over a period of nearly thirty years—made "such apparent opponents" "close to being ideally responsive readers" (431–32). Although the *Review*'s negative criticism has been stressed in recent accounts of the journal, praise for Trollope was often strong and unqualified, anticipating in the terms of its appreciation the judgments of twentieth-century critics of Trollope's "situation-structured" fiction (like Ruth apRoberts). Fielding reads these nineteenth century essays freshly, and his exploratory approach opens up some interesting questions about Trollope's realism, his status as a popular entertainer, and the unexamined assumptions of our own critical positions.

N. John Hall offers a similarly revisionist reading of Trollope's posthumous critical reputation in "Seeing Trollope's *An Autobiography* through the Press: The Correspondence of William Blackwood and Henry Merivale Trollope," (*Princeton University Library Chronicle,* 47 [1986], 189–223). The falling market value of his father's books placed Henry at a disadvantage in negotiating a price with Blackwood, but Hall rejects the view popularized by Sadleir that *An Autobiography* damaged Trollope's reputation with the public generally. Most reviews were favorable.

It has by and large not been thought necessary to speak of Trollope in terms of intellectual history, and biographical studies of him have been generally silent on the subject. But Ruth apRoberts' correction of this inherently condescending viewpoint deserves heeding: "the truth is that the breath of the *Zeitgeist* blew on him with particular effect, and filled his sail" ("Trollope and the *Zeitgeist*," *Nineteenth-Century Fiction,* 37 [1982], 259–71; p. 259). In support of this claim, apRoberts persuasively aligns the defining features of Trollope's fiction—his technique of "psychological streaming," his rejection of nature in favor of community as the ground of self, his broad canvass within which characters "make themselves" in their relationships to institutions, and his open, multi-form process-art—alongside the intellectual legacy of the German historicist gestalt. Seen this way the Victorian novel (and especially

Trollope's particular version of it) becomes a natural outgrowth of post-Darwinian disillusionment and of the efforts of Herder and others to formulate a new faith in humanity, development, and the *polis*.

That Trollope was definitively shaped by his time and place is also the premise of John Halperin's "Trollope's Conservatism" (*South Atlantic Quarterly*, 82 [1983], 56–78), an essay which seeks to expose the naiveté of critics like apRoberts, Kendrick, Kincaid, Polhemus, and Terry who have been "misled by Trollope's own assessment of his political and social views" (p. 56) into seeing him as a representative of their own democratic values. Halperin argues that "Trollope's is not the voice of the middle-of-the-road "advanced conservative liberal," as he would have us believe, but rather that of the true conservative—and, in some cases, of the reactionary" (p. 56). The essay is at once irritating and provocative. It is undoubtedly true that each generation re-writes Trollope into an image of its own political values, and Halperin's marshalling of evidence about Trollope's racist, anti-feminist, xenophobic opinions is a useful corrective to the prevailing view, if not the whole story. But one could have done without the *ad hominem* flavor of the whole argument. Halperin has a tendency to cite himself too often and too uncritically, and to lump together in quick, dismissive oversimplifications the "lazy" and "fashionable" positions of the critics against whom the essay aligns itself. Halperin's "Trollope and the American Civil War" (*CLIO: A Journal of Literature, History, and the Philosophy of History*, 13 [1984], 149–55) adds an interesting footnote to the discussion of Trollope's political views by gathering together the most important of the novelist's reflections on what he called "The War of Secession." Although he thought the South would win, Trollope was almost alone among English writers and politicians in embracing the Northern perspective. Distrusting the motives of abolitionists, and believing that some form of racial domination was necessary, he nevertheless felt that slavery had been disastrous as an institution.

If Trollope's professional and political life have been explored with greater rigor and in more detail in recent years, his childhood and personal life have slipped correspondingly into the background. In the process, the usual source for exploring such matters, Trollope's *Autobiography* has been treated with more caution. Robert Tracy and James Kincaid focus on the fictive qualities of this slippery document, and both compare it to Dickens' disguised autobiography in *David Copperfield* ("Stranger Than Truth: Fictional Autobiography and Autobiographical Fiction," *Dickens Studies Annual: Essays on Victorian Fiction*, 15, eds. Michael Timko, Fred Kaplan, and Edward Guiliano [New York: AMS, 1986], 275–89; "Trollope's Fictional

Autobiography," *Nineteenth-Century Fiction,* 37 [1982], 340–49). Tracy distinguishes between the more active, striving character depicted by Trollope and the passive recipient of unexpected benevolence David becomes. Kincaid is concerned to trace the comic pattern of the mercantile success story in each account. Sally Brown's "This So-Called Autobiography" (*British Library Journal* 8, [1982], 168–73) also addresses some of these broad themes, but for the general reader rather than the specialist.

Ira Bruce Nadel is among several recent critics to write of Trollope's biographies as, collectively, "an unwritten autobiography" (see discussion of Robert Colby's work on Trollope and Thackeray, below), arguing that, "In the lives of others Trollope unfolds a personal narrative which reticence, convention and anxiety did not allow in the posthumously published autobiography" ("Trollope as Biographer," *Prose Studies,* 5 [1982], 318–25; p. 318). The essay is strongest in its treatment of Cicero, loosest in the connections it makes between Trollope's life and his account of Caesar's. Although requiring more demonstration than this brief essay manages to encompass, Nadel's thesis is a suggestive one: "Paradoxically, in a form more public than autobiography and more historical than personal, Trollope expressed some of his most private feelings and intimate wishes" (p. 324).

GENERAL CRITICISM: FULL-LENGTH STUDIES AND COLLECTIONS

Of the six full-length studies of Trollope covered here, Andrew Wright's and Bill Overton's survey their subject from the broadest vantage point. Wright's *Anthony Trollope: Dream and Art* (Chicago: U of Chicago P, 1983) seeks to elucidate the ways in which the particular form and atmosphere of Trollope's fiction derive from its wellspring in childhood misery. Wright's subject is "Trollope the dreamer, who made of the nightmares of the waking life of his boyhood and youth, compensatory fictions" (p. 3). These "transfigurations of ordinary life," Wright urges, have an importance independent of the moral stance they embody or of their representational characteristics.

Wright's project is to read a variety of Trollope's novels through the lens of the novelist's own insight about the "dangerous mental practice" of "castle-building," a preoccupation which began in his earliest days of schoolboy isolation and which served in certain specific and defining ways as his literary apprenticeship. His Trollope is, by his own acknowledgement, "somewhat different but by no means unique" from that presented by apRoberts,

Kincaid, Halperin, and Cockshut, and his specific readings draw "gratefully" on the work of a roll-call of Trollope scholars alphabetically named and credited in his "Introduction." This sense of working within a community of respected scholars informs Wright's whole book, and is a part of its even-handed, courteous tone, but there are times when the weight of previous scholarship blurs the outlines of what is distinctive in Wright's own thesis and methodology.

For me, the book's most interesting insights lie a little to the side of its central argument. To say that Trollope sought escape in the writing of fiction and that his novels are, in one sense, wish-fulfillments ("in the shoes of Phineas Finn, he could walk with the natural grace denied him in actuality; and in the devoted statesmanship of Plantagenet Palliser he could project much of his wishful life," p. 23) is, after all, to say what is true of a great many other writers as well, Dickens, Thackeray, and the Brontës included. And though Wright is careful to distance his project from the "literature of symptoms," from questions about whether Trollope was "normal or neurotic," this way of looking at the complex relationship between a writer's life and his work necessarily involves an element of oversimplification. Still, by focusing on the points of intersection between the "wakeful" and the "day-dreaming" life in Trollope's fiction, the book is able to offer some suggestive insights about the defining character of Trollope's narrative realism. According to Wright, the distinctive quality of the Trollope narrator—and the feature that has provoked the most discussion from Henry James down to present-day critics—is his stance of "disengaged engagement," and this odd positioning of the narrator with respect to apparently realistic material can be best understood if we see it as arising "from the need to make fictions that remain false, whose ontological status includes the element of the interruptible, the provisional" (p. 6). These addresses to the reader are consonant with the peculiarly amplified realism of the novel. Trollope, according to Wright "fantasizes the domestic, and domesticates fantasy" (p. 9). His formula for fiction includes elements of the sensational superimposed on portraits of middle-class life which have been read as photographic. In the chapters that follow, on *An Autobiography,* the *Barchester* and *Palliser* chronicles, and five other novels, Wright offers a series of brief, but solid and often perceptive readings in which the dream/art premise of the book is sounded as a theme.

I found much to admire in Bill Overton's centenary reassessment *The Unofficial Trollope* (Tottowa, N.J.: Barnes and Noble Books, 1982), although the book's title and thesis seemed, on first looking, familiar enough. Overton proposes "the value of an unofficial Trollope, working beneath and at times contradicting the beliefs he maintained explicitly" (p. xi). This is of course the slant of many recent attempts to reclaim Trollope for the twentieth century. In such readings, the "real" Trollope (or at least the Trollope implicitly set forth as worth reading) is to be found in the slyly subversive subtext of the novels—in their repeated demonstrations of the cost to self and community of a patriarchal, class-based society. Overton's readings of *The Claverings* and *The Eustace Diamonds* have something in common with this kind of critical approach, but with an important difference. Noting the significant and long-standing critical gap between Trollope's appreciators and detractors, Overton postulates an explanation in the dividedness of the man himself, in the apparent irreconcilability between his conventional "official" self and that "unofficial" side which reached beyond his conscious understandings. "A proper assessment of Trollope needs to take into account both elements," Overton urges, "and especially their relationship" (p. 2). The title of this study is, then, somewhat misleading, for its originality lies in its mature and thoughtful probing of this complex symbiosis, rather than in a privileging of Trollope's "unofficial" side.

In some ways, Overton has most to offer when he deals with Trollope's "official" stance. He is one of the few serious readers of Trollope to look at—rather than dismissively through—the conventional conformist, the mouther of "reach-me-down prejudice" who was Trollope the club-man and civil servant. I found persuasive, too, the analysis of how Trollope's imagination worked in paradoxical practice: "It was the official Trollope who converted his desk into a portable production line, and, administrator to his imagination, stood over it watch in hand. Yet the result, given the unofficial Trollope's need to build castles, to tell continual stories, was a kind of freedom" (p. 61). Overton is a shrewd and sensitive reader of Trollope's prose. He understands well and has found a language to talk about Trollope's delicately nuanced ventriloquism—"the subtle notation of free, indirect speech" (p. 107)—and the chapter which analyzes a long passage from *The Last Chronicle of Barset* to demonstrate precisely how these effects are produced is brilliantly done.

Corrupt Relations: Dickens, Thackeray, Trollope, Collins, and the Victorian Sexual System (New York: Columbia UP, 1982) embodies exactly the kind of approach from which Overton's book departs. Richard Barickman, Susan MacDonald, and Myra Stark offer stimulating readings of Victorian novels as subversive texts. The authors' thesis can be briefly summarized. Dickens, Collins, Thackeray, and Trollope—despite their many differences—shared "a comprehensive ironic method" through which they exposed the corruption at the heart of the Victorian sexual system in radical, even revolutionary ways. Although their explicit statements and plot lines frequently contradicted this stance, the presence in the text of gaps, anomalies, and an unstable narrative voice—together with symbolic or analogic counterplots—persistently reveal the authors' preoccupation with a widespread and troubling victimization of men and women as a result of the prevailing patriarchal structure. "They were all feminists" (p. 235), the book concludes, adapting Rebecca West's characterization of Trollope.

In a concluding chapter which has already proved controversial, the authors go further, claiming for these male novelists a radicalism far surpassing the more overt but in the end "safer" feminism of the Brontës and George Eliot. Unlike the pattern found in novels by women in which resisting female protagonists "regularly return to the traditional value system" (p. 244) and to the now redeemed dominance of the male, the four male novelists "regularly undercut the authoritarian postures of their central male figure" (p. 248). Although Dickens, Thackeray, Collins, and Trollope are unable to imagine or embody radical alternatives, except in a satirical way, their novels taken as whole structures offer a more thoroughgoing and comprehensive critique of the patriarchy than the novels of their female counterparts. This is an intriguing line of thinking, but it requires a more patient—and less interested—demonstration than the authors give it in their rushed final chapter. And the reasons offered in explanation of these postulated differences remain unconvincingly speculative: "In part because they inherit a dominant rather than a dependent role—both as authors and in their more ordinary social roles—they are driven to explore and expose the abuses of that power to a degree that no woman novelists of the period did" (p. 242). Why dominance should necessarily result in this radical stance, rather than in complacency and identification with the status quo, is left an unexplored question.

As one might expect, the readings of individual authors vary in their insight and persuasiveness. Thackeray is perhaps the hardest novelist to fit into the book's claims about authorial ambivalence, and some wrenching of the argument is required to do so. Dickens and Trollope are well served. The reading of *Martin Chuzzlewit* as an exposé of sexual relations within the family is new and altogether convincing, and the analysis of paired heroines in Trollope, while not completely original, is made the basis for some insightful comparisons. From time to time, the book makes overstated claims for its own contributions. We are told, for example, that "prevailing critical opinion of the major male novelists" represents them as either silent or reactionary where the Woman Question is concerned, a patent oversimplification. But if *Corrupt Relations* is not quite as ground-breaking as it at times claims to be, if its wide-ranging claims about gendered authorship remain open to further question and debate, it is still an important, challenging study.

If the Trollope of *Corrupt Relations* is a radical feminist, the Trollope of Shirley Robin Letwin's *The Gentleman in Trollope: Individuality and Moral Conduct* (Cambridge: Harvard UP, 1982) is a thorough conservative. Not that Letwin herself would agree to such a characterization; indeed her whole argument is an attempt to place Trollope above and outside considerations of class and gender. The body of the book works through the implications of the title in a fairly straightforward way. In chapters grouped under the heading "The Definition of a Gentleman," Letwin looks at such characteristics as manners, occupation, and birth. How do attributes like these, popularly associated with notions of gentility, factor into the specific context of Trollope's novels? In Part III, "The Conduct of a Gentleman," Letwin explores how character is constituted by the choices Trollope's gentlemen make with respect to love, ambition, and religion. Throughout this analysis, the novels are used as illustrative case histories, each one contributing by example or qualification to an emerging definition of an ideal, complete with variants and antitheses. Letwin is especially good at teasing out the contradictions and paradoxes involved in the behavior she characterizes as "gentlemanly." She argues, for example, that a gentleman may be a woman (indeed Madame Max Goesler is the perfect embodiment of the type), that he may be rude (as Palliser was to Major Pountney), that he may abandon his strongest beliefs (as Palliser did in consenting to the marriages of his children), and that he may disregard conventionally moral behavior (as Mr. Scarborough did when he lied about his marriage). Through the accumulation and sifting of such examples as these Letwin attempts to "make explicit the grammar of a language which has been spoken without being identified" (p. 57), and within the limits of her methodology she is successful. Like Trollope himself Letwin has a fine eye and ear for nuance in word, thought, and gesture. She can take a symbolically freighted moment—such as Mrs. Finn's decision to demand an apology of the duke of Omnium—and work through its resonances with real sensitivity and insight.

One of the drawbacks of Letwin's method of surveying gentlemanly characteristics is the way in which the novels are reduced to moral exempla in the service of the book's larger thesis. We are told, for example, that "the moral of Phineas Finn's story" is that "a man who cannot keep his thoughts straight cannot be a true lover" (p. 148). And similarly: "That a gentleman's honesty is one with his individuality is the moral of a story about a liar, Lizzie Eustace" (p. 97). Moreover, Letwin's readings of these novels do not acknowledge the substantial and frequently quite relevant work of previous critics. Indeed, previous work is cited in an early chapter only to highlight somewhat snidely the inconsistency between what "some critics" and "other critics" have said.

In this entirely sympathetic reading of Trollope's fictional agenda, great care is taken to disassociate the novelist's portrayal of the gentleman from any taint of racism or snobbery. To be sure, Trollope's attitudes on matters of race and class resist easy definition, and Letwin makes the most of exceptional cases like Daniel Thwaite and Luke Rowan, "gentlemen" in spite of their servile occupations. But Trollope is also the novelist who described Mr. Emelius as "a nasty, greasy, lying, squinting Jew preacher." The characterization is notably absent from Letwin's list of examples; the question of how its descriptive terms came to be associated in Trollope's mind is not one that would have occurred to her in any event. She wants readers to overlook the constructedness of these characters and to see them instead as "like the people whom they have come to know through anecdotes in conversation or reports in a newspaper" (p. x).

Letwin has a way of writing about "myths" of aristocratic superiority as if she subscribed to them herself. "There is something to be said for the commonplace notions about noble and servile occupations," she writes at one point. And later, "Those who, in the nursery, or in the drawing room, have heard nothing coarse or sordid, who have had the opportunity to converse with the cultivated and wise and have possessed the books with the leisure for reading and reflecting, are more likely to be fit to live on an eminence and serve as a model to their fellows" (p. 127). Of course there are the obligatory qualifiers ("In reality, of course, not all nobles have received their titles for the same reasons"), but the text aligns itself close to the spirit of the ideal it describes. The notion that beliefs like these might be the creation of a particular social class at a particular moment of its history never enters the field of inquiry.

While the body of this study does indeed develop a "grammar" of gentlemanly conduct as inferred from the behavior of Trollope's characters, its application beyond these textual boundaries is not as clear. The convenient body of examples Letwin found "ready to hand" in Trollope's novels should, according to the way she has defined her project, generalize to the "neglected development in Western civilization" she takes as her true subject. But for me there's a real leap involved. Robinson Crusoe is Letwin's final example of a gentleman, and I'm not at all persuaded that he and Madame Max have anything significant in common; if you call them both "gentlemen" the term has become so broad as to be nearly meaningless.

R. D. McMaster, in *Trollope and the Law* (London: Macmillan, 1986), takes a more restricted subject but demonstrates its wider implications convincingly. McMaster's book follows Coral Lansbury's *The Reasonable Man: Trollope's Legal Fiction* (Princton: Princton UP, 1981), in which principles of advocacy and legal pleading are proposed as a paradigm for Trollope's whole methodology as a writer of fiction. McMaster's interpretation of his subject is more literal and more firmly anchored in historical detail. Here one finds clear explanations of such matters as: the differences between attorneys and barristers (and between barristers and "paper barristers"), the sources of the Old Bailey lawyers' notorious contemporary reputation, the private/public functions of Law Officers of the Crown, the complex statutes and loopholes affecting inheritance of property and the rights of women. These explanations are especially valuable to non-British readers who operate under different legal assumptions and with a different vocabulary, but McMaster is principally interested in how these practices inform the novels themselves and look beyond them to an evolving sense of the individual's place in the social fabric. Trollope, McMaster says, "had not just the average novelist's need to deal on occasion with the legal consequences of marriage, death or inheritance, but a keen interest in the intricacies of law as expressing and sustaining social order and accommodation, as spinning between individuals, families and generations the cobweb of finely adjusted interests that constitutes the English way of life" (p. 1). The reach of the law and its meaning in human life is then for Trollope at once concrete and incredibly pervasive, "from what is close at hand, a tree, a roof, a gate, through the bonds of family and social relationship to the whole network of sensibilities and associations that constitute the feeling and identity of the race" (p. 18). Thus a relatively trivial legal dispute (the definition of an "heirloom" in *The Eustace Diamonds*) or an apparently small breach of legal ettiquette (Mr. Furnival's direct consultation with Lady Mason, improper in his role as barrister) may serve as the axis on which the meaning of the novel turns. And meaning, for Trollope, as many critics have noted, is intimately bound up in a problematic ethic of truth-telling, in the tension between public acts and private scruple, and in the conflicting claims of expediency and tradition. McMaster shows how the law—with its informing metaphysical principle of justice, its complex body of definitions and regulations, and its large and various army of interpreting practitioners—provides a structure richly suited to Trollope's interests and practice as a novelist.

Trollope Centenary Essays (ed. John Halperin, New York: St. Martin's,

1982) has the appearance of being hastily assembled. The novelist's name is misspelled on the "Contents" page, and the introductory essay rehearses in a perfunctory way what most of us already know about the shifts in Trollope's critical reputation and the consistency of his popularity with the general reader. Juliet McMaster's "Trollope's "Country Estate" repackages her essay of the previous year, "The Victorian Country Estate: Anthony Trollope" (*Transactions of the Royal Society of Canada,* 19 [1981], 115–25). In general the essays play safe with their subjects and approaches. What is true of the collection as a whole, however, is not uniformly true of the individual essays. Robert Tracy's contribution, *"Lana Medicata Fuco:* Trollope's Classicism" informatively summarizes what is known about Trollope's classical education and his contributions to classical scholarship. In an essay on "Trollope's Dialogue" Robert Polhemus analyzes the novelist's richly nuanced prose in readings that are themselves supple enactments of the "good ear" his essay advocates. N. John Hall's "Trollope the Person" transcribes and shrewdly analyzes a wonderful collection of contemporary anecdotes and reminiscences—accounts by such diverse commentators as his colleagues, juniors, and superiors in the post office, literary associates like Edmund Yates, G. A. Sala, John Morley, Mark Twain, Wilkie Collins, T. H. S. Escott, and today-unknown friends, correspondents, and dinner companions.

Much more seriously flawed is Rajiva Wijesinha's *The Androgynous Trollope: Attitudes to Women Amongst Early Victorian Novelists* (Washington, D.C.: UP of America, 1982). The book attempts to demonstrate "Trollope's remarkable objectivity and realism" (p. v) by comparing his treatment of marriage and courtship to that of other Victorian novelists. Wijesinha's study offers both too much and too little. Extensive quotations from contemporary reviews and essays about "The Woman Question," coupled with a tedious succession of case studies from the novels of Dickens, Thackeray, Kingsley, Eliot, Trollope and others, reiterate the author's thesis without substantially complicating it. One can admire individual readings of scene or character, but the project as a whole founders on the narrowness of its critical agenda. The book makes no attempt to situate itself within recent critical debate on gender issues or on notions of realism (incredibly, Virginia Woolf and Henry James have the last word here). More fundamentally, *The Androgynous Trollope* would have benefitted from careful editing. The manuscript should have been cut and focussed, revised for clarity and proofread for the numerous typographical errors (including misspellings of characters' names) that mar the appearance and readability of the text.

GENERAL CRITICISM: SHORTER STUDIES

Although Trollope is pre-eminently the chronicler of church affairs and personages, few would consider him a religious writer. Stanley Hauerwas, in "Constancy and Forgiveness: The Novel as a School for Virtues" (*Religion and Literature,* 15 [1983], 23–54) is one who makes that claim. Hauerwas takes Trollope at his word that he is a "preacher of sermons" in novel form and—after some unnecessary plot summary and recapitulation of Letwin's *The Gentleman in Trollope*—proceeds to probe the implications of that assertion. His Trollope is no Christian theologian transmitting his creed into fictional paradigms; nevertheless forgiveness is at the heart of his moral vision and is inherent in the very form his fiction assumes.

The secular Trollope receives a witty and engaging treatment in Philip Collins' "Business and Bosoms: Some Trollopian Concerns" (*Nineteenth-Century Fiction,* 37 [1982], 293–315). If Trollope was a "preacher of sermons," these moral messages had a decidedly worldly flavor, Collins claims; they might be best described as "advice for making the best of things in Satan's Kingdom" (p. 296). One of the few major authors who have maintained a career in an organization distinct from his creative life, Trollope very naturally reflects a detailed preoccupation with "business" in his fiction. So much so that one could append a profit-and-loss balance sheet to most novels—"the amounts being duly carried forward in the Barchester and Palliser series" (p. 298). As for "bosoms," these were described chastely when physically attached to his heroines; in their more abstract meaning they served as the site for battles between "principle" and "expediency." Both fiscal and physical details are at the author's fingertips in this entertaining essay. Readers interested in Trollope's fetish for women's teeth can come to no better source.

Money matters are viewed within the matrix of family and society in two recent articles. Richard C. Burke's "Accommodation and Transcendence: Last Wills in Trollope's Novels" (*Dickens Studies Annual: Essays on Victorian Fiction* 15, ed. Michael Timko, Fred Kaplan, and Edward Guiliano, (New York: AMS, 1986, 291–307) offers a workmanlike analysis of the novels' patterns of bequest and inheritance. Like Juliet McMaster (see above), Burke demonstrates the near-religious value attached to the idea of the estate and hence the importance of the document that provides for its continuance and future stewardship. John R. Reed turns his attention to the opposite end of the moral spectrum in "A Friend to Mammon: Speculation in Victorian Literature" (*Victorian Studies* 27 [1984], 179–202). Reed informatively positions Trollope's fiction (specifically *The Way We Live Now*) among the ongoing Victorian response to what most regarded as "the chief economic disease of their time" (p. 183).

Laura Hapke and Sarah Gilead survey Trollope's variations on two familiar Victorian cultural symbols—the fallen woman and the orphan—while "Trollope's Girls" (*Princeton University Library Chronicle* 47, [1986], 229–47) receive appreciative tribute in Robert H. Taylor's lecture on the Trollopian *"jeune fille."* Hapke ("He Stoops To Conquer: Redeeming the Fallen Woman in the Fiction of Dickens, Gaskell and Their Contemporaries" *Victorian Newsletter* 69, [1986], 16–22) sees Trollope's treatment of Carry Brattle as protective, but ultimately condescending, in line with the paternalistic view he shares with other male writers on the subject. In an interesting, well-argued extension of Nina Auerbach's work ("Trollope's Orphans and the 'Power of Adequate Performance,'" (*Texas Studies in Literature and Language: A Journal of the Humanities*, 27 [1985], 86–105) Gilead reads Trollope against one of Victorian fiction's most characteristic patterns: an orphan undergoes a "transformative quest," the end result of which is his own accommodation or the accommodation of a surrogate or double to a "new or given social order" (p. 87, p. 86). Trollope's orphans and outsiders, she observes, seldom enact this process of self-destruction followed by spiritual rebirth. Rather, "a dark night of the soul" in a Trollopian orphan signals "a conscious and final failure to thrive," and most who do thrive do so through the eventual adoption of "ready-made, acceptable social roles" rather than through "radical revision of the self" (p. 87). Nevertheless, some Trollopian orphans simulate this process through an act of narrative self-creation, which allows them to manipulate their social environment while freeing them from the "deadly risk" of fundamental change. Gilead focuses on three characters "symbolically orphaned" by experiences which have assaulted their identity and left them victims of cultural rejection. Septimus Harding, Lady Mason, and Lily Dale are each "disinherited" and victimized by aggressive tendencies in "the hard new world of commercial England" (p. 90). Each responds by retreat, a "retailoring" of the self which amounts to a "self-mythologizing" martyrdom, a narrowing of space and withdrawal from the social and generational realm (pp. 90, 91). Gilead's reading of Lily Dale in particular is original, lifting her out of the realm of private neurosis to show her as an unconscious strategist responding to a complex and threatening psycho-social dynamic.

Arthur Pollard and Robert B. Heilman look at the character types of the Evangelical clergyman and the journalist, respectively. "Trollope and the

Evangelicals" (*Nineteenth-Century Fiction,* 37 [1982], 329–39) sets the subject in a historical framework and highlights the grounds of Trollope's disapproval (his orientation toward conduct in a social setting rather than private spirituality, his recoil from behavior he considered "intolerant and ungentlemanly," his sense that the Evangelicals spirit posed "a threat to the civilized middle way along which he chose to tread" [p. 339]. Much of this information can be gathered from other sources, but it is usefully contextualized here. Heilman's "Writers on Journalists: A Version of Atheism" (*Georgia Review,* 39 [1985], 37–54) proposes Trollope's Tom Towers as the best literary representation of journalistic arrogance and fallability.

Robert Hughes's "Trollope and Fox-Hunting" (*Essays in Literature* 12, [1985] 75–84) sets out to rescue the recurrent hunt scene from the self-deprecation of the author and from the condescension of critics who have found Trollope innocent of symbolism and inattentive to the demands of structural coherence. Hughes successfully demonstrates that these interludes are seldom simply digressions—that they stand as metaphoric equivalents for Trollope's belief in the value of social harmony, in a traditional (and increasingly threatened) class structure, and in a standard for political and moral authority rooted in an ideal, pre-industrial England. For Hughes, the hunt is also a "highly plastic image" which easily conforms to the contours of the story in which it appears, a point he demonstrates in more extended readings of three novels. A treatment of a wider range of novels, would, I believe, show Trollope re-orchestrating these same themes with only minor variations.

The Trollope reader past and present is addressed in two recent articles. Michael Lund's "Literary Pieces and Whole Audiences: *Denis Duval, Edwin Drood, and The Landleaguers*" (*Criticism: A Quarterly for Literature and the Arts* 28, [1986], 27–49) looks at the quality of "image-building" in characters and readers. The title of the essay notwithstanding, very little work is done on *The Landleaguers,* and the argument falters under the emptiness of its historical generalizations ("Just as Denis Duval, Clarisse, Grewgious, Jasper, Drood, and Rosa all desire such unlimited futures, so the Victorian citizen sought a life full of potential among the many expanding horizons of nineteenth-century life" [p. 32]. More enlightening is David Skilton's "The Trollope Reader" (in *The Nineteenth-Century British Novel,* ed. Jeremy Hawthorn [Baltimore: Arnold, 1986], 143–56). Concentrating on the 1860s, the period of Trollope's greatest popularity, Skilton explores the critical problems which arise for modern readers in valuing a literary work produced in nearly complete harmony with audience desire and identity. Although Trollope's claim to critical stature has in our generation rested on those novels perceived to be written in opposition to the spirit of the age, Skilton suggests that this may well tell us more about ourselves than about Trollope. Trollope's triumph of conformity in the 1860s, his achievement of belonging after long exclusion, went hand-in-hand with the production of "a first-class body of fiction." Trollope negotiated into a form of art "the ordinary life of his class"; in Michael Gorra's phrase, he was "The Apostle of Common Sense" (*The Hudson Review*, 36 [1983–84], 765–71).

In a pair of essays by Michael Riffaterre, Trollope's artistic sophistication is seen in relation to "the formal and semantic structures of his narrative and descriptive style" (*Nineteenth-Century Fiction* 37, [1982], 272–92, p. 273; "On the Diegetic Functions of the Descriptive," *Style,* 20 [1986], 281–94). Arguing that "After a century of criticism, much remains to be said about Trollope's technique" (p. 272), Riffaterre sets out to systematize certain features of Trollope's transparent prose by applying the methods of stylistic analysis. Riffaterre associates the subtle use of metonymic detail with artistic excellence in Trollope. He is particularly interested in that class of metonymies in which a minor physical or sartorial feature evokes in the reader's mind moral judgments. Trollope's metonymies are essentially comic, but they are elements of his realism as well. As "fragments of the larger text, immersed in it and mirroring the whole" (p. 278), metonymies play an important role in helping the reader assimilate the meaning of the novel and its overarching unity, a point Riffaterre illustrates by examining instances of a metonymic subtext at work in *Rachel Ray* and *He Knew He Was Right.* In the second essay Riffaterre writes in opposition to the notions of description as adornment or interruption, as extraneous to the narrative properly defined. Descriptions, he says, are "embeddings," "units of meaning in the narrative lexicon." They function as "the periphrases of the words we could substitute for them in a summarized version of the text" (p. 281).

SHORT STUDIES OF SPECIFIC WORKS

If Park Honan is right—and the evidence suggests that he is—"The Irish tide may be turning" ("Anthony Trollope After a Century," *Contemporary Review,* 24 [1982], 322). While the trend noted in Donald Stone's "Trollope Studies, 1976–1981" (see above) has been from Barsetshire to Palliser, the five years following that period have seen a resurgence of interest in Trollope's long neglected Irish fiction. As Owen Dudley Edwards has remarked in a recent article ("Anthony Trollope, The Irish Writer,"

Nineteenth-Century Fiction, 38 [1983], 1–42). "The latest Trollopians are forcing reconsiderations of all Trollope's Irish writing with scant respect for Sadleir's dismissal of it.... [It] is winning its place of honor in the canon" (p. 2). Recent rehabilitations include fresh readings of *The Macdermots of Ballycloran* (1847), *An Eye for an Eye* (1879), and *The Landleaguers* (1883), but critics are also stressing that Irish materials and themes weave a continuous pattern in Trollope's fiction, carrying over to novels once thought of as quintessentially English. Noteworthy among the single readings is Sarah Gilead's exploration of textual paradox in "Trollope's Ground of Meaning: *The Macdermots of Ballycloran*" (*Victorian Newsletter,* 69 [1986], 23–26). Remarking that the uncharacteristically monolithic view of human experience embodied in this novel has made it resistant to the usual forms of criticism, Gilead posits this first work of fiction as Trollope's "null hypothesis," his passage through the "realm of no-meaning," on the way to "the aggressive, risky delights of interpretive play" (p. 25). Gertrude M. White's "Truth or Consequences: The Real World of Trollope's Melodrama" (*English Studies: A Journal of English Language and Literature,* 64 [1983], 491–502) more predictably seeks to elevate the status of *An Eye for An Eye* by associating it with "modern" qualities. John Hynes's "A Note on Trollope's *Landleaguers*" (*Etudes Irlandaises,* 11 [1986], 65–70) suggests that Trollope's treatment of both Irish and English landlords is more carefully differentiated than has been formerly thought and that the novel as a whole is less uniformly morbid than previous readings would suggest. The two poles of Trollope's career as an Irish novelist are bridged in T. Bareham's "First and Last: Some Notes Towards a Re-Appraisal of Trollope's *The Macdermots of Ballycloran* and *The Landleaguers*" (*Durham University Journal:* 47 [1986], 311–17), an essay that argues for thematic continuity between Trollope's first (politically liberal) and last (conservative) novels.

Two recent essays by John G. Hynes examine Trollope's Irish fiction against its historical context. In "Anthony Trollope's Creative 'Culture-Shock': Banagher, 1841" (*Eire-Ireland: A Journal of Irish Studies,* 21 [1986], 124–31), Hynes seeks to recreate the quality and variety of Irish life as Trollope experienced it fresh from England. Interesting and colorful in the social background it develops—in the portraits of market-days and cottage life—the essay is, for my taste, a little too close to the "he must have felt," "he must have thought" school of hypothetical biography. Trollope, the contemporary historian, interests Hynes in "Anthony Trollope and the 'Irish Question': 1844–1882" (*Etudes Irlandaises,* 8 [1983], 213–28). The essay attempts to provide a twentieth-century historical perspective on the two great upheavals of nineteenth-century Ireland—the famine and the land-tenure/home rule struggle—and in the process, to test the accuracy and impartiality of Trollope's interpretations of these events. The essay is a thoughtful and balanced account which draws on contemporary travel writing, government reports, letters, and fiction to establish the fullest possible context for interpretation.

Implicit in much recent work on Trollope's Irish fiction is the assumption that the critic is dealing with something much more pervasive and deep-rooted than a self-contained Irish "period." Robert Tracy's essay "The 'Unnatural Ruin'": Trollope and Nineteenth-Century Irish Fiction" (*Nineteenth-Century Fiction* 37 [1982], 358–82) looks both forward and backward, placing the novels in the context of Trollope's wide reading among minor Irish novelists and demonstrating as well that Irish character types and motifs infiltrate Trollope's later English novels. Like Tracy, Owen Dudley Edwards, in "Anthony Trollope, the Irish Writer" (see above) sees the imprint of the "Celtic hairy heel" (p. 33) even in cloistered Barsetshire. Edwards's Trollope is an Irishman himself—or very nearly so. "His view of Ireland from first to last was that of a participant" (p. 1). More convincingly, Tracy sees Trollope as "doubly an outsider—a foreigner in Ireland, an exile from England" (p. 381) and speculates that the detachment thrust upon him by circumstance in his Irish years, "made him also approach English society as a kind of foreigner, eager to understand it and to excel English writers in depicting it" (p. 382).

Karen Faulkner takes a broader view of "Anthony Trollope's Apprenticeship" (*Nineteenth-Century Fiction,* 38 [1983], 161–88) —one which examines the influence of the minor Irish novelists Trollope read as well as his immersion in Scott, Austen, Dickens, Fielding and others. Claiming that Trollope "differs from many writers who seem to have some sense of their own voice, however unperfected, from the start of their writing careers" (p. 181), Faulkner views the early novels as a time of (mainly negative) experimentation in the subjects, points of view, style, and idiosyncracies of his literary predecessors. The narrative of Trollope's progression toward technical mastery and moral vision is made to seem neat and sequential in this essay, but this is in part a function of the care with which the author examines the sometimes subtle distinctions between one literary project and the next.

A small piece of Faulkner's general subject is given an extended and provocative treatment in Jerome Meckier's essay, "The Cant of Reform: Trollope Rewrites Dickens in *The Warden*" (*Studies in the Novel* 15 [1983],

202–23), the interesting premise of which is that *"The Warden* deserves special recognition as the only Victorian novel to parody a Dickens novel
Dickens never actually wrote" (p. 202). Meckier refers, of course, to the jibes
at Dickens taken in Chapter 15, when John Bold purchases the first number
of Mr. Popular Sentiment's *The Almshouse* and the narrator summarizes its
highly colored contents. But, he argues, the parodic elements extend well
beyond this chapter: "The anti-Sentiment section forms part of a comprehensive reconsideration of Dickens as realist and social critic, especially his use
of Juvenalian satire to promote a radical politics and encourage reform" (p.
202). Meckier's long article masterfully analyzes the implications of
Trollope's preoccupation with Dickens in *The Warden,* demonstrating how
"writing in opposition" helped Trollope to formulate in this fourth novel "his
true style, subject, and milieu" (p. 202). A study of *The Warden*'s sources in
the journalism of the day, and of its transmutation into "two" novels ("one
Trollope is writing and one that he is refuting") underscores for Meckier that
"the idea of a common reality, which an objective realism can portray for a
secularized society, was always an imperiled ideal, even in the heyday of
realism, long before postmodern critics decided that realism itself is a kind of
cant or fiction" (p. 217, p. 222).

Ross Murfin's Trollope ("The Gap in Trollope's Fiction: *The Warden* as
Example," *Studies in the Novel* 14 [1982], 17–30), perpetually hovering in
the interstices between irreconcileable positions, fits similarly within a postmodern sensibility. Murfin demonstrates with considerable cogency "the
presence of a hiatus, a gap between things that precede and things that follow" in the divisions between chapters, paragraphs and sentences of *The
Warden* (p. 21). Nearly concealed by the author's style—by his habit of arguing "one at a time and with passionate geniality, for each of the discrete opinions that are to be bridged—but never quite integrated—with their neighbors
in the text" (p. 21), this irregularity in construction seems almost by design to
defy closure and coherent interpretation. That the stylistic and structural features of this, in some ways, anomalous novel are characteristic of Trollope's
fiction generally (as Murfin's title and speculative conclusions strongly
imply) will indeed "have to be defended elsewhere" (p. 28).

Two additional essays on *The Warden* can be briefly noted. Barry M.
Maid's "Trollope, Idealists, Reality, and Play" (*Victorians Institute Journal,*
12 [1984], 9–21) uses Huizinga's game theory to explore the political realities of the novel, but the essay loses itself in repetition and jargon. Andrew
Wright's subject in "Trollope Transformed, or The Disguises of Mr Harding
and Others" (in *Victorian Literature and Society: Essays Presented to*

Richard D. Altick, ed. James R. Kincaid and Albert J. Kuhn [Columbus: Ohio State UP, 1984]) is not, strictly speaking, Trollope's novel, but the various abridgements, simplifications, and dramatizations of it, from radio scripts and novel adaptations to student "crutches." Though the essay merely suggests the cultural significance of the texts it examines, it has some insightful things to say about Trollope's style.

Recent treatments of *Barchester Towers* range from the simple note of explication to traditional formal analysis to more theoretically ambitious readings of the novel in relation to culture. Edward H. Kelly's "Trollope's *Barchester Towers*" (*Explicator* 44 [1986], 27–29), an examination of the etymology and significance of the name Quiverful, belongs to the first category. Elizabeth Langland's "Society as Formal Protagonist: The Examples of *Nostromo* and *Barchester Towers* (*Critical Inquiry,* 9 [1982], 359–78) explores the implications for novel form when society (rather than the individual) is posited as the protagonist of the novel. Gay Sibley's "The Spectrum of 'Taste' in *Barchester Towers*" (*Studies in the Novel,* 17 [1985], 38–52) examines issues of politics and rhetoric by positing a "silent" analogy between good taste and morality in the narrator's descriptions. Sibley concludes that Trollope's "rhetoric of taste" is "a sneaky business" which "the narrator is good at," rather than—as seems more likely to me—a condition of the culture within which his imagination took shape (p. 50). Jane Nardin, in "Conservative Comedy and the Women of *Barchester Towers*" (*Studies in the Novel* 18 [1986], 381–94) supplies a convincing reading of Trollope's uncharacteristic mysogyny in a novel that espouses the values of the past as a defense against its cast of hen-pecked husbands, shrews, and female over-reachers.

Issues of gender, class, and culture are joined most challengingly in D. A. Miller's Foucauldian reading, "The Novel as Usual: Trollope's *Barchester Towers*" (in *Sex, Politics, and Science in the Nineteenth-Century Novel,* ed. Ruth Bernard Yeazell, Series 10 in *Selected Papers from the English Institute* [Baltimore: Johns Hopkins UP, 1986]; later published in *The Novel and the Police* [Berkeley: U of California P, 1988]). Miller's interrogation of Trollope's text is, by design, poles apart from "the usual appreciation of [Trollope's] appreciation of the usual" (p. 1), and his impertinent central question, "Where are the police in *Barchester Towers?*" is meant to defamiliarize the transparent tissue of Trollope's prose (itself "a highly developed system of familiarizations") by foregrounding its silences and evasions (p. 1). The police are absent, Miller claims, because they have been thoroughly absorbed and subsumed. "Moderate schism"—the deflection of genuine conflict into gamesmanship that it is invisibly an instrument of terrifying social control—renders overt policing unnecessary. "Moderate schism" is shown to operate in the religious and sexual politics of the novel as well as to define plot. Moreover, Trollope's "tolerance" for the "mixed motives" of his characters models a reading practice which is the natural outgrowth of the whole system—where personality resembles "a parliamentary democracy" in constant equilibrium and where tolerance always and necessarily "includes an acute consciousness of all that needs to be tolerated" (pp. 18, 27). Miller's argument is by turns closely reasoned and sweeping in its claims. Aiming to shock as a deliberate part of its own critical strategy, it is likely to evoke admiration, resistance, and assent—sometimes all at once.

The remaining novels in the Barsetshire chronicles are less thoroughly treated during the period under consideration. Sarah Gilead's brief reading of the flower imagery surrounding Lily Dale in "Trollope's *The Small House of Allington* [sic]" (*Explicator,* 42 [1984], 12–14) is quite modest in its ambitions but nicely executed. Laura Hapke's analysis of a very different Trollope heroine in "The Lady as Criminal: Contradiction and Resolution in Trollope's *Orley Farm*" (*Victorian Newsletter,* 66 [1984], 18–21) convincingly demonstrates Trollope's domestication of Lady Mason's potentially subversive crime, but fails to define adequately the relationship between "realistic" and "sensational" in its own usage of these terms. Robert Pattison's "Trollope among the Textuaries" (in *Reconstructing Literature,* ed. Laurence Lerner [Tottowa, N.J.: Barnes and Noble, 1983]) deploys a hybrid of deconstructive approaches on *The Last Chronicle of Barset* and then stands back from the result to deconstruct it. Both the "textuary" reading (focussing on paradoxes of closure and transcendance) and the critique of it (emphasizing its trendiness and jargon) work within fairly predictable paramaters.

Among the (surpringly few) recent treatments of the Palliser novels, Robert M. Polhemus's "Being in Love in *Phineas Finn / Phineas Redux:* Desire, Devotion, Consolation" (*Nineteenth-Century Fiction,* 37 [1982], 383–95) deserves note for its deft and supple analysis of Trollopian romantic love. Polhemus positions the *Phineas* novels within the *Don Juan* tradition, as embodying a basic conflict between unrepressed sexual freedom and society's concern to protect itself against anarchy. Love—an emotion which embraces desire, affection, and responsibility—mediates this struggle, and Phineas's four love choices show him negotiating the multiple and contradictory meanings which constitute the personal and political reality of Victorian romantic love. Although its thesis is a familiar one (that Lizzie Eustace functions as a "text" variously interpreted by an expanding repertoire of fictional characters and by the reader herself), Patricia Vernon's "Reading and Misreading in *The Eustace Diamonds,*" (*Victorians Institute Journal* 12 [1984], 1–8) is also worth a look. The essay suggestively probes the paradoxical relationship between Trollope's honest, forthcoming narrator, who would withold no secrets, and a narrative truth that cannot be yielded up because the reader's participation in part creates it.

The Way We Live Now, that masterpiece of Trollope's supposed "dark" period long a favorite with critics, has received scant attention lately. Neither of the recent essays turned up in my computer search offers anything really new. I found it dispiriting just to wade through the prose style of Iva G. Jones's "Patterns of Estrangement in Trollope's *The Way We Live Now*" (in *Amid Visions and Revisions: Poetry and Criticism on Literature and the Arts,* ed. J. Burney [Baltimore: Morgan State UP, 1985]). Jones begins paragraphs with pronouncements like the following: "Not to be passed without notice is the fact that Melmotte is a Jew" (p. 53). A. Abbott Ikeler, in "That Peculiar Book: Critics, Common Readers and *The Way We Live Now*" (*College Language Association,* 30 [1986], 219–40) attempts to "close the gap" between the common readers' devaluation of the novel as anomalous and the twentieth century's elevation of it to canonical status—a goal which proves too ambitious for the essay's dimensions and critical vocabulary.

One measure of Trollope's recently assured stature as a novelist for the twentieth century is the critical attention now given to works once dismissed as minor. Even the little-read travel books have received their due, as witness Helen Heineman's appreciation of their novelistic "fairness" and Asa Briggs's more critical commentary ("Anthony Trollope: The Compleat Traveller," *Ariel: A Review of International English Literature,* 13 [1982], 33–50; "Trollope the Traveller," in *Trollope Centenary Essays,* see above) Quite simply, more Trollope is being read and with the rigor generally applied to books that matter. Two notable examples of this trend are David Pearson's essay on *Sir Harry Hotspur of Humblethwaite* and Geoffrey Harvey's on *Mr. Scarborough's Family* (*Nineteenth-Century Fiction* 37 [1982], 396–418; *Nineteenth-Century Fiction* 37 [1982], 419–29). Pearson reads Trollope as a "semi-epistolary" novelist, taking *Sir Harry Hotspur* as a case in point of Trollope's Richardsonian technique. Relying on summary and classification to illustrate his points, Pearson pays tribute to the naturalness of Trollope's letters, to their appropriate placement and language, to the ways in which they evoke (frequently juxtaposed) reactions in their readers and shadow forth paradigmatic conflict situations. Geoffrey Harvey seeks to explore more fully the extent and significance of Trollope's debt to Fletcher and Massinger's *The Elder Brother* and Middleton's *A Trick to Catch the Old One*. In both plays he finds the law mediating between social and moral claims within a context of conflict between an older landed aristocracy and a newer, more mobile commercial class, a situation which posed intriguing analogies to Trollope's own times. As Harvey convincingly demonstrates, *Mr. Scarborough's Family* owes its overall design to these sources, superimposed on which is a rhetorical strategy by which the novel's hypothetical "cases" are brought to trial before the bar of the reader's judgment. The novel finally evades any "causal certainties"—its main plot ironically bringing into coincidence abstract law and natural justice, while its comic subplot emphasizes the arbitrary, amoral nature of the law's triumph.

The role of comedy as thematic counterpoint is explored from another angle in Jane Nardin's essay on "Comic Convention in *Rachel Ray*" (*Papers on Language and Literature: A Journal for Scholars and Critics of Language and Literature*, 22 [1986], 39–50). Nardin follows Barickman et al in contrasting Trollope's "antifeminist narrators" and "reliance on conventional characters and plots" with the "interior arrangements oppositional to the conservatism of traditional comedy (p. 39). But her argument is less subtle than that found in *Corrupt Relations* (see above). In Nardin's essay, Trollope is constructed as a calculating subversive encoding feminist messages for his more sophisticated readers with one hand, while simultaneously playing safe with his "uncritical Victorian readers" on the other. Nardin's reading of *He Knew He Was Right* (*Genre*, 15 [1982], 303–13) is more compelling. Exploring the role of generic experimentation in the "unevenness" of Trollope's multi-plot novels, Nardin challenges the assumption that "Trollope is trying unsuccessfully to write dark, unified, homogeneous psychological novels" (p. 303). She concludes that tragedy and farce are meaningfully linked as subplots in *He Knew He Was Right;* only negative lessons can be learned from the heroes of each whose repetitive, inappropriate acts render them incapable of growth or change. By contrast, as the three comic subplots reveal, comedy is the genre of characters who can learn when to be firm and when to yield and by so doing create their own happiness.

Christopher Herbert defines the "problem" of *He Knew He Was Right* differently (*"He Knew He Was Right*, Mrs. Lynn Linton, and the Duplicities of Victorian Marriage," *Texas Studies in Literature and Language: A Journal of the Humanities*, 25 [1983], 448–69), but he too is concerned with the worrying inconsistencies of Trollope's fictional agenda here. His argument, which places the book quite specifically within the feminist controversies of the 1860s, makes sense of the novel for me in a way that previous readings have been unable to do. Using Eliza Lynn Linton's *Sowing the Wind* (a probable source for the novel), as a case in point, Herbert demonstrates how popular fiction attempted to negotiate the contradiction between two culturally powerful, but mutually exclusive ideals of marriage—the patriarchal and the companionate models—by sanitizing and mystifying the underlying power relationship. In the Victorian folktale the blame for marital misery and discord is displaced onto the authoritarian husband, a figure of melodramatic intensity. Trollope's move, however, is to unmask the power structure inherent in marriage itself. The "determined nullifying of moral verdicts" (p. 456) is the whole point since this is not, finally, a novel about who was right. Rather, the protagonists' quarrels about language and definitions, about roles and rules—which seem so odd and extreme on first reading—reveal what is really at stake. "In Trollope's version ... male supremacist values are not simply weapons of convenience for a pathological bully; they are discovered to be a core element of Victorian personality, to coexist with a wide range of good intentions, and—especially—to be so deeply embedded as to be largely unconscious and unacknowledged. Bringing them to the surface and exposing their contradictions is thus ... a process fraught with profound psychic consequences" (p. 454).

TROLLOPE AND OTHERS

Readers interested in Trollope's relationship to other Victorian novelists will want to look at a pair of recent essays on Trollope's rivalry/friendship with Thackeray. J. Hillis Miller's "Trollope's Thackeray" (*Nineteenth-Century Fiction*, 37 [1982], 329–39 examines the value for modern readers of the biography Trollope wrote about his friend. A largely sympathetic and appreciative account, the essay points to the ways in which Trollope's work has set the critical agenda for twentieth-century critics and biographers while communicating with rare clarity and ease a set of powerful assumptions about the art of fiction still influential today. Miller reads the Thackeray biography as another Trollope "novel," and in doing so Miller's own prose at times seems quite Trollopian ("but of that third skeleton not a word can be written" p. 351), suggesting appealingly how thoroughly he is immersed in his subject. Robert Colby's "Trollope as Thackerayan," (*Dickens Studies Annual: Essays on Victorian Fiction*, 11, eds. Michael Timko, Fred Kaplan, and Edward Guiliano [New York: AMS 1983], pp. 261–77), also a strong essay, positions itself quite differently. Colby's premise is that Trollope failed in his attempt to write a fair, accurate, and substantial biography of the man he named in his *Autobiography* as first among contemporary English novelists. As Colby demonstrates in this fascinating, well-researched article, the specific ways in which Trollope failed tell much about his own personal anxieties to define himself and his art in the face of slipping sales and critical reputation.

Henry James's critique and appropriation of trollope continues to generate commentary. Susan e. Hendricks ("Henry James as Adapter: *The Portrait of a Lady* and *Can You Forgive Her," Rocky Mountain Review of Language and Literature,* 38 [1984], 35–43) develops a convincing case that *Portrait* draws for its plot on *Can You Forgive Her,* which James had reviewed in *The Nation* in 1865, fifteen years before James's novel began appearing serially. Hendricks's naive reading of the Victorian fictional aesthetic and her unquestioning identification with James's critical assumptions limit the usefulness of her project. A more sophisticated approach to a similar theme is taken by John Halperin in "Trollope, James, and 'The Retribution of Time'" (*Southern Humanities Review,* 19 [1985], 301–8). Halperin lays out the plot parallels between *Sir Harry Hotspur of Humblethwaite* (1870) and *Washington Square* (1880), noting that James could have read Trollope's novel when it was serialized in *Macmillan's.* The essay interestingly traces the ramifications in plot and character development when "portraiture" is chosen over "pathetic incident" as the generative principle for novel development. Vivien Jones, in "James and Trollope" (*Review of English Studies: A Quarterly Journal of English Literature and the English Language* 33 [1982], 278–94) brings useful insights to bear on James's harsh reviews of Trollope's novels. Looking at four of these pieces written between 1865 and 1868, Jones demonstrates convincingly the specific ways in which they represent stages in the formulation of James" own aesthetic as he struggled aggressively to position himself with respect to realist and modern sensibilities. James's criticisms of Trollope are still the standard against which Park Honan measures his achievement in his brief appreciation and reassessment, "Anthony Trollope After A Century" (*Contemporary Review,* 241 [1982], 318–23). Honan concludes that Trollope's steady habits of composition were not necessarily harmful, and that his central achievement lay in the artistic permanence and solidity he gave to the world he created.

The experience of reading Trollope is compared, variously (!), to the experience of reading Margaret Drabble, Barbara Pym, and Murasaki Shikibu in several recent essays. Trollope is cast unfairly as a negative example of Victorian omniscience in Morton P. Levitt's "The New Victorians: Margaret

Drabble as Trollope" (in *Margaret Drabble: Golden Realms,* No. 4 in Living Author Series [Edinburg, Texas: School of Humanities, Pan American U, 1982). Kate Browder Heberlein's "Barbara Pym and Anthony Trollope: Communities of Imaginative Participation" (*Pacific Coast Philology,* 19 [1984], 95–100) rapidly sketches similarities between the two novelists that go well beyond their shared interest in the clergy and in the social activities that grow out of clerical life. Generosity of outlook and novelistic, scale link "Trollope and Murasaki" in Edward Seidensticker's essay, subtitled "Impressions of an Orientalist" (*Nineteenth-Century Fiction,* 37 [1982], 464–71). Seidensticker, whose interest in Trollope has been a pleasurable sideline to his specialty in oriental literature, notes that Trollope is not appreciated in Japan, where "Literature is taken too seriously" (p. 469) and where his elegant, ironic language baffles translation.

CONCLUSION

"Lines of investigation open invitingly all around," Ruth apRoberts wrote at the end of her essay on Trollope for *Victorian Fiction: A Second Guide to Research* (ed. George Ford, New York: MLA, 1978, p. 171), sounding the call for scholarly effort in some eighteen areas of needed study. A dozen years alter it is gratifying to see that much of apRobert's wish-list has indeed been addressed, some of the topics in a preliminary way, some quite definitively. We know more about Trollope's studies of latin classics and of Elizabethan and Jacobean drama. Trollope's politics and his understandings about the law have been well treated, as have his experiences in the postal service and his attempts to come to terms with Ireland. His ethics and moral casuistry have been scrutinized in detail, especially as these affect the structure of his novels and his techniques of characterization. Good editions of the novels are at least beginning to appear, and a significant percentage of formerly invisible titles are being read, analyzed, and taught. These accomplishments throw into relief the work that remains to be done. Little has been written about Trollope in relation to other novelists. Studies of influences on his developing aesthetic (from his mother's novels, from the Continent) remain similarly thin and impressionistic. N. John Hall's edition of the letters, together with several recent articles on the subject, have brought Trollope's role as a professional author more sharply into the foreground, but this and other issues related to his life's work await extended treatment in the (promised) biography. Trollope's texts have not been studied in any very rigorous way as illustrated novels; nor have the manuscript materials been examined at all comprehensively. The future for Trollope studies is indeed an exciting one, poised as it is on the foundations of a new (if belated) textual rigor and on recent theoretical formulations that make it possible to give Trollope, in D. A. Thomas's words, "another thought."

Index

Ackroyd, Peter, *Dickens*, 271

Act for Encouraging the Establishment of Museums in Large Towns (1853), 247

Addison, Joseph, *Spectator*, 4–5

Affron, Charles, 249

Alchemy, 1

Alison, Archibald, 236

Altick, Richard D., 193n.; *The English Common Reader*, 195, 210n., 228n., 247

apRoberts, Ruth, 288, 311; "*Trollope and the Zeitgeist*," 288–90

Arac, Jonathan, 111n., 127n.

Armstrong, Nancy, 255, 258

Arnold, Matthew, 239

Arscott, Catherine, 250n.

Art Union, 250n., 251n.

Athenaeum, 235, 250n., 251n.

Auden, W.[ystan] H.[ugh], 11, 12; "Vicarage," 12, 22

Auerbach, Nina, 127n.

Austen, Jane, *Pride and Prejudice*, 76, 203

Averill, James, 244–45

Baetzhold, Howard, 63–65

Baker, Robert, 110n.

Bakhtin, Mikhail, 38–39, 42–43, 58; *The Dialogic Imagination*, 214–15, 262; "Discourse in the Novel," 93–94n.; "The Problem of Speech Genres," 94n.; *Rabelais and His World*, 97; theory of language as a social act in *Bleak House*, 79–96

Bailey, J. W., "*The Duke's Children*: Rediscovering a Trollope Manuscript," 286–87

Baldridge, Cates, 256; "Alternatives to Bourgeois Individualism in *A Tale of Two Cities*," 269

Baldwin, William, 181

Bareham, T., "First and Last: Some Notes Toward a Re-Appraisal of Trollope's *The Macdermots of Ballycloran* and *The Landleaguers*," 302

Bargainnier, Earl F., 11

Barrickman, Richard, MacDonald, Susan, Stark, Myra, *Corrupt Relations: Dickens, Thackeray, Trollope, Collins and the Victorian Sexual System*, 292–93, 308

Barthes, Roland, 39, 43, 55, 154n., 155n.

Barnett, the Reverend Samuel, 247–48

Barnett, Henrietta, 247–48

Basche, Francoise, 127n.

Bassett, John E., 76n.

Batsleer, Janet, 210n.

Baumgarten, Murray, "*Dombey and Son* and the Industrial World," 267

Bell, Alexander Graham, 64

Bell, Charles, 243, 244

Bender, John, *Imagining the Penitentiary*, 213, 215, 227–28n.

Bentham, Jeremy, 215, 227, 228

Berman, Jeffrey, *Narcissism and the Novel*, 259–60

Bernard, Catherine, 113, 126n., 127n.

Blackwood, John, 284

Blackwood, William, 288

Blackwood's Magazine, 236, 238, 250n., 251n.

Blount, Trevor, 98, 101, 103, 109n., 110n., 111n.

Booth, Bradford, 283

Borzello, Frances, 247, 248

Boutwell, George S., 73

Bradbury, Nicola, *Charles Dickens' Great Expectations*, 265

Brantlinger, Patrick, 217, 218, 223, 228n., 229n.

Brigante, Chiara, "The Monstrous Actress: Esther Summerson's Spectral Name,"

313

Contents of Previous Volumes

Volume 2 (1972)

Volume 3 (1974)

Volume 8 (1980)

Volume 9 (1981)

Volume 10 (1982)

Volume 13 (1984)

Volume 14 (1985)

Volume 15 (1986)

Volume 17 (cont'd)

Volume 18 (1989)

Volume 19 (1990)

Volume 20 (1991)